# COCTEAU'S WORLD

Juillet
1922  Lavandou

Jean Cocteau

# COCTEAU'S WORLD

*An Anthology of Writings by Jean Cocteau*

☐

TRANSLATED FROM THE FRENCH

☐

Edited and Introduced by
Margaret Crosland

DODD, MEAD & COMPANY

NEW YORK

# Contents

# Contents

# ACKNOWLEDGEMENTS

The publishers acknowledge with thanks the co-operation of the following for permission to publish the writings of Jean Cocteau :

M. Edouard Dermit, for *Barbette, Le Fantôme de Marseille, La Leçon des Cathédrales, Le Livre Blanc, Satie, Secrets de Beauté*; Editions Gallimard and Farrar, Straus & Giroux, Inc., for *The Impostor* (copyright © 1957 by The Noonday Press, Inc.), translated (from *Thomas l'Imposteur*) by Dorothy Williams; Editions Gallimard, for *Un Ami Dort,* translated by Mary C. Hoeck, *La Crucifixion,* translated by Mary C. Hoeck (in collaboration with Margaret Crosland), 'In Egypt' (from *Maalesh*), translated by Mary C. Hoeck, 'In Japan' (from *Mon Premier Voyage*), translated by W. J. Strachan, also for *Lettre aux Américains, L'Impromptu du Palais-Royal, Le Mythe du Gréco, L'Ode à Picasso,* and *Verlaine, Place du Panthéon*; Editions Bernard Grasset, for *La Corrida du Ier Mai* and *Jeanne d'Arc*; The Harvill Press Ltd and New Directions, Inc., for *Les Enfants Terribles,* translated by Rosamond Lehmann; the late Mary C. Hoeck, for the letters written to her by Jean Cocteau and translated by her; Editions du Rocher and Coward McCann, Inc., for *Diaghilev and Nijinsky* (from *La Difficulté d'Etre*); Editions du Rocher, for *Le Boeuf sur le Toit* and *L'Ecole des Veuves*; and Editions Stock, for *Le Coq et l'Arlequin, D'un Ordre Considéré comme une Anarchie* and *Le Secret Professionnel* (from *Le Rappel à l'Ordre*), translated by Rollo Myers, also for *Le Grand Ecart,* translated by Dorothy Williams, *Opium,* translated by Margaret Crosland and Sinclair Road, *Le Potomak,* and *Sonnerie de Téléphone dans une Rue Vide* (from the poetry collection *Opéra*).

*Note* : With the exception of those specified above, the translations have been made by Margaret Crosland.

The following books, from which material has been taken for this anthology, are published in English translation by Peter Owen Ltd: *The Difficulty of Being; The Impostor; Le Livre Blanc; Maalesh: A Theatrical Tour of the Middle East; The Miscreant; My Contemporaries; My Journey round the World; Opium: The Diary of a Cure.*

# Introduction

Jean Cocteau lived from 1889 until 1963 and during fifty-four of those seventy-four years he wrote poetry, novels and plays, drew and painted, devised ballets and made films. In the complete bibliography of his work there are several hundred entries, while most biographical facts about him rest in his innumerable experiences, admirations, friendships, loves – no hatred. With Cocteau, the orthodox situations of happiness, unhappiness, success or failure cannot easily be isolated. In his case such states are found to merge or exist on different levels. Similarly it is not easy to isolate one aspect of his activity from another : each work he produced was linked to others and the diversified surface conceals a remarkably homogeneous whole. He regarded himself as a 'poet' in the Greek sense of the word, a creator.

During the last two decades few people have fascinated biographers so much. However, biographers have concentrated on establishing facts at the expense of interpreting Cocteau's work and encouraging others to study and value it. These facts perhaps need to be recapitulated. Cocteau was born in Maisons-Laffitte, an attractive, respectable small town just outside Paris. His father was a lawyer, the family were comfortably off. When Jean was born his brother was twelve, his sister eight, and as a result he spent more time with his mother than he did with them. When he was only nine his father committed suicide, a fact which aggravated the somewhat unnatural family situation. Cocteau was educated at the Lycée Condorcet, one of the best known old-fashioned day schools in Paris, where he claims to have reached no academic heights. Even had there been any need for him to take up a conventional career, the adolescent who left the Condorcet (at the school's request) would not have put his mind to it. As a schoolboy he had been hypnotized by the theatre and the gay life of *la Belle Epoque*. The world he admired was filled with actors, acrobats, circus performers, musicians, writers, painters. At twenty he was publishing poems (which he later renounced) and at twenty-two he was drawn into the exotic world of the Russian Ballet. These dancers astonished Paris in 1909 and a little later the impresario Diaghilev asked Cocteau to 'astonish' him. From that moment Cocteau's life became a non-stop whirl of creative activity which ceased only with his death. His life was lived on a kind of stage in full view of an audience, sometimes small and specialized, sometimes universal. Cocteau himself was playwright, producer and

9

actor, and all his relationships were theatrical in quality, a
mingling of the real and the unreal. The close friendships and
painful losses which were so important in his life, notably the
relationship with Raymond Radiguet, could not remain in the
wings of existence – every person, every experience, was brought onstage and used in that ballet with speech, that 'poetry' as he called
it, which was his work, the work inextricably entangled with his
life.

It is perhaps understandable that Cocteau's biographers have been
deeply preoccupied with the minutiae of his life-style, but too much
time has been spent by them in attempts to distinguish between
'objective' truth – that is, what 'really' happened – and 'subjective'
truth, the truth as Cocteau saw it and remembered it, sometimes in
different ways at different stages of his life. It is precisely in his
handling of this subjective truth that Cocteau's originality lies. If
he had searched for objective truth his work might have had
status, but of a different kind. Because his creations are always
subjective, they reach us directly, they make an impact and we
cannot remain indifferent. The products of the twentieth-century
giants, Proust, Gide, Claudel, impress on many counts and undoubtedly achieve classic status, but they are sometimes remote.
They are like well-preserved buildings surrounded with fences, and
one pays for admission.

Cocteau lived and wrote in total freedom, unattached to conventions, codes, schools or groups. As soon as he reached creative
maturity he rejected his early conventional poems. At the same
time he did not claim to be perpetually inventive or original and
was always ready to listen, either to Sophocles or the Surrealists.
He was immensely responsive to people, events and ideas, and
possessed the rare quality of creating an equal, if not similar,
response in anyone coming in contact with his work.

It is not surprising that many potential readers are daunted by
the mere size and scope of Cocteau's output and also because
Cocteau himself has called it 'poetry'. Most people who come to
know the work in detail encounter it first in the way that Cocteau
himself knew so well – by chance. Such an encounter is undemanding, and since the author's voice is always heard so directly the
reader, theatre-goer, film-goer or onlooker listens, probably unaware
that he is responding to 'poetry'. To Cocteau, 'poetry' was not
limited to 'poems'. Much verse does not achieve the level of
'poetry', that emanation which leads the reader into some state of
emotional-intellectual response, some state when he begins, however
unconsciously, to create some form of poetry himself. By poetry
Cocteau meant that dynamic, ferment-like quality that can occur

in any form of activity from writing and painting to cutting out paper shapes and conducting business deals. It is a form of intellectual laziness to call it magic, although it might perhaps be fair to say that it is as hard to define as 'love' or the principle of life itself.

It is Cocteau's lifelong dedication to 'poetry' that makes his work so continually stimulating. Some of his creations may sometimes appear dated, the themes may not be original, the intellectual concepts naïve, the details of execution may not comply with textbook standards, but none of this matters in the long run. The poetry matters, it is a vitalizing element leading to a chain-reaction of more and more poetry.

Once the first contact has been made, the explorer who wishes to enter Cocteau's world may wonder where to begin. Not everyone finds it easy to read 'poems' in the accepted sense of compositions (usually) in verse form, like the ones in this anthology. Most people, however, are drawn to a story or some form of narrative, which suggests they could start with a novel. I will not say 'the novels' because Cocteau's novels are unlike those of other novelists and cannot be isolated within his work. Reading one of them will probably lead the reader not to the next novel in chronological sequence but to some other work with a related theme or to one of Cocteau's film treatments.

As though to prove that this particular world is not best explored by orthodox methods, the *Poésie du Roman* is headed by one of the author's few obscure works, *Le Potomak*. As I explain in my introductory note, it is a book which seems confusing because it expresses Cocteau's own confusion as he reached artistic maturity. It is best read in retrospect after most of the other work.

Four years after *Le Potomak* Cocteau published two novels within the same month : *Le Grand Ecart* and *Thomas l'Imposteur*. Both use autobiographical material, both are short and highly readable, otherwise they differ widely from each other. On the surface *Le Grand Ecart* appears frivolous and Francis Steegmuller has referred to 'its ballet of students tumbling in and out of bed with each other's girl friends (they still called them mistresses), whom they sometimes found in bed with each other'. The novel has real depth, however, examining with only apparent gaiety the nature of love, hetero- and homosexual, and discovering, like Keats, the truth about 'Joy, whose hand is ever at his lips, bidding adieu'. *Le Grand Ecart* was the first novel Cocteau wrote, and he wrote it at the age of thirty-three during his close friendship with Raymond Radiguet who was completing work on *Le Diable au Corps*. It is rewarding to speculate on the lives of the two authors, their heroes

and heroines, and their way of handling the material. The reader
who would prefer to approach Cocteau through fiction would do
well to start with *Le Grand Ecart*. Later on, he will often be
reminded of this surprisingly mature early work, reproduced here in
its entirety.

*Thomas l'Imposteur*, published a few weeks after *Le Grand Ecart*,
was one of the earliest books about the First World War to be more
than reportage. Although nearly fifty years have passed since its first
publication, it is not yet as well known and appreciated as it should
be. Like all Cocteau's work it is based on his own experiences, but
we read it not for mere autobiography, or even for the brilliance of its
war descriptions, but for its philosophical implications, the closeness
of life and death, the interplay of the real and the non-real to the
extent when the two are indistinguishable. There are three short
sentences which dominate the book : *'I haven't a chance if I don't
pretend to be dead,* he said to himself. But in him make-believe
and reality were one. Guillaume Thomas was dead.' As the reader
goes further into Cocteau's world he will see how these two related
themes reappear, like the few other leitmotivs, over and over
again in widely divergent aspects of the work. Unfortunately copyright problems have restricted the number of pages from *l'Imposteur*
included in the present volume, but the extract reproduced here
should encourage the reader to turn to the novel.

Three other examples of Cocteau's 'poetry of the novel' are
included here : the first chapter from his most famous story, *Les
Enfants Terribles*, the whole of *Le Livre Blanc*, and the ironic story
*Le Fantôme de Marseille*. Few of Cocteau's creations exist in the
void and the figure of Dargelos forms a strong link between *Les
Enfants Terribles* and the very different *Livre Blanc*. The sinister
schoolboy, a symbol of adolescent sexuality, also appears in *Opium*
and in the original version of *La Fin du Potomak*, published in
1940 but not represented here.

All the 'novels', with the exception of *Le Potomak*, appeared
during the 1920s. After *Les Enfants Terribles* in 1929 the only
narrative Cocteau published was *Le Fantôme de Marseille*. From
the beginning to the end of his life Cocteau wrote poems, plays and
miscellaneous prose, mostly classified as 'critical poetry', yet only
in this one period – between the ages of thirty-four and forty – did
he devote any time to story-telling. After the Second World War
Cocteau's work as a narrator was continued in his films.

Films of course are described by Cocteau as 'poetry of the
cinema', just as plays and ballets are 'poetry of the theatre'. The
theatre always supplied the most dynamic element in Cocteau's
work, although nothing he created could be called static. As a boy

he had been educated as much by actors, actresses, playwrights and circus artists as by his parents. A reading of *Portraits-Souvenir* makes this clear and shows how Cocteau was so conscious of theatre that he tended always to see theatrical qualities in the people he met, from writers and critics to the Empress Eugénie and the Comtesse de Noailles. Poems after all are a heightened, dramatic use of language and Cocteau had been introduced to creative life through men of outstanding theatrical power – Diaghilev, Nijinsky, Stravinsky, Picasso.

Cocteau's first contributions to the theatre were in the form of ballets, which are poems in theatrical terms. He began with the conventional (in Diaghilev terms) *Dieu Bleu* in 1911 and continued with the novel but not successful *Parade* in 1916–17. The composition and performance of *Le Boeuf sur le Toit* are discussed in this anthology, where I should like also to have included that delightful creation *Les Mariés de la Tour Eiffel* (1921), but the text alone is only half the work – this *comédie-ballet* should be seen, and its accompanying music, by the composers known as *Les Six*, heard at the same time. It is a proof of how Cocteau, essentially an individualist, possessed the quality of grouping together elements which might seem irreconcilable and producing something both novel and homogeneous at once.

The writing of plays continued for the rest of Cocteau's life, interspersed with ballets such as *Le Jeune Homme et la Mort* (1946) and *Phèdre* (1950). It is through his plays that Cocteau first became internationally known, his films later increasing his fame even further. *La Voix Humaine*, that astonishing monologue which he took to the Comédie Française as soon as he had completed his disintoxication from opium in 1930, continues to provide a vehicle for actresses and has an even stronger impact now than when it was first produced, for everyone is more preoccupied today with the problem of communication. It is not reproduced here since it is easily available in translation. *La Machine Infernale* (1934) is studied in Britain by students preparing for entrance to the universities. The other major plays have been performed internationally – W. H. Auden translated *Les Chevaliers de la Table Ronde* (1937), and the controversial *Bacchus* (1951) was given its English language première, in Mary Hoeck's translation, by the BBC in London. For this anthology I have chosen two short works, previously untranslated, which are good examples of Cocteau's dramatic skill.

There is no medium in which Cocteau did not practise, and in the early 'thirties he was tempted by the cinema. *Le Sang d'un Poète* (1932) is an enigmatic and curiously cruel, un-human film, but it has known great success, especially in the United States. Its symbolism becomes clearer when seen *after* a study of other work, including the film *Orphée*, the latter being in my opinion one of the most dynamic of Cocteau's creations, for it is fast-moving entertainment and a summing-up of what he felt about death, expressed partly through an obsession with mirrors, 'the gates through which death comes and goes'. One is immediately reminded of two striking scenes in *Le Livre Blanc* in each of which the mirror plays an important part : first, the imitation mirror through which the man watches the onanist love-making of another man and experiences orgasm himself; second, the mirror which the young man kisses before shooting himself. And the reason for the suicide is significant: he could not bear the idea that the narrator, with whom he is in love, might marry his sister. The mirror, and its inevitable association with Narcissus, is never far away from the image of death and from the realization that homosexual love cannot bring total happiness in ordinary human terms because it cannot perpetuate life.

The film *Orphée* is exceptionally poetic and full of symbolic imagery. There is poetry of intensely differing kinds in most of Cocteau's films : *L'Eternel Retour* (1944), *La Belle et la Bête* (1945) and *Les Parents Terribles* (1938) prove this to be so. Some films, such as *L'Aigle à Deux Têtes*, based on the stage play of 1946, seem to me lacking in poetry; but this is a subjective response, it may exist for others. Many people have started to value Cocteau's work after a first approach through films, even though each film is different from all the others. But for those who have seen none of them I would recommend the lyrical and undemanding *La Belle et la Bête*, of which Cocteau also kept a diary while filming proceeded.

In this discursive introduction I have so far attempted to show the range of Cocteau's work, all of which he regarded as 'poetry', without mentioning any specific poems or books of poems. He wrote so many poems of all types and lengths that they could only be examined adequately in a book-length study. His style in poetry reflects that of the work as a whole – it shows infinite variations within an integrated whole. While I have chosen only a few poems, I have attempted to include examples of various phases, from the early *L'Ode à Picasso* to the relatively late *Crucifixion*, wishing that there had been space for the important *L'Ange Heurtebise* from the collection *Opéra* (1927). It is remarkable that the unconventional Cocteau wrote so much rhymed verse in regular metres.

Unfortunately there is no room here to discuss his poetic antecedents, but several clues about them will come to light in the 'critical poetry'. This includes a great number of prose works which editors today would class as non-fiction. By choosing to call them 'critical poetry' Cocteau did not mean criticism in the sense generally accepted in publishing or journalism today. Just as he thought of 'poetry' as creation of all types, he thought of 'criticism' in its Greek sense of judgment, without the destructive factor so often implied in the current usage of the word. It is important to remember here the phrase 'I love loving, I hate hatred', for Cocteau's 'criticism' often consists of what could be described as unquestioning eulogy. The reader may disagree for instance with his praise or assessment of Erik Satie, or Giorgio de Chirico, El Greco or Barbette, but the praise remains stimulating to read. Similarly descriptions of travel incidents or drug-taking or bull-fighting may sound inaccurate or unreal; but none the less, they constitute reportage in which 'truth' has supplied themes for improvisation and undergone endless changes of key. The selections given here from the critical poetry are small in relation to Cocteau's output but I hope they will stimulate the reader to explore further. It is worth noting that this section of his work contains a great deal of autobiography, while the author is careful to point out that his memory was never accurate. 'Truth' was subjective not objective for him, and the 'I' never sounds wrong – it was the only way he could think or talk.

It is in the 'critical poetry' naturally that one finds the most direct expression of the themes or concepts which characterize the whole of Cocteau's work and reappear with a frequency which can only be described as obsessive. One of the most important is the concept of 'invisibility', closely linked with the professionalism which for him implied a kind of acrobatic skill, a skill which made everything look easy. In one way the insistence on invisibility was characteristically French, for it was always concerned with elegance. Cocteau was fond of quoting Beau Brummell's remark to the Prince Regent : 'I can't have been elegant at the ball because you noticed me.' In other words true elegance is unseen, invisible, while inelegance is noticed. Cocteau believed that this concept applied to the much more worthwhile elegance of behaviour and style, for elegance is wholeness, harmony. Striking examples of Cocteau's insistence on this theme can be found in his writing about de Chirico and Barbette in *Secrets de Beauté* and of course in *Le Secret Professionnel.* A belief in the invisibility of elegance seems strange in someone so preoccupied with 'astonishing' others, as Diaghilev had ordered him to do. Yet Cocteau found no difficulty in reconciling these two notions. 'Astonishment' was to be found less in the crudity of shock than in the bold but careful execution of a stimulating theme, and the theme itself need not even be new.

The only aspect of Cocteau's work not yet mentioned is the

'graphic poetry', the drawing which he regarded as merely another aspect of handwriting. Many writers have enjoyed drawing or painting and this, to them, subsidiary form of expression often illuminated their written work. Victor Hugo's drawings, for instance, have recently received a good deal of attention from scholars for this very reason. Cocteau's visual sense was highly developed and he was no spare-time artist, as the drawings from *Opium* prove – they express states of mind which could in fact hardly be described in words. It is particularly significant that the 'Eugènes' which led to the writing of *Le Potomak* came to life originally through drawings on a blotter. Several of the novels have included drawings – although not necessarily on first publication – and some are reproduced in the present collection.

There is no room here for the reproduction of larger scale works or stage design. However, the reader will find no difficulty in relating the visual work to the books, even when it serves more as decoration than as part of the writing itself. It is of course unfair to show reproductions of paintings such as the now famous decorations for the chapel of Saint-Pierre in Villefranche, in the South of France, or for the marriage-room at the *mairie* in Menton. Work of this type can only be appreciated in its architectural context.

Finally I would recommend anyone particularly interested in the more literary and biographical aspects of the 'graphic poetry' to make a study of Cocteau's self-portraits over the years. Whatever their artistic merits they reveal a total honesty, not unexpected in the man who drew his own portrait in words in the autobiographical book *La Difficulté d'Etre* (1947) : ' ... my body is neither tall nor short, but slender and lean, fitted with hands which are admired because they are long-fingered and very expressive; my head is unrewarding and gives me a false arrogance. This is due to a desire to overcome the embarrassment I feel at showing myself the way I am, and the rapidity with which it melts away is due to my fear that it might be taken for real arrogance'.

Mention has already been made of some writings omitted here because they are generally available, but it is only right to refer to one or two others which I should have liked to include but did not do so through fear of over-involvement in biographical detail, which is not my principal concern. The *Lettre à Jacques Maritain* for instance, published in 1926, is concerned with Cocteau's friendship with the author, who, rumour had it, had brought the poet back to the Church. Cocteau maintained that he could not be brought back because in fact he had never left. He tried to link his own ideas about aesthetics and the 'divine' origin of poetry to Catholicism, but when Maritain replied to the letter, he could not accept such a programme as a testimony of faith. The preface to the play *Bacchus,* concerned with the problem of youth today, includes many themes showing a remarkable far-sightedness on Cocteau's part, but the play and the polemics surrounding it are too much involved with French personalities and politics for inclusion in this selection.

The intellectual establishment, in most countries of the world, has been continually cool towards Cocteau, regarding him as a clever tightrope walker, a kind of literate Barbette. The orthodox literary critics have remained understandably suspicious of someone who practised in so many fields and appeared to offer some intangible 'message' of no great originality. Memories of Ancient Greece and obscure recollections of Nietzsche, an admiration of theatrical and acrobatic skill, an obsession with death, the relationship between the real and the unreal, the semi-personification of the unconscious as an 'angel', the use of word-play as a form of free association : how can such random elements add up to a coherent whole? Fortunately Cocteau was not concerned with constructing a system, he merely said what he wanted to say. The elements fall into place, they are complementary but at the same time complete within themselves. Cocteau did not wish to teach or analyse, he wanted to speak as a 'poet'. His interest in social conditions and politics was often naïve or clumsy. He was fascinated by youth because youth is generally a period of creativity; Cocteau the man hoped to stay perpetually young, but being mortal he failed. Cocteau the writer remained youthful, and there is little significant change in his voice from the beginning to the end of his life. Timbre and speed may have varied, but intonation never.

It would be unfair to compare Cocteau with the monolithic classical writers of the twentieth century; for them writing was a profession, while Cocteau wanted only to be himself and say what he felt. He showed childish delight when he was elected to the Académie Française but it would be more appropriate to see him as an academy of one.

Cocteau does not solve problems or tell anyone what attitude they should take – except to be aware of poetry and live with its creative spirit. This is the only way in which we break through the barrier between life and death, the only way in which we lose concern as to whether time moves forward or backwards, as to whether the real and the unreal are in any way different from each other. Our one concern is with the perpetually creative intermingling of the two; if we maintain this concern we can dispel the invasion of materialism, the truly destructive force at work today.

Cocteau said that all a poet wanted was to be believed. No one can be believed or disbelieved until he has been read, and my main

purpose in arranging this selection from his writing and drawing
has been to enlarge his readership. For many people Cocteau has
been a vague figure associated mainly with homosexual love-affairs
and a narcissistic preoccupation with himself. His memory was
good or bad depending on his requirements of the moment. Sometimes he would tell bad jokes or fail to see a joke at all, though he
had a sense of humour. The critics of Cocteau who laughed at him
fared badly, but they survived and will always be there, in larger
or smaller numbers according to the fashion of the times. They will
never be out of work. I hope this book will establish a proper
relationship between biography and artistic production.

Rarely indeed has a writer's life been so closely interwoven with
his work and rarely has the work been so neglected or misconstrued.
During the next fifty years or so more and more of this detail will
be published and jealously examined by biographers and critics.
There will be much gossip, entertainment and certainly rewarding moments when some of the more enigmatic work will
suddenly be clarified for us. But the essential thing is not to argue
about what Cocteau did and said among friends and enemies, but
to examine and think about his creation. He was a creator, a poet.
'I shall disturb after my death,' he wrote. Creation is a dynamic
process and includes within itself an inseparable process of continued renewal. Creation is neither comfortable nor comforting,
which is why it disturbs. Cocteau's world is continually alive, and
like no other. It can be accepted or analysed, those who approach
it may react as they wish. *Je dérangerai après ma mort.*

I should like to thank Peter Owen for his encouragement during
the preparation of this book, Michael Levien for his creative edit-
ing, Rollo Myers for allowing me to reprint the first translations in
English of a Cocteau book, and for showing me unpublished
material, and finally the late Mary Hoeck, friend and translator of
Cocteau, for all the ways in which she illuminated my understanding of the poet.

Margaret Crosland

# PART ONE

*Novels and Stories*

# The Miscreant

*The Miscreant* is the English title given to Cocteau's first published novel, *Le Grand Ecart*. The French phrase means 'the splits', a term used in dancing or acrobatics. Cocteau apparently intended it to refer to the gap between innocent young men and sophisticated young women (*un écart* means a gap or deviation).

It is not difficult to see the likeness between Jacques Forestier, the hero, and Cocteau himself, for the two young men did the same things : they both made a trip to Venice with their mother, attended a cramming establishment and had love-affairs with girls and/or young men. The Germaine-Louise relationship shows some similarities with the Jeanne-Berthe situation in *Le Livre Blanc*. Cocteau introduces the same incident or set of circumstances in more than one book, as though he could never forget the experience in question.

*The Miscreant* is entertaining and even frivolous on the surface but suggests some underlying sadness. Although it has no 'message' it seems to say, without sentimentality, that love is hard to find and does not last long.

## PREFACE

Of all my books, *Le Grand Ecart* is the one that dates, and that is deliberate. I mean in which the period is caught, cruelly pinned to a cork like the entomologist's butterfly. Besides, I liked substituting swift significant anecdotes for argument and voluminous studies, threaded on the red string of love – on a unifying action, action which would bring out the awful loneliness of youth – but of a youth carried away by his relationships.

My whole work hangs on the drama of loneliness and man's attempts to overcome it. It is shown here without contrivances (except those of my youthful accomplices), and, as it were, utterly naked.

I

Jacques Forestier cried easily. Films, bad music, a romantic serial, would bring tears to his eyes. He did not confuse these deceptive signs of soft-heartedness with deep tears. These seemed to come to his eyes for no reason.

As he hid his shallow tears in the darkness of a theatre-box or alone with a book, he was considered an insensitive and witty man.

He had a reputation for wit because his mind was sharp. He would take rhymes from the four winds and link them in such a way that they seemed to have rhymed always. By rhymes we mean: anything at all.

He would force the meaning of proper nouns, faces, actions and diffident suggestions to extremes. This behaviour earned him a reputation for lying.

He also admired handsome figures and faces, regardless of their sex. Because of this last peculiarity he was given credit for loose living; this being the only thing for which credit is given without forethought.

As Jacques' appearance was not all he would have desired, and did not conform with his own ideal type of young man, he stopped trying to live up to the ideal which was too far from him. He exaggerated his weak points, mannerisms and ridiculous ways until they were no longer liabilities. He deliberately brought them out.

Through tilling barren soil, forcing and improving weeds, he had acquired a hard streak that was quite inconsistent with his gentleness.

He had been slim; he deliberately became thin: he had been nervous; he made his nerves raw. As his bristly, yellow hair was difficult to control, he kept it untidy. Besides, an appearance as artificial as possible gave him the advantages of artifice, hiding a bourgeois love of order, the unhealthy detachment which he inherited from his father, and his mother's melancholia.

If one of the skilful, ferocious Parisian huntsmen dislodged him, it was easy to wring his neck. He could be demoralized with a single word.

*

Out of contempt for the simple superiority which consists in running counter to the spirit of one's class, Jacques adopted the spirit of his; but in him it took such a different form his equals could not recognize it as their own.

In short, he was handsome in a suspicious way : like an animal.

This aristocrat, this son of the people, who could not bear the aristocracy or the masses, deserved the Bastille and guillotine a dozen times a day. He was not satisfied with the Right or the Left, which he thought weak. Only his extremist nature could see no golden mean.

In accordance with the axiom *extremes meet*, he dreamt of a virgin extreme Right so close to the extreme Left that it almost merged with it – but where he could act independently. The chair would not exist, but if it did, it would be unoccupied. Jacques nominated himself to take it, and from that seat he surveyed all politics, art and behaviour.

He was not trying to engineer a reward. That provokes censure.

From schemers, because detachment brings a certain good luck which they could not admit to be independent of intrigue. From those who give the reward, because they are never asked for it.

To continue. Jacques wondered where successful people get to. Did Napoleon get to the Coronation or St Helena? Does a train get anywhere if it makes a sensation by running off the lines and killing the passengers? Does it get farther if it reaches the station?

A closer search for a profile of Jacques leads me to denounce him as a parasite on earth.

Indeed, where was the document that authorized him to enjoy a meal, a fine evening, a girl or men? Let him show it. All society confronts him like a civil servant and demands it. He is confused. He stammers. He cannot find it.

This pleasure-seeker whose feet were planted firmly on the ground, this critic of scenery and man-made things, was holding on to the earth by a single thread.

He was as heavy as a diver.

Jacques dug around on the bottom. He could sense it. He had acclimatized himself to it. No one brought him up to the surface again. They had forgotten him. To come up, to take the helmet and the suit off, was to pass from life to death. But a breath of illusion blew down the tube, bringing him to life and overwhelming him with nostalgia.

*

Jacques spent his life struggling with one long fit of fainting. He felt unstable. He built no foundations except for amusement. He hardly dared sit down. He was the kind of sailor who cannot get over his seasickness.

*

Beauty which is strictly physical has an assuming, arrogant manner of being at home everywhere. Exiled, Jacques coveted it. The less desirable it was, the more it affected him; for it was his fate to be hurt by it always.

He saw a dance through the windows : the race who have their papers in order, who are glad to be alive, in their proper element with no use for diving-suits.

So he wove dreams around unkind faces.

\*

This is what the ideal graphologist would learn from the handwriting of Jacques Forestier who is now studying himself in his wardrobe mirror.

Make no mistake. We have just drawn Jacques in full face, but even here we have no more than a profile of his character. That is why we were speaking of an ideal graphologist. In disentangling the strokes of the pen, he would have to disentangle the whole line of a life. Jacques will become the man who precedes partly as a result of what is to follow; and what is to follow will happen partly as a result of what precedes.

\*

Objects and atoms take their business seriously. If the mirror were not concentrating, Jacques could doubtless put in one leg and then the other, until he was standing at a vital angle so new as to be inconceivable. No. The mirror was playing safe. The mirror was a mirror. The wardrobe a wardrobe. The room a room, on the second floor, Rue de l'Estrapade.

He was still thinking of the Englishman who committed suicide having written : *too many buttons to do up and undo, I'm killing myself.* For Jacques was unbuttoning his jacket.

Waiting. What was he waiting for? Jacques would have liked to have been waiting for something definite, to simplify the wait. He did not believe, or his belief took such a muddled form that his mother prayed for him, considering him an atheist.

Having a vague belief makes the mind dilettante. He believed too much. He did not limit his beliefs or define them. Limiting one's beliefs fixes a spiritual attitude just as defining and limiting one's beliefs in art fixes an attitude of mind.

\*

He studied himself. He inflicted the sight on himself.

\*

We are full of things which make us hate ourselves. Since his childhood he had longed to be one of those whom he thought handsome and not to be loved for it by them. He did not like his own good looks. He thought he was ugly.

Memories of human beauty stayed with him like wounds. One evening at Mürren, for example. At the foot of the mountains, visitors gulp down cold beer that shoots directly to the head and blows it to smithereens. The cable-car moves off through the blackberry-bushes. Their ears are gradually blocked, their noses clear; they have arrived.

Jacques was eleven years old. He remembered a priest who had lost his trunk, being half asleep, the hotel with its sweet smell of resin, their grimy arrival in the lounge where the ladies were playing patience, the men smoking and reading the papers. Suddenly, as they stopped in front of the lift-shaft, the lift came down and dropped a couple. A young man and a girl with dark faces and starry eyes, laughing and displaying magnificent teeth. The girl was wearing a blue dress with a blue belt. The boy was dressed for dinner. There was a clatter of crockery and a foul smell of cooking in the corridors.

Once in his room, which looked out on to a wall of ice, Jacques looked at himself. He compared himself to the couple. He would gladly have died.

Later he got to know the young pair. Tigrane d'Ybreo, the son of an Armenian from Cairo, collected stamps and concocted sickly sweets over a spirit-lamp. His sister Idgi wore new dresses and dilapidated shoes. They used to dance together.

The dilapidated shoes and the honey cakes denoted a royal but sordid race. Jacques dreamt of this cooking and the holes. He desired them. He saw in them the only means of identifying himself with these two sacred cats. He wanted to collect stamps, make almond toffees. He wore his tennis pumps out by an artificial method.

Idgi was always coughing. She was tubercular. Tigrane broke his leg skating. Their father used to receive telegrams. One morning they went away coughing and limping, followed by a dog as mysterious as Anubis.

Jacques coughed. His mother was desperately worried. He let her suffer for him. He was coughing for love. On the road he would limp when no one was looking.

Every evening after dinner, when he sat in the straw-bottomed chair, he fancied he could see Idgi, in her Virgin Mary dress, framed in the lighted lift between the pageboy and Tigrane, as she was borne up by angels into heaven.

From eleven to eighteen years old he burnt himself up, like the Armenian paper that flares up quickly and has an unpleasant smell.

Finally, the journeys to Switzerland came to an end. Mme Forestier took him from the Italian lakes to Venice.

*

By Lake Maggiore he met a student teacher who was annotating Bergson and Taine. He had a fair moustache, an eye-glass, and his humour was a parody of Barres'. His intellect was sharp. He savoured it like barley sugar as he wore it away. This undisciplined disciple thought nothing of the Borromean Islands. He nicknamed them 'The Isola sisters'.

This witticism was Jacques' first revelation of how freely the senses can be used. He accepted these islands without investigation.

*

By day, Venice is the shattered pieces of an ornate shooting-range on a fairground. By night, she is an amorous Negress lying dead in her bath with her tawdry jewels.

On the night of their arrival the hotel gondola is as entertaining as a fairground amusement. It is no ordinary vehicle. Unhappily, parents do not see it that way. Venice begins the next day. Tonight they do not take a gondola; they take a bus. They count the trunks. The town is like the Opéra, backstage; they do not look at it.

The following morning Jacques saw the crowd of tourists. Trapped in the theatrical setting of St Mark's Square, this fashionable crowd discloses every secret it has, as it might at a masked ball. The most immodest frankness overrides age and sex. The shyest finally venture the gesture or the dress which they hardly dared contemplate in London or Paris.

The masked ball is certainly revealing. It might be a medical board. With her footlights and spotlights Venice lays hearts bare.

For Jacques, the pangs of love were to take a more deceptive turn than at Mürren. As he lay under his mosquito-net at night, he could hear guitars, tenors. He suspected clandestine meetings. He cried because he was not the town. Heliogabalus, in his wildest flights of fancy, demanded no more.

The student from Baveno was passing through Venice. He introduced Jacques to a young journalist and a dancer. They often went out together.

One night when the journalist was going back with Jacques as far as his hotel, he said : 'I live a vile life in Paris. I am in love with this girl who has no inkling of it. When I go back, I can't possibly continue my old relationships, and on the other hand I know I shall find it very hard to break them off.'

'But ... if Berthe is in love with you?' (this was the dancer's name).

'Oh! She doesn't love me. You ought to know that. In any case, I intend to kill myself in two hours.'

Jacques jokingly reminded him of the classic suicide of Venice and wished him good night.

The journalist committed suicide. The dancer was in love with Jacques. He had not seen it and only came to know of it years later through a third person.

This episode left him disgusted with the nauseating poetry of disease. He still had an intermittent fever caught on a walk in the Eaden Garden which was an unpleasant reminder of his stay.

*

Mme Forestier was afraid of colds, bronchitis and motor accidents. She did not distinguish spiritual dangers. She let Jacques play with them.

*

Venice had disappointed Jacques like a stage-set that is warped with use, because every performer erects it for at least one act of his life.

After two hours of walking and concentrating in the museums, the splendour fell on his shoulders like a dead weight.

Half dead with exhaustion and cramp, he came out, went down the steps, saw the Palazzo Dario bowing to the boxes in front like an old singer, and returned to his hotel. He admired the vigour of the couples who go round Venice with insect-like activity. Those who know her by heart and have dipped their trumpets hundreds of times before into the golden pollen of St Mark show their new sweethearts round the square. This Ciceronian role rejuvenates them. They only pause to sit down in a shop, where the object of their affections buys glass jewellery, volumes of Wilde and D'Annunzio.

Stimulated by his slight fever, Jacques, like us when we recall it, was filled with mounting distaste for this charming brothel where the rarest spirits slake their thirst.

Our very insistence proves how far he had succumbed to a spell which his dark side repelled.

\*

Half dark, half light : this is the way of the planets. One half of the world rests, the other works. But from the half that is dreaming there emanates a mysterious strength.

In man, the sleeping half contradicts the active. It is the voice of nature itself.

If the lesson bears fruit, the man listens and puts his light side in order, the dark side will grow dangerous. Its role will change. It will give out poisonous fumes. We are to see Jacques struggling with this night of the body.

For the time being it was protecting him, providing him with antidotes, files and rope-ladders.

\*

All help does not achieve its end. Paris is a more cunning town than Venice, in the sense that its pitfalls are better hidden and its equipment is not so simple. You know in advance with Venice, as with certain houses, that there is water, the chamber of mirrors, the Veronese room, the Bridge of Sighs, weary beauties in pink petticoats, and the danger of infection.

You can hardly recognize yourself in Paris.

Jacques, the Parisian, the privileged, returned to Paris from the provinces.

He had come from there five months before, but on the way he had crossed the narrow borderline to the age at which the mind and the body can choose.

His mother thought she was bringing back the same person, rather disturbed by the panoramas of Italy. She was bringing back another person. And it was precisely in Venice that the change had occurred. Jacques only felt it through his uneasiness. He attributed that to the suicide and the unexpected meetings at night in the arcades. In reality, he was leaving a dry skin floating on the Grand Canal, like a snake's slough hanging on a wild rose-bush, as light as foam, slit at the eyes and mouth.

## II

The map of our life is folded in such a way that we cannot see one main road across it, but, as it is opened out, we are constantly seeing new side roads. We think we are choosing, and we have no choice.

*

A young Persian gardener said to his Prince : 'I met death this morning. She made me a sign of warning. Save me. By some miracle I should like to be in Ispahan tonight.'

The good Prince lent him his horses. That afternoon the Prince met death.

'Why did you make a sign of warning at our gardener this morning?' he asked.

'I did not make a sign of warning but a sign of surprise,' she answered. 'For this morning I saw him far from Ispahan, and I am to take him in Ispahan tonight.'

*

Jacques was working for his baccalauréat. His parents, obliged to live in Touraine for a year after the loss of a perfect bailiff, sent him to M. Berlin's boarding school in the Rue de l'Estrapade.

M. Berlin rented two floors. He kept the first to himself and put the boarders together on the second, five rooms off a sordid corridor, lit by a gas burner so encrusted with dirt that it would not turn full on.

Jacques' room was between those of Mouheddin Bashtarzi, the son of a rich merchant from Saint-Eugène, which is the Auteuil of Algiers, and of an albino : Pierre de Maricelles. A very young boy with a weak but engaging face lived opposite. He answered to the pseudonym of Petitcopain.

The year before, in the Sologne, he and his younger brother had wanted to play a trick on their tutor. But just as they were going to enter his room at midnight, dressed up as ghosts, the door opened, and their mother came out in her night-gown, with her hair rumpled. They were hidden by the door. She crossed the hall, put her ear to their father's door, and returned to the tutor's room without seeing them.

Petitcopain was never to forget the moment when they got back into bed without saying a word.

*

The last room was chaos. There in the flotsam of textbooks, exercise-books, ties, shirts, pipes, ink, tubs, sponges, fountain-pens, handkerchiefs and blankets, camped Peter Stopwell, long-jump champion.

*

Mme Berlin was far more sprightly than her husband, left a widower after his first marriage. She simpered and thought that the boys were in love with her. Occasionally she would go into one of their rooms, where the boy would be standing in a stupid position after rushing to hide some occupation unconnected with his work. She would look the reddening boy up and down, and burst out laughing.

She would declaim Racine in places where it is appropriate to be quiet. One day, when she realized that she was caught out, the boys heard her change her oration into a cough which gradually lapsed into silence.

One significant feature of Mme Berlin was this. When they were first married in the country, Berlin and she had taken in a lodger, a divorced woman who was a pianist. Berlin came home on the seven o'clock train every evening after college. One evening he had to stay in town. Mme Berlin, who was very frightened, begged the pianist to sleep near her. The pianist made the best of it and moved into the family bed. Berlin slept out twice in one week, and his wife put her question again. The pianist wished her bedfellow good night, turned to the wall, and returned quickly to her room the following morning.

Seven years later, when a group of people were talking about the pianist, all accusing her of having doubtful morals, Mme Berlin smiled mysteriously and declared that to judge from her personal experience she had every reason to believe that the woman absolutely flaunted her vices.

She was a naïve actress, hoping for example to take in her guests when she served the tea lukewarm by pretending to burn her tongue.

'Don't drink!' she would cry. 'Wait! It's boiling!'

Berlin surveyed his wife, his boys, and life with lacklustre eyes behind pince-nez.

He wore a white beard and slippers. He had trousers like the man acting the hind legs of an elephant at the circus. He taught at the Sorbonne, played cards in the Café Voltaire and came home to sleep. His pupils took advantage of his sleepiness to recite whatever they liked.

The maid completes the picture. There was never the same one. They were changed every fortnight, generally because they dusted a Boule clock which M. Berlin always wound up himself and allowed no one else to touch.

At midday and eight o'clock they all met for a meal at which Mme Berlin served out leathery meat.

Her husband ate mechanically. Now and then he would be shaken by a gloomy hiccup which made him quiver like a mountain of snow.

*

Peter Stopwell would have had the beauty of a Greek if the long jump had not drawn him out like a photograph taken from the wrong angle. He had just come down from Oxford. Hence his fatuity, his boxes of cigarettes, his navy-blue muffler, and the multiform immorality beneath the sportsman's uniform. Petitcopain loved him.

On Sundays he carried a bag containing his sports clothes and bathrobe to the Parc des Princes.

To love and be loved, that is the ideal. Providing, of course, that the same person is involved. The opposite often happens. Petitcopain was in love and he was loved. Only he had a student in a laboratory in love with him and he was in love with Stopwell. His love stupefied him.

He was a victim of the half-light where the senses meet the emotions.

This love flattered Stopwell. He showed no sign of it. He snapped at the poor child.

'That is not done,' he would say in response to the slightest childish caresses. Or : 'You are not clean, you know. Wash yourself. Have a bath. Rub yourself down. You never have a bath. If you don't bath, you will *smell*.'

Stopwell's rebukes were often a kind of English teasing. But Petitcopain knew nothing but the A B C of laughter and tears. He did not understand. He thought he was dirty, wicked and stupid.

One evening when Petitcopain, seated on the edge of the bed where Peter Stopwell was smoking, put his hand religiously on his shoulder, Stopwell pushed him away and asked him if he was a girl to hang round men's necks.

Petitcopain dissolved into tears.

'Oh, you are always begging things of me, crying, touching me, petting me,' said Stopwell lighting a cigarette from the stub which he threw carelessly away. 'You'd do better to go out with girls. You can find one for sixpence behind the Panthéon.'

*

Maricelles was the sixth son of a family of delicate country squires. Constipation kept this albino endlessly in a place which he made inaccessible. With the Maricelles it was the rule that patience alone must solve such problems, the youngest brother having died of a ruptured aneurism for having tried to force fate.

'You love dirt, you French,' said Stopwell to Petitcopain. 'Molière talks about nothing but purges.'

Petitcopain hung his head and did not dare go through that ridiculous door.

*

Mouheddin Bashtarzi, of Turkish extraction, sported the tarboosh. He owned one in red, one in soft grey fur and one in astrakhan. He was big, fat, puerile. His visiting-cards bore the strange inscription:

### MOUHEDDIN BASHTARZI
#### INSPECTOR

He wrote poems, inhaled ether. One day when the smell of ether was growing too strong, Jacques went into his room and found him sitting on the sill of the open window with his tarboosh on his head, slavering and holding his left nostril with one hand and putting a medicine bottle to the right nostril with the other. Not hearing Jacques he was swaying, deafened by the cicadas that were frozen by the drug.

Was that the ideal environment in the mind of a delicate mother, afraid of germs and draughts?

*

After a few difficult days Jacques had just settled into the Berlin place, when a tragicomical interlude broke the peace. Petitcopain fell ill in such a way that there could be no doubt as to the cause of his pains.

M. Berlin got the truth from him. He learnt that the poor child had taken Stopwell's advice literally. Petitcopain was sobbing.

'It's unbelievable,' cried Mme Berlin. 'But the story ought not to be spread.'

Jacques went to see him every day. One evening, in an expressionless voice, Petitcopain begged him to ask Peter why he had never come to his room.

Stopwell was annotating Auguste Comte, in a haze.

'Why, simply because he disgusts me,' he said. 'Do you think I would want to see a boy who sleeps with diseased women. *I* don't sleep with anyone.'

'You are hard,' murmured Jacques. 'The poor child; he is not asking much . . .'

'Not much! What if my regiment could see me with him, fiddling about with my hands? I think you must be going mad.'

His 'What if my regiment could see me?' sounded like a girl saying 'What if my mother could see me?'

Jacques was preparing to go when Peter pulled him back by the sleeve, opening a box of cigarettes.

'What? Are you going back to that ape? At Oxford we treat them like servants. Leave him alone and stay with me.'

His hand was gripping Jacques with Herculean strength. He made him sit down on his trunk.

Was his gesture enough to remove a mask? Roses lose their flaw-less cheeks in the same way once we have struck the vase. Jacques saw a new face, utterly naked, without a trace of composure.

He rose.

'No, Stopwell, it's late,' he said, 'I have to write a letter.'

'Just as you like, old man.'

With the skill of a trickster, Stopwell turned round to show a face repaired, a new mask, supported by a cigarette.

*

In short Petitcopain did not like Jacques, being jealous of the pretended favours bestowed on him. Stopwell loathed Petitcopain and deliberately misled him. Bashtarzi resented him for having come in while he was inhaling ether. Maricelles despised the whole lot of them.

There remained the Berlin family.

Occasionally at mealtimes a pertinent remark from Jacques would bring a light to the master's eye and Mme Berlin appointed as supervisor by her husband would always stay longer in his room than in the others. She did not think Stopwell a 'gentleman'. The Arab 'frightened' her. The others were children.

One Saturday night when all the boys had gone out either to their families or to the theatre, Jacques, who had a sore throat, was left alone on that floor. Mme Berlin brought him some herbal tea, felt his forehead and his pulse. Jacques soon saw that the mistress of the house was playing Stopwell's game; but this time instead of his coldness being enough to quench the flames, it was fanning them, and Mme Berlin was unconsciously abandoning the role of second mother.

Jacques pretended not to understand, and while he coughed, moaning like an invalid trying to sleep, he watched Mme Berlin through his eyelids, a Mme Berlin driven mad by desire, just as her shadow was driven by the candle to left and to right against the walls of the room.

In the end, with an amazing grip, she grabbed his hand.

'Jacques, Jacques, what are you doing then?' she murmured.

The sound of a side door saved him. Mme Berlin let go, put herself straight and rushed out.

Mouheddin was coming back from the theatre. Jacques heard him whistling a popular song. He went wrong and repeated the mistake.

The following day at mealtime Jacques did not dare look at Mme Berlin. She, on the other hand, faced him bravely, reassured him, forgave him.

*

Jacques was living in complete solitude, and working like a real slacker. What did he know? Nothing. Only that our every movement brings us into conflict with our fellow-men. He would gladly have died of his sore throat. But he had almost stopped coughing.

Mouheddin suggested that they should go to the Scala together. You can get a stage-box very cheaply for the matinées on Sundays and Thursdays. Jacques tried to be pleasant. He agreed. They lured Petitcopain. He received nice little sums of money from his family who lived in the north.

In this way, on the third Sunday, Jacques met Mouheddin's mistress : Louise Champagne.

Louise was better known than her dancing and had a better position in the demi-monde than on the theatre bills. She was one of the women who make two pounds at the theatre and two thousand at home. She told Jacques that he could not live alone and that she would find him a friend : Germaine.

This popular girl played four parts in the revue which was ready to flop exhausted after 350 performances.

Germaine smiled high up between the orchestra and the drum. Her beauty was near ugliness, but in the same way as an acrobat is near death. It was a way of arousing emotion.

This black and white attracted Jacques.

Unfortunately the kind of liberty we enjoy allows us to misbehave in a way which plants and animals avoid. With Louise's lamp Jacques felt his desire again.

After the first contact in her dressing-room, Louise took on the final arrangements and asked Jacques to go and see her at her home in the Rue Montchanin.

The following day he cut lessons, as schoolboys say, left Mouheddin there and ran to the place where they were to meet.

\*

He found Champagne crestfallen. Germaine did not like him. She thought him attractive. He was not her type.

Louise felt sad to have to pass on bad news.

'Poor little thing!'

She stroked the back of his neck, tweaked his nose, in short openly offered to console him.

Peter, Mme Berlin, well and good. It was growing more difficult to refuse. Louise Champagne was beautiful and there was no way of getting off the sofa. They deceived the Arab.

Bashtarzi had no suspicions and cursed Germaine, for she had a larger car than Louise's little runabout, and Mouheddin already saw a harem life ahead of him.

One Sunday Jacques was walking backstage past Germaine's dressing-room. She called him, shut him in, and asked him why he had backed out after the steps Louise had taken and her own favourable reply and gone so far as to make Louise behave as rudely as himself.

Jacques was amazed. Germaine saw that his amazement was not simulated, talked him round, consoled him, and stopped speaking to Louise.

On the pretext that he loathed to deceive Mouheddin, Jacques followed up his new conquest. Louise went to Mouheddin and accused Jacques of having made advances to her. She refused to see him.

The neighbours in the Rue de l'Estrapade lived as strangers to one another.

### III

In Paris, art, especially the worst, removes stains like magic. It does not wash them out, it mounts them. From then on a bad reputation, given top billing, is as useful as a good one. It needs to be as carefully guarded. Many kept women use the stage to make them immune. The theatre is a tax they pay, but it interferes with their work.

After the theatre treatment Germaine and Louise gave themselves a holiday. They made it a long one. They did not make a living out of art.

Germaine had a rich lover, so rich that his name alone meant wealth. He was called Nestor Osiris, like a box of cigarettes. Lazare his brother kept Loute, Germaine's younger sister.

Germaine was loving and would gladly have sent Osiris to the devil, but her sister was thinking of the future.

She disapproved of Jacques. Although she herself had deceived Lazare with a painter she knew that her sister would not play the trick cautiously and was afraid of the consequences.

She was as much like Germaine as a plaster cast is to the original marble. That is to say they were alike, except in every way.

\*

In spite of the abominable air Jacques had been breathing since his seizure, his heart was still in a state of innocence and capable of an ideal love.

\*

Germaine's bloom came from the manure-heap. She fed on it as greedily as a rose; and while the rose presents the picture of a long mouth sucking up perfume from the dead, her laugh, her lips and cheeks owed their brightness to the failures of the Bourse.

\*

The indifference of a landscape gives us every opportunity of sneering at it. Had Venice offered herself, would Jacques have sneered at Venice?

\*

The heart lives in confinement. Hence its outbursts of melancholy, its fits of deep despair. Ever ready to pour out its riches, it is at the mercy of its membrane. What does it know, the poor blind thing? It watches anxiously for the slightest sign that would relieve the tedium. Thousands of nerves bring the news. Is the object for which its help is sought a worthy one? It does not matter. It pours itself out trustingly, it drains itself dry, if it is ordered to stop, it writhes and gasps out its last.

Jacques' heart had just been told to start. It did so with a beginner's clumsiness and enthusiasm.

So Jacques was afraid of the first effects of the capsule which opens inside us and releases a powerful drug.

As quickly as a tiny woman in a group on the cinema screen is followed by the woman's face in close-up six times life size, Germaine's face filled the world, concealed the future and hid from Jacques not only his examinations and his friends but his mother, his father, himself. All around, darkness prevailed. This darkness also concealed Osiris.

There is a story in which children sew stones into the stomach of a sleeping wolf. When he awoke, Jacques felt an unknown weight, an unsteadiness that could have drowned him like the wolf as it bent over the water to drink.

Without a doubt, Germaine loved him. But her little heart was no beginner. It was not an equal match.

At the circus, a careless mother may let her child take part in the experiments of a Chinese magician. He puts him in a box. He opens the box; it is empty. He closes it again. He opens it; the child reappears and goes back to its seat. Now it is no longer the same child. Nobody doubts it.

\*

One Sunday Jacques saw his mother. She came to collect him at the boarding school. How could she sense his recent metamorphosis, after failing to realize that she had brought a changed son back from Venice? She thought he looked well, but rather thin. She was translating his exhaustion and burning cheeks into maternal language.

Mme Forestier was short-sighted and lived in the past; two reasons which prevented her from forming an accurate idea of present things. In her son she worshipped the resemblance to a grandmother, in her husband the father of Jacques. She appeared cold because she carried her scruples so far as to form no liaisons, being afraid of what she called infatuations. Her only friend was dead. Her life was divided between the Church, her husband, who was a good one, and her fears for Jacques' future.

Alone with him, she harassed him with tender criticism, but in front of strangers or her husband, she heaped praise on him.

If we leave M. Forestier in the background it is because he himself kept in the background. When he was young he suffered from a demon similar to the one that tortured Jacques. He kept it down by study and marriage. But a demon is difficult to keep down. His upright nature was atrophied. It felt that it had been bent. Now M. Forestier guessed what was disturbing Jacques and, recognizing it, he was as dismayed as a man with a sarcoma in his shoulder which has been cured, who feels the pain start again in his knee.

'So are you feeling well, Jacques?' said his mother.

'Yes, Mother.'

'Are you working?'

'Yes, Mother.'

'Your friends?'

'Nothing special. An Arab, an Englishman and two youngsters.'

'You should take the opportunity of living with an Englishman to learn his language.'

This sentence took Jacques so far from reality that he did not reply. He was usually glad to go shopping with his mother, but he now felt that the time they spent together was time wasted.

Deception irritated him, enveloped everything in a stifling atmosphere of artificiality. As he could not tell his mother about Germaine, he would have preferred her to go away, so that she would not force him to keep his distance from her.

He was in love.

He did not want to be Germaine. He wanted to possess her. For the first time, his desire did not manifest itself in the form of a sick feeling. For the first time, he did not hate his own reflection. He thought he was cured.

The vague longing for beauty is death to us.

We have explained how Jacques was wearing himself out with desire for thin air. Surely the figures and faces unmoved by our wild glances are thin air.

This time the desire met a sensitive surface, and Germaine's response was the very reflection of Jacques, just as the screen releases the film which, if there were no barrier, would only spread out in a white sheaf. Jacques saw himself in this desire, and for the first time he was overwhelmed at meeting himself. In Germaine he loved himself. He became unconscious of the character he would develop later, without trying to live up to his ideal.

Until then the women who liked him were not the ones he liked. He knew their weak profiles. All the heads in the world can be put into a few categories. He knew in advance that certain high-bosomed brunettes would fall in love with him.

Germaine did not belong to the generation of great intimidating girls with the same names as racehorses. But there was something unattainable, supernatural about her, the thing which can turn the sailor on the quay at Naples or a tennis player at Houlgate into a memory of unhappiness.

So one of the thousands of passers-by had stopped. He had

caught him in his trap. In him he would love all streets, all towns on his first night there, the disturbing temperature of ports, Idgi and Tigrane d'Ybreo, the jackal dog, the troupe of acrobats in Geneva and the circus rider in Rome.

He thought of these things uninterruptedly until the train left, taking Mme Forestier to Tours.


# IV


'Now don't worry, Loute,' said Germaine to her sister. 'Nestor won't notice anything. You'll have to introduce Jacques as a friend of your painter' (for moneybags knew that his brother was being deceived, which he as an egoist found entertaining). 'He loves being let into secrets, and we shall run less risk.'

Osiris was prodigiously credulous. His mistress was fostering this security in letting him into the conspiracy against Lazare.

On one of the first nights when Nestor was lying asleep by her side, a young actor whom she liked rang her bell through having mistaken the date.

'Hide, it's my old man,' she said to Osiris.

Osiris got up, collected his things, got into a wardrobe, was nearly suffocated in there while Germaine let the young man in, and went away bursting with pride.

Their relationship dated from this stroke of genius. Do not draw the conclusion that Germaine was dishonest. She was protecting herself. Her action was not calculated.

*

When they were very young her sister and she had dreamt of the Palais de Glace which they imagined as a hall of mirrors. They went in one Sunday and came out followed by a train of handsome men. One of them seduced Germaine.

When he left her, she took a job with a milliner in Montmartre. The milliner said one day, 'I am going to be arrested the day after tomorrow, my dear. Look after the shop, I'm clearing out.' She took her pearls and her clothes.

Germaine stayed, put a card in the window announcing that four-shilling hats were to be sold at sixpence, sold out in a morning, replaced the window display with soiled hats she found in the cellar, hired a cart with the money, moved the chairs, table and cheval glass out of the shop to the room which still belonged to her and let the bailiff take the rest.

She had the demon of the streets. She was not at all ashamed of it.

While dining with Loute, Nestor and Lazare in a fashionable restaurant, she had knocked her wine over. The head-waiter sprang forward and spread a piece of oilcloth over the stain until a table-cloth arrived. This piece of oilcloth reminded both sisters of one and the same thing. They glanced at each other. Loute blushed, but Germaine cried : 'Oh ! that oilcloth. It takes me back to Belle-ville, the lamp, the soup, and Father.'

Their real name was Rateau. Since Nestor, the Rateaux were not to be pitied. They were the owners of a delightful farm near Paris.

\*

The sisters, the Rateau farm, the Osirises, Jacques, his family and his dream make an explosive mixture. Yet it is shaped by fate, fond of handling men like chemicals.

\*

If Jacques' multitudinous desires were to crystallize, and we were to approach them in the same way as we approach Germaine, would the result be any the more fit to tell?

Narcissus was in love with himself. For this crime the gods turned him into a flower. The flower gives us headaches and its onion-like bulb does not even make us cry. Would he deserve any more tears?

The story of our Narcissus is more complex. He was in love with the river. But rivers flow on heedless of the bathers, the trees they reflect. Their desire is the sea. At the end of a perpetual journey they kiss and plunge voluptuously into her waters.

Jacques always felt that human beauty, like rivers, had a bed and a goal. It moved on, it went elsewhere. A ship weighs anchor, a curtain falls in the music-hall, the Ybreo family returns to its gods.

He recalled Idgi saying to him during a tennis match that he looked like Seti I. This was the only time he remembered the river looking at him.

This time the water stopped, ardently showing him his reflection. He deceived the sea. Perhaps he thought the water-sprite's voice was the water talking. But he did not analyse. His heart no longer gave him the time.

\*

We have said that frequent demands were made on Germaine's heart. This habit did not lessen the enthusiasm she put into her escapades. She was in love every time for the first time. She wondered how she could ever have loved other men and played her new game showing all her cards. She did not try to make the fire last by banking it up with cinders. She flared up as high and as quickly as possible.

Her ability to put herself into a primitive state with sincerity prevented her from meeting Jacques' passion with the mechanical passion of a thoroughly experienced woman.

The storm threw their possessions together, regardless of their source.

For if Jacques had wasted a lot but brought his dreams, Germaine who had given much, had received much. And so she did not meet him empty-handed.

The last sentence lends itself to a double meaning. There too Jacques' passion was stronger than his scruples. Moneybags would be a husband, a deceived husband.

Deceiving Nestor seemed so legitimate to Germaine that she did not feel a shadow of uneasiness. The failure to realize things is contagious. The trick of pretending to be a friend of the painter seemed natural to Jacques.

The dinner at which they met amused him. During the dessert Germaine unthinkingly addressed him as darling. He was on her right.

'Darling, did you read X's article. . . ?'

'*You might reply, darling,*' she added almost without a break turning to the left to a Nestor stunned by this stupendous three-card trick. Afterwards they laughed at the warning.

Osiris took a liking to Jacques. He found he had a feeling for figures. Such an absurd opinion was due to the fact that Jacques listened to him. People either listened to him or they did not. He saw only this crude difference between men, not having the turn of mind which shows us the originality of each one.

The place where the young people really met was in the Rue Daubigny, on a ground floor as dark as that painter's canvases.

The chambers belonged to Germaine. She argued that she needed a place to escape to when Nestor was visiting her. According to her explanation, she was going to find this place most convenient for the first time. She believed it. She was afraid of the caretaker Mme Supplice. And not in case the caretaker would think 'another one', but in case she would be shocked to see that she no longer went in alone.

*

There is a limit to caresses, even the deepest. To all intents and purposes a virgin, Jacques was trying to satisfy a boundless desire. The first embrace disappointed him. In the course of time, as his dizziness subsided, he regained his quickness of sight and mind.

Then, when he studied this Desdemona lying back lifeless against the pillow, terrifyingly pale, her teeth bared, her face filled him with a host of shameful memories and he drew himself away from her like a knife.

Germaine distributed her full-blown caresses quickly. They were as extravagant as a florist's bouquet. When one bouquet fades, you buy another. But Jacques was taking root. His abnormal love was growing normally, slowly. He loved himself, he loved travel, he loved too many things, in his mistress. Germaine loved only her lover.


V


This existence necessitated tricks in the Rue de l'Estrapade, where Jacques idled away the hours that Germaine and Osiris spent together.

For the afternoons, he invented some work in the Sartre-Geneviève Library.

This library is the alibi of the young rascals in the Latin Quarter. If everyone who was supposed to be going there actually went, they would have to build a new wing. Jacques, who was friends again with Mouheddin and Louise, slept out one night in four. The Arab and he left the side door half open. They shut it at dawn when they returned from their mistresses.

Louise saw Mouheddin in her room. The two accomplices met at the gates of the Parc Monceau, and waited for the first Métro.

There was nothing funny in the way they left, guillotined. They sat half asleep among the factory girls who were going to work.

＊

It needed no great cunning to trick Berlin. He saw nothing and did not want to see anything. He asked no more than that his pupils and his salary should arrive on time.

His wife did use her eyes. They misled her. She was convinced that Jacques, smitten with love for her, incapable of deceiving his master, was fleeing her presence and drowning his sorrow with the girls at the Café Soufflet. She recommended the Arab to keep an eye on him.

*

Every Sunday Stopwell found a mysterious incentive to win the jumping contest. During the week he was a rag, watching anxiously for the postman who was always supposed to be bringing him a cheque, living in the cloud rising from his pipe and teapot. His great body was splayed out all over the room. After dinner, he put on a silk suit and fell into a heavy sleep intoxicated with tobacco.

Petitcopain waited on this despot with the same expression as the girls who look after lunatics in hospitals. He divided his time between this job and the duty of look-out which he did for Mouheddin.

He had no grudge against Peter. Beneath his pose he discovered a host of weaknesses of a nature which he did not understand, but from which he inferred that he was vulnerable.

With the smell of Virginia tobacco he breathed in the poetry of England.

He loved Stopwell in the same way as the Latin races slowly succumb to London, the town with healthy red cheeks and a heart of black coal, a sleeping poppy.

In him he loved sleepiness, a royal chessboard, does on the grass, dukes marrying actresses, Chinese beside the Thames.

Stopwell's infrequent remarks were in praise of Oxford, paradise of colleges and little shops, with the best Hellenists and the finest gloves in the world.

Through sitting hopefully by an attic window, like a princess in her tower, young Maricelles had fallen ill.

He was curing himself at the Château de Maricelles, near Maricelles-les-Maricelles, an address which was enough to amuse the boarders and provide a topic of conversation at dinner.

*

One Wednesday in November, when Germaine and Jacques were to meet Bashtarzi in Louise's room, they saw a small thin woman in the sitting-room, hatless, and wearing an emerald pendant. It was her mother. Jacques was astonished to recognize Mme Supplice, the caretaker in the Rue Daubigny. The house belonged to one of Louise's ex-protectors. Germaine had never said anything about it.

'Good afternoon,' said Germaine. 'What a dress you're wearing! Is Louise in?'

'No,' replied the caretaker in a monotonous voice, *'the young lady has not come in yet.'*

They sat down. They coughed. But Mme Supplice quickly grew more friendly. She launched into praises of Mouheddin, whom she believed to be a Turkish prince.

In any case Mouheddin was quite shy with intelligent people and hid his stories from them, lost all control with tradesmen and stupid people. You could see that Mme Supplice's sentences, reeled straight off without full stops or commas, were the stories that he had to tell her since he could not shine in more distinguished company.

Jacques did not dare look at Germaine. He would have been very surprised to see that she was not laughing. She smiled. She stood up.

'Good old Mother, always the same!' she exclaimed, and gave her a familiar pat on the knee.

Louise and Mouheddin came back. They seemed annoyed about the meeting, particularly Mouheddin.

*

Can a writer slip a story into the middle of his book when that story is superfluous to it? Yes, if the story brings out a character. Now it is important to bring out the fact that Louise was a good girl, but a good Supplice-Champagne girl.

Before our book begins, Louise used to dance at the Eldorado. Four schoolboys always went to applaud and throw her bouquets of violets. On 1st January they wanted to give her a pendant. The pickpocket of the group pinched an emerald from an old relative. He naïvely agreed that they should draw lots to decide who should present it. The lot fell on the shyest boy. Louise thanked him with a caress. They told themselves that to an actress an emerald is a drop of water in the ocean. They forgot that the ocean exists on drops of water.

A long time after the closing episode in this book the shy one, now a diplomat, met Louise. They revived old memories.

'You know the false emerald?' she said. 'I gave it to my mother. She always wore it. She wanted it to be buried with her.'

The diplomat confessed that the emerald was stolen, and that it was real. Louise paled.

'Will you swear it?' she asked. And he dared not swear because Louise had just assumed the expression of a gravedigger.

*

Let us return to the Rue Montchanin.

The two couples often used to go to a skating-rink. They went there now. They knew the instructors and the barman.

A young man with a face like a washerwoman, wearing a cape and a pearl necklace, was walking around the tables, smiling at some, bumping into others, shouting that spinning round had made him sick. His cultivated voice was like the ridiculous curves of art nouveau.

This monster would have got himself hanged anywhere. There, he was a fetish. They fawned on him, they were honoured if he spoke to them. He shook hands with Germaine and Louise and simpered coquettishly at the men.

Jacques' dark side vainly sent a feeling of moral uneasiness to his light side. He had adopted a limping rhythm. He liked it. He was walking along the roof-tops without feeling giddy, like a sleepwalker.

The monster allowed them to sit down for a minute. In a voice which was now quite faint he was guessing the value of Louise's rings. He was showing his own. He was telling stories about police raids.

When everything is moving at once, nothing appears to be moving.

For Jacques to realize his spiritual laziness there would have had to be a fixed point. That he should have imagined his father or mother walking across the promenade, for example.

But his actions were far from them, far from himself. He was lying happily in the dirty water.

He would have felt disgusted had he been alone in such a place. As he was blended with Germaine who talked to the fetish on equal terms, he did not rebel, and had an easy time.

The orchestra was playing a fashionable dance.

Fashions die young. That is what makes their gaiety so grave. The dance was swollen with the assurance of success and with melancholy because it would soon be forgotten. One day every note of it would pierce Jacques' heart. They skated.

During a pause in which the monster performed a number, Louise gave a little scream : 'You!' And looking away from the rink, they all saw a jovial Osiris leaning on his stick, with the electric-light bulbs reflecting on his nose, his top hat, his pearly tiepin.

'Yes, children, me, me. And quite satisfied too. For several days I have been assailed with anonymous letters saying that Germaine spends all her time at the skating-rink with a lover. I wanted to verify it and I consider it to be untrue. And that's it,' he concluded, laying his hand on Jacques' shoulder, 'for between you

and me, my friend, I don't want to say anything nasty (tastes differ)
but you are not her type.'

He sat down. Germaine beat him with her fists, spoke threaten-
ingly to him, and put on a straight face.

'In any case,' he said, opening a card-case, 'I think I recognize
Lazare's writing. Perhaps this is his revenge. Here, Jacques my boy,
take these letters, study them. You young people are being brought
up on traveller's tales. You can make a better guess than an old
fool like me.'

'Do we love our old fool?' he lisped, tickling Germaine under
the chin, 'do we love him?'

And Germaine, now securely mounted in the saddle again,
replied, 'No, we don't love him. We don't love sneaks.'

*

Jacques' life was like the rooms of Montmartre women that are
never cleaned because they get up at four o'clock and slip a coat
over their night-gown to go downstairs and eat.

This state of affairs always gets worse. Nestor stopped showing
letters, stopped laughing. He did not suspect Jacques, in spite of
precise accusations; he suspected Germaine. Blinded by conceit, he
would gladly have admitted that she might deceive him with a
man as stout and as old as he, what he ingenuously called his
type, but that it might be with little Jacques would have been too
much for him to believe. He did not hesitate a moment. He confided in him and asked him to keep an eye on Germaine.

'I have to live at the Bourse and I often work at night. Follow
her. Do not leave her. Do be so kind.'

Now, Nestor Osiris began to make scenes. He had not started
threatening yet, he broke ornaments. Germaine had noticed that he
gave her a Copenhagen ornament every time they made it up. In
this way he could break things without doing much damage. He
avoided Chinese vases and earthenware.

When he broke a Dresden china group, Germaine knew that
the vaudeville had turned to tragedy. He broke open cupboards,
hunted for fingerprints, bribed manicurists, lost his head.

Returning from the dentist one evening he found Germaine on
the chaise-longue. He asked her if she had had company. She
replied that she had not, that she had been sleeping and reading
since lunch. It was true.

Nestor went out to hang his fur coat in the cloakroom. He
reappeared brandishing a cane with a tortoise-shell top.

'And what's this? What's this?' he shouted. 'Since your gentleman friend leaves his canes in my room, I'll use this to teach you a lesson.'

Germaine closed the book.

'You're crazy,' she said. 'Get out.'

The telephone rang.

'Don't touch the receiver,' shouted Nestor. 'If it's the man with the cane, I'm the one who will speak to him.'

In fact, it was about the cane. The dentist asked Mr Osiris if there had not been a mistake, as his patient had found one with the initials N.O. instead of his own, which had a tortoise-shell top.

Germaine enjoyed the modest triumph. The episode gave her four days' peace.

*

The Osiris brothers went shooting on Sundays. They left at five o'clock on the previous evening. So Germaine was free. This Saturday, Nestor stayed, sacrificing his shooting. It was a chivalrous way of making her forgive him.

Germaine hid her disappointment. She warned Jacques. He was to be sensible and stay in the Rue de l'Estrapade, and go to bed early.

At nine o'clock Jacques was reading in his room like the other boys (except Mouheddin) when they heard a timid ring at the bell on their floor.

After answering the bell and whispering, Petitcopain, who acted as caretaker, knocked on Jacques' door. He announced a visitor. It was Germaine. She was carrying a bag. Jacques couldn't get over it.

Some reflex made him kick an old pair of socks under the chest of drawers. Germaine teased him for being so dazed.

She was bored with Nestor at dinner-time. She had said, 'Wait for me; I am going to make a salad in the kitchen for a surprise.' She had taken clothes, toilet things and had escaped down the service stairs.

'Don't scold me, my love,' she begged. 'I am free, free, free. Let him break everything. I am taking you on a honeymoon trip.'

*

A road can sometimes look so different on the way out and on the way back that the traveller, coming home, thinks he is lost.

The village where one lives, seen suddenly from a hill, can be mistaken for another village.

Because of Germaine's presence in the Rue de l'Estrapade, Jacques hardly recognized his mistress, and no longer recognized his room.

It took him a minute to admit the proposition, namely : to go away by train and spend Sunday on the farm that belonged to the Rateaux who had gone to Le Havre.

After the initial shock, Jacques was as madly enthusiastic as she. They christened the trip *Round the World*. Jacques would have to go down and see the master's wife, tell her that he was going out and would not be back until Monday morning, to work.

Not wanting to leave Germaine in his room, as Peter might have gone in, he shut her in Maricelles' empty room with a lamp and cigarettes. She was in no danger there.

On the floor below, Jacques found the master and his wife in the process of setting the clock. They had to wait for it to strike all the hours and half-hours. Then Jacques, who usually went out every Saturday night, announced that he was going to spend Sunday in the country at a friend's house.

The Berlins gave their permission, on the condition that the boy reported to his master's study on Monday morning. Jacques went upstairs, released Germaine, and they got their things ready.

Everything went into one bag. This delighted them. They smothered their hysterical laughter. Still playing at *Round the World*, Jacques said in a whisper that they would have to be careful on the crossing outside the cabin that belonged to a fierce Englishman, with a red moustache, a bag of bank-notes, and a veil made out of a butterfly-net. He had been on their track since Liverpool and was plotting their downfall.

They went downstairs without any difficulty, using a box of matches, and found the cab that Germaine had left at the corner of the Rue Mouffetard.

## VI

To describe the journey I would need all the delightful apparatus of a conjurer. Flags, bouquets, lanterns, eggs and goldfish.

Miraculously, Germaine still had the down of her girlhood. It had often been plucked. Jacques had a protection against the mud like the grease which prevents water from making swans wet. But both of them passed the first snow-laden trees, the first animal, like a sleepwalker passing the refuse-carts in Les Halles on his way home at five o'clock in the morning.

But this was unimportant. The country was part of Germaine's heritage. She was returning to a lost paradise, and Jacques was Jacques no longer, but Germaine, that is to say one of the high carts so fresh at dawn in the Place de la Concorde where the market gardeners lie asleep, cradled like idle kings on their litters of cabbages and roses.

Germaine really was misleading him. The conjurer could almost have been the Spring in person, using his boxes for false bottoms.

How could this early harvest, false as it was, seem anything but real to Jacques who had borne with the fetish at the skating-rink.

*Thousands of roads lead away from the white, one leads towards it,* says Montaigne. Jacques went for the white. He held Germaine close, kept her warm in the carriage and let himself behave like a child.

Jacques disliked himself, but he was not disliked. Germaine and he made an attractive couple. They were taken for two innocent lovers on an excursion.

What spontaneity, what surprises! But the only place where the poor girl had any surprises left was up her sleeve.

Jacques could not see the strings any more than the children who clap. It is a good start to be able to make children clap.

Germaine, whose old tricks were well practised, sincerely believed that she was gathering watches and doves. The illusionist shared in the illusions of the public.

So this trip was the only ethereal happiness they had.

The farm was small. Germaine was on familiar terms with the servants and the cows. She walked about with a pack of young dogs snapping playfully at her heels. She shouted, jumped about, took her hair down.

They lunched in a room where the fire was a great blaze. They ate the clean food that one cannot eat in town. The cheese, knowledgeably ripened in a vine-leaf, was the only thing which contrasted vividly with the meat and the white cream.

After lunch, Germaine showed him the room that belonged to her father, an old drunkard. It was impossible to cure him of his vice.

In the middle of the room hung a multicoloured paper chandelier. On the chest of drawers stood pale photographs of sailors, weddings, and, under a piece of glass, half a frigate stuck on to painted green waves.

'Here I am as a virgin,' said Germaine, holding a frame of seashells in front of Jacques. It surrounded a naked baby.

She had her own room. They went to bed there and adored each other for the last time. Did Jacques foresee it? Not in the slightest.

Neither did Germaine. They were right, as they were often to make love afterwards.

*

They left at dawn two days later, not at all tired. They could hear the cocks taking up the infectious cry one after the other like the burners of a huge chandelier lighting up. Everything was frozen, wet, virginal. Germaine went about jauntily with a red nose. She had not a single wrinkle to disturb the pure morning.

She had discovered an old photograph in her chest of drawers. She was screwing up her eyes as if she were short-sighted. Jacques thought this face was divine. Germaine gave it to him.

Besides that they brought back eggs and cheese. They really did go round the world.

*

In that short time Germaine had forgotten what the streets of Paris looked like. This surprise prolonged the escapade. She was getting back to her normal life again without feeling sorry. The cries of the tradesmen, the lean runners training behind the cyclists, the maids beating carpets out of the windows, the steaming horses, reminded her of her childhood.

They decided that after his work Jacques should have lunch at Germaine's flat. They took a taxi, for she wanted to go back with him.

The chauffeur drove like a madman, skidded, mounted the islands. Germaine and Jacques enjoyed themselves, kissed on the mouth, bumped their teeth, were thrown all over each other. At each new feat, the driver turned round, shrugged his shoulders, and winked at them.

Germaine dropped Jacques in the Rue de l'Estrapade about ten o'clock, after a long embrace. He went on watching her waving her glove as the car went on its way. He arrived like Phileas Fogg, just in time to change and appear at the right moment with his fellow-students in the study, where M. Berlin was trying to teach geography.

*

Germaine went into a post office and telephoned her flat. Josephine, who had been told on the famous evening to say to Osiris that she had not seen Madame go out, described the poor man's fury, the way he searched, begged and cursed. He had broken a mirror and cried, being superstitious. He had spent Sunday anxiously walking up and down, watching the telephone and the cars. Finally, on Sunday night, he said quietly, 'Josephine, whether Madame comes back or not, I am leaving her. You can tell her that from me. Sort my things out. I am leaving the rest for her. Let her do whatever she likes with it.'

'Phew!' sighed Germaine. 'Good luck.'

She knew that a beautiful girl is never in difficulties for long.

On her way in she met her sister.

'Didn't I tell you often enough what would happen?' cried Loute. 'Nestor won't see you again. When people talk about you, he spits.'

'Let him spit,' replied Germaine. 'I'm suffocated. I have just come back from the country with Jacques. Nestor is stuffy.'

'How will you live?'

'Don't worry, little Loute. Besides, Nestor is a fly-paper; he sticks. I should be very surprised if he didn't try to come back.'

Osiris came back so quickly that he passed Loute on her way out. Germaine, who had gone to bed, kept him waiting.

When he came in, he stopped, bowed, and went to sit down on a chair at the foot of the bed.

'My dear Germaine,' he began.

'Is this a speech?'

He struck an attitude.

'My dear Germaine ... everything is over between us, ov-er. I have written you a final letter, but as I know how careless you are and the way you read letters, I have come to read it to you.'

'Do you realize that you are being ridiculous beyond bounds?'

'That is possible,' continued Nestor, 'but you must hear my letter.'

He took it out of his pocket.

'I won't hear it.'

'You will.'

'No.'

'Yes.'

'No.'

'Very well. I shall read it all the same.'

She put her fingers in her ears and hummed. In the voice of one used to calling the prices at the Bourse, Osiris began.

'My poor little lunatic ... '

Germaine burst out laughing.

'The lady laughs, the lady is listening,' remarked Nestor. 'So I shall continue.'

But this time Germaine hummed her loudest and it was impossible for him to read. Nestor put the letter down on his knee.

'Very well, I'll stop,' he said.

She took her fingers out of her ears.

'Only I warn you' (he shook his first finger admonishingly) 'that if you don't let me read it, I shall leave. And you will ne-ver see me again.'

'Because it is your final letter.'

'There are ends and ends,' stammered Osiris, who had a gift for ciphers; that is to say, for poetry, and who was absolutely stupid in love where such poetry does not exist.

'——I wanted to end it in a nice way, in a proper way, and you are hounding me out. Supposing I called you to account!'

'I have nothing to account for,' burst out Germaine, who was exasperated by this play-acting, 'and if you want an account, here it is: yes, I am deceiving you. I have a lover. Yes, I sleep with Jacques.' And with every yes she tugged at her plait as if it were a bell-pull.

'My word!' said Osiris, standing up, stepping back and screwing up his eyes like a painter. He accused Germaine of pinning the suspicion on an obliging boy, hoping that he, Osiris, would rush off to find him while she entertained her real lover.

He added that he was not taken in; that he might be the rich man being taken for a ride, but being rich was a profession; an exacting profession that makes one observant.

\*

Germaine was full of admiration. Despite the plays she had seen, she had not believed that anyone like this existed.

'You are superb, Nestor,' she said. 'I sleep with Jacques. In any case' (the bell rang) 'this is sure to be him. He is coming to lunch. Hide, and you will see the proof for yourself.'

She wanted to end it.

'Hide,' said Osiris with a derisive laugh. 'That is too easy. You have plenty of tricks in your bag, and you will signal. I am staying.'

And as they heard a door opening, and Jacques' voice offstage, he shouted: 'My dear Jacques, do you know what Germaine has thought up?'

Jacques came in.

'You sleep with her!'

\*

From his contact with Germaine Jacques had learnt her tricks. He understood the scene at a glance, and saw that his mistress, tired to death, had given everything away.

'Let us keep calm, Monsieur Osiris,' he said. 'You know that Germaine likes teasing. She teases you because she loves you.'

The pure-hearted Jacques did so well that Nestor stayed to lunch and opened a box of cigars.

Queens of Egypt! The contents of that richly painted box were like tiny mummies with their golden girdles.

Osiris ate, smoked, laughed and left for the Bourse.

Germaine sulked and reproached Jacques for his cunning.

'Then you don't want to be the only one?'

'I don't want to be responsible for such a serious thing and for you to blame me for it one day.'

The farm, the milk, the eggs, were far away.

*

When Lazare questioned his brother, Nestor gave him a pat on the shoulder.

'Germaine is a character,' he said. 'That is her charm. We shan't change her. She was at her farm. She needed cows. We men of the Bourse don't understand it. Loute is simple, what shall I say – less lively, less colourful. Again, she has her points. I am keeping Germaine.'

This episode appeared to restore Osiris to his former position. Insinuations, anonymous letters, made him smile in a superior way as if he knew a secret which might mean that Germaine laid herself open to scandalmongers, but which was to the advantage of her rich lover. This vague secret had something to do with his mistress's superiority, her love of nature, and her rearing dogs.

If he was asked 'Where is Germaine?' he would reply, 'I give her a great deal of freedom. I don't interfere.'

Loute was amazed. As she herself lacked an easy manner and talents, she considered her sister very strong.

## VII

Like dirty clothes, boxes and combs lying about an hotel room, the affair was dragging on. Jacques had no reason to suffer from this disorder. He no longer saw it. He saw only through the eyes of his mistress, who had been accustomed to live in this way since her childhood. A new element came to swell the disorder.

For three weeks Germaine had been having bad news of her father. She did not like him and burnt the letters.

'It's our business to go out at night, you know,' Louise would say.

But Germaine, who thought herself more 'respectable', rather looked down on Louise, and imagined that shutting her eyes to her father's condition would leave her more freedom. She even pretended to think that her mother was exaggerating, flying into a panic for nothing.

One evening when she was dressing to go to a revue with Jacques and Osiris, Jacques found a telegram half hidden beneath the telephone : *Urgent father dying come love.* She hid it so that she could go to the theatre. Jacques showed it to her in silence.

'Leave it alone,' she said, as she put on her lipstick, pressing her lips together afterwards, 'I'll go tomorrow.'

During the interval Rateau passed away on his farm at eleven o'clock.

For two weeks Mme Rateau had been reading him *La Maison du Baigneur,* in which Siete-Iglesias is crushed by a mechanical ceiling. Rateau confused this chapter with reality. He thought he was Iglesias and died lying on the floor, his face turned to one side, trying to take up as little space as possible, crushed by the ceiling of his room, in front of his horrified wife.

\*

M. Rateau left to his wife all he had had from his daughter, and insisted on being buried in the family vault at Père-Lachaise. Osiris ordered a motor hearse.

Loute had quarrelled with her mother.

As Germaine refused to go alone to the farm to fetch the body, Jacques asked for special leave from the Rue de l'Estrapade. Nestor lent his car which would hold the road better than the limousine. The hearse left half a day in advance.

This trip to the farm was not as delightful as the other. The driver had a little mirror so that he could see behind. It was important for them to be on their guard.

Germaine organized the return. She liked her mother. She would put her up for a fortnight in Paris. She took three rooms below her flat which were used for storing furniture. Orders were given for some of the furniture to be taken down to the linen-room, and for the three rooms to be furnished with the rest. Mme Rateau would have a little home of her own.

Her daughter made plans and grew sentimental.

Incapable of pretence, except with Nestor, she did not shed a

single tear over the drunken father who had beaten her too often.
In her eyes her mother was freed.

\*

Mme Rateau came to meet them. She was weeping, holding a
handkerchief in one hand and a Spanish fan in the other.

Since she had stopped working she had let her nails grow and,
not knowing where to put her hands, she was never parted from the
fan.

Her figure looked like a Lotto bag. She had regular commonplace
features, a blotchy skin, and a white wig which emphasized her
complexion – that of an English judge.

Her daughter introduced Jacques. The widow looked at him
like a person suffering from seasickness.

The coffin was in the room where the young people had lunched
on their trip *Round the World*.

Germaine managed to play the part tactfully. She decided that
Mme Rateau should go in the car and the hearse should follow.

Every time the hearse was mentioned, Mme Rateau shook her
head and repeated : 'A motor hearse . . . a motor hearse.'

The return journey was pitiful. Germaine tapped on the windows.
She was restraining the driver so that M. Rateau could follow.

Suddenly she turned round, looked through the window and
exclaimed : 'Where is it?'

The road stretched away into the distance with no hearse.

They halted and turned back to look for the body. They found
it. It was in a side-street with a puncture. The wheel would have
to be changed. The jack was not working properly. Jacques and
the driver set to work.

After an hour's struggle, with Mme Rateau shaking her head in
encouragement, worn out with hiccups and tears, they set off
again.

As luck would have it, Jacques' silence irritated Germaine and
she dropped him in the Rue de l'Estrapade, so that for one
moment the drivers could imagine that they were conducting the
body of a famous man to the Panthéon.

\*

Mme Rateau's mourning-dress kept the fashionable dressmakers
and milliners busy. Feeling it to be respectable to have a widowed
mother, Germaine put her on show. She took her to her shops.
Mme Rateau appreciated this luxury. She picked up bits of crêpe

everywhere. She had crêpe dresses, dressing-gowns, tippets, toques, cloaks and hoods. What is more, she took care of her mourning-dress, and never went out if there was a chance of rain. *'Crêpe is like sunshine for lunch,'* she said.

No one hesitates to lay a wreath of brightly coloured flowers on a tomb, and Mme Rateau did not give up her fan.

One Sunday when Germaine was taking her to Versailles, inflicting this duty on Jacques, the silence which reigned in the car as far as the Bois de Boulogne gave him the opportunity of studying the fan.

It depicted the death of Gallito.

\*

Nothing is more like a sunset than a corrida. Gracefully lowering its powerful neck, its Antinous' brow, wide and curly, the bull was watching the crowd and goring the fallen matador in the stomach with its right horn. In the middle distance, to the left, a picador on a bloody horse whose ribs could be counted like the Spanish Christ was trying to prick the simple beast which was shaking the bunch of bandilleros on its neck.

A man was scaling the outer wall on the extreme left, and like the Aeginian archer who is said to be on his knees shooting to fill up a corner, a hump-backed ring-hand filled up the extreme right with his hump.

\*

Jacques was growing bored. The crêpe intimidated him. He did not dare take Germaine's knees between his legs.

'Gallito,' he kept saying stupidly, 'Gallito, Gal, gal, gal.' And the gal reminded him of Victor Hugo's lines :

> Gall, amant de la reine, alla, tour magnanime
> Galamment, de l'arène à la Tour Magne, à
> Nîme.

So he recited them under his breath as if he were humming.
'What are you reciting?' asked Germaine.
'Nothing. I remembered two lines by Victor Hugo.'
'Say them again.'

> 'Gall, amant de la reine, alla, tour magnanime
> Galamment, de l'arène à la Tour Magne, à
> Nîme.'

'What does that mean?'

'Gall : a M. Gall who was the queen's lover; went on a magnanimous journey : chivalrously – from the arena, as on your mother's fan : to a tower called Magne : at Nîmes, the town.'

'Animates the town?'

'No. Nîmes, Nîmes, Nîmes the town.'

'So what?'

'So nothing.'

'Victor Hugo was trying to make fools of everyone the day he wrote those lines.'

'But it's deliberate, it's a joke.'

'I don't think it's funny.'

'It wasn't meant to be funny.'

'Now I really don't understand.'

'They are two lines that sound the same and look different.'

'Explain.'

'Instead of rhyming at the end, these two lines rhyme the whole way through.'

'Then they aren't rhymes, if they are the same.'

'But they aren't the same because they say something different. It's a triumph of wit.'

'I don't see how it's a triumph of wit. I'd have dozens of triumphs of wit if all I had to do was to repeat the same thing twice running and call it lines of poetry.'

'Look, little Germaine, listen; you aren't listening.'

'Thank you. Treat me like a fool.'

'Oh! Germaine.'

'Don't let's talk about it any more, if I am incapable of understanding.'

'I never said you were incapable of understanding. You ask me to explain the lines. I explain, and you get angry ... '

'I get angry, do I. Well! I don't care two hoots for your Victor Hugo.'

'To start with, Victor Hugo is not mine. Secondly, I love you. Those lines are silly. Don't let's talk about them any more.'

'You didn't think they were silly a minute ago. Now you think they are silly so that I'll leave you alone.'

'We have never argued. Are we going to do so for something so ridiculous?'

'Just as you like. I ask you nicely, and because you are thinking about something else and I am disturbing you, you give me a lump of sugar.'

'This is not like you.'

'Nor you.'

*

This vulgar scene, the first between Germaine and Jacques, had been going on since the Bois de Boulogne. After her *nor you* Germaine turned away and looked at the trees. Mme Rateau went on fanning herself.

They reached Versailles and had tea at the Hôtel des Reservoirs without Germaine or her mother speaking. On the way back Germaine broke the silence and said in a submissive voice : 'Jacques, my love, those lines . . . '

'Oh !'

'Will you teach them to me?'

'Listen. I'll give them to you in detail : Gall – amant – de – la – reine – alla – tour – magnanime. Galamment – de – l'arène – à – la Tour Magne – à Nîme.'

'You see, it's the same thing.'

'No it's not.'

'You say it's not and you don't prove anything.'

'There's nothing to prove. It's a famous example.'

'It's famous?'

'Yes.'

'Very famous?'

'Yes.'

'Then how can it be that I don't know it?'

'Because you are not interested in literature.'

'That's what I said. I'm a fool.'

'Listen, Germaine, you are the reverse of a fool, but you are frightening me today. You are deliberately trying to frighten me.'

'That's the last straw.'

'How sad that we should hurt each other for such an asinine thing.'

'You're telling me !'

'That's enough. I don't feel well. I demand silence, it's my turn.'

And so they went on until they were on the verge of sticking pins in one another. Then Mme Rateau came out of her dumb silence.

'You see, children,' she said, folding up her fan, 'none of that prevented this Gall from being the queen's lover.'

These words from a mother disclosed a perfect grasp of the facts.

Mme Rateau spoke little, but well. It was either 'My poor husband was carried away in one hour' or 'What? Paris was called Lutetia, M. Jacques? That's news.'

As she was enthusing over 'a superb statue of Henri IV', Jacques asked her mechanically if it was an equestrian one. She hesitated, only to reply 'so-so', spontaneously defining the centaur.

Germaine held her sides. Mme Rateau was annoyed. Jacques was completely at sea.

*

The day after the Gall business he woke up feeling unhappy.

Just as a patient after an operation thinks of cold drinks, a man with an injured spine, being unable to sit down, draws chairs, he dreamt of the discreet wives who help their men in their work and start a family. But he thrust this thirst for cold water away as if it were a thirst for alcohol.

*

One night when he was holding Germaine tight, he whispered that he would like a child. Germaine confessed that this pleasure was denied to her.

'I should already have had one if it were possible,' she said. 'I make up for it by rearing fox terriers.'

The peach reveals its worm. Most of them conceal one. Poor Jacques; it would have been very rash for him to have changed his lot for that of the king's beasts, as he longed to do. On assuming their form, surely one would feel some deep-seated infirmity apart from the flaws which cannot be seen through park trees or bar smoke.

These successive blows in no way estranged him from Germaine. On the contrary, he pitied her. So he pitied himself. His love grew, and slept like a baby rocked in its cradle.

*

There was a surprise party at Germaine's. The Castor Sugar crowd came to tea unexpectedly.

Castor Sugar was sixty and looked twenty-five. Her diet consisted in drinking nothing but champagne and never sleeping, except with jockeys and dancing teachers. She kept an opium den. There were Japanese robes of crêpe de Chine to wear. Everyone lay smoking in a tangled heap on a rug. They listened to the late Caruso singing *Pagliacci*.

This delightful company shouted, jumped and boxed.

About seven o'clock they all crammed into a black maria with a white chauffeur, blind deaf and dumb like a statue of cocaine.

When Jacques and Germaine went up to Mme Rateau's room
they could see her sitting down with her back to them. Her fan
alone was moving.

'Hello, Mother.'

'Hello, Germaine.'

'You sound queer.'

'No ... no.'

'Yes you do.'

'No I don't.'

'Yes you do, Mme Rateau, you do sound queer. Jacques can
tell that there is something wrong with you.'

'Well, since you force me to it,' said the widow, 'I admit I find it
strange that people should give parties without asking me to come
down.'

'But look here, Mother, your mind is on other things. To start
with, you are in mourning' (her daughter forgot that she was in
mourning too), 'and then I really can't take you to meet Mlle
Sugar.'

*

This extraordinary excuse opened a secret door to Jacques. A
woman can look at a magazine cover and see the same woman
looking at the same magazine and so on until the point where the
picture stops for lack of space, but it continues as before when we
think we have come to the bottom of one class of society. There
are still millions capable of saying with a certain king : 'I am
further from my sister than my sister is from her chief gardener.'

Jacques accepted all that. He was too much part of his mistress
to judge her actions or her family. Now his dark side was sprinkling
clouds of ink over his light side like a cuttle-fish. After helping
him, it was gently making him blind.

Louise offered herself to Mouheddin and Mouheddin to Louise.
This loveless exchange exhilarated them. Parallel to the Jacques-
Germaine drama they were having an indecently gay time.

Louise received cheques from a foreign prince. This prince was
coming to the throne and rarely left his future kingdom. He came
to London for the conferences where great men meet. Then he
spent two weeks with Louise. He told her the secrets of Europe,
and how the puerile kings, cooped up together, played practical
jokes on each other and moved the shoes around outside the doors.
He even wrote to her, and Mme Supplice often said in her 'exceptionally lucid woman's' voice, 'if ever His Highness leaves little
Louise, she shall take his letters to the frontier. It amazes me that a

prince should write such things. She shall take them. She has him.'

In short, Louise lived in freedom except when there were big political upheavals.

On the fifteenth of every month an officer with a blue moustache turned into the Rue Montchanin, clicked his heels and delivered an envelope.

Mouheddin admired his uniform through the lavatory ventilator.

One morning, about six o'clock, when Mouheddin was dressing to meet Jacques, he had the idea of a joke. Louise was asleep. On the bedside table there was a box full of loose change and rings. This joke, which was more or less funny, consisted of dropping one coin noisily on top of the others, and wakening the sleeper, as if they were a couple at a shady hotel.

Sleep has its own universe, geographies, geometrics, calendars. It may take us back to the Ark. Then we rediscover a mysterious knowledge of the sea. We swim, and we seem to be flying with no effort.

Louise's memories did not go back so far. The noise of the coin brought her back from a dream nearer the surface.

'Gustave,' she sighed, 'do leave me something for lunch.'

Her sigh was ten years old.

This episode astonished Mouheddin. He laughed all alone in the empty street. Jacques was waiting for him. He told him what a coin can do when it falls into a sleeping marsh.

'Poor girl,' said Jacques, 'don't tell her anything about it.'

'You dramatize everything,' burst out Mouheddin. 'You're wrong. You poison your own life.'

In the Métro Jacques noticed that he had forgotten his wristwatch. He did not see Germaine the next day. The day after that, he went to the Rue Daubigny at ten o'clock to get it back.

Mme Supplice was not in the caretaker's room. He put the key in the lock, turned it, crossed the hall, opened the door. What did he see? Germaine and Louise.

*

They were asleep, intertwined like a monogram, in such an extraordinary way that the limbs of one seemed to belong to the other. Imagine the Queen of Hearts without her robe.

At the sight of these white forms spread out on the sheet, Jacques went as stupid as Perrette at the sight of her spilt milk. Should he kill? This would have been very ridiculous and, what is more, a pleonasm. It seemed impossible to make this dead couple any more dead. Except that Germaine's open mouth was moving, and Louise's legs were twitching like a sleeping dog's.

It was striking how natural the sight appeared.

You would have said that these candid positions brought out their beauty. Having always known vice, they found it a relaxation.

From what sea had this drowned couple risen? Doubtless they had come a long way. They had been tossed by all the waves and all the moons since Lesbos to be laid out there under a foam of lace and muslin.

*

Jacques felt so awkward that he thought of going out and leaving no traces. But, as Jesus revives a sinner, so his presence revived Louise.

'Is it you, Mother?' she said with half-open eyes. She opened them and recognized Jacques.

He had to smile or fight. Jacques muttered : 'This is a fine thing.'

'What a fine thing?' cried Germaine. 'Would you rather I deceived you with a man?'

If she is still in love, this kind of woman thinks of a lie. But without realizing it, she was no longer in love. Since the Sunday at the farm, the light had gone out and her love was only a habit.

'You are young,' Louise concluded, yawning.

Jacques took the wrist-watch and ran out.

Once in the Berlin establishment he realized his stupidity. After a burst of individuality he was again seeing things from Germaine's angle. He told his discovery to Mouheddin who knew about the relationship between the girls.

'You're working yourself up,' he said. 'Moral laws are the rules of a game at which everyone cheats, and has done so since the beginning of the world. We shan't change it. Go and meet them at the skating-rink at four. I have a lesson. I'll come for you at six.'

Jacques shaved, studied the short-sighted picture, congratulated himself on having an Osiris and a Louise as rivals, scribbled off a Greek translation, and ran to the skating-rink. They were having a benefit gala for a musicians' charity fund.

## VIII

The skating-rink was crowded. The Vesuvian rumble of the skates
on the concrete was deafening, even during the intervals. A Negro
band alternated with an organ. The Negroes flung trumpet notes
at one another like lumps of raw meat.

Near the organ, which was vomiting behind a flimsy staircase,
a woman in mourning was writing letters at a little table. She
changed the bands. A dismal crowd spun round, each thinking he
was surrounded by empty space. On the lower floor there was a
delightful slate shooting-range decorated with pipes, red targets,
a host of rabbits, palm trees, zouaves. The fountain with an egg
bobbing on top was a tulip plant. A shot would cut the flower off.
The woman in charge of the range leant over and put the flower
back on again. Men in sweaters played bowls. Heard from above,
between the two kinds of music, the bowls thudded like shoe-trees
being thrown about a room.

On the balcony, from which there was a view of the whole hall,
stood two American marines with profiles like Dante and Virgil,
their ribbons whipped crazily by the ventilators as they leant over
the gulf. The decorations were banners and floodlights.

One number consisted of a revival of the cancan. Eight women,
survivors from the golden age, shook a real bird-cage to the rhythm
of Offenbach. Sometimes nothing could be distinguished but their
black legs in silks and satins from the Palais-Royal; sometimes they
threw their feet up in the air with their hands like champagne
corks and were drowned in the froth below. There is no more foam
in the *Birth of Venus*.

This dance rouses the Parisian as the corrida rouses the Spaniard.
It finishes with the splits, a group on a transparent postcard on
which the Eiffel Tower, old stager that she is, smiles, bursting her
steel bodice, split open to the very heart.

*

In spite of the crush, Jacques found the two girls sitting down.
The picture of them as a Hindu idol haunted him. He had to
make an effort to see them apart.

'Here,' said Germaine, 'it's too cold; take my glass.'

Jacques was drinking, happy to put a straw through which
Germaine had drunk into his mouth, when a bump knocked down
the fence surrounding the rink so that it hit the table. Two red
hands grasped the plush balustrade. Jacques looked up. It was
Stopwell.

'Hello Jacques! Excuse me, I was skating, and recognized you. I always fall like a thunderbolt. I didn't know you came to the rink.'

'But if you come often,' Jacques shouted, because of the organ which prevented him hearing himself, 'why have I never seen you here before?'

'I went skating elsewhere. Tonight I'm here for the music.'

He disappeared across the rink.

'Who is he?' asked Germaine.

'It's that Englishman, the dreadful Englishman in *Round the World.*'

'Ask him to join us,' said Louise, 'he's alone; you never even asked him to sit at our table.'

\*

This is the way clouds group together, the air is freshened, plants lean over and the water takes on a pearly hue.

\*

Jacques went to find Stopwell and Stopwell came and sat between Germaine and Louise.

As Verlaine said of Lucien Létinois: *'He skated marvellously.'* He wore knickerbockers, charming English trousers which buckle below the knee and hang down over the leg, tartan stockings, a soft shirt, and a tie with his club stripes. His easy grace impressed Jacques.

He always saw him as part of the Berlin set-up: and, like a canvas which makes a poor effect without a frame and lighting and only appears in its full power when it is finally framed against a wall in harsh lighting, so Stopwell took on new proportions at the skating-rink.

Germaine was talking about masculine elegance. Jacques, who was riled, was arguing that the elegance of Englishmen was regimented, that French elegance was superior by its very originality. He cited the dress of various members of the Jockey Club who had a charming originality which was all their own. He wanted to evoke the fiery silhouette of the Duc de Montmorency, threadbare, stained, taking his opera hat to the dining-table.

He missed his effect. Approaching disaster deprives a man of all his resources.

Stopwell upheld his speech. Stopwell spoke. He stressed his mistakes in French. This was the first time he had talked. At the Berlins' he did not condescend to do so. He was talking about

England. He was a sailor talking about his ship. Jacques was right; Stopwell thought him noble. He leant out of his chair on the extreme right. His head was bowed.

Now Stopwell was crushing him with an indirect reply. He was speaking of elegance. He broke up his sentences with polite *you knows,* as terrible as his handshake.

'There is true elegance in London, you know,' he said. 'Opposite Rumpelmayer, for example' (he was speaking to the women). . . . 'Lock's little hat shop. It is a very dark, very small thing; so small that the assistants nail up the boxes in the street. All the coal of England' (and Stopwell assumed the voice of Lady Macbeth when she speaks the famous phrase 'All the perfumes of Arabia . . . '), 'all the coal of England went to make this little diamond. Behind his window, as you say, you can see very, very old head-gear, a century old, white with dust. Mr Lock never brushes them. And when Lord Ribblesdale tries his hat on . . . then, you know . . . *c'est magnifique.*'

He scanned the *magnifique* and stressed the *mag* and *fique,* thrusting his hands into his trouser pockets, stuffed with chains and nickel keys.

The women were silent.

Germaine was drinking in his words. She was goggling at him. Jacques was desperate, for he saw the woman with whom he was united separating herself from him without any transition, and himself diminishing as she went away. Like the cobbler in the *Arabian Nights* he was resuming his original shape. He was turning back into the man he was before their love-affair.

The physical and mental agony was too much for him.

'What is the matter with you, my little Jacques?' asked Louise. 'Your lips are trembling.'

But Germaine heard neither the question nor the answer.

'Up!' commanded Stopwell, standing up on his skates. 'Come and skate with me.'

Germaine left the table and followed him like a slave.

*

Jacques watched the rink. It was drawn out and bent in the distorting mirrors. The music was changing too, as it does when you play at putting your fingers in your ears and taking them out again while you listen to an orchestra. He saw Peter and Germaine, monks by El Greco. They were lengthened, they turned green, they rose skywards in a swoon, caught in the lightning of the mercury lamps. Then they floated far away, very far away : a fat, dwarfish Germaine; Stopwell as a Louis Philippe armchair flinging its **feet** out on both sides. The bar was pitching. Louise came up with a blurred face like something out of an art film. Her mouth moved, and Jacques did not hear a single word.

He was no longer luxuriously encased in Germaine. He could feel his bones, his ribs, his yellow hair, sharp teeth, freckles, everything he hated and had ceased to notice.

Below the amplifiers of the waltz which was strangling him, Germaine and Stopwell swept from one end of the rink to the other on one leg, holding hands, in the same position as the Auriga. Stopwell threw his chest out. He thought he was Achilles. For a second Jacques found him absurd, and naïvely thought that Germaine would notice it, run away from him, come back alone, admit that it was a joke.

Louise was not spiteful, but she was a woman. She remembered. She studied the victim complacently.

Mouheddin came up. Louise winked, pulled a long face and jerked her chin in the direction of the waltzing couple.

Mouheddin replied to these explanatory gestures with another which consisted in pushing his lower lip out and hanging his head, opening his eyes enormously wide.

Jacques' severed head was lolling on his chest.

'Take him home,' said Louise to her lover. 'He is going to die.'

Jacques refused. He was not the kind to go away. He belonged to the cursed race that stays to drink the last drop. The waltz ended. Germaine and Stopwell returned, catching hold of the chairs and the diners. Germaine fell over a fat woman. She laughed. The woman insulted her. Stopwell shrugged his shoulders. The woman's husband stood up. The woman calmed him and forced him to sit down again.

Jacques realized there was trouble. None of it seemed very much to the point.

With the same jerk of the chin, Louise pointed out the miserable Jacques to Germaine, as if she were warning a talkative friend at a funeral that he is standing behind a member of the family.

'He'll get over it,' she said. This comment was humane in the sense that the bullet fired by an officer, from point-blank range, at a wounded man who is still breathing, is an act of mercy in the eyes of the law.

'A cigarette?' Stopwell suggested.

A delightful gesture on the part of the hangman.

*

Now that the retreat had sounded, they went out. They got into Germaine's car. Hoisted up, tossed about, enfeebled, Jacques saw a confused setting on either side. A profile : Mouheddin; the Odéon, posters, the Luxembourg, the Gambrinus Restaurant, the pool. They were taking Stopwell back.

The car stopped near the Panthéon. Stopwell got out. As Jacques remained seated, 'Come on, are you asleep?' said Germaine. 'We're here.'

He stammered, jumped out, and went in silently with Stopwell. Mouheddin went home with Louise.

Peter went to his room and Jacques to his. There, falling on his knees at the bedside, he vented his tears, which hung like a liquid lens from his eyelashes and made his universe look grotesque.

*

Jacques did not see how he could live, go to bed, get up, wash, work or go on at all, with his unbelievable agony which seemed as if it could hardly last an hour.

He excused himself, had no dinner and went to bed. He was hoping that sleep would declare a truce.

*

Sleep is not at our command. It is a blind fish which swims up from the depths, a bird which swoops down on us.

He felt the fish swimming round in a circle, outside its bounds. The bird folded its wings, perched on the edge of insomnia, twisted its neck round, smoothed its feathers, hopped up and down, but did not enter. Jacques held his breath like a bird-catcher. At length the bird took wing, flew away, and Jacques was left face to face with the impossible.

Impossible. It was impossible. Because of the swiftness of Germaine's love, a swiftness which he had acquired from her, Jacques could not distinguish any transition.

From one second to the next, he had seen a face miles away. He had felt the hand, now limp, which only yesterday had still sought his own. The eyes that met his own were examining, not playful.

He kept on telling himself, it's impossible. I am dreaming. Stopwell looks down on women and the rest is pretence, an Oxford pose. He is a virgin. He winces the moment physical love is mentioned. 'That is not done,' he says and adds, 'how can people sleep together?'

Even if Germaine is following up a whim she will meet a blank. Stopwell distrusts France. On the other side of the Channel, his father the parson, his football team, and his regiment are watching him. The alarm will have no sequel.

\*

Suddenly his eyes were overcome with heaviness. His jaw contracted. The bird was in the snare, the fish in the jar. He was asleep.

He is dreaming. He is dreaming that he is not dreaming, and that Stopwell, wearing a Scottish kilt, forces him to believe he is dreaming. Then he is skating, flying. He flies round the rink where trees are growing. Stopwell is trying to humiliate him, telling Germaine that he is dreaming, not really flying. Germaine is skipping along at Stopwell's side with the aid of a parasol. They use the parasol as a parachute. Stopwell's kilt grows very long, with a train.

Accompanied by a church organ, Germaine is singing *The Silent Honorat*. This meaningless title has a meaning in the dream.

Jacques was falling. He landed at the bottom of a hole full of linen. He was awake. He could hear Mouheddin going to bed. So it was morning. He fell asleep again. He was back at the rink, the part he was skating on was revolving. That is why it looked as though Stopwell were skating. He denounced it to Germaine as a trick. She laughed, kissed him. He was happy.

Petitcopain shook him to go and work. He got up and bathed his face in cold water.

\*

One by one, like soldiers at the command, his sleeping memories awoke and lined up. The skating-rink memory also came, but it had hardly arrived when the others shrank. It alone grew larger, and became colossal.

A murdered man can live on, ignorant of his wound, as long as the knife is there. When it is pulled out he bleeds, and his flesh shrivels up.

The cold water drew the knife out of Jacques' wound.

Although Germaine was asleep at this time he decided to run to her to be kissed and scolded, to have his wound closed.

\*

When we wake up it is the animal, the plant in us, that thinks. Naked primitive thought. We see a dreadful universe, because we see aright. Soon afterwards we are loaded with the tricks of the intellect. It brings us the playthings which man invents to hide the emptiness. It is then that we think we see aright. We attribute our uneasiness to miasmas of the mind passing from dream to reality.

*

Jacques was reassured. His work began at nine o'clock. There he shook Peter's hand. At ten o'clock he dived into a car, bought flowers on the way and stopped at Germaine's door.

A surprised Josephine opened the door. Germaine was asleep.

'I'll wake her up,' he said.

Jacques went in. Transported by her dreams into the past, Germaine wore her old expression. He examined it and was delighted. He laid the fresh flowers against her cheeks.

She was one of those alert people who wake up quickly.

'It's you!' she said. 'You must be crazy to disturb anyone at this hour.'

'I couldn't stand it,' he replied. 'I dreamt you left me. I jumped into a cab.'

Germaine had no hesitation in breaking hearts. She felt as maids do, that a precious thing, when broken, can be stuck together again.

'That was no dream, little man. Keep your bouquet. I am frank. I love Peter and he loves me. You will find plenty more like me. Let me sleep.'

She turned to the wall. Jacques lay on the floor and sobbed.

'Look here, this room isn't a hospital,' said Germaine. 'I loathe men who cry. Go back to the Rue de l'Estrapade and work. You don't lead the life of a student preparing for examinations.'

Jacques pleaded with her. She had put on the paraffin-, the gas-mask of those who are no longer in love. She measured Jacques' love by her own affairs. She thought this fit would pass off in a day. She rang.

'Bring M. Jacques a little brandy, Josephine.'

She was imitating the dentist who knows that an extraction makes the patient feel sick and upsets him, but that it soon passes off.

Jacques drank to please her. Josephine stood him up, gave him his hat and cane, and pushed him out, still behaving like the dentist's housemaid. She knows what follows the shock of the operation but has to let in a new patient who is growing restive.

*

From that moment Jacques' life was blurred like a bicycle wheel after a fall, like a photographic plate when the camera is partly opened.

'Be kind to him, he is suffering,' Mme Berlin kept saying to the schoolmaster.

'What from?'

'Never mind. Women can guess certain things.'

For she was continuing her romance.

Mouheddin kept on seeing Louise; his comings and goings harrowed Jacques. Their proximity was poor consolation.

Waiting is the most diminishing occupation. It leaves one vacant like a beehive during a swarm, left only with the rudiments of cheerless work. If our frivolous senses disturb it, they are paralysed by the bees of suffering. We must wait, wait, wait; eat mechanically to provide energy for the factory of false sounds, calculations, memories, hopes.

What was Jacques doing? He was waiting.

What was he waiting for? A miracle. A sign from Germaine, an express letter.

Lying on his bed, his heart twisted like navigators' knots that are loosened or tightened by the movements of the rope, he listened anxiously for the messenger who brought the telegrams upstairs.

He invented noises in the archway and on the stairs. Distant noises died away in the corridor.

Did he go out? He would not dare return. He would ask the caretaker.

'Has an express letter come for me?'

'No, M. Forestier,' she would reply.

Then he thought that the caretaker might not have seen the messenger. He counted up to twelve on every stair. In his credulity he fancied that during this procedure the letter could be generated spontaneously on the table.

One morning he received it. *Come to Louise's at five, I want to talk to you*, wrote Germaine.

He kissed it, folded it, put it away with the short-sighted photograph and was never parted from it, even afterwards.

How could he be patient until five o'clock?

He walked around, talked and went a little way towards killing the time which was to a great extent killing him.

Stopwell avoided him, only met him at the dining-table. Mouheddin thought he was cured, Mme Berlin thought him heroic.

She felt her love-affair with Jacques was like that of the Duc de Nemours and the Princesse de Clèves.

At four o'clock Jacques went to the Rue Montchanin.

There he found the two women. Louise was pretending to polish her nails. Germaine was pacing up and down. She had a hair-style which revealed her ears, earrings, a new face, a black and beige check suit which Jacques did not know.

'Sit down,' she said. 'You know my frankness. I am not the kind of woman who makes believe. Stopwell doesn't want ... ' she laid emphasis on it, 'does not want us to go together without you knowing and agreeing. I admit I don't know many friends who would behave like that. We are going out to dinner at Enghien tonight. Is it yes or no?'

'Come on ... my little Jacques,' said Louise, and stopped polishing her nails, 'come on, a nice gesture.'

She was not displeased.

The 'nice gesture' infuriated Jacques. He found the strength to reply.

'There are no nice gestures, Louise. Ministers and patronesses are the ones who make nice gestures. I bow. Love cannot be stopped.'

*

There is hope left even on the guillotine, since the law spares the offender if the knife doesn't work. Jacques still hoped that his magnanimity would touch Germaine and bring her back to him.

'Shake hands,' she said.

He recognized the English handshake.

'Tea?' asked Louise.

'No, Louise ... no. I am going.'

He closed his eyes. Looking at Germaine's dress through his eyelids he turned her cheeks red, making them swing slowly over to the right, regain their shape on the left and swing over again.

In the Rue de l'Estrapade Jacques knocked at Stopwell's door.

'Stopwell, she has told me everything,' he declared. 'She is free.'

Did Peter think that she had admitted everything, or was he seizing the opportunity to drive the point home?'

'We are gentlemen. You ought to know that I did not suspect there was a woman in Maricelles' room. I heard movements. I thought I should catch Petitcopain.'

After these incomprehensible words Jacques found himself back in the corridor, just as if he were *it* in blind-man's-buff and the others had made him dizzy.

Mouheddin was going out. Jacques stopped him and interrogated him. He learnt that on Germaine's evening in the Rue de l'Estrapade, during the rite of the clock, Stopwell, informed by Petitcopain, had gone into Maricelles' room and apologized. Germaine had kept him, told him that she was waiting for Jacques, asked him about the number of pupils, the work, and English schools. Stopwell thought that French schools did not provide enough sport and asked her if she went in for sport. She replied that she did not. She confined herself to roller-skating. She had told him which was their skating-rink.

'I'll hurry away,' Stopwell exclaimed, 'for I'm afraid Forestier may come back up. He is touchy, you know. He would think I came on purpose. Promise not to tell him I opened this door.'

Jacques remembered his jokes about the Englishman in *Round the World*.

He returned to his room. He had just found a stain on his brightest memory.

\*

And this was where we met him at the beginning of the book. He was bracing himself. He was putting up a resistance. He had become Jacques again; he was looking at himself in the mirror.

A mirror is not Narcissus' pool; there is no plunging into it. Jacques laid his forehead against it and his breath concealed the pale face that he loathed.

\*

Dark glasses or depression dim the colours of the world; but through them we can stare at the sun and death.

So he envisaged suicide without wincing, as if it were a luxurious pleasure cruise. These cruises seem unreal. One has to force oneself to make the preparations.

Jacques was afraid of an unworthy end. He pictured the journalist in Venice, green, cheeks bulging. He remembered a suicide at Maisons-Lafitte after the races, on the banks of the Seine, the forehead a pulp, the feet dancing in the eddying water where he was half afloat.

The previous night a doctor, a tenant on the fifth floor, had been deploring the number of deaths due to drugs. He told the story of one of his patients telephoning him at night, almost insane. Her lover whom she thought to be asleep was dead. He had taken an overdose of powder.

The doctor went there, clothed the body and, supporting it under the arms, carried it in a cab to an obliging clinic, to save the married woman and kill the scandal that would have attached itself to the name of a well-known industrialist.

\*

Jacques made up his mind.

\*

About eleven o'clock in the morning he went to the skating-rink. Deserted, the room had a different atmosphere. The barman was sweeping his bar. Jacques said good morning to him, and, very red in the face, began : 'You know that I never take drugs.'

'Yes, M. Jacques,' replied the barman, who knew the expression of the novice.

'Have you any? It's for a Russian girl.'

The barman went behind his till, peered round to see if they were alone, took a Jeroboam down from the sideboard it decorated, removed the false bottom, and asked : 'How much would you like? Four grammes, twelve grammes?'

'Give me ten grammes.'

The barman counted out ten little envelopes at twenty francs each, pocketed the two notes, and advised that the greatest care should be taken.

'Depend on me,' said Jacques, and putting the doses in his pocket he shook hands with him and left the rink.

To get out more quickly, he went across the rink. This rink was his execution block. It strengthened him in his resolution.

He went back calmly like a man who has taken his ticket and sleeper and no longer has to worry about the tiresome details of the journey.

## IX

Regardless of class differences, life carries us on all together, in the same train, to death.

It would be wise to sleep until that terminus. But alas, the journey allures us and we take such inordinate interest in what should only be a way of passing the time that on the last day we find it hard to fasten our cases.

The corridor linking the classes has only to bring two souls together secretly and blend them, for the certainty that one of them will get off, that the journey will come to an end, to make the thought of the destination unbearable. They would like long halts in the open country. They look at the door; with the telegraph wires moving by it is like a clumsy harpist working at an arpeggio and beginning it over and over again.

They try to read; someone comes up. They envy those who at the moment of death fearlessly put their affairs in order, thinking like Socrates of the barber for Phaedo and the Cock for Aesculapius.

Too lonely, Jacques had leapt out of the moving train. Or perhaps this diver wanted to rid himself of the human form that suffocated him. He wanted to find the communication cord.

He undressed, wrote a few lines on a pad which he put in an obvious place and undid the packets of powder.

He emptied them out by the corner into an old cigarette box. The contents sparkled like mica.

On his table stood a bottle of whisky, a syphon and a glass, a habit he had caught from Stopwell. He poured out a whisky, mixed in the powder, and drank it in one gulp. Then he went and lay down.

*

He was invaded from all sides at once. His face hardened. He remembered a similar feeling at the dentist's. With a coated tongue he felt strange teeth set in wood. A cold vapour like ethyl chloride played on his eyes and cheeks. Waves of gooseflesh ran over his limbs, coming to rest around the heart which was beating as if it would break. The waves swept up and down from his toes to the roots of his hair, like the sea when it is too low and keeps taking from one beach to give to another. A mortal cold replaced the waves; it played, spread out, disappeared and reappeared like the patterns on watered silk.

Jacques felt a weight like cork, like marble, like snow. It was the angel of death completing his task. He lies down on those who are going to die and waits until their attention is ever so slightly distracted, to turn them to stone.

Death has sent him; he might be an ambassador extraordinary, the ones that take the place of their prince at his marriage. So they do it with indifference.

A masseur is no longer affected by the skin of young women. The angel works coldly, cruelly, patiently, until the spasm. Then he flies away.

His victim could feel that he was implacable, like a surgeon

administering chloroform, a boa about to eat a gazelle, expanding
gradually like a woman with child.

'The man of snow ... the man of snow. ...' A confused refrain
bewitched his hearing. When children want to stay up with the
grown-ups at night and fall helplessly asleep, we tell them about
the sandman. They awaken when their chins nod on their chests,
and come to the surface bewildered.

Jacques heard a voice intoning, 'The man of snow ... of snow
... of snow. ...' He must not let himself succumb to it, and he
floated, head back, with his ears alone immersed in the unknown
element. For what the angel did had this terrible quality; being
unlimited, it worked above, below and within. It was not brutal;
the angel would rest and begin again with a new vigour.

What a distance between the decision to drown oneself, the
action, and the shock it reserves for the system. Many weak men
begin to swim when the water has hardly entered their nostrils, or
if they cannot swim they improvise it in desperation.

Jacques was overcome with fear. He wanted to pray, fold his
hands. They were heavy, immovable.

When your arm has gone to sleep because you have slept on it,
it can be revived quickly with soda water; it is animated, ready to
obey. Jacques' hand remained inert.

A man in an aeroplane cannot feel the movement. The machine
keeps still. Enclosed in helmet and goggles, he sees houses shrinking
and spreading, a lifeless town split apart by its river. The town
sways or stands like an atlas map against the wall. Suddenly looping
the loop, he can see it painted above his head. This movement of
the world around the pilots has disturbing effects. The passenger's
stomach seems to fall away. His ears are blocked up. Dizziness cuts
clean across his chest. He may touch down thinking he is at an
altitude of 3,000 feet : he mistakes the bracken for a forest.

On his bed Jacques began to confuse his symptoms with external
phenomena. The walls were breathing. The ticking of the clock
came first from the inkwell, then from the wardrobe. The window
was either shut or wide open on a sky full of stars. The bed slid,
tipped over, was held in unstable equilibrium. It overbalanced and
slowly righted itself again.

Jacques' head grew clearer, although it was humming like a
beehive. He saw Tours, his poor mother opening the telegram,
going rigid, his father fastening their bags.

'This is the end,' he thought. 'At our death we see our whole life.'
But he saw nothing more. His mother's face changed. It was
Germaine. It was Germaine or his mother. Then Germaine alone.
He found it appallingly difficult to remember her. He got her eyes

and mouth mixed up with the eyes and mouth of an English girl, one of the beasts he had desired, glimpsed in the casino at Lucerne. Everything was submerged by an edelweiss. He had a magnifying-glass and was studying this tiny starfish of white velvet which grows in the Alps. He was nine years old. They missed the train to Geneva because he was making a fuss, wanting them to buy him one.

'Memories ... ' he said to himself. 'My memories are coming back to me.'

But he was wrong. The performance closed with the edelweiss.

Nocturnal animals hide by day; a fire will drive them out of their holes. At the end of a corrida the audience in the shade and the audience in the sun are mixed; the drug had such tumultuous effects that it mixed Jacques' dark and light sides. He was vaguely aware of some disaster unconnected with the physical drama. He did not remember his wasted love or the dissolute weeks he had spent; he threw them up like a drunkard returning wine which he has forgotten drinking.

*

Jacques rose. He was losing his bearings. He could see the backs of the cards. He was not conscious of the system he was wrecking but he had a feeling of responsibility. The night of the human body has its nebulae, suns, earths and moons. A mind less subject to sluggish matter could tell how simple is the mechanism of the universe. If it were not, it would break down. It is as simple as a wheel. Our death destroys universes and the universes in our sky are inside a person of alarming size. Does God contain all? Jacques fell back.

Speculations of this extent are common in men who have taken poison. They delude many mediocre men about their intelligence. They imagine they can solve eternal problems.

After a lull the watered silk, the shivering, the cramp began again. Jacques felt he was losing strength for the fight. He was inundated with sweat. His heart-beats were not strong. He felt them even less because they had recently been too strong. His shoulders were touching the angel above him. He sank down. The water rose above his ears. This phase was endless.

Jacques had stopped resisting.

'There ... there ... there ... ' the angel was saying, 'you see we are getting there ... it's not so painful. ...'

Jacques replied : 'Yes ... yes ... it's very easy, very easy ... ' waiting submissively.

At last, like a torpedoed yacht as heavy as a house giving the salute and plunging slantwise into the sea, Jacques went under.

\*

He was not dead.
The angel was obeying an unknown countermand.

\*

Petitcopain was coming back from a school dance (his first dance) at five o'clock in the morning, and partly to get matches, partly to establish proof of his exploit, he went into Jacques' room, seeing a light under the door.

He saw the apparent corpse, the pad on which Jacques had written, woke Mouheddin, Stopwell, the Berlins, and the doctor on the fifth floor.

They made hot-water bottles, poultices. They gave Jacques a rub down. They forced black coffee between his teeth. They opened the window.

Mme Berlin, who thought she was the cause of the suicide, wept bitterly. Berlin put a shawl round her shoulders.

They began to organize help. They found someone to watch him. At eight o'clock the doctor affirmed that Jacques was safe.

To what did he owe his life? To a thief. Once again his dark side saved him, but in reverse. The barman had sold him a relatively harmless mixture.

# X

His convalescence was long, as he caught jaundice from the poison in his blood. After the jaundice he had symptoms of neuritis in his left leg; they disappeared. He was glad of the sharp pains which were the only things that took his mind off his obsession; medicine admiringly calls them *exquisite*, putting them on a level with illuminations in a missal.

In spite of the seemly disappearance of the long-jump champion, the Rue de l'Estrapade aggravated his exhaustion.

When he could be moved, his mother, who was staying in the house and had been sitting up with him for thirty days, enlisted the help of Petitcopain, and finally took Jacques away to Touraine.

\*

It was there on a February afternoon that Jacques awoke, cured of poison and remedies.

The wallpaper of his room depicted an old hunt. The embers of the fire were intense, furry, striped and feline from a distance and dreadful when seen close to, like the form of a tiger. His mother was near the chaise-longue, knitting.

Jacques was prolonging his state of numbness. He was pretending to be still asleep. He stopped his memories of childhood from disturbing his new memories. Clumsily, endlessly, he was moving the chessmen : Germaine, Stopwell, Osiris, Jacques Forestier. He corrected his mistakes, worked out impossible moves.

The game wore him out and wasted the little strength he had gained during convalescence. After a few seconds the chessboard went dim; Osiris, Stopwell, Germaine surrounded him. He was beaten, still beaten. Jacques wondered if there was a mistake, if Germaine were not a false image of his desires, tricking them by a resemblance. No. Desire does not deceive us. She did belong to that race.

For there is one race on earth which does not turn back, does not suffer, love or fall ill; a diamond race which cuts through the men of glass. Jacques worshipped the type from afar. It was the first time he had met it. What harm could a Germaine, or a Stopwell, do to each other. But Stopwell could cut Petitcopain to the heart.

A river race too. Petitcopain and Jacques belonged to the race that was drowned. Jacques made a lucky escape. A little longer, and he would have stayed there. In any case what was the use of his escaping? It would need only one of those rivers to flow, one of those stones to sparkle, and he would run into it to his death.

No! No! He would struggle. Will-power changes the lines on our hands. Fate can be diverted by dams. Ulysses tied himself up; he would tie himself up. He would have a home where he could be safe from sirens. It was easy to recognize them. A man had only to stop listening to them credulously to realize the vulgarity of their musical repertoire.

What was a diamond? The son of coal merchants who have grown rich. We should not sacrifice our hopes of happiness to it. Either to the river or to the diamond. He would no longer shed tears over soft or hard water.

So Jacques played with words. He thought he was defining a type, closing in on the enemy, looking him in the face, laying the ghost, guarding against a known danger. The words river, diamond, glass, siren, are Negro fetishes. A description would be better. But what description? The real monster has too many different heads, so many that they hide its body.

Jacques shifted, smiled at his mother. She stood up. She was
about to make a delightful mistake, to admit her jealousy.

'Jacques, Jacques, my dear, you must stop torturing yourself for
a bad woman,' she said.

Jacques dropped his decisions all at once. He shrank up, rebelled.
Mme Forestier sat down again. He found his card-case on the table,
opened it and out of bravado produced Germaine's photograph.
What did he see? An actress. He closed his eyes. His harness came
back. He hung on to it. His mother forgave him, and, to break the
silence : 'You remember Idgi d'Ybreo, at Mürren?'

She was counting her stitches. . . .

'Her death in Cairo is announced in the paper.'

This time Mme Forestier dropped her work. Jacques fell back.
Tears, deep tears, ran down his cheeks.

'Jacques, my angel . . . ' she cried, 'what's the matter? Jacques !'

She kissed him, wrapped her shawl round him. He sobbed without
answering.

He could see a bed. At the bedside stood the god Anubis. He had
a dog's head. He was licking a little face, a proud, noble face,
already mummified by suffering.


EPILOGUE

By the end of the month Jacques was fitter than he had been before
his illness, rest being good for people who are highly strung. He
had to take up his work again. It was decided that he should go
back to Paris with his mother, they should live there together, and
Mme Forestier should give rooms to a tutor. Jacques had suggested
this system. He still felt too unsteady to live without support. He
knew that his mother and he would be sure to murder each other,
but a fixed point of love and respect would enable him to see
whenever he was drifting. His own nature was not straight enough
to warn him. It yielded and drifted smoothly away.

M. Forestier no longer needed a plumb-line. He gave his wife to
his son. He would go and see them in May.

The morning they returned to Paris Jacques could tell from his
regret that he was not arriving alone, how indispensable Mme
Forestier's presence would be. He was suffocated. He dared not join
the crowd. He was not good at going into the sea. He found it cold
and mad.

Mme Forestier had to air the flat, make arrangements with the
staff, remove the dust covers and the camphor. Jacques was to meet
her at seven for dinner in town.

The street stimulated his body now that he was well. My eyes are open, he told himself. I am seeing Paris as I used to see Venice. There has to be drama to wake me up.

Then he sank inert again under a chaos of flats, buses, signs, barricades, kiosks, whistles, underground rumbling. He remembered the young men in Balzac who set their foot on the first rung of a golden ladder when they arrived in Paris. He could not get a foothold. He was heavy, floating over the surface of this buoyant city. He was oil on the water; wreckage. He made himself sick at heart.

He had to go and see a possible tutor his father knew, in the Rue Réaumur. As it happened, the tutor was not in. Jacques left a card.

Just as he was passing an office of the Bourse a man came up from below ground level. He recognized Osiris. Osiris coming up from a necropolis beneath a temple, this was the god Osiris, representing the past. Jacques' heart beat violently. He quickened his pace.

'Hey! Jacques! Jacques!'

Nestor was calling him. It was impossible to escape.

'Where are you going in such a hurry? Really! I didn't expect to see you! Germaine said your family was keeping you isolated in the country. Between you and me, I called you a fly-by-night. I wondered whatever we did to you. You made short work of good manners so far as we were concerned.'

Jacques stammered that he had been ill, had just come back from Touraine, and was spending a day in Paris.

'A day in Paris? I shan't let you go. Come and have a vermouth with me.'

The Osiris office was a few yards away in the Rue de Richelieu.

While Nestor was opening the door, taking his coat off, finding the vermouth and the glasses in a cupboard, Jacques saw a recent photograph of Germaine on the mantelpiece. His eyes filled with tears.

'You are well, but you look pale; drink this,' said Nestor. 'Vermouth does lymphatics good. Do you smoke? No. I have stopped smoking. I am on a diet. Look at my stomach.'

He settled down in the leather armchair and crossed his legs, holding his foot with his left hand, his glass with the right.

'Good old Jack! Germaine kept telling me your family had forced you to leave at once, but I wondered if you were sulking. Does one ever know with Germaine? She is such a tease. She'll be very pleased to hear that I've seen you. You know our latest craze, our great favourite? No, of course, you don't know anything.

I bet you anything you won't guess. Mouheddin! Yes, my dear boy, Mouheddin. Now we swear by nothing but Mouheddin. Mouheddin is a poet. Mouheddin is handsome. You can see that she doesn't change.'

Jacques did not expect the Arab's name. Nestor was delighted at his surprise. He clapped his foot and laughed.

'Fashion changes. I see them come and go, come and go. Germaine smokes amber-tipped cigarettes, eats Turkish delight and burns harem incense. All of which disgusts me. I am an old fool. Mouheddin is always right. Note that if I made her take my bazaar over she wouldn't have it at any price. That's women. That's Germaine. I allow her freedom. We won't change her.'

'And Louise?'

'Louise? Germaine has stopped seeing Louise. That's another story. Can you imagine, Mouheddin didn't sleep with Louise. It was platonic love. Then Germaine got Mouheddin from her by some trick, and so on and so forth. Her poet was captured. In any case I'm not sorry she doesn't go and see Louise any more. More jiggery-pokery. Just fancy, before Mouheddin everything had to be English. We were sportsmen, we played golf, rode, ate porridge and read *The Times*. You would have died laughing. As England was the order of the day, we had to have an Englishman. We had an Englishman; a very pleasant one too. You know him: Stopwell. Stopwell, the great favourite just after you left. Jacques bows himself out, we must have something new. Are you with me? England lasted thirty-seven days. A week after the English crisis she discovered your Stopwell. A month after the discovery I received anonymous letters. "Germaine is deceiving you" – you know the style – "she has rooms in the Rue Daubigny." Very well. I don't jib at that. On my way back from the shooting I go to the Rue Daubigny. I ring. Someone opens the door. Do you know who I catch? Stopwell. Stopwell and Louise. That's right. Poor Stopwell was as red as a tomato. Louise laughed till she cried. She took the rooms to hide from the prince who was staying in Paris incognito. You see how evil tongues get their information. On my way home I hesitated. Ought I to tell Germaine? It's a toss-up how she'll take things. She took it as a tragedy. She thought Stopwell was a virgin. She cried. She was losing her mascot, her plaything, her pet, her England. It was no use my defending Stop, telling her that flesh is weak, that Louise. ... "It's no good. He's a beast. Men are vile." Etcetera etcetera. She wouldn't let Stop set foot in the house again. She shouted that the house was not a dance-hall, that she would live alone on the farm. I've been hearing things, I can tell you.'

*

Jacques listened, quite embarrassed. Quintus Curtius relates how Alexander gradually assimilated the faults of the Barbarians through his contact with them. But if Jacques had acquired a card-sharper's sleight-of-hand through his contact with Germaine, he had lost it. He was no longer the Jacques of *Round the World*. He could not admit to having been so blind. He was like the detective who guesses that the banker's moustache disguises a thief and fingers the grip of his revolver. He wondered whether Osiris was making fun of him, whether he knew, whether he was leading up to a nasty blow.

Nestor went on.

'I'm afraid she's a devil, a real devil, my poor friend. I love her, and as long as she doesn't deceive me that's the main thing.'

Jacques spilt the vermouth on the chair.

'Leave it, leave it, it doesn't matter,' said Osiris.

'She needs to be amused. I can't amuse her. I house her, I clothe her, make a fuss of her, but I have the bank. My head's full of settlements. If I were a Stopwell, a Mouheddin, I'd still be keeping donkeys in Egypt.'

He stood up. He drummed on the window.

*

These words magnified Osiris so greatly in Jacques' eyes that he stepped back to look at him. He wondered if he could only see the base. It was as if an Osiris of granite seated on the top of five tiers of dead men was smiling down from an incalculable height in a sky studded with ciphers.

Osiris cut short the silence.

'There you are,' he said, 'that's how we stand. That's the full result of the races. I must go out. Will you come with me? Where are you going? I'll drop you in the car.'

Nestor picked up his coat and his top hat. No. Jacques recognized the gullible Nestor. His horns were not the horns of Apis the bull.

*

In the office outside a young telephonist was stamping envelopes.

'What are you doing, Jules?' asked Osiris. 'Are you putting 50-centime stamps on letters for the town?'

'There were no others about, M. Osiris, and I thought ... '

'You thought wrong; you are dismissed.'

Osiris looked inflexible. The employee was trembling.

'Don't argue,' shouted Osiris. 'Collect your pay. You are dismissed.'

The door was slammed.

On the stairs Jacques recalled the shattered face of the dismissed employee. In the doorway his mind was made up. On the pavement, he said : 'I'm sorry, M. Osiris, I have a call to make in the Rue Réaumur. But do me a favour. For Jules. He cost you one franc. You are unfair. Why did you dismiss him?'

'Why?' Osiris paused. 'Because *that,* my dear Jacques, *that* is something I can avoid.'

Then his expression changed and he took affectionate leave of Jacques. The car disappeared.

Alone in the Place de la Bourse, Jacques could still hear Osiris's emphatic *that*; he saw the oriental tugging at the revers of his coat as he said it, as if he were tweaking someone's ear.

To him the phrase seemed vague, lofty, mysterious. In it he could see the smile of a colossus once more.

Doubtless it only held a financial meaning, only gave one example of the powerful method of the Osirises, capable of accepting the heaviest losses without a frown, providing that they were inevitable. But Jacques' mind was running on, adding to it.

He decided, whatever happened, to build his character on this phrase, to keep his feet on the ground, to put on a uniform.

I am irresolute in myself, he thought, and *that is something I can avoid.* The rest by the grace of God.

*

As he was walking round the Bourse for the fourth time he saw Osiris's ex-employee behind the railings. Jules looked inordinately gay. He was playing prisoner's base with cyclists from the Havas agency.

'Funny place,' muttered Jacques.

These were the very words of an angel who visits the world and hides its wings under a glazier's sheet.

He added, 'What uniform can I wear to hide my heavy heart? It is too heavy. It will always show.'

Jacques felt himself growing gloomy again. He was well aware that to live on earth a man must follow its fashions, and hearts were no longer worn.

# Le Potomak

The Cocteau enthusiast who studies the author's bibliography is usually puzzled by the first entry under *Poésie du Roman* : *Le Potomak* (1913-14) : 1919. *Précédé d'un Prospectus* (1916) et suivi des *Eugènes de la Guerre* (1915). Cocteau refers to this book frequently as the first work he wrote after 'falling asleep'. The three books of poems he had composed and published between 1909 and 1912 were, he realized, artificial and self-conscious, and they have never been reprinted. His contacts with Diaghilev and Stravinsky made him suddenly aware of the true nature of creative work, which proceeds not from the conscious but from the unconscious or, as he maintains, 'sleeping' mind.

Critics and biographers of Cocteau invariably refer to *Le Potomak* as important but few have attempted to add the explanatory analysis and commentary which the uninitiated reader seeks. This is not laziness on their part but a justifiable admission that its message is not clear. The book, dedicated to Stravinsky and including a poem addressed to him, does not start at the beginning and go on to the end. Its characters were named after strange words read on old jars in a chemist's shop. These characters hold discussions and write letters to each other on a variety of topics, while the narrator eventually takes his friend Argémone to see the Potomak, a strange monster.

One of the most intriguing parts of the book is an evocation of the creative process, which started in this case with some drawings. From a doodle on a blotter the face of the Eugènes came into existence, horrible greedy creatures who attacked and devoured the helpless Mortimers. The cartoonlike drawings can only be described as pre-Cocteau. Their ugly angularity expresses a coarse sexuality. The only other drawings which seem to belong to the same era are some of the so-called 'atrocity' drawings, satirizing the German army, which were published during the First World War in Paul Iribe's magazine *Le Mot*.

*Le Potomak* is a confusing book in some ways because it expresses the confused state of Cocteau's mind at the time. He has described it as the book which shows him undergoing a change like a bird moulting, and he felt that his voice was breaking. Occasionally we find a sentence which seems to forecast the style of the early *poésie critique* such as *Le Coq et l'Arlequin,* and there are also descriptions, somewhat baroque, of people he wrote about later. The portrait of Pygamon for example seems to be an early draft for the brilliant description of Catulle Mendès which appeared in *Portraits-Souvenir* and was included in *My Contemporaries.*

One French critic has described *Le Potomak* as Cocteau's 'first death and first resurrection', a kind of draft of his entire future work, tightly rolled up as it were and almost indecipherable.

## AFTERWARDS

### I

1. First I met the Eugènes.
2. I drew, without a text, the album of the Eugènes.
3. Through them I felt the need to write.
4. I thought I was going to write a book.
5. I had a great number of scattered notes.
6. I dictated these notes.
7. I saw that it wasn't a book but a preface. A preface to what?
8. I leave everywhere the word 'book' and the naïve puffed-up promises. In childhood one lists the titles of works and one does not write them.
9. Nothing makes you read a book.
10. Argémone* will say : 'What is it? No connection between the drawings and the text and there's never any connection between one line and another.'

Canche's opinion reassures me : 'An idea is born from a phrase just as a dream varies according to the changing poses of the dreamer who turns over.'

---

*I was in a chemist's shop in Normandy with a friend I had in common with Gide. Look at the containers, I said to him, you might think they were names from Gide's books. This was how I christened the characters in *Le Potomak.* This and several other examples of friendly teasing should not be taken the wrong way.

## II

I was writing in a disorderly manner. At the centre we noticed that my voice was breaking, as it were, that I was writing in one of those crises in which the organism changes. In this way one dies several times before death and when one finally reaches death one resembles the sacred dancers of Spain.

These dancers dance in the church and the ancestral costumes are handed down through them. From century to century pieces of the costumes are replaced and now the costumes are still the same and not the same.

\*

Tomorrow I could be no longer capable of writing this book. It will stop when the changing stops : the last day of convalescence. Then, I could write it, but it would no longer be a book, for what composes, directs and blocks it is the state in which I momentarily find myself. Later, I speak to you about an acrobat : 'Every step cheats the fall.' He does not know where the cord ends and even with his foot on firm ground he walks carefully.

\*

If you encounter a sentence which irritates you, I put it there not like a reef to make you keel over, but
    in order that
as though it were a buoy,
you can discover how far I have gone.

\*

Too many diverse milieux cause harm to the sensitive man who adapts himself. There was (once upon a time) a chameleon. In order to keep him warm his owner placed him on a multicoloured Scottish plaid.

The chameleon died of exhaustion.

I didn't know why I created the Eugènes, the Potomak, the butterfly, or what relationship could in fact be established between them. Secret architecture. 'What are you preparing?' Canche asked me. I blushed. Impossible to answer him.

\*

'Your pockets,' said Canche, 'are full of matches and you never use them.' That, I replied to Canche, is the elegance of riches. Abuse seems to me vulgar and use is already a lack of tact. I give you a thousand matches. You are free to light your pipe.

*

What the public reproaches you for, cultivate : it is you.

*

My modesty : to be completely naked, tidy up my bedroom and put the light out. And everyone brings his lamp.

*

Beware of those who preserve old anarchies.

*

I'm going to confess to you one of my first symptoms.

In the past press cuttings would have made me weep and now I find strength in them. The more people laugh at me and the more this 'me' vanishes, I want people to laugh at it. One evening Axonge congratulated me. 'I was sure of you,' he said, 'but I expected this crisis to occur later.'

I didn't succeed in understanding him.

I shall save nothing from my burning past. Won't I become a pillar of sugar if I turn round?

*

Travel, Persicaire told me. If you change without moving, objects and people move round about you. When you travel do you know if your vision is new or do you simply see new things?

And then you return home like a stranger.

Now as I remain motionless I like this vertigo and my ingratitude.

In this way the following peeled away from me like the bark of a eucalyptus :

A . . . , the modest,

B . . . , the dilettante,

C . . . . who was more intelligent than his world and not intelligent enough for others,

D ..., the eclectic,
E ..., who was amusing,
F ..., who wasn't,
G ..., the bitter one,
H ..., the coward,
I ..., the simple one,
J ..., the complex,
K ..., the unfair,
and many things which had disturbed me and which no longer
did so.

*

I know, now, the evening of the carillon, what is happening at
Malines. Bourdaine was there. He told me.
　In the glass cage the bell-ringer leaps from
cord to cord, quite naked : and
over the town
the angels danced the ballet from *Faust*.
　It was mild ... the stars ... a street going up.
　If you don't stop, says Bourdaine, and if you don't concentrate
your sensitivity, the timpani grow soft and the bronze music
becomes confused.
　When Bourdaine tries to put the others in the atmosphere of that
evening in Malines, he puts his hand on his heart.


## HOW THEY CAME

### I

Persicaire, have you forgotten this garden? I have difficulty in
finding it again. But I'm sure I walked in it one evening with you.
　He went down to the edge of the sea.
　We heard a little sound of lament. 'The buoy at ... ' you said
then, and it is the name of the beach which escapes me.
　Here, still, I stop and dive.
　I am the element where sleeps the pearl. I sink into it. My head
buzzes. I don't move.
... careful!
jellyfish, fans, sponges,
phosphorescences,
the shadow of an island,
biological night.

My eye looks at a yellow book, a bottle of ink, my fountain-pen. I search.

Scraps of memory, dates, period remnants, faces, things done or said, and suddenly, without importance, an armchair that absorbs everything, which finds its outline again to the detriment of the rest towards which I am striving.

Spirals.

Astonishment at being myself, at having to die.

I open my diver's helmet a little.

Phew! (No, I haven't got the pearl.) But let me at least breathe.

Oh, I remember well. The name of this dreary gulf where our buoy uttered his lament, is hidden by a clump of hydrangeas. We were going down an avenue and we saw a young Indian escaping. He was crouching behind the clump and wore tennis trousers. Persicaire, it was a vast property, at dusk : a dawning of night.

We couldn't hear the sea.

Wait, we used to turn to the right.

A scent of heliotrope.

I count seven steps.

We heard the sound of a piano being played.

I'm wrong. It would be better to start again.

Persicaire, it was a vast property, at dusk : a dawning of night. We couldn't hear the sea. We crossed, if I remember aright, four little cloister courtyards in the Italian style. When we reached the threshold of the fourth, another young Indian ran away as fast as he could. It was a courtyard of morning glory and heliotrope. (Here, the scent of heliotrope.)

And it was then that somebody played the piano.

A detail we noticed : at the corners of the house there were windows so narrow and so high that we couldn't understand what they were illuminating inside.

At that precise moment I began for you the APOLOGIA FOR THE BUTTERFLY.

Apologia for the Butterfly

Once upon a time in the town of Tientsin, there was a butterfly.

Persicaire, I'm afraid that my apologia will tire you.

'I reproach you,' you say then, 'for interrupting, but advise you not to weigh heavily on the butterfly's wings. Night is falling.'

(We passed near a magnolia. It stood against the wall like a genealogical tree of doves.)

So, I went on, it was a splendid butterfly. This was why the young artist **Pa Kao-tsai.** . . .

Is your story Chinese?
Yes, I replied, lowering my eyes, I admit that, but it isn't bad all the same.
What's your young artist called?
Chou To-tse.
Well now, I thought I heard another name.
Your assurance disturbed me. 'I've forgotten the end of the story,' I stammered. 'It's a pity,' you said, 'I would like to have known it.'
We said goodbye at the edge of the lawn.

(I told Persicaire all this at the corner of the Rue de Sèze and the Boulevard de la Madeleine.)
'Strange,' he said, 'I wouldn't want to doubt your good faith, but I recall nothing of this walk. And I deplore it all the more because I find once again my curiosity about the hydrangea garden and I want to know the end of the apologia.'
'Goodbye, Persicaire; Argémone has been getting impatient for the last quarter of an hour. I will write to you tomorrow.'
The next morning I wrote to Persicaire :

My dear Persicaire,
I've found the end of the apologia again. The young Chinese artist was walking along and he caught sight of the butterfly. He had never seen such a beautiful butterfly. He became inspired and began to paint its portrait, from memory.
He painted on rice paper
with a hand which at first drew
in minute detail,
for in the town of Tientsin
there's much less to do than in Paris.
This patience took him to the age of a hundred. At last, one evening, before dying, he added the final touch.
Then the butterfly left the page and flew away.
Goodbye.

PERSICAIRE'S EXPRESS LETTER

I like your apologia. It leads me to add a more humble anecdote
to my thanks. I was inventing a fairy-tale for my son; now we
came to a monster.

I tried to describe it.

'Fat, melancholy and wild, it perpetually smells the heat of the
mud beneath its stomach. Its skull is so heavy that it cannot carry
it. It rolls it round slowly and with its jaws half open it pulls up
with its tongue the poisonous weeds watered by its breath. On one
occasion it devoured its feet without noticing.*

Excuse me if I interrupt. One must accustom children to
beautiful things and I was sleepy.

Nobody, I went on, has ever seen its eyes, or those who have seen
them are dead. If it raised its eyelids, its pink and swollen eyelids ... oh, Papa, Papa, stop, I beg you, cried Mélique. Then in a
voice without expression, he cried : 'I'm frightened of the animal.
Suppose it came out of the story !'

Here, I apologize.

In order to take up this passage later, I had made some pre-
sumptuous appointments.

The temptation I had to write the conclusion made me put off
indefinitely some work which demanded to be done at once. The
clay is dry.

I've made this mistake several times.

My incapability to make revisions and the frankness of the book
lead me not to resort to subterfuge.

I print these notes in their crude state :

Wish to reply again to the reply – Fatigue.

The pen, in the margin and on the blotter, begins to live.

In my ear ... that angelic whistling sound which occurs if you
run a wet finger slowly around the rim of a glass.

All at once : T H E  E U G E N E .

## II

I recall one of those faces with abundant detail which are dictated
to us by insomnia.

It was at Cameline's place, in the country. At the corner of a
sheet of pink blotting-paper, a woman with a large eye and a
round ear.

* Temptation of Saint Anthony.

A year later I rediscovered my room and the profile. I could not resist adding in caricature fashion a scar, a mark, a wrinkle and bags under the eyes. The next morning I felt remorse as a result, as though I had committed a sort of crime, as though I had absent-mindedly, by magic, been able to make a young mistress look older.

As soon as a face is drawn we become responsible for it, possessing the right to suppress it if we don't like it and to take care of it if we do.

The Eugène, the first Eugène, 'the Eugène envoy', fascinated me. He derived from the priodontes, grubs, the chemical retort, the aortic curve, the orb, the gyroscope adorned with a sound of murmuring, I didn't christen him. 'Well now,' I said to a Eugène like those Negroes crying 'Christopher Columbus!' and adding: 'We are discovered!'

The Eugènes transmitted their name to me as if they had sent me the outline of a silhouette equivalent to their shapeless mass.

The fact remains that a Eugène was there, without remembering that I had ever drawn him, standing up, with fixed gaze, a sly mouth and short sleeves.

Their hair still intrigues me. I am assured that it is a light metallic sheet, curled up at the base; but these appearances matter little. If they had mattered, I should have been highly astonished by their dress which is so like ours. I repeat that it has no importance. All at once I realized that this little man who came from my pen was, in relation to the infinite, the number, the golden starfish which represents stars, a conventional sign.

I experienced the appalling discomfort of a weak man who finds himself at last face to face with his enemy.

Now, while I invented (or thought I was inventing) everything about the Mortimers in a mood of half-laughter and half-anxiety, and also their name which conceals nothing, except for the fact that the word *mort*, meaning 'dead', is embedded within it, I invented nothing about the Eugènes. They continued to impose themselves in squadrons. The people who surrounded me saw that I was barely responsible. They saw them alighting from my pen, as in those aneroid barometers which are sensitive to storms and register alpine curves.

Soon the Eugènes became an index of sensitivity for me. It was only necessary to place them opposite the patient and wait. A decisive experiment. People who are impervious to miracles do not interest me. They will always be incapable of liking what I like or at least of liking it in the same way.

I learnt gradually that the Eugènes like an s in the plural through the persistence with which I began ten times over again what we thought at first was a spelling mistake.

I had therefore been given, if not the order, at least the habit of bringing the Eugène off the blotter where I could see him in just such a plastic and indecipherable state as a hieroglyphic which represents a crocodile and recounts a battle. I considered him, not even looking any further for the cause of his strength. I accustomed myself to him in a docile fashion.

My efforts to free him from his flat prison !

I do not recall having said to myself : 'It would be amusing to draw all the poses which would be possible for him,' but I do remember : 'I must arrange a relative escape for this Eugène.'

Since I am a poet, I draw badly. I experienced the surprises of the first man who discovered the existence of three-quarters without doing so on purpose.

Imagine a little man who, by means of a clumsy line, walks towards the interior of the room *for the first time*.

The way in which the Eugène communicated to me his wish to move in three-dimensional space comes back to me in a manner as precise as that September night. By dint of looking at him and being followed by his little eye, I noticed that two lines near the curve of the nose and at the back of the head, one which Ramsès would have taken for a mark and the other for a crook, only awaited, in order to bring into relief the nose and the hair, a slight retouching. The first was the angle of a curved section of the nose; the other, the backbone, as one might say, of half-rolled-up parchment.

It only remained to me to follow the example. After the nose and the hair came the cheek, the mouth, the collar, the tie, the stomach, the legs and the ridiculous little boots. Soon there were Eugènes everywhere and, since no two of them were identical, I imagined that they were one and indivisible like zero, the necklace of the infinite.

Had I already seen something that the Eugènes recalled to me? I felt I was grasping, losing and grasping again, moving up and down like a Cartesian diver in the element of thought, a circumstance analogous to that of their terrestrial birth, a vague old connection between this blotter and another blotter, between the self of this gesture and another twin self that I could not reach.

I learnt later that this was a joke played by the Eugène women. To make me imagine suddenly, in the space of a thousandth of a second, that I had already seen or heard elsewhere and in the same circumstances a sight or phrase which strikes our eye and our ear.

The Eugène women stimulate the neurones of memory a little

before the image or the sounds touch the senses, and the imbroglio provokes this lack of equilibrium which makes us remember a perception, at the very instance when it reaches us, as something old and already dead.

I see you smile, Axonge. What can I reply to your knowledgeable gravity?

Where a wall forces philosophers and scholars to meticulous halts, the poet begins.

Science only serves to verify the discoveries of instinct.

I would like to quote two phrases to you. They were spoken to me by Henri Poincaré a few days before his death. I was very young and I had met him at Alysse's place. Here is the first sentence : 'Why are you shy? It's for me to be shy. Your youth and poetry are two privileges. The chance of a rime sometimes makes a system emerge from darkness, and gaiety catches mystery on the wing.'

The second was better. 'Yes, yes,' said this upright man, 'I guess what it is. You would like to hear how far we have got with the unknown. Each day brings a miracle into our laboratories, but responsibility obliges us to maintain a professional silence. I see things, I see things. . . . (And he took off his eye-glasses.) The confidence that is placed in us can only be maintained by certainty. The unknown ! . . .'

I heard the samovar and a passenger boat on the Seine.

'We hear it, at the present time, as miners excavating a tunnel hear the violent muffled sounds and the first pickaxe blows of the miners on their way to meet them.'

Admit it, Axonge, not bad, was it? Moreover, it killed him. Outside forces made him die – the police force of the unknown.

But I'm digressing; where was I? Ah, yes, your smile after the hypothesis of the Eugène women's behaviour, which motivates (let's be orderly) enlightenment about their appearance.

How did the Eugène women appear? One evening, and of their own accord, on a page where my hand was wandering in lifeless fashion.

You must have seen, Persicaire, the early dawn, the vegetable carts in the Place de la Concorde. You're going back home. You put off the effort of undressing and going to bed. It's beyond one's strength. To be honest I didn't see the thing until the next day, among the scribblings. One of the women, flabby and serious, was mixed up with a Eugène. The line from which she was made came out from his ribs.

I drew the couple.

Then a troupe of them.

Then the album.

THE EUGENE ALBUM
or
A STORY
WHOSE HAPPY ENDING
ONLY MAKES
FOR A
WORSE CONCLUSION

*Here is the Eugène album.*
*In the end I granted myself the right to link a text to the drawings after feeling that they did not include one.*

Seek Mortimers only within yourself.
This couple are ending their delightful honeymoon by a lake at Geneva.
Lake Geneva! One more drop and it overflows. God is a very uneven landscape painter.

\*

Depending on their appetite the Eugènes choose a couple who are upset easily or not.
This time, face to face with 'typical Mortimers', the Eugènes are not afraid of waiting and they even whet each other's appetites.

## FIRST VISIT TO THE POTOMAK

'Argémone, get ready, I'm taking you to see the Potomak.'
'Your Potomak gets all the attention,' said Argémone. 'In the first place, why name it after a river?'
'My Potomak ends with a K (insist on the K). And then, would you ask me why Cambacérès was named after a street? The river which flows, if I am not mistaken, into Chesapeake Bay, owes its name to this *megaptera coelenterous*.
'He didn't belong to the Ark. The crew took him for a madrepore. He swam, he swam to survival, Argémone. He dreams about the phenomena of the infinite of which his gelatine is the image.
'He plays little jokes on his keeper. He's spoilt at the aquarium.'
ARGEMONE : Where is your aquarium for monsters?
WE : But, dear Argémone, in the Place de la Madeleine.

ARGEMONE : One might have known.

WE : In the case of men, as soon as a prodigy escapes from the realm of the unreal, he ceases to be a prodigy. There were twelve spectators for Farman's first flight, and if we read on posters that a troupe of centaurs were galloping round the Zoo, we wouldn't go or else we'd go a week after reading the poster.

ARGEMONE : Are there many people at your aquarium? What dress should I put on?

WE : Wear what you're wearing now, Argémone. My aquarium attracts nobody. A rich American and I are the only regulars.

*

Nourished on mandragoras and montgolfier balloons, the Potomak was dozing in his glass container.

'I don't like your Potomak,' said Argémone.

'I didn't think you would,' I replied.

The Potomak swallowed a mouthful of oil and sighed.

The rich American threw him white gloves and spelling mistakes.

'This dried-up aquarium doesn't mean a thing to me,' repeated Argémone.

Her insistence annoyed me.

The Potomak raised towards heaven one eye drowned in prisms and his large pink ears, formed like marine shells, listened to the unending murmur of an interior ocean. (*Bravo.*)

WE : Ah, to place one's ear against this cold soft flesh and surprise the ebb and flow of antediluvian waves and the silence of the meteors.

ARGEMONE : How dirty you are!

The Potomak fascinated me more and more. My anxiety received a response from him. A wave came and went between us. 'Pet, pet,' the keeper called out. The Potomak unfolded his paws. He smiled. He was certainly tender-hearted.

'Let's go,' said Argémone, who was pulling at my jacket. 'It's seven o'clock.'

They had just lit arc lamps and mercury lights. The Potomak became phosphorescent. You could sense the darker mass of the viscera and the near-black presence of the gloves he had eaten. Alfred the keeper was playing on a small hydraulic flute.

We moved away.

Quickly, as we passed, I looked at
the hexapod Opoponax that counts its

feet and gets the number wrong,
the Pharynx which moans,
the Cadenza which dances up and down on his abdomen,
the Aratory with its red carcass that has fallen on
the rough ground,
and
the Orpheon who devours geraniums.

It was as hot as an oven. *The coolness of the Boulevard de la Madeleine astonished us.*

'We can breathe!' cried my companion. 'I'll never go into your cellar again.'

'Then I'll go alone,' I sighed. 'I know it's impossible for an enterprise of this type to succeed.'

'Well,' she concluded irritably, 'people are right. That cellar is unhealthy. You run the risk of catching a cold there. Your Potomak frightens me and I prefer calf's head. It's all imagination again, like your Eugènes. I'm normal. I don't understand anything about all that and I don't want to. It's a principle. I reject it.' (She was quivering.)

'Yes,' I went on, 'the Potomak disturbs me. What kind of moiré do his sleeping and waking form between each other? My confused life and the coherence of my dreams link me to this Potomak. The same fluid runs through us. I walk in the twilight. I continue to live in my dreams and to dream in my diurnal mechanism. Sometimes I can appear absent-minded enough not to reply to signs and not to pursue encounters; but this is because I believe I am the only one aware of it, as happens in dreams.

I go to bed just as one might pick up a book. Sometimes I go to bed for ten minutes, for an hour, fully dressed between the sheets. In this way I prolong and delay my course, for the life of dreams opens the box of human dimensions.

You have often seen me, Argémone, coming out of my room with my face still confused. Didn't Pascal wonder if dreams added to experience? Sometimes I believe it. Dreams direct me and I direct my dreams. I record many spectacles from the day before in an unmethodical way, just as one might pick up fragments of multicoloured glass so that sleep could co-ordinate them and rotate them in the depths of a dark telescope. I am regarded as frivolous, unstable, unreliable, egotistical : I dream. And not, understand me, Argémone, not those dreams that Murger dreamt in which the dreamer marries a Chinese princess.

Landscape
tunnel
landscape

tunnel
tunnel with blue eyes.

My reality resembles my dream so strongly that when I believe I am in one room it happens that I find myself in another. Some of my painful dreams resemble my reality so strongly that I consider the hope that they might be only a dream, alas, to be void, in order to subject myself to it.

I've read accounts of dreaming. People who are dead or familiar to us play absurd parts in them, supported by memory. Their labyrinth is developed by the stomach within and by noises without. They are the warmth of a make-believe corpse. They do not derive from my lucid lethargy. I regard them as no more comparable to mine than a phenomenon of Daltonism to the interpretation of a painter.

Argémone, when I emerged from my dreams, you always received me unkindly. I brought no news from the Bourse and I didn't know the names of the ministers. I'm wrong. I know it. Even if you believe yourself a cog in a communal error, you still have to play your part. That of the Potomak is to be the Potomak, mine is to travel, to learn, to go up in a plane, to invent a form of dynamite. You get angry because I question you about the mysteries of your childhood and I inform you about mine.

Argémone, did you walk along a groove in the pavement four times?

Did you go, Argémone, to the right of certain lamp-posts and to the left of certain trees?

Did you go back ten times, Argémone, to touch a door-bell until your palm was satisfied with it?

Did you re-establish, in order to relieve the strain on your shoulders, imaginary equilibrium with the faces you used to pull, and were too ashamed of to let your maid discover unexpectedly?

Argémone, I used to see days in colour and I stopped seeing them when I was twelve. Until I was seven, Argémone, I thought I had lived in China.

You reproach me about my nerves and my literature. Your faith was flagrantly good, but I paid you the supreme politeness of believing it was bad.

O sweet Argémone, the most loving people clash.

One evening in Padua (it was on a bench by the river) I saw two lovers exchanging caresses. It was warm and the slightest sighs, traversing the softness of the atmosphere, reached me.

Can I ever forget their laughter
when their elbows and their
clumsy knees bumped against each other?

We were exceptionally cut off.

Argémone, you're frightened of death. In the past, appendicitis converted you. You go to Mass and once through the door you no longer give it a thought. A small coin drops from your muff into the cap held by the legless cripple. You feel very sorry for this cripple and you say to me : 'How can one complain when one has legs?'

Everyone has his problem, Argémone. As for me, I sometimes think that death is the only certainty that brings no peace; at other times I think it is a reward, the greatest of all surprises on this earth; at others. . . . But, later, people will talk to you about death. Argémone, I could find consolation (of a selfish kind) in the spectacle of your cripple, but his desire for legs gives me, who have legs, a desire for wings.'

'I'm sleepy,' said Argémone. 'I would like not to dream about your Potomak. I dream a lot at the moment. No doubt I have indigestion. Do you dream, dear friend?'

'No,' I replied, 'for my digestion is good and I'm wonderfully well.'

That evening we did not go any further.

# The Ghost of Marseilles

*The Ghost of Marseilles* (Le Fantôme de Marseille) is listed in the *Poésie du Roman* section of the Cocteau bibliography, but it is of course what we would call a short story, and the only one of this length Cocteau ever published. It first appeared in 1933 in the November issue of *La Nouvelle Revue Française* and was republished in 1947, together with *Le Numéro Barbette,* under the title *Deux Travestis.* There is an obvious link between the pieces – the curious appeal of a man dressed in women's clothes, drag in fact. Barbette was a professional acrobat who seemed to confirm Cocteau's theories about 'professional secrets'; the characters in *The Ghost of Marseilles* are in no way commendable, and perhaps we should laugh at them, but we feel sorry for poor Monsieur Maréchol and admire the logic of Marthe's closing remarks.

This theme, with its Marseilles background, remained in Cocteau's mind for many years and in 1955 the theatrical sketches collected in the *Théâtre de Poche* included a version of the story in monologue form which he had written specially for Edith Piaf. The monologue consists of the girl's address to the magistrate when she is apprehended after the shooting.

There is no similar story in Cocteau's writings and its style is different from that of the novels.

For four days Achilles had been living in the women's apartments disguised as a woman. But we are not concerned, as you might think, with the Achilles of legend and you are not beginning a Greek tale. The Achilles I'm telling you about was an Arab and his mother belonged to Marseilles; he was twenty and looked fifteen. He was good-looking and his good looks were feminine without being effeminate. I mean that his firm beardless face and slim waist, his slender wrists and ankles allowed this young rascal to wear with dazzling effect the clothes dictated by a fashion whereby women try to resemble ephebes; and when worn by him these fashions became feminine by contrast and endowed him with a charm that was indescribable, fabulous (in the proper sense of the word) and equivocal.

Why was our Achilles wearing a woman's dress, stockings and necklaces? Where was he wearing them? For the scrupulous accuracy of our story we have to admit that he was hiding or, more precisely, he was being hidden and shielded from the police. This ruse, arranged by a woman named Rachel, amused her companions greatly and these companions and this Rachel, much more scantily clad than our hero, surrounded him with ritual and acts of kindness in a secret room within a place of much ill-fame in Marseilles.

In short Achilles, in spite of his youth, acted as pimp for two girls. One, Rachel, worked in the brothel and the other, Marthe, worked on the Canebière and in the neighbouring streets.

Rachel and Marthe loved Achilles. Achilles loved them. He showed just enough cruel indifference to maintain his role in the milieu, a milieu where, except in rare circumstances, affection is not in evidence.

All these nice people were very naïve, in spite of what one might suppose; many customs of high society would have appeared deeply shocking to the members of this little trio who intended no harm and observed the ritual of an age-old tradition.

Misfortune willed it that Achilles allowed himself to be led by Victor (a colleague) into a less official enterprise – a burglary, to be honest – and that, since the police were looking for him, Rachel and her companions had the audacity to dress him as a girl and include him in their troupe. Madame was won over by Achilles' niceness and became an accomplice in the stratagem; for four days Achilles could be found like the Achilles of legend, in women's clothes, in the women's apartments.

Alas, all good things come to an end. Madame anticipated a domiciliary visit and, in spite of the improper aspects of the situation, it was decided that our hero should leave the *Flamboyant* and walk the dark alleyways until further instructions.

His first steps along the street amused Achilles. The disguise made his flight look like a full-dress carnival and the entertainment concealed the drama from him. It concealed it so well that instead of remaining, as agreed, in the darkness of the narrow streets surrounding the market, Achilles took the risk, about eight o'clock in the evening, of appearing, first on the quayside, opposite the boats which go out to the Château d'If, with the gramophone playing, and then, right out on the Canebière.

It was there that he noticed Marthe walking up and down along the pavement. Wishing to avoid her and fearing a scene he rushed headlong towards the road. As he took to his heels an astonished glance from a policeman reminded him that his sprint could not have been in keeping with his actual appearance. He tried to slow down too quickly, stepped back, became entangled in the Marseilles traffic, which is notorious for confusion, and stumbled as a limousine touched him and almost knocked him down.

Within a moment he found himself at the centre of a gesticulating crowd, he was lifted up by the strong-armed chauffeur of the limousine and deposited on the cushions beside an extremely grave gentleman who with one hand told the chauffeur to drive on and with the other indicated to the crowd and the policeman that he was taking responsibility for everything, that the incident was closed, that they could disperse and seek other delights.

The owner of the limousine was called Monsieur Fabre-Maréchol, he was one of the richest men in Marseilles, manufactured olive oil (Maréchol oil) and was returning home from his club. He had just acted, he thought, under the influence of an entirely natural human reflex and gradually, while the vast limousine glided along beside the sea, he wondered, as he looked at his victim's suggestive profile and figure, if his human reflex was not, rather, an example of our remarkable aptitude for making contact with chance, for leaping astride the miracle which all men summon in secret and which is demanded by the least imaginative people even when they think they are accepting the inevitable.

Monsieur Fabre-Maréchol patted Achilles' hands and asked him if he was hurt, if he was still suffering from his fall.

When it was a question of inventing a story Achilles was never at a loss. He played the scene marvellously. He sighed, said he was a silly girl, made out that he was a poor girl called Lily, turned his head away when speaking of his fall, so that this fall might look like attempted suicide, wiped away a tear, spoke of his loneliness and his disgust for the means of livelihood available to young people in Marseilles when their families were dead, in short, he moved the worthy Monsieur Fabre-Maréchol to the point when this very worthy man wondered, without daring to believe it too much, whether destiny had not just touched him with a snowy finger and if the sentimental heart which he concealed beneath his paterfamilias-cum-businessman's jacket had not just, at last, found a reason to start beating.

Monsieur Fabre-Maréchol had a wife, two daughters and a son, all unbearable; he was one of those charming men of whom people say : he's stupid but he has a first-class wife, daughters and a son.

These first-class characters were at that moment on holiday at Pourville. Monsieur Fabre-Maréchol was enjoying bachelor life and sighed as he thought of the pied-à-terre which he kept empty and which he hoped to use one day for some dream. Casual romances would have shocked his sensitive soul; he dreamed vaguely, waited, built up ideas, hoped, I say, and now, suddenly and as though some fairy had waved a wand, there was a young woman in his car, a young bird-woman, a young face as sweet, as blonde, as anonymous as Melisande.

Monsieur Fabre-Maréchol deemed this conquest worthy of pursuing into the still virgin pied-à-terre. It was in this way that Achilles, instead of prowling dangerously about before the eyes of the police, landed in a luxurious milieu prepared lovingly and carefully by a rich businessman, where he could gild an idol and worship it.

Achilles' plan was not complex : 'If he touches me,' he calculated, 'I'll fly at him, I'll knock him down, relieve him of his wallet and run away.'

But Monsieur Fabre-Maréchol decided differently. And gradually, confronted by the septuagenarian's respectful attitude, Achilles modified his plans. They changed from rapid to long-term. After a few hours it was a question of actually installing Lily, placing her among her furniture, having her cooking done by the old concierge and waiting for the moment when, through his care and attention, Monsieur Fabre-Maréchol would manage to break the ice, succeed in overcoming legitimate modesty and experience the consummation of his desire.

'You realize,' Achilles had said, 'you're not like the others. I wouldn't want to give you false hopes and put on an act. You speak to my heart ... I shall wait until my heart responds. ...' It can be seen that he knew how to behave and that, as the phrase goes, he could be allowed out on his own.

I add, and this is the finishing touch, that Monsieur Fabre-Maréchol, intoxicated with love and trust, asked if she did not have some girl friend who could act as maid, and that our hero, following blindly the plot of Italian *opera-buffa*, suggested and obtained the services of Marthe.

I leave to the imagination Marthe's surprise, the couple's giggles and the strange scenes that the poor businessman would have interrupted if he had not been afraid of intruding and had not exhibited incredible tact in the timing of his visits.

The extraordinary situation lasted. The couple took good care of each other. Marthe went out and told Rachel. The police lost interest.

Monsieur Fabre-Maréchol hoped.

For a week his hope had even been tinged with a slight impatience, for he saw with some fear that the date of his family's return was coming closer and he dreaded, with justification, the imbroglios of a double life.

Marthe felt this impatience. She immediately advised the young man to relax slightly, to show a little abandon and suggest for example an 'outing', which would flatter the old man's vanity. This outing was very dangerous. Achilles risked it. People saw them together and talked. Questions were asked at the club. Fabre-Maréchol blushed, lowered his eyes, defended himself weakly and accepted the unkindness.

Things became so tense, so strained, that Marthe, who was more nervous, less oblivious, decided that they must be brought to an end. They must buy a gun (can one ever tell?) and risk what the apaches call *une mise en l'air,* that is a sudden attack which would leave the poor businessman gagged, bound and alone one night amidst the ruins of his dream.

This plan made Achilles very gloomy. He agreed about the value of bringing things to an end, but he liked this existence and he did not see how he would easily take up any other, which would be strangely complicated by fresh police inquiries.

For the dénouement the couple selected an evening when Fabre-Maréchol proudly took his conquest to a kind of dancing-club. Marthe would await their return, with the gun in her soubrette apron pocket, they would attack the defenceless old man, immobilize him and beat a retreat.

The dance-hall was full of people and noise. Nobody dared approach the mysterious little table where Fabre-Maréchol was relishing his triumph. Achilles, who was no longer concentrating on his role, presented a strange sight to the spectators. 'If I were Maréchol, I would have my suspicions about that girl's way of life,' stated a very beautiful young woman who lorded it over a table where the town bigwigs were crowded together.

The fact was that Achilles, beneath his make-up and false eye-lashes, his feathers and tarlatan, was assuming a boyish look that was less and less disguised. He no longer heard the orchestra, no longer saw the lights, no longer caught the multicoloured balls. His heart sank into vague sorrow, he was not skilful enough to deal with the feelings that made him rebel against his base ingratitude, he relapsed into strange fantasies, saw himself dragging Maréchol into the car, throwing himself at his feet, confessing everything, begging him to be kind, to keep him as a son; then there were other images. He was constantly prowling about, his hands in the pockets of a short jacket. He had to avoid the police, he had to disappear into Chinese shops, wait and wait, slip out, start walking again down the Rue de la Rose, the Rue Saint-Christophe, through the sinister docks. No! He would confess the truth to Maréchol! Maréchol wouldn't drive him out, he'd understand, forgive. He was kind, tender-hearted. . . .

He jumped : and Achilles found himself in the dance-hall once more, brushed against by the dancers, contemplated by Maréchol, who was slightly drunk, inspected by a hundred pairs of eyes. 'Let's go,' he said.

It was at the top of the marble staircase leading down into the foyer that the catastrophe took place, with the fearful mischievous quality of lightning. Achilles, absorbed by recollections, gave as little as possible to his role of elegant woman, and had just had his fur coat placed round his shoulders when, at the bottom of one of the flights of the vast staircase, he recognized Victor, his accomplice in the burglary, wearing the uniform of a page. The rest, I repeat, happened so fast that I must resort to a kind of slowing down in order to describe it to you.

After shouting 'Victor!' and giving a strident whistle obtained with outlandish effect by the insertion of ring-laden fingers between scarlet lips, Achilles, as though mounted on speed and death, jumped astride the marble balustrade, leaving behind him the wide-open mouths of the maître d'hôtel and Fabre-Maréchol. The poor boy, victim of a crook's reaction, caught up in his dreams and his skirts, had forgotten his fetters. There was a cry and suddenly, from one second to the next, this celestial slide was transmuted into something terrible, fatal, immobile, red, pale, definitive, given over to the solemn silence of ruins.

The crowd rushed forward. Fabre-Maréchol, his eye-glasses in disarray, went down step by step, with fixed gaze, towards a scarecrow of cock feathers and tarlatan, a flat little creature, crushed on the ground and, due to a funereal disorder, about whose sex there could be no doubt.

A white tablecloth was placed over the body, but everyone had had time to relish the spectacle of the businessman, his eyes fixed on the telltale indecency. A derisive murmur therefore followed Maréchol as, still respected by the police, he staggered towards his car. The murmur was even more derisive, it can be understood, when the wretched man took with him Victor, sole link between the possible and the impossible, a strange Antigone in the uniform of a page.

In the car, while Maréchol's head rolled on his chest as though decapitated, Victor talked and talked. 'Don't be upset,' declared this optimist. 'Achilles wasn't the only one in the world. You'll get over it. Like me, now, I'm telling you, I don't look anything; but when I'm dressed as a woman, my word! You'd take me for Marlene Dietrich!'

They arrived, went upstairs, rang the bell. Marthe, strained to breaking-point, was waiting for it to ring. As she was about to open her mouth ... 'Don't bother,' said Victor. 'Don't bother, Monsieur knows everything.'

Monsieur knew nothing, understood nothing. For the last hour he had been living in a fateful world, that topsyturvy world where even the smallest signs no longer have any meaning, where the broken heart wondered how it could beat.

In a state of collapse, slumped in an armchair, he looked in turn, uncomprehending, at Victor, Marthe, the furniture, the haunted décor that had been assembled in the vague hope of living there happily.

A great tear trickled down the side of his nose, lodged in the bristles of his grey moustache, hesitated, continued its way into his beard. Marthe saw this tear and was taken in. Victor had just told her what had happened. 'Oh,' she cried, 'the bastards! They were in league together!'

She seized the revolver, aimed and fired.


The scandal at the court and the way the papers juggled with the details of the trial are well known.

When questioned by the magistrate Marthe said that she ought to feel sorry for her action, since Monsieur Maréchol was a decent man and that she couldn't understand why he had wept, but that in fact she wasn't sorry at all, as she couldn't live without Achilles and that poor gentleman couldn't have lived either, 'because he was in love with a ghost'.

# The Impostor

Of the few novels Cocteau wrote, *The Impostor* (Thomas l'Imposteur) is the most subtle. It is isolated within the main body of his work in the sense that none of its characters appear in other books, but typical of Cocteau in the use of autobiographical material and in its general style – that is, the presentation of the narrative-character relationship.

The book appeared in 1923, only five years after the end of the First World War. Cocteau did not set out to write a 'war novel', but certainly he based the story partly on his own adventures of 1915–16 when he went to the Belgian front with a specially formed ambulance unit and spent some time as the 'mascot' of a company of Marines. He used his hero Thomas and the war to express an aspect of his personal philosophy. Guillaume Thomas, aged sixteen, who pretended he was the nephew of a general, possessed a privilege; not, like Dargelos, the privilege of beauty, but of being believed. Everyone believed him, and finally he believed in himself, to the extent that truth upset him as lies upset the honest. The novel tells the story of how he was forced to escape from himself, since everyone had been bewitched by him. His death is an irony, not a tragedy, and it is brilliantly related, for Thomas attains the supreme moment of *déformation professionnelle* at the instant when he is shot. If he had continued to live he would never again have had such a magnificent chance for imposture. The double lie is always in danger of becoming the truth.

Their baptism of fire awaited Clémence de Bormes and Guillaume at Rheims. As they approached from the hills they saw the martyred town lying below them. A dark pall of smoke hung over it, stretching far beyond, like the smoke of a ship at sea.

Grass grew in the town, trees sprouted from windows. Houses gaped open, showing the flowered wallpaper of their bedrooms. In one there was still a chest of drawers and a picture-frame on the wall. From the edge of another hung a bed.

The cathedral was a mountain of old lace.

The military doctors, unable to carry out their duties because of
the heavy bombardment, awaited a lull in the cellars of the Golden
Lion. There were three hundred casualties at the convent and the
hospital. No one could be evacuated and no one could be fed,
because, in wartime, Rheims was under the protection of a town
that would offer her no assistance. The wounded died of their
wounds, of hunger, thirst, tetanus and the enemy fire. At the
hospital a gunner had just been told that the only hope of saving
him was to amputate his leg without chloroform; pallid, he
was smoking a last cigarette before the ordeal when a shell
smashed the surgical instruments, and killed two medical officers
outright.

No one dared to face the gunner again. Gangrene must have
crept over him like ivy over a statue.

Such scenes took place a dozen times a day. For a hundred and
fifty wounded the Sisters of Mercy had one glass of sour milk and
half a pork sausage. In a long shell-riddled room a priest
administered the sacrament from man to man, forcing teeth apart
with the blade of a knife.

The convoy could offer little assistance, but the officers gave
Gentil messages asking for help. They lived with the noise of their
own ear-splitting shells whistling above them, and the German
shells, that set a black seal of thunder and death on their smooth
despatches.

In the town, confusion had reached its height, nerves were at
breaking-point. Spies seemed to be everywhere, and spies were soon
shot. The princess, Madame Valiche and Guillaume found a patrol
actually threatening the Russian painter with his life. He had been
found sketching the cathedral. The name of Fontenoy saved him,
and prevented the other members of the party from having to share
his experience.

This unbearable atmosphere stimulated Clémence and Guillaume.
They were second only to Madame Valiche, who amazed everyone
at the two dressing stations with her boundless enthusiasm.

She suggested that they should fill the cars with casualties, leave
her at Rheims with the doctor, and return the following day for
another load. The princess and Guillaume wanted to stay behind
too.

'When my car is empty, it holds two men,' said Clémence. 'We
can't possibly take their place.'

Wrapped in blankets, they slept in the cellars of the Golden Lion.
Shells rocked the town as storm-waves rock a ship. It was shaken
to the very core.

The enemy guns were aiming at the gasometer. They circled it, they groped hesitantly, like a blind man groping for a door-knob. This threat finally set their nerves on edge.

Guillaume admired the courage of Clémence de Bormes; she admired his. It was soon clear that Guillaume's courage was a product of immaturity and the princess's of inexperience. The princess had seen the very worst. She had seen a horse trampling in its own entrails as it turned a street-corner, a group of gunners blown to pieces at their stations. Yet she thought herself to be invulnerable. Being almost the only woman in the town, she fancied that death had a well-bred respect for her sex, and she courted it fearlessly. But when she was on her way from the convent to the hospital, and saw a poor townswoman and her child struck down in an explosion only fifty yards away, she suddenly realized that shells do not spare women, and was smitten with such fear as only complex natures can feel. She began to scream, and ran round in circles calling for Guillaume.

When Guillaume arrived he was limping. He had been blown over while he was ferreting in the rubble, and had come out unhurt but for a blow on the knee from a falling beam. He was green.

Clémence wrung her hands. She called herself an unworthy mother, and begged Guillaume to bring her daughter to the spot at once.

This was easier said than done. The cars were not due to return until the evening.

The rest of the day was purgatory. Madame Valiche took care of Clémence, who was trembling in every limb.

All the cars came back except one – the one which was driven by the Parasite. This was their nickname for the man who was out of work. The Germans had aimed at the convoy, a suspect anthill on the hill-slope, trying to pick off cars like pawns. One of them had succeeded in making queen at the expense of the Parasite's pawn, and not a trace of him remained.

They were to wait for nightfall to cover their departure.

The princess refused to wait. While the Russian painter was turning the starting-handle, a heavy shell, directed at the gasometer, fell on the house in front of their car. They were covered with plaster and their windows were blown out.

In this car, uncomfortable but covered with glory, Clémence and Guillaume left Rheims, oblivious of the Russian's reckless steering.

And then Guillaume heard that incorrigible woman murmur, 'Come on, let us go back. How absurd to have been afraid!'

*

There are some men who have everything and cannot convince one of it, rich men so poor and noblemen so common that the incredulity with which they meet makes them shy and gives them an unconvincing manner. The most beautiful pearls are artificial on some women. On the other hand, artificial pearls look real on others. In the same way there are some men who inspire blind confidence and enjoy privileges which they cannot claim by right. Guillaume Thomas was of this happy breed.

He was believed. He did not have to take precautions or count the cost. A star of falsehood led him straight to his goal. And so he never had the preoccupied, hunted look of the trickster. Without knowing how to swim or how to skate he could say 'I skate and I swim'. Everyone had seen him on the ice and in the water.

A special fairy casts this spell at birth. Some men who have gifts from no other fairy are successful.

Guillaume never did reflect on his behaviour or think 'How will I get out of this?' 'I'm cheating', 'I'm a wretch', or 'I'm a clever man'. He went on, wrapt in his fairy-tale.

The more he lived his part, the more absorbed in it he became, playing it with convincing verve and frankness.

For some time he had had a new toy : to describe the death of his cousins before their father's very eyes. His ridiculous story was crudely drawn and coloured, like a chap-book illustration.

His synthesis, like these illustrations, was striking, and seemed more lifelike than life itself. It appealed to that element of childishness in his listeners which is present in every one of us. Occasionally he touched up the picture with a bit of gold. He was taken in himself. Tears came to his eyes. No one could listen to him without being moved.

As he never had to be on his guard – which causes the rogue's downfall – he would relate this heroic episode in the princess's home, at table, in the presence of expert soldiers. He took in civilians and soldiers alike, proving that truth, even when it is false, comes out of the mouths of babes.

# Les Enfants Terribles

In order to judge Cocteau's mental state during the writing of his third and most famous novel, *Les Enfants Terribles*, one should first delve into *Opium*. There, Cocteau describes how he came to write the story.

As Francis Steegmuller has pointed out, Cocteau has frequently quoted precise figures relating to numbers of days, pages, etc., apropos this book, and just as frequently revised them. Its atmosphere is so enclosed and intense that this could only have been written *d'un trait*. Cocteau may have dramatized this situation when he wrote about it, but many writers have had similar experiences. Cocteau has also stated that while writing the novel he was obsessed by the music of *Make-Believe* from the film *Show Boat*, and much later he told André Fraigneau that his characters and plot were all ready, waiting in his unconscious mind.

The figure of Dargelos, whose snowball thrown in the first chapter initiates the entire action, haunted Cocteau most of his life. He crystallized this memory of his schooldays at the Lycée Condorcet by giving his 'hero' the name of a real school friend whose photograph appears in various biographies of Cocteau. Dargelos is described in rather cruder terms in *Le Livre Blanc*, he is referred to in a short poem at the end of *Opium* and he again returns, like a recurrent dream, in part of *La Fin du Potomak*.

The English version of the story was originally published as *Children of the Game*. Rosamond Lehmann, the translator, has commented (in a personal letter to the editor of the present anthology) : 'It is a hypnotizing novel, and to translate it was a very odd and in a way disturbing experience : as if reality kept disappearing and images kept turning inside-out – as if they, or I, were hallucinated. Impossible to translate literally. I had to reach out with an inner ear, to try to re-create some approximation to his language and rhythm – both of which are unique, I think.'

That portion of old Paris known as the Cité Monthiers is bounded
on the one side by the Rue de Clichy, on the other by the Rue
d'Amsterdam. Should you choose to approach it from the Rue de
Clichy, you would come to a pair of wrought-iron gates : but if you
were to come by way of the Rue d'Amsterdam, you would reach
another entrance, open day and night, and giving access, first to a
block of tenements, and then to the courtyard proper, an oblong
court containing a row of small private dwellings secretively disposed beneath the flat towering walls of the main structure. Clearly
these little houses must be the abode of artists. The windows are
blind, covered with photographers' drapes, but it is comparatively
easy to guess what they conceal : rooms chock-a-block with weapons
and lengths of brocade, with canvases depicting basketfuls of cats,
or the families of Bolivian diplomats. Here dwells the Master,
illustrious, unacknowledged, well-nigh prostrated by the weight of
his public honours and commissions, with all this dumb provincial
stronghold to seal him from disturbance.

Twice a day, however, at half past ten in the morning and four
o'clock in the afternoon, the silence is shattered by a sound of
tumult. The doors of the little Lycée Condorcet, opposite number
72b Rue d'Amsterdam, open, and a horde of schoolboys emerge to
occupy the Cité and set up their headquarters. Thus it has
reassumed a sort of medieval character – something in the nature of
a Court of Love, a Wonder Fair, an Athletes' Stadium, a Stamp
Exchange; also a gangsters' tribune-cum-place of public execution;
also a breeding-ground for rags – rags to be hatched out finally in
class, after long incubation, before the incredulous eyes of the
authorities. Terrors they are, these lads, and no mistake – the
terrors of the Fifth. A year from now, having become the Fourth,
they will have shaken the dust of the Rue d'Amsterdam from their
shoes and swaggered into the Rue Caumartin with their four
books bound with a strap and a square of felt in lieu of a satchel.

But now they are in the Fifth, where the tenebrous instincts of
childhood still predominate : animal, vegetable instincts, almost
indefinable because they operate in regions below conscious memory,
and vanish without trace, like some of childhood's griefs; and also
because children stop talking when grown-ups draw nigh. They
stop talking, they take on the aspect of beings of a different order
of creation – conjuring themselves at will an instantaneous coat of
bristles or assuming the bland passivity of some form of plant life.
Their rites are obscure, inexorably secret; calling, we know, for
infinite cunning, for ordeal by fear and torture; requiring victims,
summary executions, human sacrifices. The particular mysteries are
impenetrable, the faithful speak a cryptic tongue; even if we

chanced to overhear unseen, we should be none the wiser. Their trade is all in postage stamps and marbles. Their tribute goes to swell the pockets of the demigods and leaders; the mutter of conspiracy is shrouded in a deafening din. Should one of that tribe of prosperous, hermetically preserved artists happen to pull the cord that works those drapes across his window, I doubt if the spectacle thereby revealed to him would strike him as copy for any of his favourite subjects : nothing he could use to make a pretty picture with a title such as *Little Black Sweeps at Play in a White World*; or *Hot Cockles*; or *Merry Wee Rascals*.

There was snow that evening. The snow had gone on falling steadily since yesterday, thereby radically altering the original design. The Cité had withdrawn in Time; the snow seemed no longer to be impartially distributed over the whole warm living earth, but to be dropping, piling only upon this one isolated spot.

The hard muddy ground had already been smashed, churned up, crushed, stamped into slides by children on their way to school. The soiled snow made ruts along the gutter. But the snow had also become the snow on porches, steps, and house-fronts : featherweight packages, mats, cornices, odds and ends of wadding, ethereal yet crystallized, seemed, instead of blurring the outlines of the stone, to quicken it, to imbue it with a kind of presage.

Gleaming with the soft effulgence of a luminous dial, the snow's incandescence, self-engendered, reached inward to probe the very soul of luxury and draw it forth through stone till it was visible, it was that fabric magically upholstering the Cité, shrinking it and transforming it into a phantom drawing-room.

Seen from below, the prospect had less to recommend it. The street-lamps shed a feeble light upon what looked like a deserted battlefield. Frost-flayed, the ground had split, was broken up into fissured blocks, like crazy paving. In front of every gully-hole a stack of grimy snow stood ominous, a potential ambush; the gas-jets flickered in a villainous north-easter; and the dark holes and corners already hid their dead.

Viewed from this angle the illusion produced was altogether different. Houses were no longer boxes in some legendary theatre but houses deliberately blacked out, barricaded by their occupants to hinder the enemy's advance.

In fact the entire Cité had lost its civic status, its character of open mart, fairground, and place of execution. The blizzard had commandeered it totally, imposed upon it a specifically military role, a particular strategic function. By ten minutes past four the operation had developed to the point where none could venture from the porch without incurring risk. Beneath that porch the reservists were assembled, their numbers swollen by the newcomers who continued to arrive singly or two by two.

'Seen Dargelos?'

'Yes.... No.... I don't know.'

This reply came from one of two youths engaged in bringing in one of the first casualties. He had a handkerchief tied round his knee and was hopping along between them and clinging to their shoulders.

The question had come from a boy with a pale face and melancholy eyes – the eyes of a cripple. He walked with a limp, and his long cloak hung oddly, as if concealing some deformity, some strange protuberance or hump. But nearing a corner piled with school haversacks he suddenly flung his cloak back, exposing the nature of his disability : not a growth, but a heavy satchel eccentrically balanced on one hip. He dropped it, ceased to be a cripple; the eyes, however, did not alter.

He advanced towards the battle.


To the right, where the footpath joined the arcade, a prisoner was being subjected to interrogation. By the spasmodic flaring of a gas-lamp he could be seen to be a small boy with his back against the wall, hemmed in by his captors, a group of four. One of these, a senior boy, was squatting between his legs and twisting his ears, to the accompaniment of a series of hideous facial contortions. By way of crowning horror, the monstrous, ever-changing mask confronting the prisoner's was dumb. Weeping, he sought to close his eyes, to avert his head. But every time he struggled, his torturer seized a fistful of grey snow and scrubbed his ears with it.

Circumnavigating the group, threading a path through shot and shell, the pale boy went on his way.

He was looking for Dargelos, whom he loved.

It was the worse for him because he was condemned to love without forewarning of love's nature. His sickness was unremitting and incurable – a state of desire, chaste, innocent of aim or name.

Dargelos was the Lycée's star performer. He throve on popular support and equally on opposition. At the mere sight of those dishevelled locks of his, those scarred and gory knees, that coat with its enthralling pockets, the pale boy lost his head.

The battle gives him courage. He will run, he will seek out Dargelos, fight shoulder to shoulder by his side, defend him, show him what mettle he is made of.

The snow went flying, bursting against cloaks, spattering the walls with stars. Here and there, some fragmentary image stood out in stereoscopic detail between one blindness and the next; a gaping mouth in a red face; a hand pointing – at whom? in what direction? ... It is at him, none other, that the hand is pointing: he staggers, his pale lips open to frame a shout. He had discerned a figure, one of the god's acolytes, standing on some front-door steps. It is he, this acolyte, who compasses his doom. 'Darg. . . .' His cry is cut short; the snowball comes crashing on his mouth, his jaws are stuffed with snow, his tongue is paralysed. He has just time to see the laughter, and within the laughter, surrounded by his staff, a form, the form of Dargelos, crowned with blazing cheeks and tumbled hair, rearing itself up with a tremendous gesture.

A blow strikes him full on the breast. A heavy blow. A marble-fisted blow. A marble-hearted blow. His mind fades out, surmising Dargelos upon a kind of dais, supernaturally lit; the arm of Dargelos nerveless, dropping down.


He lay prostrate on the ground. A stream of blood flowed from his mouth, besmearing chin and cheek and soaking into the snow. Whistles rang out. Next moment the Cité was deserted. Only a few remained beside the body, not to succour it but to observe the blood with avid curiosity. Of these, one or two soon made off, not liking the look of things, shrugging, wagging their heads portentously; others made a dive for their satchels and skidded away. The group containing Dargelos remained upon the steps, immobilized. At length authority appeared in the shape of the proctor and the college porter and headed by a boy, Gérard, whom Paul had hailed upon entering the battle, and who had run to fetch them after having witnessed the disaster. Between them the two men took up the body; the proctor turned to scan the shadows.

'Is that you, Dargelos?'

'Yes, sir.'

'Follow me.'

The procession started.

Great are the prerogatives of beauty, subduing even those not consciously aware of it. Dargelos was a favourite with the masters. The proctor felt the whole baffling business to be excessively annoying.

They bore the victim into the porter's lodge, where the kindly porter's wife did her best to bathe him and restore him.

Dargelos stood in the doorway, backed by a throng of curious faces. Gérard knelt beside his friend, tearfully clasping his hand.

'Tell me what happened, Dargelos,' said the proctor.

'There's nothing to tell, sir. Some of the chaps were chucking snowballs. I chucked one at him. It must have been a jolly hard one. It hit him smack in the chest and he went "Ho!" and fell down. At first I thought his nose was bleeding from another snow-ball that had hit him in the face.'

'A snowball wouldn't crack a person's ribs.'

'Sir, sir!' cried the boy who answered to the name of Gérard. 'He put a stone inside that snowball.'

'Is that true?' inquired the proctor.

Dargelos shrugged his shoulders.

'Haven't you anything to say?'

'What's the use.... Look, he's opening his eyes. You'd better ask him.'

The victim was beginning to show signs of life. Gérard slipped an arm under his head and he lay back against it.

'How are you feeling?'

'Sorry ... '

'There's no need to apologize. You're ill, you fainted.'

'I remember now.'

'Have you any idea what made you faint?'

'A snowball hit me in the chest.'

'A snowball? Why should that make you faint?'

'It's the only thing that hit me.'

'Your friend has given me to understand that this particular snowball had a stone in it.'

The patient saw Dargelos shrug his shoulders.

'Gérard must be cracked,' he said. 'You're cracked. It was just an ordinary snowball. I was running, I expect I sort of blew up.'

The proctor breathed a sigh of relief.

Dargelos seemed about to take his leave, then changed his mind and advanced a few paces in the direction of the victim. But when he reached the porter's counter, on which were displayed such goods as ink, sweets, pen-holders, he stopped short, pulled a couple of coins from his pocket, flung them down, picked up a twist of liquorice – the kind so popular with boys, that looks like bootlaces – crossed the hall, raised one hand in a sort of military salute, and disappeared.

The proctor had already called a cab, intending to see the patient home, but Gérard objected that it was unnecessary. He declared that the sight of the proctor would alarm the family, and that he himself would be his escort.

'Anyway,' he added, 'he's much better now – you can see.'

The proctor needed little persuasion. It was snowing hard. The lad's home was in the Rue Montmartre.

Having seen them into the cab and observed Gérard in the act of removing his cloak and woollen muffler to wrap them round his friend, the proctor concluded that he was justified in washing his hands of further responsibility.

# Le Livre Blanc

*Le Livre Blanc*, attributed to Jean Cocteau, has a twofold interest: first because of its appeal to bibliophiles as a collector's item, and second because of its assumed authorship. Cocteau never formally acknowledged the book, except in so far as he allowed it to appear in the 'authorized' bibliography drawn up in connection with his Complete Works.

The usual reason given for Cocteau's refusal to acknowledge the book when it first appeared is that he did not wish to upset his mother, who was then still alive. His reasons for not conceding authorship seem to constitute a game he was playing both with himself and with his readers. Rarely has any so-called anonymous book contained such strong internal proof of its creator's hand.

Admittedly the actual episodic construction of the book, which is written in the form of a short novel, is unlike any other by Cocteau. The narrator tells of his love for boys and young men, relates a few incidents from his childhood, mentions his father's latent homosexuality and then describes his own unhappy affairs. Two of the episodes include moments of self-deception when he believed himself to be in love with women. In one case he had an affair with the girl's pimp, in another with the girl's brother.

Each episode ends in death or heartbreaking separation. Dargelos the schoolboy dies from angina in hospital; Alfred is abandoned sobbing on the pavement; PAS DE CHANCE is deserted in an hotel bedroom, shedding tears over the narrator's gloves; and Mademoiselle de S's brother shoots himself. The general impression is that homosexual love is doomed to failure, disappointment, treachery or death, but there is no feeling, even implicit, that these sufferings represent punishment in any way. Only towards the end of the book is there a cumulative effect of sadness and isolation, when the narrator feels that even the monastery has rejected him – like everything else.

There is certainly no incitement to adopt the homosexual way of life and love, and in fact the book is calculated to dissuade anyone from following such an inclination out of mere curiosity or emulation. The plea at the end of the book for the love of man for man to be recognized for its own sake is heartfelt and moving; the thought of mere tolerance is represented as the most painful reaction of all.

The mention of Cambacérès in the final paragraph is a reference to the brilliant jurist who drafted the first version of the Code Civil for Napoleon. He was well known for his homosexual nature and was often laughed at because of his effeminacy in dress. As Arch-Chancellor it was he who approved the measures suggested by an enlightened committee working on the Code Napoléon and deciding on the treatment of sexual offenders.

It should be remembered that in the vocabulary of public affairs 'livre blanc' is the term used to describe official parliamentary documents in France, just as 'white paper' is the term used in England. In other words, this novel is not written for the sake of special pleading – it is a statement of the facts relating to a specific subject, drawn up with care in order to clarify a controversial issue.

The details belong, like those of all Cocteau's writing, to the imaginary but convincing world which he created from a blend of reality and fantasy. The strongest factual evidence that Cocteau wrote *Le Livre Blanc* comes from the inclusion of that symbolic hero who appears in so many of his books, Dargelos. The attractive, destructive adolescent schoolboy, named after one of Cocteau's acquaintances at the Lycée Condorcet, is a key figure in many of his mature works and he constitutes a theme upon which Cocteau composed variations in works of a widely differing type and in different media. *Le Livre Blanc* is the only one of these works, apart from *La Fin du Potomak*, where Dargelos is described in his sexual reality and not merely as a symbol. Significantly enough *Le Livre Blanc*, on the other hand, is the only book in which Dargelos dies. Textual comparison between the description of Dargelos here and those in the other books points to the unlikelihood of their being the work of more than one author.

Elsewhere, the clearest identification with Cocteau is the scene in the *établissement de bains*, which presents the image of the man who makes love to his own reflection. Fulfilment for the homosexual lover lies partly perhaps in the world of fantasy – which is why the hero of *Orphée* breaks through the mirror. The description in *Le Livre Blanc* of the man who thinks he is acting out his love only with his own image, unaware of the onlooker behind the mirror who in fact 'responds to' his love, is among the most memorable in the book. Only Cocteau could have written it with such dramatic intensity, transforming what might otherwise have been an erotic fantasy into a poetic reality. Significant also is the reintroduction of a mirror at the suicide scene towards the end of the book.

Many of the incidents narrated in *Le Livre Blanc* are in themselves unreservedly sensual; it is the spirit and style of the writing that give them another dimension. The narrator himself is almost an anti-hero; he tries to behave well but never succeeds. He is unafraid of sexual description and even when he lets his lovers down, as he does most of the time, the frankness of his admissions disarms the reader. André Gide thought that 'some of the obscenities' were 'described in the most charming manner'. Throughout Cocteau's work there are many hints of latent homosexuality, but the clearest expression of it is in *Le Livre Blanc*.

There is little point in searching for the identity of the people described – Alfred, H or PAS DE CHANCE. Cocteau has written freely of his admiration for many real people : Radiguet, Jean Desbordes, Jean Marais and a host of others. The identity of the figures in *Le Livre Blanc* may be known to some, but I prefer to think of them as enhanced versions or even composite figures of anonymous people whom Cocteau had no doubt met and loved, people who remained individuals and were in no way concerned with literature. The fact that they served in the creation of this book gives them immortality enough. PAS DE CHANCE, and similar figures, have been drawn by Cocteau on many occasions, but hitherto they have not been sketched or described so vividly – *Dargelos en marin* – and brought to life.

An actress named Jeanne Reynette makes an appearance in the predominantly cheerful *Portraits-Souvenir*, but there is no mention of any love-affair with her, only a drawing. This may be the Jeanne of *Le Livre Blanc*, but there is no proof of it. Jeanne deceived the narrator with Berthe, just as Germaine in *Le Grand Ecart* deceived Jacques with Louise. The appearance of the Abbé X leads the reader to think of Cocteau's friendship with Jacques Maritain and other Catholic leaders, and of his partial return to the Church, but, as he himself has said, he could not be converted in the conventional sense for he had never ceased to be *croyant*. For a time he did in fact become *pratiquant*, but the meaningful account of this incident in his life should properly be read in the *Lettre à Jacques Maritain* and in Maritain's reply. The discussions with the Abbé X in *Le Livre Blanc* are superficial, but probably have some basis in reality.

It would be a mistake therefore to overrate the autobiographical element in *Le Livre Blanc*; it is present in some degree, as in nearly everything that Cocteau wrote, but to approach the book as a *roman à clef* would imply failure to accept the book as Cocteau wrote it : a work of fiction which expresses some of his deepest experiences and their symbolic interpretation.

As far back as I can remember and even at the age when the mind still has no power over the senses, I find traces of my love for boys.

I have always loved the stronger sex and believe that it can legitimately be called the fair sex. My misfortunes are due to a society which condemns anything out of the ordinary as a crime and forces us to reform our natural inclinations.

Three decisive incidents come back to me. My father lived at a small château near S. This château possessed a park. At the end of the park were a farm and a watering-place which did not belong to the château. My father allowed them to remain unfenced in exchange for dairy produce and eggs which the farmer brought up every day.

One morning in August I was roaming round the grounds carrying a loaded rifle. I was pretending to be a sportsman, and since I had hidden behind a hedge, on the look-out for some animal, I saw from my hiding-place a young farm-boy taking a cart-horse to have a wash. He knew that nobody ever came down to the far end of the grounds and had taken his clothes off so that he could go into the water. He made the horse start cleaning itself a few yards away from me. The sunburn on his face, neck, arms and feet contrasted with the whiteness of his other skin and reminded me of sweet chestnuts bursting out of their husks; but these dark patches were not the only ones. My attention was attracted by another, and in its midst was an enigma visible in all its detail.

My ears buzzed. My face flushed. My legs felt weak. My heart pounded as though I had committed a murder. Without realizing it I fainted and was only found after a search lasting four hours. Once I had recovered I instinctively took care not to reveal the cause of my weakness and at the risk of appearing ridiculous I said that a hare had rushed out from the thick clumps of trees and startled me.

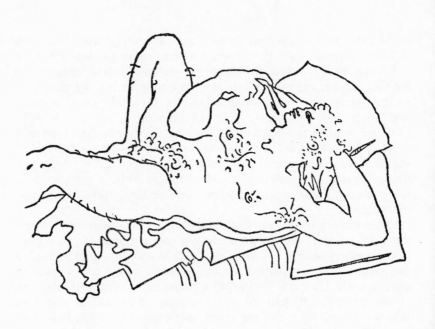

The second incident occurred the following year. My father had allowed gypsies to camp in the same place at the end of the park where I had lost consciousness. I was going for a walk with my nursemaid. Suddenly she pulled me away, calling out to me that I mustn't turn round. The heat was blinding. Two young gypsies had taken their clothes off and were climbing the trees. The sight of them terrified my nursemaid and my disobedience gave the scene an unforgettable aura. If I live to be a hundred that shout and that chase will always make me remember a caravan, a woman feeding a newborn baby, a smoky fire, a white horse cropping the grass and, up in the trees, two bronze bodies, each with three patches of black.

The last occasion, if I am not mistaken, concerned a young servant named Gustave. When he waited at table he had difficulty in restraining his laughter. This laughter delighted me. Through turning over and over in my head the memories of the farm-boy and the gypsies I began to hope eagerly that my hand might touch what my eye had seen.

My plan was extremely naïve. I intended to draw a woman and take the sheet of paper to Gustave. I would make him laugh, encourage him and ask if I could touch the mystery whose existence I saw in my imagination while he waited at table, beneath a significant bulge in his trousers. My nursemaid was the only woman I had ever seen in her shift and I believed that artists invented women with firm breasts, whereas in reality they were all flabby. My drawing was realistic. Gustave burst out laughing, asked me who my model was and I, taking advantage of the fact that he was shaking, went straight to the point with inconceivable audacity. He repulsed me, went very red, pulled my ears, alleging that I was tickling him and, desperately afraid of losing his job, led me to the door.

A few days later he stole some wine and my father dismissed him. I interceded, I wept, but all in vain. I went to the station with Gustave, who was carrying an Aunt Sally game which I had given him for his little son whose photograph he often used to show me.

My mother had died giving birth to me and I had always lived alone with my father, a sad and charming man. His sadness preceded the loss of his wife. Even when contented he had been sad and this is why I sought reasons for a sadness which lay deeper than his bereavement.

Pederast knows pederast as Jew knows Jew. They sense each other beneath the mask, and I undertake to discover them between

the lines of the most innocent books. This passion is less simple
than moralists might suppose. For just as pederastic women exist,
women who look like lesbians but seek out men in the same special
way that men do, there exist pederasts who are unaware of their
own nature and live to the end of their days in a state of uneasiness
which they ascribe to poor health or a jealous nature.

I have always believed that my father was too much like me to
differ on this major point. He was no doubt unaware of his inclination and instead of pursuing it he strenuously followed another
without knowing what made his life so unbearable. His tastes were
revealed to me by odd phrases, his way of walking and endless
details about his person, but if he had ever discovered them or
found the opportunity to develop them, he would have been
astonished. At that period people killed themselves for less. But no;
he lived in ignorance of himself and accepted his burden.

It is perhaps to this blindness that I owe my existence. I regret
the fact, for if my father had known the delights which would have
prevented my misfortunes, we should both have been happier.


I went into the fourth form at the Lycée Condorcet. Our senses
were awakening in uncontrolled fashion, growing like weeds. ·
Nothing but pockets with holes in them and soiled handkerchiefs.
The art class in particular emboldened the boys because they were
concealed by a wall of papers. Sometimes, during an ordinary class,
a sarcastic teacher would suddenly question a boy who was on the
point of an orgasm. The boy would stand up, his cheeks burning,
and stammer out whatever came into his head, while trying to turn
a dictionary into a fig-leaf. Our laughter made him even more
embarrassed.

The classroom smelt of gas, chalk and sperm. This combination
nauseated me. I should add that what seemed a vice to the other
boys did not seem so to me; or, to be more precise, since it was the
cheap parody of a type of love that my instinct respected, I appeared
to be the only one to disapprove of this state of affairs. This led to
endless sarcastic remarks and attacks on what my comrades
regarded as prudery.

But the Lycée Condorcet was a day school. These practices did
not go as far as love-affairs; they hardly went beyond the limits of
clandestine play.

One of the boys, called Dargelos, possessed a virility far in
advance of his age, and enjoyed great prestige as a result. He
exhibited himself in cynical fashion and would do so, even for boys
from other forms, in exchange for rare foreign stamps or tobacco.

The seats which surrounded his desk were special seats. I can still see his brown skin. His extremely short trousers and the socks hanging down over his ankles showed that he was proud of his legs. We all wore short trousers, but because Dargelos had a man's legs he was the only one to have *bare* legs. His open-collared shirt revealed a broad neck. A strongly curled lock of hair fell over his forehead. His face, with its rather thick lips, slightly narrow eyes and somewhat flat nose, was characteristic of the type which for me was to prove fatal. When fatality appears in disguise it gives us an illusion of freedom and in the end always leads us into the same trap.

The presence of Dargelos made me ill. I avoided him. I lay in wait for him. I dreamt of some miracle which would make him notice me, destroy his arrogance and reveal to him the meaning of my attitude which he was bound to regard as ridiculous prudery but which in fact was simply due to my frantic desire to please him.

My feeling for him was vague. I did not succeed in defining it. It led me to feel merely embarrassment or delight. The one thing I was sure about was that he was in no way similar to my friends.

One day, when I could bear it no longer, I talked about it to a boy I sometimes saw outside school, whose family knew my father.

'You're silly,' he told me. 'It's easy. Invite Dargelos one Sunday, take him behind the trees and that'll do the trick!'

What trick? There wasn't any trick. I muttered that it wasn't a question of the kind of pleasure that could easily be had in class and I tried in vain to describe my dreams in words. My friend shrugged his shoulders. 'Why create problems when there are none?' he said. 'Dargelos is stronger than we are.' (He used other terms.) 'The moment you flatter him he'll do what you like. If you want him, all you've got to do is get him.'

The crudeness of this reply overwhelmed me. I realized that it was impossible to make myself understood. Suppose, I thought, that Dargelos did agree to a rendezvous. What would I tell him, what would I do? My urge would not be to amuse myself for five minutes but to live with him for ever. In fact I adored him, and I resigned myself to suffering in silence. Without actually describing my suffering as love, I sensed that it was very different from what went on in the classroom and that it would find no response there.

This story had no beginning but it had an end. Urged on by the boy I had confided in, I asked Dargelos to meet me in an empty classroom after five o'clock prep. He came. I had relied on some miracle to determine my conduct, but in his presence I lost my head. I could see nothing except his strong legs and his scarred knees, emblazoned with scabs and ink.

'What do you want?' he asked me with a cruel smile. I guessed what he was thinking and also that my request could have no other significance in his eyes. I invented something.

'I wanted to tell you,' I stammered, 'that the Vice-Principal's got his eye on you.'

It was a ridiculous lie, for the magic of Dargelos had bewitched our teachers. Beauty holds vast privileges. It acts even on those who appear to take the least notice of it.

Dargelos lowered his head and pulled a face. 'The Vice-Principal?'

'Yes,' I went on, finding strength in fear, 'the Vice-Principal. I heard him saying to the Headmaster, "I'm watching Dargelos. He's going too far. I've got my eye on him"!'

'So I'm going too far, am I?' he replied. 'Well, old chap, I'll show it to the Vice-Principal. I'll show it to him when it's ready for action! And as for you, messing me about just to tell me stupid stories like that, I warn you that if you try it once more you'll get a kick in the pants.'

He vanished.

For a week I pretended I had stomach-ache, to avoid coming into class and having to face Dargelos. When I came back I heard that he was ill and was keeping to his room. I didn't dare ask about him. But there were rumours. He was a boy scout and there was talk of a reckless bathe in the Seine, icy cold water and then angina. One afternoon, during a geography lesson, we heard that he was dead. Tears forced me to leave the classroom. Youth is not tender-hearted. For many boys this news, which the teacher announced to us standing, was merely a tacit authorization to do nothing. The next day habit closed over their mourning.

In spite of everything, eroticism had received its death-blow. Too many little pleasures were disturbed by the ghost of the handsome animal whose charm had moved even death itself.

In the fifth form, after the holidays, a radical change had taken place in my friends. Their voices were breaking; they were smoking; they were shaving off shadowy moustaches, going out bareheaded and wearing English-type shorts or long trousers. Onanism gave way to boasting. Postcards circulated. All these young things now turned towards women as plants turn to the sun. It was then, in order to follow the others, that I began to falsify my nature.

As they hastened towards their own truth they dragged me towards falsehood. I ascribed my revulsion to ignorance. I admired their casual approach. I forced myself to follow their example and share their enthusiasm, but I kept having to overcome my feelings of shame. In the end this self-discipline made my task fairly easy. In addition, I would repeat to myself that debauchery was no fun for anyone, but that the others put more goodwill into it than I did.

On Sundays, if it were fine, we would set off in a body with our tennis rackets, saying that we were going to play at Auteuil. On the way we deposited the rackets with the concierge at a fellow-pupil's house – his family lived in Marseilles – and hurried off to the brothels in the Rue de Provence. Outside the leather-covered doors the natural shyness of our age returned. We would walk up and down, hesitating like bathers beside cold water. We would toss up to see who would go in first. I was always terrified that I might be chosen. Finally the victim would creep closely along the walls, go through the door and lead us in after him.

Nothing is more intimidating than children and whores. Too much separates us from them. We don't know how to break the silence and put ourselves on their level. In the Rue de Provence the only meeting-place was the bed where I lay down beside the girl and the act which we performed together without the slightest enjoyment.

These visits made us bolder, we accosted street-walkers and in this way made the acquaintance of a young person called Alice de Pibrac. She lived in the Rue La Bruyère in a modest apartment that smelt of coffee. If I am not mistaken, Alice de Pibrac received us but only allowed us to admire her in a sordid dressing-gown and with her thin hair hanging down her back. This state of affairs irritated my friends but pleased me greatly. Eventually they got tired of waiting and opted for something new. We pooled our resources, took the stage-box at the Eldorado for the Sunday matinée, threw bunches of violets to the singers and waited for them outside the stage-door in the freezing cold.

I mention these insignificant adventures in order to show how tired and empty our Sunday outings left us, and how surprised I was to hear my comrades describe the details all week long.

One of my friends knew the actress Berthe who introduced me to Jeanne. They were both on the stage. I liked Jeanne and told Berthe to ask her if she would agree to become my mistress. Berthe brought me back a refusal and persuaded me to deceive my friend with her. Shortly afterwards, on learning from this friend that Jeanne was complaining about my silence, I went to see her. We discovered that she had never been given my message and decided to take our revenge by surprising Berthe with our happiness.

This romance made such an impression on my sixteenth, seventeenth and eighteenth years that it is still impossible for me to see

Jeanne's name in a newspaper or her picture on a wall without a shock. And yet I am unable to describe any part of this ordinary love-affair, which was spent in waiting at milliners' shops and playing a somewhat unpleasant dual role, for the Armenian who kept Jeanne held me in great esteem and made me his confidant.

The scenes began during the second year. After the most violent of them, which took place at five o'clock in the Place de la Concorde, I left Jeanne on a traffic island and ran off to my own home. In the middle of dinner I was already contemplating a telephone call when someone came to tell me that a lady was waiting for me in a carriage.

It was Jeanne.

'I'm not upset,' she said, 'at being left standing in the Place de la Concorde, but you're too weak to go through with it. Two months ago you would have come back to the island after crossing the square. Don't flatter yourself that you've shown strength of character – you've only proved that your love has cooled off.'

This dangerous analysis enlightened me and showed me that my slavery had come to an end.

My love could only be revived by my discovering that Jeanne was deceiving me. She was deceiving me with Berthe. This situation reveals to me today the basis of my love. Jeanne was a boy; she loved women, and I loved her with the feminine part of my nature. I discovered them in bed, curled up together like an octopus. I had to win; I pleaded with them. They laughed and consoled me, and this was the pitiful end to a romance which died of its own accord yet none the less upset me enough to make my father anxious and force him to shed the reserve he still maintained towards me.


One night, when I was going back to my father's house later than usual, a woman with a soft voice accosted me in the Place de la Madeleine. I looked at her, found her delightful, young and fresh. Her name was Rose, she enjoyed talking and we walked up and down until the time when the market people, sitting sleepily on their vegetable-carts, drove their horses across a deserted Paris.

I was leaving for Switzerland next day. I gave Rose my name and address. She sent me letters on squared paper, enclosing a stamp for my reply. I wrote back willingly. When I returned I was happier than Thomas De Quincey at finding Rose in the place where we had first met. She asked me to come to her hotel in the Place Pigalle.

The Hôtel M was dismal. The staircase stank of ether, which provides consolation for whores who come home too tired to speak.

The bedroom was typical of those in which the bed is never made. Rose smoked in bed. I complimented her on her looks.

'You mustn't see me without make-up,' she said. 'I haven't any eyelashes. I look like a white rabbit.'

I became her lover. She would refuse the smallest gift. Truly! However, she did accept one dress, merely because it was no good for *le business* – it was too smart and she would keep it in her wardrobe as a souvenir.

One Sunday there was a knock at the door. I quickly got out of bed. Rose told me not to worry, it was her brother and he would be delighted to see me.

This brother resembled the farm-boy and the Gustave of my childhood. He was nineteen and everything about him was in the worst possible taste. He was called Alfred or Alfredo and spoke an odd kind of French, but I didn't worry about his nationality; he seemed to me to belong to the country of prostitution which has its own patriotism, and possibly this was its language.

The slope which led me towards the sister was slightly uphill, but it is easy to guess the headlong descent which took me to the brother. He was, as his compatriots say, on the ball, and we soon resorted to apache-like tricks so that we could meet without Rose's knowledge.

For me, Alfred's body was more like the one I saw in my dreams than the young, powerfully equipped body of an adolescent: a perfect body, rigged out with muscles like a ship with ropes, its limbs appearing to open out like a star around that fleece where there rises, in contrast to woman, who is built for concealment, the only thing about a man which cannot lie.

I realized I had taken the wrong turning. I vowed that I would not get lost again, that in future I would go straight along my own path instead of going astray on someone's else's, and that I would listen more to the dictates of my senses than to the counsels of morality.

Alfred returned my caresses. He confessed to me that he was not Rose's brother. He was her pimp.

Rose continued to play her part and we ours. Alfred would wink, dig me in the ribs and sometimes start to giggle. Rose looked at him with surprise, not suspecting that we were in league and that there existed between us links that were strengthened by deceit.

One day the hotel bell-boy came in and found us lying together, with Rose between us. 'You see, Jules,' she cried, indicating both of us, 'my brother and my fancy-man! Everything I love.'

Alfred, who was lazy, began to find lying wearisome. He confided to me that he could not go on with this life, working on one side of the road while Rose worked on the other, and walking up and down this open-air shop where the sellers are themselves for sale. In other words, he asked me to extricate him from it.

Nothing could have pleased me more. We decided that I would book an hotel room in the Ternes district; Alfred would occupy it at once, and I would go to join him after dinner and stay the night. Meanwhile I would pretend to Rose that I thought he had disappeared and go to look for him, which would set me free and allow us much valuable time.

I booked the room, settled Alfred in and dined with my father. After dinner I rushed to the hotel. Alfred had flown. I waited from nine o'clock until one in the morning. Alfred did not return and I went back home with a broken heart.

At about eleven o'clock next morning I went to find out what was happening. Alfred was asleep in his room. He woke up, and whimperingly told me that he couldn't help going back to his old habits, that he couldn't do without Rose and that he'd been looking for her all night, first at her hotel where she was no longer living, then from one pavement to another, in every brasserie in the Faubourg Montmartre and in the dance-halls of the Rue de Lappe.

'Of course,' I told him, 'Rose is out of her mind, she's slightly feverish. She's staying with one of her girl friends in the Rue de Budapest.'

He begged me to take him there at once.

Rose's room at the Hôtel M was a festive place compared to her friend's. We argued in a thick fog of smells, washing and dubious sentiments. The women were in their shifts. Alfred lay on the floor in front of Rose, groaning and kissing her knees. I was pale. Rose turned towards me, her face streaked with make-up and tears. She stretched her arms out to me : 'Come on,' she cried, 'let's go back to the Place Pigalle and live together. I'm sure Alfred agrees. Don't you, Alfred?' she added, pulling his hair. He remained silent.


I was due to follow my father to Toulon in order to attend the wedding of my cousin, daughter of Vice-Admiral G.F. The future looked dark to me. I told Rose about this family expedition and left her, with a still silent Alfred, at the hotel in the Place Pigalle and promised to come and see them when I was back.

At Toulon I noticed that Alfred had taken a little gold chain of mine. It was my lucky charm. I had put it round his wrist and had forgotten doing so, while he had taken good care not to remind me.

When I returned I went to the hotel. As I entered the room Rose flung her arms round me. It was dark. At first glance I did not recognize Alfred. What was so different about him?

The police were scouring Montmartre. Alfred and Rose were afraid because of their doubtful nationality. They had obtained false passports and were preparing to make their getaway while Alfred, intoxicated by the romance of the cinema, had had his hair dyed. Beneath these inky-black locks his small, fair-skinned face stood out with anthropometric clarity. I demanded my chain back from him. He denied ever having had it. Rose gave him away. He threw a tantrum, swore, threatened her, threatened me and brandished a weapon.

I rushed out and went down the stairs four at a time with Alfred on my heels. In the street I hailed a taxi. I called out my address, jumped in quickly and as the taxi moved off I looked round. Alfred was standing motionless outside the door of the hotel. Big tears were running down his cheeks. He stretched out his arms; he called my name. Beneath his badly dyed hair he was pitifully wan.

I wanted to tap on the window and stop the driver. Confronted by this solitary distress, I was undecided about returning like a coward to my home comforts, but then I thought of the chain, the weapon, the false passports, the flight in which Rose would surely ask me to join. I closed my eyes. And even now I have only to close my eyes in a taxi to conjure up the small figure of Alfred and his tearful face beneath that gangster's hair-style.

Since the Admiral was ill and my cousin away on her honeymoon, I had to return to Toulon. It would be tedious to describe that delightful Sodom where the fire of heaven falls without danger, striking by means of caressing sunshine. Before dusk an even softer atmosphere floods the town and as in Naples, as in Venice, a fairground crowd moves through the squares ornamented with fountains, noisy shops, waffle-stalls and street-hawkers. Men in love with masculine beauty come from all corners of the globe to admire the sailors who walk about idly, alone or in groups, respond to glances with a smile and never refuse an offer of love. Some nocturnal salt transforms the most brutal jailbird, the roughest Breton, the most savage Corsican, into those tall, flower-decked girls with low décolletés and loose limbs who like dancing and lead their partners, without the slightest embarrassment, into the shady hotels by the port.

One of the cafés with a dance-floor was kept by a former café-concert singer who had a woman's voice and used to exhibit himself in women's clothes. Now he sported a pullover and rings. He was flanked by colossal men wearing caps with red pompoms; they worshipped him and he ill-treated them; his wife called out lists of drinks in a harsh, naïve voice, and he noted them down in large, childish handwriting, with his tongue hanging out.

One evening when I opened the door to the place kept by this astonishing creature, surrounded by the respectful attentions of his wife and his men, I remained rooted to the spot. I had just caught sight of the ghost of Dargelos, a man I could see from the side leaning against the pianola. Dargelos in sailor's uniform.

This double possessed in particular the arrogance, the insolent and absent-minded air of Dargelos. On his cap, which was tilted forward over his left eyebrow, could be read in gold letters *Tapageuse*, he wore a tight black scarf around his neck and those trousers with tabs which in the past allowed sailors to roll them up to their thighs and are today forbidden by regulations on the pretext that they are worn by pimps.

In any other place I would never have dared stand in the orbit of that arrogant gaze. But Toulon is Toulon; dancing avoids the awkwardness of introductions, it throws strangers into each other's arms and forms a prelude to love.

To music full of ringlets and kiss-curls we danced a waltz. The backward-leaning bodies were linked together at the groin, profiles were grave and eyes lowered, faces moved round more slowly than the feet which wove in and out and sometimes came down like horses' hooves. The free hands assumed the graceful pose affected by the working class when they drink a glass of wine and when they piss it away. A springtime ecstasy excited those bodies. Branches grew in them, hardness crushed hardness, sweat mingled together and the couples would leave for the bedrooms with clock-case lampshades and eiderdowns.

Stripped of the accessories which intimidate a civilian, those which are affected by sailors to give themselves confidence, Tapageuse became a timid animal. He had had his nose broken by a wine carafe during a fight. A straight nose might have made him colourless. The carafe had added the final thumb-stroke to the masterpiece.

This boy, who for me represented good luck, bore on his chest the words PAS DE CHANCE tattooed in blue capital letters. He told me his story. It was short. He had just come out of a naval prison. After the mutiny on the *Ernest Renan* he had been mistaken for a colleague; this is why he had a crew-cut, which he hated and which suited him wonderfully well.

'I'm unlucky,' he repeated, shaking his little bald head, like some antique bust, 'and I always will be.'

I put my gold chain round his neck. 'I'm not giving it to you,' I told him, 'that wouldn't protect either of us, but keep it for this evening.'

Next, with my fountain-pen, I crossed out the ominous tattooing. Beneath it I drew a star and a heart. He smiled. He understood, more with his skin than with anything else, that he was safe, that our encounter was not like those he was used to : brief moments of self-gratification.

PAS DE CHANCE! Was it possible? With that mouth, those teeth, those eyes, that belly, those shoulders, those iron muscles, those legs? PAS DE CHANCE, with that fabulous little under-water plant, lying dead and crumpled on the moss, which unfolded, grew bigger, reared up and threw its seed far away as soon as it found the element of love. I couldn't get over it; and in order to resolve this problem I sank into a feigned sleep.

PAS DE CHANCE remained motionless beside me. Gradually I felt that he was embarking on a delicate manoeuvre in order to free his arm on which my elbow was resting. Not for a second did it enter my head that he was contemplating some sly trick. This would have meant disregarding naval ceremonial. 'Honesty, good behaviour' illuminate the vocabulary of sailors.

I watched him through barely closed eyelids. First he weighed the chain in his hands several times, kissed it and rubbed it on his tattoo. Then, with the terrible slowness of a player who is cheating, he tested my sleep, coughed, touched me, listened to my breathing, brought his face close to my right hand which lay wide open near my face and gently leaned his cheek against it.

I was the indiscreet witness of this attempt by an unlucky boy who could feel a lifebelt coming close to him on the open sea, and I had to restrain myself from losing my head, pretending to wake up and ruining my life.

At dawn I left him. My eyes avoided his, which were full of all the hope which he felt but could not express. He returned the chain to me. I embraced him, tucked him in bed and put out the light.

I had to return to my hotel and write down on a slate in the hall the time (five o'clock) when sailors wake, beneath countless other requests of the same kind. Just as I picked up the chalk I noticed that I had forgotten my gloves. I went back upstairs. Light shone through the glass over the door. Someone must have switched the lamp on again. I couldn't resist putting my eye to the keyhole; it made a bizarre frame for a small shaven head. PAS DE CHANCE had buried his face in my gloves and was weeping bitterly.

I hesitated outside that door for ten minutes. I was about to open it when the face of Alfred superimposed itself with great precision on that of PAS DE CHANCE. I went downstairs on tiptoe, asked for the door to be unlocked and banged it behind me. Outside, a fountain was conducting a grave monologue over the empty square.

No, I thought, we don't belong to the same order. He's already beautiful enough to move a flower, a tree or an animal. Impossible to live with.

Day was breaking. Cocks were crowing over the sea. A dark coolness gave away its presence. A man emerged from a street carrying a shotgun. I went back to the hotel weighed down with a heavy burden.


Sickened by emotional adventures, incapable of reaction, I dragged my feet and my soul. I sought the consolation of a more secretive atmosphere. I found it in a working-class *établissement de bains*. It was reminiscent of the *Satyricon* with its little cells, its central courtyard and its low room decorated with Turkish divans where young men sat playing cards. At a sign from the proprietor they would get up and stand in a row along the wall. The owner would feel their biceps, squeeze their thighs, uncover their intimate charms and offer them as a salesman offers his wares.

The clients were sure of their tastes, quick and discreet. I must have been a problem for these young men who were accustomed to precise demands. They looked at me without understanding; for I prefer talk to action.

My heart and instinct combine in such a way that I find it difficult to commit either without the other following. This is what leads me to cross the boundaries of friendship and makes me wary of casual contacts in which I risk catching the malady of love. In the end I envied those who do not suffer vaguely from beauty, know what they want, bring a vice to the point of perfection, pay, and satisfy it.

One man wanted to be insulted, another weighed down with chains, another (a moralist) could only find enjoyment in the spectacle of a Hercules killing a rat with a red-hot needle. How many sensible people I saw, who knew the exact recipe for their pleasure and whose existence was simplified because they bought themselves, on a fixed day, at a fixed price, an honest, bourgeois complication! Most of them were rich industrialists who came from the north to satisfy their needs and then rejoined their wives and children.

In the end I spaced out my visits. My presence was beginning to look suspicious. The French find it difficult to tolerate a character that is not true to type. The miser must always be miserly, the jealous man jealous. This explains the success of Molière. The proprietor thought I was attached to the police. He gave to understand that one was either buyer or seller. One couldn't be both.

This warning jolted me out of my laziness and forced me to break with unworthy habits, to which was added the memory of Alfred perpetually floating over the faces of young bakers, butchers, cyclists, telegraph boys, zouaves, sailors, acrobats and other professional masks.

One of my few regrets was the two-way mirror. You went into a dark cabin and opened a shutter. This shutter revealed a metallic canvas through which the eye could see a small bathroom. On the other side of the canvas was a mirror that reflected so well from such a smooth surface that it was impossible to guess that it was full of eyes.

When I had the money I would spend a Sunday there. Out of the twelve mirrors in the twelve bathrooms it was the only one of this sort. The owner had acquired it for a very high price and had had it brought from Germany. His staff were unaware of the observatory. The young working-class men supplied the show.

They all followed the same routine. They undressed and hung up their new suits carefully. Once they were out of their Sunday best their delightful professional deformities made it possible to guess their jobs. Standing up in the bath, they would look at themselves (and me) and begin by a Parisian grimace that bares the gums. Then they would rub one shoulder, pick up the soap and make it lather. The soaping turned into a caress. Suddenly their eyes left the world, their head would fall back and their body spit like a furious animal.

Some of them sank down exhausted into the steaming water, while others began the same procedure all over again; the youngest ones were distinguishable because they climbed out of the bath and wiped from the tiles the sap that their blind stems had hurled distantly, madly, towards love. Once, a Narcissus who was pleasuring himself brought his mouth up to the mirror, glued it to the glass and completed the adventure with himself. Invisible as a Greek god, I pressed my lips against his and imitated his gestures. He never knew that the mirror, instead of reflecting, was participating, that it was alive and loved him.

Chance led me towards a new life. I emerged from a bad dream. I had fallen into all that was worst, an unhealthy idle existence equivalent, in the love of man for men, to clandestine rendezvous and meetings with whores in the love of women.

I knew and admired the Abbé X. His touch was near-miraculous. He could make everything appear less burdensome. He knew nothing about my intimate life, he merely sensed that I was unhappy. He talked to me, comforted me and introduced me to highly intelligent Catholics.

I have always been a believer. My belief was confused. Through frequenting a pure milieu, seeing so much peace on people's faces, and understanding the stupidity of unbelievers, I moved towards God. Dogma was certainly not at all in keeping with my decision to give free rein to my instincts, but this last period had left me with feelings of bitterness and satiety in which I wanted to see only too quickly proof that I had taken the wrong road. So much milk and water, after forbidden beverages, revealed to me a future of transparency and whiteness. If I had scruples, I would dismiss them by remembering Jeanne and Rose. Normal love, I thought, is not denied me. Nothing prevents me from founding a family and returning to the straight and narrow path. In fact I merely yield to my inclinations through fear of making any effort. Nothing beautiful exists without effort. I will fight against the devil and I will be victorious.

Divine period! The Church cradled me. I felt I was the adopted son of a divine family. Bread for chanting, bread enchanted, transformed limbs into snow, into cork. I rose towards heaven as a cork rises to the surface of the water. During mass, when the star of sacrifice dominates the altar and heads are bowed, I prayed ardently to the Virgin Mary that she would take me under her holy protection : 'Hail to you, Mary,' I would murmur. 'Are you not purity itself? Can there be any question with you of precedence or freedom? What men believe to be indecent, surely you see it as we see the amorous exchanges of pollens and atoms! I will obey the orders of your son's ministers on earth, but I know very well that his goodness does not stop with the chicanery of Father Sinistrarius and the rules of an old criminal code. Amen.'

After a religious crisis the soul has a relapse. This is the difficult moment. The grown man does not shed his skin as easily as the snake that leaves its light robe hanging on the briars. There is love at first sight, betrothal with the beloved, marriage and austere duties.

At first everything took place in a kind of ecstasy. A prodigious zeal takes hold of the neophyte. It becomes hard, when this has

cooled, to get up and go to church. Fasting, prayers and orisons possess us. The devil, who had gone out through the door, comes back through the window, disguised as a ray of sunshine.

It is impossible to find one's salvation in Paris; the soul is too divided. I decided to go to the sea. There I would move between the church and a boat. I would pray on the waves far from all distraction.

I booked a room at the hotel in T. From the first day at T the heat counselled enjoyment and undressing. To reach the church meant going up stinking streets and climbing steps. This church was deserted. The fishermen did not go into it. I wondered at God's failure, which is the failure of masterpieces; yet this does not mean that there are no famous masterpieces or that people do not fear them.

Alas, I spoke in vain, this emptiness influenced me. I preferred my boat. I would row out as far as possible and there I would drop the oars, take off my trunks and stretch my limbs out freely.

The sun is an old lover who knows his role well. He begins by holding you down all over with firm hands. He puts his arms round you. He seizes hold of you, throws you down, and then suddenly I would find myself coming to in a stupefied state, my belly soaked with a liquid resembling mistletoe berries.

I was on the wrong track. I hated myself. I tried to take myself in hand again. In the end my prayer was reduced to a plea for forgiveness : 'God, you forgive me, you understand me, you understand everything. Have you not desired everything, made everything : bodies, sexes, the waves, the sky and the sun which loved Hyacinth and turned him into a flower?'

I had discovered a little deserted beach where I went to bathe. I would pull my boat up on the shingle and dry myself among the seaweed. One morning I found a young man there bathing in the nude; he asked me if I was shocked. My frank reply enlightened him about my tastes. We were soon lying side by side. I learnt that he was staying in the neighbouring village and that he was convalescing after suspected tuberculosis.

Sunshine speeds the growth of feelings. We moved fast and, thanks to numerous encounters in the midst of nature, far from objects which distract the heart, we came to love each other without ever having spoken of love. H left his inn and came to stay at my hotel. He wrote. He believed in God, but affected a puerile indifference towards dogma. The Church, this likeable heretic would repeat, demands from us a moral prosody equivalent to that of a Boileau. If you place one foot in the Church, which maintains that it does not move, and one foot in modern life, you are trying to live with your feet apart. I say that active obedience is the opposite of passive obedience. God loves love. In loving one another we prove to Christ that we know how to read between the lines, which are inevitably those of a severe legislator. Speaking to the masses entails forbidding anything that mixes the common with the rare.

He laughed at my remorse which he regarded as weakness. He disapproved of my inhibitions. I love you, he would repeat, and I congratulate myself on loving you. Perhaps our dream could have endured beneath a sky where we lived half on land, half in the water, like mythological divinities; but his mother summoned him back and we decided to return to Paris together.

His mother lived at Versailles, and since I was living with my father we rented an hotel room where we met every day. He had many women friends. They did not alarm me unduly, for I had often observed that perverts enjoy the society of women, while men who like women despise them utterly and, apart from the use they make of them, prefer the company of men.

One morning when he spoke to me from Versailles I noticed that the telephone, which favours lying, brought me a voice different from the usual one. I asked him if he was really speaking from Versailles. He became upset, quickly arranged to meet me at the hotel at four o'clock the same day and hung up. I was chilled to the marrow, and, spurred on by the terrible desire to know the truth, I asked for his mother's number. She replied that he had not been home for several days and was sleeping at a friend's house because his work was keeping him late in town.

How could I wait until four o'clock? Countless incidents which had only been waiting to emerge from the dark became instruments of torture and began to persecute me. The truth became clear to me. Madame V, whom I had believed to be a friend, was his mistress. He met her in the evening and spent the night with her. This certainty pierced my breast like the claw of some wild animal. Although I knew this beyond any doubt, I still hoped he would find an excuse and would be able to give proof of his innocence.

At four o'clock he admitted that in the past he had loved women and that he kept going back to them, led by some invisible force; I mustn't be upset; it was something different from his love for me; he loved me, he was disgusted with himself, he could do nothing about it; every sanatorium was full of similar cases. This twofold sexuality must be put down to tuberculosis.

I asked him to choose between women and me, believing he would choose me and try to renounce women. I was mistaken.

'I am taking the risk,' he replied, 'of making a promise and breaking my word. It's better to break it off. You would suffer. I don't want you to suffer. A break would hurt you less than a false promise and lies.'

I was standing against the door and I was so pale that he was frightened. 'Goodbye,' I murmured in a lifeless voice, 'goodbye. You were all I lived for, I had nothing else but you. What will become of me? Where will I go? How will I wait for the night and after the night the day, and then the next day? How shall I spend the weeks?'

I could see only a confused room moving through my tears, and I was counting days and nights on my fingers with moronic gestures.

Suddenly he awoke as though from a hypnotic spell, leapt out of bed where he had been biting his nails, put his arms round me, asked my forgiveness and swore to me that women could go to hell.

He wrote a letter to Madame V breaking things off. She feigned suicide by swallowing a whole tube of sleeping tablets and we lived for three weeks in the country, leaving no address. Two months went by; I was happy.

It was the day before a big religious festival. Before attending mass I was in the habit of going to the Abbé X for confession. He more or less expected me. I warned him as I came through the door that I was not coming to confess but to tell my story; and that unfortunately I knew his verdict in advance.

'Monsieur l'Abbé,' I asked him, 'do you love me?'

'I love you.'

'Would you be glad to learn that at last I feel happy?'

'Very glad.'

'Well, know that I am happy, but in a way that the Church and the world disapprove of, for it's friendship that makes me happy and for me friendship has no limits.'

The Abbé interrupted me. 'I believe,' he said, 'that you are the victim of scruples.'

'Monsieur l'Abbé, I will never offend the Church by believing that it comes to terms and deceives people. I know what happens in "friendships that go too far." Who is being deceived? God is watching me. Shall I measure to the inch the slope that separates me from sin?'

'My dear boy,' the Abbé X told me in the vestry, 'if it were only a question of risking my place in heaven, I wouldn't be risking very much, for I believe that God's goodness surpasses what we imagine. But there is my place on earth. The Jesuits are watching me closely.'

We embraced. As I went back home, along walls over which came the smell of gardens, I thought how admirable was the economy of God. It gives love when one lacks it, and, in order to avoid a pleonasm of the heart, refuses it to those who have it.

One morning I received a telegram : *Don't worry. Have left on trip with Marcel. Will telegraph time return.*

This telegram astounded me. There had been no question of a trip the day before. Marcel was a friend from whom I need fear no treachery, but I knew he was wild enough to decide on a trip on the spur of the moment, without reflecting how vulnerable his partner was or that dashing off like that was likely to prove dangerous.

I was about to go and question Marcel's servant when the bell rang and Mlle R was brought in, her hair dishevelled, her face pale and drawn. 'Marcel's stolen him from us ! Marcel's stolen him from us !' she cried. 'We must act ! Do something ! Why are you standing there like a block of wood ? Move ! Quickly ! Avenge us ! The wretched man !' She wrung her hands, paced the room, blew her nose, fastened up strands of hair, clung to the furniture and tore her dress.

Fear that my father would hear and come in prevented me from understanding immediately what was happening to me. Suddenly the truth became clear and, concealing my anxiety, I propelled the crazy woman towards the hall, explaining that I was not being deceived, that there was nothing except friendship between us, that I was completely unaware of the incident which she had just explained so noisily.

'What ?' she went on at the top of her voice. 'Don't you know that this boy adores me and comes to see me every night ? He comes from Versailles and goes back there before dawn ! I've had terrible operations ! My stomach is covered with scars ! I'm telling you he kisses those scars, rests his cheek against them before going to sleep.'

It is pointless to describe the state into which this visit threw me. I received telegrams : *Long live Marseilles!* or *Leaving for Tunis.*

The homecoming was terrible. H thought that he'd be scolded like a child after a joke. I asked Marcel to leave us alone and I flung Mlle R's name at him. He denied it. I insisted. He denied it. I bullied him. He denied it. Finally he admitted it and I hit him. Pain intoxicated me. I beat him like a brute. I took hold of his head by the ears and banged it against the wall. A trickle of blood ran out of the corner of his mouth. In a moment I became sober.

Crazed with tears, I wanted to kiss that poor bruised face. But I encountered only a flash of blue over which the eyelids closed in pain.

I fell on my knees in the corner of the bedroom. A scene of this kind drains deep-lying resources and can break us up like puppets. All at once I felt a hand on my shoulder. I raised my head and saw my victim looking at me. He slid along the floor, kissed my fingers and my knees, choking and groaning : 'Forgive me, forgive me ! I'm your slave. Do what you like with me.'

There was a month's truce. A sweet and weary truce after the storm. We were like dahlias leaning over when soaked with water. H looked unwell. He was pale and often stayed at Versailles.


Nothing embarrasses me when talking about sexual relationships, but modesty holds me back when I come to describing the tortures which I am capable of suffering. So I will describe them in a few lines and not mention them again. Love breaks me in two. Even when I'm calm I live in constant fear that this calm might cease and this anxiety prevents me from enjoying its pleasures. The slightest setback ruins everything. I find it impossible not to see the worst side of things. Nothing prevents me from losing my foothold, even if I have only slipped. Waiting is one form of torture; possession is another, through fear of losing what I possess.

Doubt caused me to pass wakeful nights walking up and down, lying on the floor, hoping that the floor would sink down, eternally down. I promised myself that I would not say a word about my fears. As soon as I was in H's presence I plied him with complaints and questions. He said nothing. This silence either drove me into a frenzy or else made me weep. I accused him of hating me, of wanting to kill me. He knew very well that replies were useless and that I would start again the next day.

That was in September. 12th November is a date I shall never forget for the rest of my life. We were due to meet at the hotel at six o'clock. The proprietor stopped me downstairs and, highly embarrassed, told me that the police had raided our room and that H had been taken to the police headquarters, with a large case, in a car containing the commissioner of the vice-squad and plain-clothes men.

'The police?' I cried. 'But why?'

I telephoned some influential people. They made inquiries and told me the truth, which was confirmed at eight o'clock by an exhausted H, who had been released after interrogation.

He had been deceiving me with a Russian woman who gave him drugs. Learning that there was to be a raid, she asked him to take his cigarettes and powders to the hotel. Some thug he had met and in whom he had confided had immediately given him away. He was a police spy. So, at the same moment, I learnt that I had been betrayed twice over in an underhand fashion. His discomfiture disarmed me. He had been boastful at the police headquarters and on the pretext that he was an addict had smoked lying on the floor in front of the astonished police while being interrogated. Now he was reduced to a rag. I was unable to utter a word of reproach. I begged him to give up drugs. He replied that he wanted to, but the addiction was too far advanced for him to turn back.

The next day they telephoned me from Versailles to say that he had begun to spit blood and had been rushed to a nursing home in the Rue B.

He was in Room 55 on the third floor. When I came in he barely had the strength to turn his head towards me. His nose had become slightly flattened. He looked sadly at his transparent hands.

'I'll tell you my secret,' he said to me when we were alone. 'There was both woman and man in me. The woman was subjected to you; the man rebelled against this subjection. I didn't like women. I sought them out to sidetrack myself and prove to myself that I was free. The vain, stupid man within me was the enemy of our love. I'm sorry about it. I love only you. I'll obey you unquestioningly and I'll spend my time making up for the harm I've done.'

I hardly slept all night. Towards morning I went to sleep for a few moments and had a dream. I was at the circus with H. The circus became a restaurant consisting of two small rooms. In one of them a singer seated at the piano announced that he was going to sing a new song. The title was the name of a woman who dominated the world of fashion in 1900. This title, after the introduction, was an insult in 1926. This was the song :

> The lettuces of Paris
> Go walking through Paris.
> There's even an endive,
> So live and let live,
> An endive in Paris.

The magnifying power of the dream made this absurd song into something celestial and extraordinarily funny.

I woke up. I was still laughing and this laughter seemed to me a good omen. If the situation were serious, I thought, I wouldn't have had such a ridiculous dream. I had forgotten that the exhaustion of grief sometimes does produce ridiculous dreams.

In the Rue B, I was about to open the door to the private ward when a nurse stopped me. 'Number 55 is no longer in his room,' she informed me frigidly. 'He is in the chapel.'

How did I find the strength to turn and go back?

In the chapel a woman was praying by a slab where my friend's body had been laid. How calm it was, that beloved face that I had struck! But what did the memory of my blows or caresses mean to him now? He no longer loved either his mother, or women, or me, or anyone. For death interests only the dead.

In my terrible solitude I did not think I would turn again to the Church; it would be too easy to use the host as medicine and to find some negative strength at the Holy Table, too easy to turn to heaven whenever we lose what delighted us on earth.

There remained the expedient of marriage. But I had no hope of making a love-match; I would have considered it dishonest to deceive a young girl. At the Sorbonne I had known Mademoiselle de S whom I liked because of her boyish air and I had often said that if I had to marry, I would prefer her to anyone else. I renewed our acquaintance, frequently visited the house at Auteuil where she lived with her mother, and gradually we came to consider marriage as a possibility. She liked me. Her mother had been afraid she might remain an old maid. We became engaged quite effortlessly.

She had a young brother whom I had not met because he was completing his studies at a Jesuit college near London. He came back. Why had I not foreseen this new trick of fate which persecutes me and conceals beneath other guises a destiny which is always the same? The things I had liked about the sister were striking in the brother. The moment I saw him I understood the tragedy and the fact that a pleasant existence would be denied me. It did not take me long to learn that the brother, in true English fashion, had on meeting me been struck with love at first sight. This young man was in love with himself. In loving me he deceived himself. We met in secret and the consequences were inevitable.

The atmosphere of the house became charged with evil tension. We concealed our crime skilfully, but this atmosphere disturbed my fiancée all the more because she did not suspect its origin. Eventually, the love her brother felt for me turned to passion. Did this passion possibly conceal a secret need to destroy? He hated his sister. He begged me to withdraw my promise, to break off the engagement. I slowed things down as best I could. I worked to obtain a relative calm which merely postponed the catastrophe.

One evening when I was coming to see his sister I could hear the sound of weeping through the door. The poor girl was lying full length on the floor, with a handkerchief in her mouth and her hair hanging down. Her brother was standing over her. 'He's mine!' he was shouting. 'Mine! Mine! Since he hasn't the courage to tell you, I'm doing so myself!'

I couldn't bear this scene. His voice and manner were so cruel that I struck him on the face.

'You'll always regret you did that,' he cried, and shut himself in his room.

While I was trying to revive his sister I heard a shot. I rushed out. I opened his bedroom door. Too late. He was lying at the foot of the wardrobe-mirror on which, at head-height, I could still see the grease-mark of his lips and the blurred mist left by his breath.

I felt I could no longer live in this world where ill-luck and mourning haunted me. I could not resort to suicide because of my faith. This faith and the disturbed state in which I had remained since relinquishing religious practices led me to the idea of entering a monastery.

The Abbé X, whose advice I sought, told me that one could not take these decisions hastily, that the rule was very severe and that I could try out my strength by means of a retreat at the Abbey of M. He would give me a letter for the Superior and would explain why this retreat was something more than the whim of a dilettante.

When I reached the Abbey it was freezing cold. The snow was melting into icy water and slush. The porter arranged for me to be conducted by a monk, beside whom I walked in silence beneath the vaults. When I asked him about the times of the services and he answered me, I jumped. I had just heard one of those voices which tell me more about the age and beauty of a young man than do faces or figures.

He lowered his hood. His profile was silhouetted against the wall. It was that of Alfred, H, Rose, Jeanne, Dargelos, PAS DE CHANCE, Gustave and the farm-hand.

I reached the door of Dom Z's office in a state of collapse. Dom Z's greeting was warm. On his desk was a letter he had already received from the Abbé X. He dismissed the young monk. 'Do you know,' he said to me, 'that our house is without comfort and that the rule is very severe?'

'Father,' I replied, 'I have reasons to believe that this rule is still too lenient for me. I shall confine myself to this visit and I shall always preserve the memory of your welcome.'

Yes, the monastery drove me away like everything else. So I had to leave and act like those Carmelite Fathers who burn themselves out in the desert and whose love is pious suicide. But does God allow us to cherish him even in this way?

However, I shall depart, leaving this book behind me. If someone should find it, let him publish it. Perhaps it will help to make people understand that in exiling myself I am not exiling a monster, but a man whom society will not allow to live, since it considers one of the mysterious cogs in God's masterpiece to be a mistake.

Instead of adopting Rimbaud's gospel, *The time of the assassins has come,* young people would do better to remember the phrase *Love must be reinvented.* The world accepts dangerous experiments in the realm of art because it does not take art seriously; but it condemns them in life.

I fully realize that an ideal fit for termites, like the Russian ideal which tends towards the plural, condemns the singular in one of its most lofty forms. But nobody will ever prevent certain flowers and fruit from being smelt and eaten only by the rich.

A vice of society makes a vice of my rectitude. I withdraw from this society. In France this vice does not lead me to prison because of the way Cambacérès lived and the longevity of the Code Napoléon. But I will not agree to be tolerated. This damages my love of love and of liberty.

PART TWO


*Plays and Poems*

# School for Widows

Cocteau wrote *School for Widows* (L'Ecole des Veuves) for the famous actress Arletty for performance at the Théâtre de l'ABC in Paris in 1936. Its theme is based on a story by the Roman writer Petronius, *The Matron of Ephesus*, as was Christopher Fry's play *A Phoenix Too Frequent*. Throughout his life Cocteau found inspiration in classical literature. His first play, apart from *Les Mariés de la Tour Eiffel* which is classified as a *comédie-ballet*, was an adaptation of Sophocles' *Antigone*, first performed in 1922 and published in 1928.

None of Cocteau's biographers has given *School for Widows* any attention; presumably they do not regard it as particularly original or characteristic of its author. It is, however, skilful and entertaining, proving like *Les Parents Terribles* that Cocteau was a truly professional man of the theatre; he was not limited to writing for the avant-garde and could construct an 'orthodox' play calculated to amuse an 'orthodox' audience. *School for Widows* was not published until 1949, when it was included in the *Théâtre de Poche*.

CHARACTERS

The Nurse
The Widow
The Guard
The Sister-in-law

*A tomb in the cemetery at Ephesus, decorated with great luxury. Two openings at the back: in the centre, a square skylight about six feet from the ground; on the right an open door, through which can be seen moonlight and masses of flowers. Between the skylight and the door is an upright sarcophagus, facing the wings opposite prompter. On the left, forward, a huge day-bed covered with furs. On the right, also forward, tables and chairs. On the table night-lights, and funeral cakes in the shape of human statuettes.*

THE NURSE : Madam!

THE WIDOW : If you want to tell me the same thing all over again, don't talk.

THE NURSE : Your husband would have been the first person to tell you ...

THE WIDOW : My husband's dead – I'm a widow. He has nothing more to say. I'm in charge now.

THE NURSE : When it was light I felt brave, but as soon as it was dark ... a cemetery, a tomb ... two women alone with ... (*She points to the sarcophagus.*)

THE WIDOW : With?

THE NURSE : With ... the Master. Madam will understand. The Master was very good, very fair ... but he's dead, and in a cemetery, the dead can live again ...

THE WIDOW : Don't be stupid. The Master couldn't possibly want to do you any harm. Personally I like him being here. His presence reassures me. Behind the little window, I can see his dear face ...

(*They go nearer to the sarcophagus.*)

THE NURSE : How the Master has changed since ...

THE WIDOW : Since when?

THE NURSE : Since he was stuffed.

THE WIDOW : Embalmed, embalmed.

THE NURSE : Oh, well, embalmed! Personally I find those Jews rob the rich, and the Master could have been anyone.

THE WIDOW : Perhaps the eyes aren't quite right ... and the nostrils ... and the mouth and the cheeks a bit too round. Yet on the whole, no, I recognize him and his presence comforts me.

THE NURSE : To think that a beautiful, rich young woman, the most beautiful and the richest in town, should resolve to die in her husband's tomb!

THE WIDOW : And to think that you insist on following me.

THE NURSE : That's natural, I'll never leave you.

THE WIDOW : If I condemn myself to death because my husband is dead, that's my affair, but if you die because I die, that's suicide. It's crazy! It's barbarous! I command you to let me die alone.

THE NURSE : Crazy and barbarous! I'll tell you a thousand times that it's crazy and barbarous to make a fatal decision and then carry it out. What could have put such a monstrous notion into your head?

THE WIDOW : The frivolity of fashionable women, led by my sister-in-law. They were greedy and dried up and they began to wink at each other about my newly won liberty. I had to show an example. I had to show these worldly women what a worldly woman is capable of. Don't try to dissuade me from my plan. It's impossible. I shall die in this tomb. In future years men will remember my name. Perhaps too my statue in gold will stand beneath the porch of the temple and erring wives will blush as they pass in front of me.

THE NURSE : So you'll die out of obstinacy and you want to surprise the world out of pride.

THE WIDOW : Not the world, just worldly women. Do you remember the magnificent procession which accompanied me to this door? The music, the scents, the choirs of priests, and those women, all those women on their knees. . . .

THE NURSE : They were only too glad, the bitches! They were overwhelmed by your beauty, your intelligence, your riches and your clothes. If it was the custom to burn the widow alive on the dead man's funeral pyre, each of them would bring a torch! On their knees, were they! They were weeping loudly but they were laughing up their sleeves. How could you be taken in by such vulgar play-acting?

THE WIDOW : You're being unfair and any method of saving me seems all right to you.

THE NURSE : Madam!

THE WIDOW : Oh be quiet, and don't insist on following me to hell. In any case you ought to know that I've left all my fortune to you, and only you.

THE NURSE : To me?

THE WIDOW : To you. I'm keeping this surprise in store for my charming sister-in-law.

THE NURSE : To me!

THE WIDOW : To you.

THE NURSE : What a pity!

THE WIDOW : What do you mean, what a pity?

THE NURSE : Because I've got no family and there's no one to enjoy all that money.

THE WIDOW : Enjoy it yourself.

THE NURSE : I'll be dead.

THE WIDOW : Oh, I can't be angry with you. You're too kind, too faithful. But listen, you must go on living. My death must remain a unique example. I've announced my decision.

THE NURSE : That's a fine thing! Don't you realize you'll upset everyone much more by announcing that you'll go back home?

THE WIDOW : In the end I'll forbid you to open your mouth and put me off like this. You won't change my plan. You may make it more difficult to carry out.

THE NURSE : I'll protect you against yourself. If I have to I'll hoot like an owl. Why, there's spring, moonlight, flowers, marble, fabrics and furs, everything that ought to make you think of love, and there's a woman who's never known love ...

THE WIDOW : Will you stop it?

THE NURSE (*shouting*): Who's never known love, and who on the pretext that her old husband is dead and has been stuffed in a box ...

THE WIDOW : Embalmed ....

THE NURSE : Pretending that the licentiousness of our town ought to be shown an example and that gossips must be punished, punishes herself first of all and lets herself die of hunger in a tomb. Oh, if you'd ever been in love, we wouldn't be here.

THE WIDOW : In love with whom?

THE NURSE : Not with your husband, certainly. But there are other men in the world and they don't all get their good looks from the embalmer ...

THE WIDOW : I loved my husband ...

THE NURSE : Naturally.

THE WIDOW : And I was never tempted to deceive him with anyone.

THE NURSE : Good heavens! You've never seen a man.

THE WIDOW : You're joking.

THE NURSE : The young men about town who're after your money can't be called men. I suspect them of playing a double game, they're not interested in the charms of our sex, and when they look you up and down they wear tunics as loose as yours and women can't see what they're thinking.

THE WIDOW : The moonlight and the scents of this springtime night have made you lose all restraint. So none of our young men are men as far as you're concerned. Where shall I find this ideal man? Where shall I meet him? Does he exist? Will he come down from the heavens on a griffon and take me out of this tomb?

THE NURSE : You needn't look so far afield. The first ordinary young man you'll meet will provide you with an example. You'll only have to look at him once.

THE WIDOW : Give me an example.

THE NURSE : I can. The guard.

THE WIDOW : What guard?

THE NURSE : The guard who looks after the cemetery.

THE WIDOW : That insufferable half-wit who drops in every other minute to ask how I'm getting on?

THE NURSE : You think he's a half-wit because he's shy and because he has feeling and your riches frighten him. Your death upsets him. He can't bring himself to believe it's true.

THE WIDOW : And with him at least, do you know what he's thinking?

THE NURSE : That shouldn't be difficult.

THE WIDOW : Is he young and handsome?

THE NURSE : Haven't you ever seen him?

THE WIDOW : I've got other fish to fry. Why do you think I spend my time looking at soldiers?

THE NURSE : Well, when you've fried your fish just take a look at our young guard and you'll understand that a woman mustn't leave this life without trying to meet a real man, not like one of the gilded youths of the town, or like this ... thing which frightens me so much.

THE WIDOW : I forbid you to speak of the Master in that tone.

THE NURSE : The Master looks so little like the Master. He looks no more like himself than do those statue cakes that your friends bought. The dead are lucky. They can eat!

THE WIDOW : That's enough. Stay or go. The door's wide open. But if you stay, respect my silence and let death take me slowly.

THE NURSE : Look, here's the guard. Don't forget to look at him. He's worth it.

THE WIDOW (*lying down quickly on her bed*) : Quickly, quickly, I'm going to sleep. Speak quietly, if you want to; but for goodness' sake don't let him speak to me.

THE NURSE : Close one eye and look at him with the other. Women are past masters of that art.

THE WIDOW : To think that one can't even die in peace. (*She lies down in a rage.*)

THE GUARD (*coming in shyly*) : She's asleep.

THE NURSE : Yes, come in a moment.

THE GUARD : Poor woman!

THE NURSE : Obstinate woman, you ought to say.

THE GUARD : She hasn't eaten since last night.

THE NURSE : Oh, you know, she could go for a week without eating if she was slimming. I'm dying of hunger!

THE GUARD : I offered to share my meal with you.

THE NURSE : Madam won't eat. I do as Madam does. Madam wants to die mad, I shall die mad too. That's what a loyal servant ought to do.

THE GUARD : I can only think of this great love.

THE NURSE : What great love?

THE GUARD : A love which forces you to die after the death of those you love. Was he young and handsome?

THE NURSE : Come here. (*She leads him in front of the sarcophagus.*) That's what it's all about.

THE GUARD : It's not possible! It's for a man like that, that a woman like this. . . . I admire her even more. Passion leads to madness, but to die out of duty, out of mere duty! I didn't know that such noble women existed.

THE NURSE : Such stupid women.

THE GUARD : You can't understand. Soldiers know only common girls. They never meet any women, real women. . . . Couldn't I have a closer look at your mistress?

THE NURSE : You could, if she was strong enough to stand on her feet. I won't feel very steady tomorrow.

THE GUARD : I must go and look after my three corpses.

THE NURSE : What three corpses?

THE GUARD : Three thieves – the State won't allow them to be buried. They're exhibited on a pillory and our chiefs are afraid their gang or their families will try to take their bodies down. I've got to hurry. If you want anything, just call me. (*He goes out.*)

THE NURSE : Well? Were you asleep?

THE WIDOW : No.

THE NURSE : Did you see him?

THE WIDOW : Just.

THE NURSE : What do you think of him?

THE WIDOW : He seemed to me to have a wonderful figure. I think he's probably very tall.

THE NURSE : Very tall.

THE WIDOW : He'll make some woman of his own class happy. The gods will help him. (*She comes and sits by the table with the funeral cakes. She sits there leaning on one elbow, dreaming.*)

THE NURSE : Have you thought about it?

THE WIDOW (as though coming out of a dream. She jumps.) : Thought about what?

THE NURSE : About what the Master would say if he knew.

THE WIDOW : Firstly, he does know . . . he approves, he calls me, he looks at me. Secondly, what the Master thinks has nothing to do with the matter. I've always been very independent. The Master always left me very free . . .

THE NURSE : Precisely. He preserved both Madam's liberty and his own too. Perhaps he doesn't want Madam to follow him where

he is. He often used to say to me : Don't tell Madam when I
go out and when I come back, I hate being spied on.

THE WIDOW : Good heavens, whatever are you saying? My husband
went in and out secretly?

THE NURSE : Secretly isn't the word. He liked his liberty and knew
how to take it.

THE WIDOW : And I who never.... (*She strikes the table.*) Women
are always deceived. And to think that you were helping him
to take me in. It's too much! I'll have my revenge.

THE NURSE : Perfect. Have your revenge by not sacrificing yourself.
Leave this tomb at once. But don't tell me that I helped the
Master to deceive you. I helped him to preserve domestic bliss.

THE WIDOW : The deceitful wretch!

THE NURSE : There you go exaggerating again. The Master was
anything but a deceitful wretch. He was a very kind master.
He was frankness personified. He hated scenes and that's why
I suspect he must hate the part you're making him play.

THE WIDOW : Take his side! Go on with your game! Fortunately
my husband's person has very little to do with my death and
higher interests force me into it.

THE NURSE : Higher interests! Your sister-in-law's selfishness and
a few silly gossiping women – that's what causes your death!

THE WIDOW (*to herself*) : So he used to go out, and come back, and
ask your opinion. (*As she speaks, closing her eyes and looking
into the distance, she takes one of the funeral cakes and without thinking eats it.*) Whatever next! I'm glad that I'm going
to rejoin him quickly and settle our differences.

THE NURSE : You won't tell the Master what I said....

THE WIDOW (*eating another cake*) : I'm not the type who says 'she
said that you said'. Understand that. But it's strange. We think
we know the people close to us. Just because we live together.
We think (*she eats another cake*) we know whom we're living
with. But we live with people we don't know. It's unbelievable,
unbelievable. And only yesterday, I was thinking ... (*she
notices that she is eating*) Oh!

THE NURSE : What?

THE WIDOW : I've absent-mindedly eaten the funeral cakes ... I
was talking ... dreaming.

THE NURSE : It's sacrilege.

THE WIDOW : And I had promised myself not to eat a thing. I
specially promised that.

THE NURSE : Since Madam has eaten something and since I do
what Madam does, there's no longer any reason why I
shouldn't eat. Does Madam allow me? (*She eats a cake.*)

THE WIDOW : Oh, very well. This first day won't count. We'll start fasting tomorrow. The vital thing is that nobody should suspect it. Our guard mustn't know that we've been eating.

THE NURSE : On the contrary. He wanted to share some solid food with us. And since everything's been put off until tomorrow, I propose to accept his offer.

THE WIDOW : Listen to the advice of the stomach.

THE NURSE : Now you're behaving better.

THE WIDOW : ... and ... what did the young man say about me? He must think I'm completely mad.

THE NURSE : I've tried to contradict him, but he won't change his mind. Your mistress, he says, must have reached the stage when women don't know how to retire. She's cleverer than the others. She'll be regarded as a magnificent widow when she ought to be a middle-aged woman who's retiring at the right moment.

THE WIDOW (*standing up*) : He said that! He dared to say that!

THE NURSE : Well, he didn't see you very clearly in the darkness.

THE WIDOW : He's there!

(*The head and shoulders of the guard appear in the skylight of the tomb.*)

THE GUARD (*at the skylight*) : Ladies!

THE NURSE (*aside*) : I've gone a bit far.

THE WIDOW (*loudly*) : Guard! Stay where you are. (*She turns her back to the audience and unfastens her dress in front.*)

THE GUARD : Oh!

THE WIDOW : And now you can tell the ladies and gentlemen of the town that I'm neither one-legged, nor hunchbacked, nor too fat, nor too thin, that I've left life on top of my form and that I've not just taken the first opportunity to disappear.

THE GUARD : But Madam ...

THE WIDOW : Don't behave like a fool. Come down from that skylight. You look like the full moon. (*Guard comes down to the door. She continues violently.*) Either come in or go out. Don't stand there on one leg looking at me stupidly.

THE GUARD : I'm going Madam, I'm going ... (*He dashes out.*)

THE WIDOW : Now he's running away. Run after him. Catch him, the idiot.

THE NURSE : Good, I'll get him back for you.

(*Just as the nurse is going out lights are seen outside, and drums can be heard.*)

THE WIDOW : What is that music and those torches?

THE NURSE : It's a vampire!

THE WIDOW (*looking through the skylight*) : Almost. My sister-in-law is visiting us. It's true her slaves are with her. But for her to venture into a cemetery at such an hour she must have a strong motive. Go and catch up our young idiot. I'll send my sister-in-law away as fast as I can.

(*As the nurse goes out she passes the sister-in-law, who is strikingly elegant, and bows very deeply to her.*)

THE SISTER-IN-LAW : Are you going out? Among the tombs.... Ugh!

THE NURSE : I'm going on an errand for my mistress. (*She disappears.*)

SISTER-IN-LAW : Darling!

THE WIDOW : Darling!

(*They kiss.*)

SISTER-IN-LAW : Darling, darling, how ghastly!

THE WIDOW : What do you mean, how ghastly?

SISTER-IN-LAW : Living in such a place. This morning, with the procession and the sunshine, it didn't look so dreary. Darling, something made me come, I just had to. I felt I must make a supreme effort and snatch you away from this unnatural death.

THE WIDOW : My mind is made up. In any case, I'm already too weak to get up from this bed.

SISTER-IN-LAW : It's awful. I do admire you! Oh yes, I really do, we all admire you. ... You look very well.

THE WIDOW : I'm resting. I've only done what's very natural.

SISTER-IN-LAW : Of course. As for me, I have my faith, my own approach. I believe it's more difficult to give up the small things than the big ones. I could easily sacrifice my life, if I had to, at once, but I couldn't sacrifice my shower-bath or my rusks. I could bear to see someone beheaded : I could stand it, and yet I've only to scratch a finger to feel upset. Little things upset me, alas ... and that reminds me, I want to ask you about a detail that will seem terribly vulgar to you.... What about your will?

THE WIDOW : I've made one. After my death I've a surprise in store for you and for everyone.

SISTER-IN-LAW : It's in your interest that I mention it to you. I was afraid that your heroism would prevent you from thinking of details which are sometimes indispensable. (*She gets up.*) Oh, well!

THE WIDOW : I won't come with you.

SISTER-IN-LAW : Oh, darling! In any case, I don't believe in this horrible thing. We must take you away. Sleep brings counsel. The daylight tomorrow morning will drive all these ghosts away. You'll come back to town! You'll bury us all! Do you like my dress? Well then, good night. (*As she passes the sarcophagus she places her hand on the window.*) Good night to you!

THE WIDOW (*shocked*) : Listen . . .

SISTER-IN-LAW : Oh, nobody can make me change my tune just because someone's alive or dead. I keep my style. I have a mystique. I don't need to die in order to live with my dead. Goodbye, darling!

(*She disappears. The torches and drums fade away.*)

THE NURSE : Madam! Madam!

THE WIDOW : What is it?

THE NURSE : Are you alone?

THE WIDOW : Yes, hurry up.

THE NURSE (*to the guard*) : Come in. Madam, our guard has had a misfortune.

THE WIDOW : Misfortune? How red you look!

THE NURSE : I've had something to eat and drink.

THE GUARD : Alas, Madam. I was watching over three corpses condemned to the pillory without the right to burial. I felt myself so drawn by this window (*he lowers his head*) that I abandoned my post. The family of one of the brigands has stolen the corpse. I shall lose my job and will never be able to see you again.

THE WIDOW : Is that what's upsetting you?

THE GUARD : I admit it and I'd do anything to find a fresh corpse to put in the place of mine.

THE WIDOW : My husband would be delighted, I'm sure, to do you this small service.

THE NURSE : What!

THE GUARD : Madam! That's impossible!

THE WIDOW : What's impossible? The living help the dead enough for the dead to help the living a little. A dead man is a dead man. My husband will not die any more because he replaces your dead man, and as for you, you will take his place. Misfortune serves some purpose. The important thing is to see on which side the damage is worse.

THE GUARD : I'll never dare . . .

THE WIDOW : Don't make excuses. This sarcophagus was beginning to give me nightmares. (*To the nurse*) Help us.

THE NURSE : Do you want to take out the sarcophagus?

THE WIDOW : Three of us won't be too many for this job. (*To the guard*) Push, you're the strongest. We two will pull.

(*They go ahead.*)

THE NURSE : You see, Madam, we can't get it out. It would be enough to unwrap the Master.

THE WIDOW (*stamping her foot*) : He got in, he can get out. It's too silly!

THE GUARD : We must turn it sideways.

THE WIDOW : Exactly.

THE NURSE : The face will be damaged. . . . The embalmer said . . .

THE WIDOW : The face! The face! It is so little like him. . . . We're not going to let this boy be ruined because of ridiculous, hysterical sentimentalism.

THE GUARD : It's going through.

THE WIDOW : Fine. It's gone!

(*The sarcophagus disappears outside.*)

THE GUARD : Madam . . . how can I thank you?

THE WIDOW : Easily. (*To the nurse*) Explain it to him.

THE NURSE : Oh, all right. . . . (*She whispers in the guard's ear.*)

THE GUARD (*red in the face*) : Oh!

THE WIDOW : I'm going to whisper my name to you. Listen. (*She tells him. A long embrace.*)

THE NURSE : Madam was clever to leave me her fortune. It won't leave the family vault. We're rich!

THE GUARD : Rich! To live here, how blissful! Silence . . . flowers . . . and you will live!

THE WIDOW : I thought my first husband was extremely independent by nature, that the bridle had to be left slightly loose, so as not to make it look as though he was being supervised.

THE GUARD : She thinks of everything!

THE NURSE : She's an intelligent woman . . .

THE GUARD : And she's got a heart!

THE WIDOW : I've reached the age of reason, alas!

THE GUARD : Naughty! It's my turn to whisper my name in your ear. (*He embraces the widow.*)

THE WIDOW : Nursie, he'll be the death of me!

THE NURSE : Since you make him live, that's all right. Death's death. Now speak only of life!

# The Ox on the Roof

When I first wrote about Cocteau in 1955 I regarded him as a choreographer, and I used the word in both the literal and figurative sense, for he was a creative person who by means of dance-design united music and décor into a ballet, which is a theatrical poem. It is impossible to repeat too often that Cocteau regarded himself as a poet.

It was the ballet, notably that directed by the great Russian impresario Serge Diaghilev, which roused Cocteau to creative existence in 1909 and the years immediately following. All through his life Cocteau remained close to the world of ballet and his creation in 1946 for Jean Babilée, *Le Jeune Homme et la Mort*, will always be important in the history of theatrical dancing. His participation in ballet was of varying kinds, the first being as writer (with Federico 'Coco' Madrazo) of the scenario for *Le Dieu Bleu*, a Fokine ballet created for Nijinsky in 1911. The story was based on a Hindu legend, the costumes and sets by Bakst were magnificent, the music by Reynaldo Hahn is now forgotten and the ballet was not a success. Cocteau had not yet 'found' himself, or to use his own phrase he had not yet 'fallen asleep', not yet learnt how to write what was in his unconscious mind. After the traumatic experiences of watching Nijinsky dance in Stravinsky's *Petrouchka* and *Le Sacre du Printemps* Cocteau longed to express himself through dancers on the stage.

Naturally, he had no ambitions to work as a choreographer within the framework of the classical tradition. His ballet would be a Cocteau ballet, a synthesis of all that was new and stimulating at that moment. In 1917 came *Parade*, 'a realistic ballet' with the collaboration of Picasso and Erik Satie. It was danced by the Ballets Russes of Diaghilev, and it is interesting to note that the choreography was by Léonide Massine 'after plastic indications given by the author'. The ballet used lifelike gestures, and consisted of the music-hall turns and acrobatic performances admired by Cocteau. He relished virtuosity for its own sake.

Cocteau wrote a great deal about the reception of *Parade*; the ballet caused much excitement and *scandale* but was a failure. Its half-page synopsis tells us nothing, it is no more than history, embellished now by a drawing of Picasso smoking a pipe and embracing one of the characters, the 'little American girl'. The author claims, in a note at the end, that in this ballet 'gestures from life were, for the first time, amplified and magnified into dance'.

Three years later, in 1920, came a 'ballet' which is described by Cocteau as a 'Farce, imagined and directed by the author'. This was *The Ox on the Roof* (Le Boeuf sur le Toit), or *The Nothing Doing Bar*. The work came into being, like most ballets of any interest, through a form of spontaneous combustion. The starting-point was a score by Darius Milhaud, a member of the *Groupe des Six*, and Cocteau, who had now moved away from Diaghilev, decided to create a pantomime which could use the three famous Fratellini brothers, who were superb clown-acrobats. He acted as a choreographer here at all levels – he created his ballet out of elements apparently unrelated to each other and, having fused them together, he showed his interpreters exactly what he wanted them to do.

It did not have an entirely smooth passage on to the stage, for Guy-Pierre Fauconnet, who was designing the sets and costumes, died of a heart-attack before his work was finished. He was quickly replaced by Raoul Dufy and the work was produced at the Comédie des Champs-Elysées on 21st February. It was a success and was performed in London five months later, with its English subtitle and an English cast. It formed one item in a curious programme staged at the London Coliseum, a programme which included Ruth Draper, the famous clown Grock, and various other performers unremembered today.

The performance in Paris was such a success that Louis Moysès, the proprietor of the Bar Gaya, asked Cocteau's permission to call his new bar *Le Boeuf sur le Toit*, and the place became a favourite rendezvous for Cocteau and his friends, a centre of literary and artistic activity.

Milhaud's score is still played and there is still a bar of the same name in Paris, in the Rue du Colisée. People have asked how the ox got there, which raises the question of whether Cocteau's inventive genius was matched by the accuracy of his memory. It is known that Darius Milhaud composed the music after a visit to Brazil, and had thought that it might be used as an accompaniment to a Chaplin film. In a footnote to the scenario of the ballet Cocteau wrote (in 1949) : 'The title *Le Boeuf sur le Toit* was an

emblem of Brazil. It was given to me by Paul Claudel.' The latter
of course had been French Ambassador there for several years. In
1970 Cocteau's biographer Francis Steegmuller reported that a
specialist in Brazilian folklore had asserted that there was no legend
on the subject – 'the title is merely a picturesque combination of
words'. This is one of many minor mysteries encountered in a study
of Cocteau and his work. Fortunately it is not essential to find the
solution, but the situation illustrates how easily Cocteau could blend
fact and fantasy together.

It would be cheering to think that the work might one day be
performed again, for it symbolizes a whole era, but without the
Fratellini brothers, and without Cocteau, the supreme *animateur*,
this seems unlikely. However, a reading of the scenario can revive
some of its delights. When it was first produced the ballet was
intensely modern, even anticipating the future. Now it typifies and
perpetuates a moment which inaugurated the 1920s. It is included
here because of its undeniably theatrical story line.

The Ox on the Roof is a bar with harsh lighting. A contorted screen in yellow wood conceals the wings on the right. The corner of a billiard-table protrudes beyond the left flat, on which plum-coloured drapery is painted. To the left, forward, a leather arm-chair. To the right, forward, a table. Table and chair, visible in front of the curtain, announce the vulgarity of the décor like a sort of prologue. They take their place in the set as soon as the curtain rises. Fan in the ceiling. The fan turns slowly and casts shadows over the performers. They are wearing cardboard head-dresses three times as big as their heads. They behave in accordance with the style of the décor. They are *moving décor*. With the heaviness of deep-sea divers, each of them executes in slow-motion, and in opposition to the music, the gestures essential to his or her role.

The accessories, bottles, glasses, straws, cigarettes, chalk and saucers are on the same scale as the postiche heads.

From the front border, which is painted with multicoloured flags, hang five smoke-rings made out of tulle which start from the armchair and move towards the centre. As the curtain goes up the barman, who is all pink and white, is alone. He is shaking cocktails behind the bar. A cigar as big as a torpedo is burning on a table behind the armchair. Enter, left, the Negro boxer with the sky-blue pullover, coming from the billiard-room. He orders a cocktail, flexes his muscles, falls into the armchair, crosses his legs and picks up his cigar again. Immediately the smoke-rings belong to him. A Negro boy, in shirt-sleeves, comes out of the billiard-room, moving backwards. He marks a billiard cue with chalk. The boxer asks the barman to cut his cigar which is drawing badly. The barman cuts it by firing his revolver. The shot knocks the Negro boy over backwards. During all the first part of the performance he can be seen playing billiards in the wings, raising his leg, and taking aim, as in American lithographs.

Enter, one after the other : the décolletée lady, in a red dress, very mannered, very common. The red-headed lady, with hair made of paper, pretty, mannish in style, slightly round-shouldered, her hands in her pockets. The man in the rexine suit, who looks at his wrist-watch and does not leave his bar-stool again until he goes out. A scarlet bookmaker, with gold teeth, who wears a grey bowler and a sporting tie kept in place by a pearl as big as a round garden ball.

All these strange people sit down and play dice. (The dice game between the man and the bookmaker should be a mechanical tableau composed of their heads, the barman's head behind a newspaper with type as large as on a poster, and the two dice, real cardboard boxes which they move by spinning them round on their axes.) The elegant lady powders her face and discovers the Negro boy. He climbs on to a stool. She takes him on her shoulder and carries him into the billiard-room. The red-headed lady crosses the stage, takes away the smoke-rings with her arm, puts them round the barman's neck and winks at the boxer. The boxer leaves his chair to follow her. The bookmaker sees them, becomes angry, quivers with rage, comes up quietly, takes out his pearl tie-pin and hits the Negro over the head with it. The Negro collapses. The Negro boy drops his billiard cue, helps the boxer up, puts him down in the chair and fans him with a towel.

A little dance of triumph by the bookmaker. Tango by the women. A whistle. It's the police ! Everyone shudders. The barman hangs up a notice, *Only milk served here*, hides the glasses and bottles, hands out bowls and whisks the milk in a churn.

The giant policeman puts his head through the wings. He enters. He looks round. He goes up to everyone to smell their breath. He tastes the milk.

Under the influence of the bucolic atmosphere he performs a pleasant little dance.

While he revolves in the centre with the grace of a ballerina the barman operates a lever. The fan comes down and decapitates the policeman. He sways. He looks for his head, tries to put it back the wrong way round and falls down dead.

Nothing surprises the night-birds. After some brief rejoicing, during which the Negro sings a romantic song with his hand on his heart, the barman presents the head on a tray to the red-headed lady who has remained indifferent, looking into the wings on the left.

She dances. Her dance is a caricature of all Salome dances in general. She stretches, smokes, shakes the policeman's head like a cocktail. Finally she walks on her hands like the Salome in Rouen Cathedral, goes round the head and, still walking on her hands, leaves the bar, followed by the bookmaker.

Before disappearing after them, the décolletée lady turns round, takes the rose from the buttonhole of the man in the suit and throws it at the barman. The man pays and they go out.

The boxer wakes, stands up, staggers and goes out in his turn, followed by the Negro boy, who refuses to pay the barman.

Left on his own, the barman tidies up. He sees the policeman's body. He drags it as best he can up to a chair behind the table. The dead body tries to find its equilibrium. Once the body is wedged in position the barman brings piles of saucers which he puts on the table and a bottle of gin which he empties into the body. He picks up the head and puts it back between the shoulders. He tickles it and mesmerizes it. The policeman comes back to life. Then the barman unrolls a bill three yards long in front of him.

PS. The title *Le Boeuf sur Le Toit* was an emblem of Brazil. It was given to me by Paul Claudel.

# Telephone Ringing in an Empty Street

Of all Cocteau's collections of poems *Opéra* is one of the best known. It contains the famous *L'Ange Heurtebise* which evokes the poet's struggle with himself during the creative process, and has been associated also with memories of Radiguet, *Prière Mutilée* and the extraordinary collection of short prose poems *Musée Secret*. Many of these pieces were written at the Hôtel Welcome in Villefranche where, as Cocteau wrote in his preface to a new edition of the collection in 1959, 'so many modern myths were born. My few readers confused the oracular style of certain pieces with puns. What was more, I was far from thinking that the atmosphere of this little book would finally put out to sea. In our Villefranche there were the kind of secrets one whispers into one another's ears. And I can still see myself circulating between my room and those of Glenway Wescott and Monroe Wheeler in order to read them the texts of *Musée Secret*, texts in which I endowed our enigmas with the chilly air of a trial'.

Puns are usually regarded now as a low form of humour but Cocteau used them in all seriousness as signs of free association. The play *Orphée*, which dates from the same period (1925, the year the poems were written), is full of them. It is hard therefore to produce a satisfactory translation of these poems, for the additional overtones of meaning are inevitably lost. In the prose-poem from *Musée Secret* which follows, the word *plinthe* – meaning 'plinth' of 'column' – has the same sound in French as *plainte,* a complaint or lament. Several other examples of this word-play occur in this short poem and the 'Greece/grease' link gives some idea of Cocteau's style at this time. Some readers will find it dated, but others will no doubt agree with the French critic Jacques Brosse who wrote of Cocteau's 'technical discovery : how to use language in order to make it express the unsayable'.

The atmosphere of strange still silence following some unexplained violent crime is typical of much writing by Cocteau at this period and occurs also in the film *Le Sang d'un Poète*.

Among the friends who stayed at the Hôtel Welcome in Ville-franche during the composition of *Opéra* was the artist Christian Bérard who became famous later as a theatrical designer. He made a suitably dramatic design for the first edition of *Opéra* which included a red curtain.

The window through which the criminal entered was dark. His leg climbed over it and one of his hands cried Help! while leaving a very clear mark on the plinth. A crime soils everything. It dragged along an incredible amount of filth, empty bottles, ribbed glasses beside them. Rough wine dripped from the handle of the knife, from a disgusting parcel badly tied up and sealed with red sealing-wax. The curtains torn down by the woman as she fell had dragged the bust with them. She herself was dead asleep in her ball dress and her right hand still held the anonymous letter. Life had ebbed away backwards from the body, striking with anything whatsoever, breaking a gilt chair whose remains floated in a pool of blood which is moving across and beginning to soak through the ceiling of the floor below. The unfortunate man had fled over the roofs without knowing that Ancient Grease not only leaves marks on every mirror but also leaves no doubt about the nature of bodies cut into pieces.

Now I remember very well having gone down the street on the night of the crime and hearing the telephone ring and feeling surprised that nobody answered it because of a chandelier that one could see through the window lighting up this ghastly scene with the indifferent brilliance of stars.

# Ode to Picasso

In Cocteau's life Picasso was as important as Stravinsky. The poet and the artist met in 1915, went to Rome together and worked on the ballet *Parade*, which was to cause such excitement in Paris two years later.

Picasso contributed two monograms and a portrait of Cocteau to *Le Coq et l'Arlequin* in 1918. Cocteau's own drawing of Picasso, with pipe and bowler hat and talking to Stravinsky, has become a classic. Cocteau refers to Picasso at many points throughout his work and in 1953 he gave a brilliant extemporised talk about him in Rome. Fortunately it was recorded and was published in *La Corrida du Ier Mai* four years later. It is included in my own anthology of Cocteau's portraits of people, *My Contemporaries*. An early essay about Picasso (1923), reprinted in *Le Rappel à l'Ordre* three years later, may also be found in the *Poésie Critique*, Volume I.

In spite of Cocteau's lifelong admiration for Picasso there were periods of coolness between the two men from time to time, attributable to various causes, but even Picasso's lack of response did not lead Cocteau to lose his enthusiasm towards the painter.

The *Ode to Picasso* (L'Ode à Picasso, 1919) might be regarded as an 'essay in indirect criticism'. It evokes Picasso as a tamer of the muses through a daring use of magic, card-games and mathematics. A few examples of word-play defy translation, but Picasso's work is as recognizable in this poem as is the human head in the most controversial periods of his semi-representational painting.

## I  THE SEATED MAN

The mirror's gold
circles roundabout.

The tamer of muses, who ties
a saucepan

to the poodle in the troupe,
is punished in his turn
and contemplates
a dirty trick,
a spoke in the wheel, for,
having teased them, he was
caught in their fearsome dance,
and he's looking

for a way to get out.


II   THE MUSES

The accident which could have happened
ends in flight.

>        CASTING OUT NINES;
>        he was playing alone
>        and his hand puts the muses out of place.

Four queens :
a hinge doubles the number;
eight of them now
        and the idler, Polyhymnia.

The
nine
new
muses,
all but one, for
the surplus Polyhymnia
(she lives with me)
takes me to the picador's place;
but the master's eye sends her
back at once
to number 9
and her thumb spreads out the group
like a fan.

Even in this cloister
little Erato is angry
through being lovely without any hair.

A tonic sol-fa of thicknesses
drapes Euterpe;

once they conducted orchestras
in the palace of the note factory,
whose motor beats
it's your heart.

Terpsichore, taking care
to support all these ladies
well balanced
on her hip,
with a costume of velvet and gold.

Listening to your magic guitar,
objects follow you Orpheus
until they acquire the shape you wish.

Bar-counter Clio, Calliope
telephones news items
and Urania lights the gas-lamps
which beautify the chestnut trees below.

Punch and Judy       the guillotine
      Thalia
      and
      Melpomene.
Then the drums of Santerre
make you silent, chattering queens.

           The solitary man
           eats the city.

His distributor delivers you
completely different.
    He shares out
   the sun      the shade
and since he's broken his guitar
over Clio's big head,
she sways and she forgets
the order of dates.

     He marries you. He sends you away.
     He walks along the asphalt pavement

so soft at half past seven in September
beside the great ink-anchor cafés
where death wrote its letters
beneath a Christmas chandelier.

Where? Who? What? What? He frees you
and consults obedience.

The bat opens a right-angled eye.

Dancer dressed in paint.

*Maison close* in every sense :
astonishing discovery.

A rope-soled silence
precedes the pimp
whom Mnemosyne pays nine times,
for she keeps precise accounts
concerning her daughters.

Nothing in his sleeves      Nothing in his pockets
                Would some gentleman
                    lend his hat
to the harlequin from Port-Royal.

# A Friend Sleeps

Cocteau, as we know, regarded himself as a 'poet', in the original sense of the Greek word meaning creator. All his life he wrote poetry, publishing many collections and sometimes single poems such as *L'Ode à Picasso* or *La Crucifixion*. Both these poems were written in the form dictated to the poet by their content, the second one in unrhymed stanzas of varying length, the first in a style of total freedom.

It may seem paradoxical perhaps that Cocteau, who was always interested in anything new, wrote so much poetry in orthodox verse forms with regular or mainly regular rhyming stanzas, such as *Léone* (1945), *Le Chiffre Sept* (1952) and *Cérémonial Espagnol du Phénix* (1961). The poem here entitled *A Friend Sleeps* (Un Ami Dort, 1948) is also written, like the others mentioned, in rhymed quatrains, a fact which obviously makes translation even more difficult than usual. Before reading Mary Hoeck's translation one should remember a few telling sentences that Cocteau wrote in *Coupures de Presse* : 'A poem is not written in the language used by the poet. Poetry is a language of its own and cannot be translated into any other, even into that in which it seems to have been written.' I have heard many poets say that they need only a slight knowledge of a language to read poetry, whereas they remain cut off from even simple prose.

*A Friend Sleeps* is perhaps the first time a poet has written a loving and deeply meditative poem about his feelings as he watches the man he loves sleeping. The poem evokes a man's love for a younger man and is a kind of nostalgic leave-taking. The speaker has reached that stage of emotion where he regards himself as a friend, not a lover. He does not wake the sleeping man, as a lover would have done, but watches his sleep.

There are references to Cocteau's play *L'Aigle à Deux Têtes* and the poem *Plain-Chant* of the early 'twenties.

Your hands upon the sheets were my dead leaves,
    My autumn loved your summer glow.
The wind of memory bangs doors and leaves
    Nothing of where we went or go.

I let your selfish sleep spin out its lies
    Where dreams will hide your trace.
You think you are sure-placed. How sad the ties
    Which link us to an unsure place.

You lived bemused within another self,
    And from your body freed so well,
You seemed set stone. How hard upon this shelf
    To see only the beloved shell.

Still, but awake, I visited the rooms
    Where we shall walk no more,
Sped through the air while still my hands as tombs
    Cupped head as they had done before.

When I returned to where my body sat,
    Once more I dully saw
Your eyelids closed, your breath, and, open flat,
    Your hand, your mouth full of night's awe.

Could we but be an eagle with two heads,
    Or Janus looking East and West,
Siamese twins, shown in the circus sheds,
    Or single-threaded book at best.

Love makes of lovers but one monster, joy
    Full of their cries, their mane,
This monster joy, its own self will destroy
    With four devouring hands again.

What then can friendship do to loneliness,
    Whither can friendship go?
What is the maze where all our study's less
    Than sleep-found friends can know?

But what is happening to me? Can sleep
    My eyelids close down fast?
I would not sleep, unless by dreaming deep
    I dive into your dreams at last.

How beautiful a face which nought disturbs!
  Sleep which holds back the breath,
Embalms and polishes, all feeding curbs,
  Like Egypt's gold-masked death.

I contemplated by your side your face
  Which knows nought of my grief.
Your waves died on my shore and left no trace
  For my tired heart's relief.

Radiance of friendship shines, so this world dares
  (Grudging the life of friends)
To cast the name of 'love', with all its snares
  On friends, and friendship ends.

Time holds its breath before our cloister walls,
  What time or day is this?
When either love may find, no silence falls
  To hide our swift-shared bliss.

You run, but not the way I ran before.
  Which is your way, whence mine?
Not ours the way of China's monsters, nor
  Hindu flutes divine.

Fused at the height of ecstasy in love,
  Lovers in love by loving joined,
You are winged ogres, perched above
  The Norman capitals engroined.

We who have parted arms but knotted souls
  (The body seeks this knot),
Our hell has no lit flame. The void has goals
  For dead who need to share their lot.

Elbowed beside your bed, I see the beats
  Your heart proves on your brow.
Before your blood's red sea, my lamp retreats . . .
  No look may plumb it now.

While one of us in mirrored memory dips,
  The other sees in pictures light
The sunshine and the sea in watered strips,
  Through windows paint the ceiling bright.

Meanwhile your inner eye a vision sees.
    I only need to take
Your arm, when toppling down your temple flees
    The dream you wrought – you wake.

Motionless I waited while you slept,
    Elbow on knee, chin high.
I could not pass the sign-post, closely kept.
    Unlinked our flesh by any tie.

I dreamt, you dreamt, things gravitate around,
    Blood, constellations turn.
Time, which is meaningless, is swiftness bound;
    With swift hate nations burn.

Your clothes thrown down, the folds, their stuff took on
    Their shadow-play, their bits
Resembled bodies after some clash-on,
    Make them scare-crow hits.

Far from your bed, upon the ground, your shoe
    Lay dying, with a life which waned. . . .
These strayings from your life – they can hurt too –
    Can sleepers be constrained?

Your shoe took on your life, the way you walked,
    It held your step enclosed.
And had your sleeve held pointed as you talked
    A gun aimed and posed?

Here in the suburb, death may pay a call,
    A villa be a tomb.
Your placid face could mirror and forestall
    All these in its closed room.

I went my way, sick to the heart of dreams,
    As in my 'Plain Chant' time.
My time on earth now less, the sunshine streams,
    Long-shadowed as I climb.

Amongst all other shadows, this is mine,
    I know the way it goes.
This on the desert sand I can divine
    As my form's form, shadowed, it flows.

The shadow-picture my ill-luck portrays ...
    Can any hope my shadow fill?
Only the ending day, and moonlight lays
    Myself behind me on the hill.

Enough, I will return. Confused remain –
    Only you can change your gait
While love may wake the loved one and so gain,
    In deference friends wait.

Automatons, false stars, now fill the sky,
    And eagles, human-faced abound,
So, when you wake, to battle you must fly.
    Sleep-plundered you must not be found.

# The Palais-Royal Impromptu

In his preface to the short play that follows Cocteau explained how he came to write it. Since he had always liked actors he agreed to write an 'impromptu' or curtain-raiser to be played just before Molière's famous comedy *Les Fourberies de Scapin* by a group from the Comédie-Française who went on a tour in Japan in 1961.

Molière himself had written 'impromptus' and critiques of his own plays, to which Cocteau refers in this text. Cocteau found himself inspired to write it after seeing a children's matinée performance of *La Critique de l'Ecole des Femmes* and remembered also improvised performances given by his actor friends. 'I planned to marry together,' wrote Cocteau, 'without the slightest prudence, the actors and the characters whom they incarnate, to make them into one mixture, comparable to the tales of Selma Lagerlof, Lewis Carroll and the fables of La Fontaine, in which animals speak the language of men. For Molière was being affectionate when he wrote : "Ah, what strange animals actors are when you have to direct them." In short I had to solve the problem of a one-act comic play which would be serious and allow me, through the intervention of a slightly pedantic actress-spectator, to say certain things of importance to me about the inexplicable phenomenon of Time.'

In some ways the play might appear to be a kind of private joke only accessible to those with a knowledge of social and cultural life under the Sun King. The French critic Jacques Brosse has described the *Impromptu* as 'not only a brilliant divertissement, but an extremely original essay in theatre within theatre and even theatre within theatre within theatre, taken to infinity and even to the extent of making us dizzy'.

CHARACTERS

First Marquis
Woman spectator (in the balcony)
The Duke
Second Marquis
The Marquise de Montespan
The stage manager (in modern dress)
Molière
The King
Saint-Simon
The gorgon Sthéno
Monsieur, the King's brother
The prompter
Extras : Third and Fourth Marquis

*In front of the curtain the lights come on. The minuet from*
Le Bourgeois Gentilhomme *can be heard in the distance. The*
*First Marquis enters at the side in front of the curtain. He is*
*just putting on his jacket and is carrying his plumed felt hat*
*under his arm. He signals to the audience to be patient, goes*
*to look on to the stage either through the observation slit or*
*between the curtains and advances mysteriously towards the*
*prompter's box as he finishes dressing.*

FIRST MARQUIS : Quickly, ladies and gentlemen, quickly. It's
urgent. Our author's a famous chatterbox and I'm taking
advantage of the fact that he's probably going round from
dressing-room to dressing-room imitating what Baudelaire
tells us about his meeting in Belgium with Victor Hugo. Hugo
abandoned himself, he says, to one of those monologues which
he called conversation. That leaves me a few moments free
before the curtain rises. And if you ask why a marquis from
the Court of Versailles is talking about Hugo and Baudelaire
I will explain that in spite of my costume I'm not a marquis
at all but an actor, that is to say a man who travels in time
and assumes its faces, a man who is what he is, believes he's
something he isn't and if he doesn't believe he's something he
isn't he tries to make other people believe so. Now, our author
holds very strange ideas about the problem of time. He believes
for example that time is all rolled up in advance like a film in

its can, that we can only see this film shot by shot, but there's nothing to stop some indiscreet person from picking out some shot by chance, in the middle of the reel.

There's the essential thing about this *Impromptu*; a ghastly mixture of what we are and what we aren't. A trap! For apparently we're being given our head. 'I'm leaving you as free as possible', those were the author's very words. There's a subtle trap that he conceals beneath his praise. It means that if we improvise, and improvise boldly enough to ruin the play, he'll make us responsible.

Don't be mistaken. The remarkable things you're going to hear are definitely by him and we've learnt them. It's possible that one of us might move away from the text and embroider, but on the whole it's the author alone who's expressing himself and I wouldn't want to be the victim of this imbroglio.

WOMAN SPECTATOR : Imbreuio.

FIRST MARQUIS : I beg your pardon?

WOMAN SPECTATOR : One doesn't say the Prince de Broglio but the Prince de Breuil. Imbroglio should be pronounced *imbreuio*.

FIRST MARQUIS : One always learns something new.

WOMAN SPECTATOR : Quite so. Young people are racist in the sense that they are one race and old people are another. And since I don't yet belong by any means to the other race I address myself not to your age but to our lively race by crossing the conventional and unfair barrier which condemns the public to silence.

FIRST MARQUIS : There's proof already of the adventures we are liable to encounter through this famous liberty the author offers us. I've made a note of it. Where was I?

WOMAN SPECTATOR : You were at *imbreuio*.

FIRST MARQUIS : Oh yes. I wouldn't want to be taken in, I was saying, by this imbreuio. (*He pronounces the word with difficulty.*) What's more I haven't been mandated by my friends and I'm taking the risk of being expelled by the management, but I wanted to be of service to our troupe by putting the audience on guard and not letting the author play one of his tricks on us and get away with it.

WOMAN SPECTATOR : Tell me now, marquis, there's a word for your behaviour – aren't you being a sneak?

FIRST MARQUIS : Very well. Let's say I'm a sneak. But it occurs to me, perhaps you're not a real spectator and you're going to pay me back in my own coin?

WOMAN SPECTATOR : You know me very well, my friend. Don't pretend to be innocent. It's true that I belong to the Theatre.

Only I've come to this play as a spectator and I take advantage
of the freedom the author allows us to interrupt the acting
and in a way I can make the audience play its part. After all,
why not?

FIRST MARQUIS : Just what I was saying. You're going to give the
show away, sneak on the sneak and report to the management
the courageous initiative I've taken.

WOMAN SPECTATOR : Don't be frightened. It's precisely because I
dare to take a risk myself and because the adventure amuses
me that I won't repeat anything.

FIRST MARQUIS (*going to look through the observation slit or
between the curtains*) : Good heavens! Time may be an illusion but we have to live through it. I'm off. We'll soon be
hearing three knocks. I don't want to be caught in the act.

(*The three knocks are heard.*)

WOMAN SPECTATOR : Too late, my friend, too late. Now you're a
victim of that chattering of which you accused the author.
You'll have to manage. The curtain's going up.

(*The curtain rises or parts. There is no scenery. The stage is
empty, ready for what follows. There are in addition three
panels with doors, standing freely, so that the actors can be
seen approaching them. One of these doors opens on to the
back of the stage. The two others open at an angle, one facing
the left of the stage, the other the right. Three chandeliers
hang in the middle. As the curtain goes up the Duke is
arranging two chairs at a gaming-table covered with a cloth.
He places them in such a way that one faces the audience and
one has its back to it. On the table is cardboard food and
a bucket from which emerges the neck of a champagne bottle.
Four red velvet stools are lined up far left and far right. The
three Marquises come towards the front of the stage.*)

SECOND MARQUIS (*to the First Marquis*) : So, dear sir, we've been
looking for you and ringing for you. What are you doing on
the other side of the coin?

FIRST MARQUIS (*leading the others towards the centre of the stage*) :
Do forgive me! I had strayed into the world of the audience
and I was trying to get back to our world.

SECOND MARQUIS (*in a falsetto voice*) : Dammit, marquis, since
we've found you, have you heard the news?

FIRST MARQUIS : I have, marquis.

SECOND MARQUIS : Isn't it the most unbelievably awful news in the world?

FIRST MARQUIS : The most awfully unbelievable!

THIRD MARQUIS (*shouting*) : The most . . .

SECOND MARQUIS (*interrupting him*) : Be silent, sir! You're still a pupil at the Conservatoire and you haven't the right to speak. That doesn't prevent you from observing us in silence and, in silence, learning to mime your dissatisfaction. (*The Third Marquis throws his hat down on the ground and is about to stamp on it.*) You're overdoing it! Moderation, whatever happens. Moderation. . . . (*The Third Marquis picks up his hat and raises his arms to heaven.*)

THE DUKE (*who had gone out through the door, left, and returns with some plates which he arranges on the table*) : My head's splitting. Couldn't we be living through one of those bad jokes inflicted on us by sleep?

FIRST MARQUIS : It's no dream, alas, but the craziest piece of reality.

THE DUKE : The King invites Monsieur Molière to his table!

SECOND MARQUIS : And we have to obey.

FIRST MARQUIS (*to the Duke*) : And you have to wait on him and take the soups and a napkin to this cad.

THE DUKE : Just as it is glorious to serve the King so do I feel ashamed to humiliate myself in front of a scoundrel.

SECOND MARQUIS : I understand you, my dear duke. It must be painful to submit to the orders of the knave who satirizes us and irritates us in his buffooneries.

THE DUKE : So, gentlemen, I have decided to tell His Majesty what I think of it and to complain about the task which he is imposing on me.

FIRST MARQUIS : I'm very doubtful about that.

THE DUKE : I'm not. You'll see me hard at work.

SECOND MARQUIS (*nudging the First Marquis with his elbow*) : Bravo, your grace.

FIRST MARQUIS : For it's not a good thing to thwart the King's whims. I find it admirable that you're planning to do so and you're showing a heroism that nobody here can envisage.

THE DUKE : His Majesty cannot enjoy dishonouring a gentleman of his suite and I assume that he will approve of my attitude, however strange it is.

SECOND MARQUIS : Sound the horn, your grace, and drive your point home.

THE DUKE (*holding his head high*) : I certainly shall.

FIRST MARQUIS (*aside to the audience*) : Farewell, Versailles. . . .

*(Enter through the door at the back the Marquise de Montespan.)*

THE MARQUISE : Gentlemen, I see astonishment written on your faces and that my presence disconcerts you. To be honest, there is no reason why I should come onstage before His Majesty. But I was tempted to appear in this *Impromptu* and I was looking for a pretext. Don't think that it's just to show off one of the fine costumes of Françoise Athénaïs de Mortemart de Rochechouart, Marquise de Montespan. I've made the author my accomplice. Let's imagine with him that you've interceded through me to convince His Majesty that it isn't good for his *amour propre* to set an example for an extraordinary reversal of Etiquette and dissuade him from his plan of admitting Monsieur Molière to his table. I have given the King seven children and you must admit that I have a certain hold over him. But there is a limit to it. When the King wants something he really wants it. He enjoys throwing his Christians to the lions and paying homage to his beast-tamers. We'll all have the same fate, gentlemen, however great we are. Unfortunately Monsieur Jourdain will not be his only scapegoat. Imagine now that I've failed in my embassy and that His Majesty has turned a deaf ear to me. I realize, your grace, that you're pulling a long face now and the Marquises are ruffling their plumage. But apart from the fact that we must obey the King, we're playing a double game here. Won't this be the moment to pretend that we're jealous of the good fortune which falls to one of our friends, the chance to play the part of the man whose name our theatre has the honour to bear? That we plotted to deprive him of a part that was bigger than ours? In short, don't let's make confusion worse confounded. I've said my say. I pride myself that my words were strong enough to justify their brevity and support what you have to say. I return to the glorious shade in which I rest and abandon you to your dance of death. Dance, gentlemen. May one of the minuets which once accompanied our splendours accompany you. Gentlemen, we had more than our fair share. A period in which France believed itself to be the centre of the universe with the rest of the world at its beck and call. Dance, with one foot on the ground and one foot in dream. Dance between heaven and earth. Limp like Jacob after he had wrestled with the angel. It is through this divine limp that the gait of poets can be recognized. Dance at the end of the strings that the invisible author manipulates above us. I leave you.

Monsieur Molière must be already waiting in the ante-room for the doors to be opened.

THE DUKE : What are you insinuating, madam, that I will also have to open the door to him?

THE MARQUISE : No, your grace. The stage manager is responsible for that. Goodbye. (*She moves towards the door at the back and, just as she is leaving*) That doesn't mean that I wouldn't rather be in my shoes than yours. (*And with a laugh she goes off.*)

THE DUKE : It's the limit! My head's splitting. I can't make head or tail of it.

FIRST MARQUIS : Obedience without understanding is the loftiest dignity of duty, your grace. And what's more, aren't you going to rise to the attack?

THE DUKE : I am still aware of an injury to my pride which will take a long time to heal. (*Raising his eyes to heaven, with indignation*) Monsieur Molière!

SECOND MARQUIS : Silence. There he is.

(*The door at the right opens.*)

WOMAN SPECTATOR : Don't look so miserable. Face up to things.

THE DUKE : If the audience joins in, that makes it even worse. My head's splitting!

(*Enter the stage manager in modern dress.*)

STAGE MANAGER (*announcing*) : Monsieur Poquelin.

MOLIERE (*entering*) : Are you out of your mind?

STAGE MANAGER : I thought it would be amusing ...

MOLIERE : You amuse no one. Our job consists in confusing the true and the false. I beg you to announce me by the false name that I have made famous enough for nobody to be unaware of it and, although I'm flattered that you know me well enough to be aware of my real name, I advise you to introduce me as you should.

THE DUKE (*half aloud while Molière goes off again*) : The pride of this good-for-nothing staggers me.

STAGE MANAGER (*announcing Molière's second entry*) : Monsieur Molière. (*He goes off.*)

MOLIERE : Gentlemen, I am not unaware of the scandal I am causing and that a man of my station does not deserve to be your equal. Understand that I am the first to feel the embarrassment of it and if it were not by order of the King I would never have dared aspire to it and impose my presence upon you.

THE DUKE : It is true, sir, that we give way against our will.

MOLIERE : Everyone has his prerogatives, your grace.

THE DUKE : I should be amused to know yours.

MOLIERE : They are those of a man of the theatre. And, for example, they force me to point out to you that these chairs are by no means placed as they should be.

THE DUKE : Sir !

WOMAN SPECTATOR : He's right.

MOLIERE : Your grace, ask this spectator, who seems to know about these things, why these chairs are not placed where they ought to be.

*(Everyone turns towards the woman spectator.)*

WOMAN SPECTATOR : The chairs force one of the characters to turn his back on the audience.

MOLIERE : Me, as it happens.

WOMAN SPECTATOR : Which is what an actor doesn't like.

MOLIERE : Especially when the places have been worked out by a friend.

THE DUKE : Sir ! I'd like to be a real duke and persuade the King to ennoble you so that I could provoke you to a duel and run my sword through you.

MOLIERE : These hypotheses are overweening.

THE DUKE : The devil take you !

FIRST MARQUIS : I swoon !

SECOND MARQUIS : I die !

MOLIERE : Swoon, gentlemen, die. Here is the King.

*(A deathly silence. The door at the back opens. The stage manager enters.)*

STAGE MANAGER *(at the top of his voice)* : The King, *le Roué* !

THE KING *(entering)* : What do I hear?

STAGE MANAGER : I thought it would be amusing, since the author puts us at our ease, to adopt the pronunciation of the period.

THE KING : Firstly there is nothing to prove that it was the pronunciation of the period. Secondly you think too much. Thinking prevents action. You are only required to open and close the doors. You amuse no one.

STAGE MANAGER : It's hard for an actor to watch others act without joining in.

THE KING : I summon you to the administrator's office between ten and eleven tomorrow morning. He will decide on the suitable consequences to your impertinence. Furthermore, it is not part of your responsibility to inaugurate traditions.

THE DUKE (*shrugging his shoulders*) : Traditions?

THE KING : I know a little about the theatre. That kind of tradition has nothing to do with ours. Molière, will you please enlighten the Duke and explain to him the meaning of this term.

MOLIERE : With pleasure, sire. (*To the Duke*) The first time I played the part of Alceste in *The Misanthrope* I suddenly discovered the trick, as I came onstage, of breaking a chair, which amused the audience. The next day I broke another chair, the day after that yet another one and so on. But since the play met with some success, I didn't break the fifth chair. Chairs are expensive, your grace, and we're not very rich. Well, if I had gone on breaking chairs and my successors had imitated me, this angry gesture, in perpetuating itself, would be called a tradition.

THE KING : You see, duke, when a man is king in his own country you can always learn something from him. (*He claps his hands.*) To table! To table!

MOLIERE : Opposite the prompter, sire, naturally.

(*The King takes his seat opposite the prompter and Molière faces him. The Marquises sit down on the stools.*)

THE KING : Shall I admit to you, dear fellow, that when I'm not playing the part of King I take care of my figure and only have one meal a day. This means that I would be incapable of eating what Louis XIV ate. And since I'm pretending to be King, you're pretending to be Molière and this food is pretending to be food, we'll pretend to eat and the Duke will pretend to serve us. Except for the first soup; for it demands obedience to one of the rules of etiquette.

(*The Duke has entered, carrying a soup-tureen with distaste. With the tureen in his hands, he stops beside the King.*)

THE KING (*to Molière*) : Some regicidal kitchen-boy could have put poison in it. (*To the Duke*) Taste it.

(*The Duke looks obstinate.*)

MOLIERE : Sire, I assume that the Duke would be proud to exchange his life for yours. But he must be given time to commend his soul to God.

THE DUKE (*aside*) : A plague upon him!

THE KING : Taste it. Taste it, I tell you! (*The Duke raises the soup-ladle to his lips.*) I almost waited. (*The Duke staggers.*)

Could this imaginary soup be acquiring some reality in its turn? You're quite pale.

THE DUKE (*in a faint voice*) : No, sire, it's fear. (*He pretends to serve the King and Molière and says, as he goes out*) Does one know, in this devilment, where imitation begins? I'll never get used to it. (*He disappears through the door, left, with his soup-tureen.*)

FIRST MARQUIS : The scene's amusing and his expression's priceless.

(*The Marquises applaud and roar with laughter.*)

THE KING (*turning towards the Marquis*) : Stop, gentlemen. I was tolerating you as décor. But décor that starts to applaud ceases to be décor. Leave, gentlemen, and return to your chatter. Your lack of discipline forces me to summon you to the administrator's office. You are free. (*The Marquises leave through the door, right, after low bows.*) I thought they were too concerned with themselves to take any interest in our affairs. I was mistaken. This time we are alone. (*Molière smiles and indicates the audience to the King.*) Does one know if the three walls of our life are not four and if this fourth invisible wall does not conceal a crowd that is observing us?

WOMAN SPECTATOR (*laughing*) : That's 100 per cent Cocteau and King Louis XIV would never have had such an idea.

MOLIERE (*calling her to order*) : Madam ... madam ...

THE KING : I must, madam, communicate rapidly things of the greatest importance to Monsieur Molière and I command you not to intervene any more. (*To Molière*) Whether our solitude be true or false like the rest of the performance, I must, far from everyone, set out to you one of the reasons for our tête-à-tête. I'm keeping the main part as a titbit for the end. I must make a confession, Molière, I owe you an apology ...

MOLIERE : Is Your Majesty joking?

THE KING : Listen to me without interrupting. I should be dis-pleased if the Duke could hear us. If he brings in the second soup I shall be silent and I shall wait until he goes. Now then. I consider myself in some way as your collaborator and even as your accomplice. I have handed you victims, stimu-lated your verve against my doctors, my pedants, my cuckolds and my bores. When the court smiled in sickly fashion *because I was laughing,* we rejoiced over it in secret. Only the threats which were aimed at me through you were mere blusterings and you got away with it. The next offensive will be serious, very serious. And it will be my fault.

*(The Duke enters with the second soup. Silence. The King hums the Lulli minuet and drums on the table. The Duke serves, then he reaches the door, left, not without a glance from the wings towards the table.)*

THE DUKE *(to the audience)* : One might say that the sauce is curdling. *(He goes out.)*

THE KING *(to Molière)* : I had entrusted you with the entertainment that would result from exposing to ridicule one of those falsely devout people, one of those impostors whose airs compromise the faithful members of our Holy Mother the Church. I remember, alas, that our *Tartuffe* has fierce attacks in store for you and that my ministers let themselves be convinced by those who are waiting to see you make your first mistake.

MOLIERE : Sire, the phrase 'our *Tartuffe*' fills me with pride.

THE KING : I know, Molière, I know. The fact remains that I have terrible scruples about having dragged you into an adventure where I shan't be able to follow you and where I shall have to pretend to be in league with your enemies. This time the thunderbolt falls from on high.

MOLIERE : I shall therefore have the glory of sharing a secret with Your Majesty.

THE KING : Would it not be wise to give up *Tartuffe*?

MOLIERE : The devil! Don't let Your Majesty force me to disobey him.

THE KING : I know your obstinacy, but my conscience isn't good. . . .

MOLIERE : Be reassured, sire. Others have encountered these setbacks and have overcome them. In order to use the pathos of Monsieur Lysidas in my critique of the *School for Wives*, according to the 'continuum in which one puts oneself', our author has had or will have a bone to pick with similar cabals. He could write a critique of his play *Bacchus* in which witty people would utter words about him with an objective truth which forces him to make them responsible. Your Majesty knows this story. We have barely turned our backs before people slip into our pockets the mistakes, vices and crimes of our characters in order to show ironic and virtuous astonishment, after searching, to find on us things which we allege to belong to others and only know through hearsay.

THE KING : No doubt, but if circumstances oblige us to ratify the verdict of our judges I run a definite risk of being judged in my turn.

MOLIERE : What court would allow itself to judge the King.?

THE KING (*pointing to heaven*) : The supreme court.

MOLIERE : Sire, on the arms of one of your dukes can be seen the Holy Virgin saying to him : 'Put your hat on, cousin.' Your Majesty can imagine, in view of this celestial privilege, those to which, from a hierarchical point of view, Your Majesty can aspire.

THE KING : Words! We are only linked together by words.

WOMAN SPECTATOR (*putting her hand up as in school*) : Montaigne!

THE KING (*as though he had not heard*) : But God doesn't worry about words. He judges us by our deeds. As to my dukes ... my dukes ... it happens in fact that I suspect one of them of taking a little too much interest in our discussion. (*The King rises.*) Remain seated. (*Leaning towards Molière, as he stands*) I have sharp ears and you'll see if I'm mistaken.

(*During the last few seconds a little nobleman has come up through the wings to the door on the right and has started to listen. Behind him stands a young girl in the peplum of a tragedienne. The King puts a finger to his lips and walks on tiptoe to the door. He opens it suddenly. The nobleman falls over on to the stage.*)

THE KING : So, Monsieur de Saint-Simon, you listen outside doors?

SAINT-SIMON : I would be ungracious in denying it. Only, if I was listening at this door, it was in order to await a favourable moment which would allow me to introduce a young actress in whom I am interested and who wishes to make a request to you.

THE KING : You digress. I'm beginning to think that the freedom with which you all interrupt the show is indecent.

SAINT-SIMON : I remembered that one of the gorgons, Medusa's sister, was called Sthéno. Now, since I like scribbling notes ...

THE KING : Gauge, sir, the bad taste of that ridiculous joke.

SAINT-SIMON : Ridiculous, I admit. It would allow our young plaintiff to show herself to you in a light which makes her request more convincing.

THE KING : But, good heavens, the audience has nothing to do with this business and you're in front of the audience here.

(*The young actress enters.*)

STHENO : Precisely, sir. I wanted the audience to embrace my cause along with you.

THE KING : Get on with it, then. We haven't any time to waste. What's the problem?

STHENO : It's this. One of our doyennes used to say, 'I'm no longer young enough to play old parts.' In the past the big leading parts demanded robust caryatids and age didn't count. Mounet-Sully played Hippolyte and Ruy Blas at sixty and nobody found it funny. Films came and the public insisted that the heroes should have the age attributed to them by history or legend. But films offer opportunities less subtle than the boards. Then came *Le Cartel* in which the big leading roles were those of the producer and scene designer. Soon afterwards young artists showed themselves capable of taking over. We saw them giving marvellous renderings of ...

WOMAN SPECTATOR : Néron and Le Cid.

STHENO : Thank you, madam. Today the old caryatids make way for new ones who no longer wait to get old before being worthy of bearing the burden of masterpieces on their shoulders.

THE KING : Quite so, mademoiselle. We no longer go about in carriages.

STHENO : Neither the ministers nor the administrators listen to us. They only meet us *en passant*. I'm taking the bull by the horns and using the leeway the author grants us in order to demand publicly what is my right : work which corresponds to my youth and strength, which I'm in the process of losing.

THE KING : That's all very fine, mademoiselle, but it only concerns the administrator. Go to his office tomorrow morning between ten and eleven. He is the only one who can give you the part of Junie or Agnès, unless he throws you out – which is likely.

STHENO : I'll manage to convince him.

THE KING : The precedent created by this interlude is intolerable. Your comrade, who was weak enough to take part in it, will accompany you to the administrator. Go back to your dressing-room, mademoiselle. I have good reasons for doubting that the Duke needs any help from you to refresh his memory. You, sir, remain with us. (*The young actress leaves after curtseying. The King to Saint-Simon*) Be seated, sir. When I think the moment is opportune I reserve the right to tell you what makes me allow you to be present at our meal.

SAINT-SIMON (*taking a pencil and pieces of paper out of his pocket*): A meal which fascinates me all the more, sire, because it never took place.

THE KING : Now, really !

MOLIERE : True, sire. It never took place. That is why I prefer legend to history. History is made up of realities which turn false in the end and become lies. Legend, on the other hand, is made up of lies which grow stronger in the end and become realities.

SAINT-SIMON : Noted! Noted! Monsieur Molière, that is a remarkable maxim.

MOLIERE : To be honest, it isn't I who said it, but the author. But that doesn't prevent it from becoming mine, since he attributes it to me.

SAINT-SIMON : Noted! Noted!

WOMAN SPECTATOR : Rouget de Lisle neither composed nor sang: he is regarded all the same as the author of *La Marseillaise*. A famous picture shows him to us and proves what tricks are exploited by fable so that it can take shape and achieve its ends.

(*She assumes the pose of Rouget de Lisle singing* La Marseillaise. *The Duke, who had entered a moment earlier with a large soup-tureen, stops on hearing the woman spectator.*)

THE DUKE : Now what's this?

THE KING : I feel in fact that I don't remember this historic meal.

SAINT-SIMON : Perhaps Your Majesty intended to arrange it.

MOLIERE : Or he may have spoken about it in jest in order to mystify some fool.

SAINT-SIMON : As it goes from mouth to mouth a fable gathers strength.

MOLIERE : And it is at this moment, here, on this stage, that the imaginary meal is really taking place. (*Lulli's minuet has been played softly for a moment.*) Now, sire, that minuet. When Lulli brought it to me, for *Le Bourgeois Gentilhomme*, I didn't regard it as important.

WOMAN SPECTATOR : *Le Bourgeois Gentilhomme*, 1670. *Tartuffe*, 1669.

MOLIERE : Madam, we are not at school but in the kingdom of shades. We drank the water of Lethe. Dates matter little to us. (*He takes up the thread again.*) When Lulli brought it to me, for *Le Bourgeois Gentilhomme*, it was just another minuet, but time reverses the phenomenon of the perspectives of space. The things that move away from us in space grow smaller and those that move away from us in time grow bigger. Now his minuet is transfigured and transports me. I suddenly find it possesses solemnity and a kind of funereal magnificence comparable to that of the rhythms which accompany some Negro ceremonies.

(*The Duke goes out, raising his eyes to heaven and shrugging his shoulders.*)

THE KING : Molière, aren't you putting rather a lot of yourself into it?

MOLIERE : No, sire, for unlike that savage who, seeing his hut for the first time from a distance, thought it had become too small for him and turned back, some things to which we had allotted no importance emerge suddenly from our memory and resemble that genie in the Arab tale who comes out of a bottle and grows in size until he frightens us. . . .

SAINT-SIMON : Noted! Noted!

WOMAN SPECTATOR (*rises and recites like a somnambulist*) :

> Versailles a candlestick guided your walk.
> Through what shade did they go, down what muddy path
> Those great idle kings on their ceremonial beds
>     Drawn by the oxen of death?
>
> Princes the minuets that move with pomp
>     Do you dance them now
> Now that you dance with your scarlet heels
>     In the kingdom of the dead?
>
> In the kingdom of the dead do others show you
>     Another way to be
> Or will you dance in your heavy wigs
>     Throughout eternity?

(*The woman spectator, like a medium, sits down again. A silence. The King and Molière have stood up and advanced towards the footlights, from where they listen.*)

THE KING : Who wrote these verses and why is this lady declaiming them to us?

(*The King and Molière take their seats again.*)

SAINT-SIMON : I think these verses are by the author, or perhaps by this lady, who is slightly pedantic at the edges.

THE KING : Gentlemen, I no longer understand very clearly what's happening to me. I'm floating. I feel I'm the ghost of a king in the ghost of a château. Have I been drinking?

MOLIERE : No, sire, unless this make-believe champagne isn't beginning, through contagion, to mythify – which should not be confused with mystify. Your Majesty is no doubt sinking slightly, thanks to intoxication from this theatrical champagne, into that element where the patient muses' *loser takes all* triumphs over the *winner take nothing* attitude assumed by the puppets of reality. The muses wait underneath the stage.

Reality is active on top of it.

SAINT-SIMON : Noted! Noted!

MOLIERE : You might say that the devil's involved. Let's shake off our ashes and suppress our tears. This *Impromptu* is going off course and turning into mourning. I propose to bring it back to that straight line followed by sensible people and not to stray any longer down those cross-roads which diverge from it and open up forbidden perspectives on to the future and the past.

SAINT-SIMON : Superb! What a haul! Noted, noted ...

MOLIERE : Would Your Majesty like me to attempt a less melancholy experiment concerning this perspective presented by the things we believed in, seen under a new aspect?

THE KING : I confess it would be nice for me to be no longer lost in the vagueness between what I represent and what I am. Neither the gardens of Versailles nor my box in the Rue de Richelieu has prepared me for your behaviour.

MOLIERE : Sire!

SAINT-SIMON : Sire!

THE KING : As for sire, I think of Ulysses and the sirens and the wax with which I should stop my ears. You, gentlemen, are dangerous sirens. If I didn't stop up my ears and have myself tied to the mast, you would lead me I don't know where and very far from my usual habits.

*(The Duke has come onstage. He stands to one side, with a napkin under his arm, as stiffly as a maître d'hôtel.)*

MOLIERE : For my experiment, it is important that Your Majesty persuades the Duke to give up his title and the distance which separates us, that he returns to his theatrical work and agrees to interpret the scene with Oronte, in which he excels.

THE DUKE : I accept all the more willingly because it will give me a rest from playing the part of a maître d'hôtel.

THE KING : Come now, come, you played this part better than anyone in *Le Sexe Faible*. Come here.

*(The Duke comes up to the table, facing, between the King and Molière.)*

MOLIERE : I will give you the lead-in. And above all, stress the comic side.

SAINT-SIMON : I can guess where you are going.

MOLIERE : If you can guess, say nothing and don't make my experiment go wrong. *(He remains seated.)* We shall see, sir.

THE DUKE *(standing)* :

Moreover, you should know
I wrote it in a quarter of an hour.

MOLIERE :

Come, sir, time has no part in this affair.

THE DUKE (*exaggerating the ridiculous aspects*) :

Hope 'tis true can comfort us
And turn our woe to laughter.
But Phyllis, how very sad it is
When nothing follows after !

MOLIERE (*adopting the voice of Philinte*) :

Already I'm delighted with these lines.

(*In his own voice*) :

What, are you bold enough to call them fine?

THE DUKE :

You showed some kindness to me;
In truth you must show less,
And do not go to such great lengths
If you never can say yes.

MOLIERE (*in the voice of Philinte*) :

Ah ! what gallant things he says !

(*In his own voice*) :

Good God ! You hypocrite, to give him praise !

THE DUKE :

If I must wait for ever
Despite my zeal and ardour,
All hope for life is spent.

Your care will not keep me from death;
Fair Phyllis, all hope is lost,
If you will never relent.

MOLIERE : And now, since Your Majesty permits, I shall recite the sonnet without making it ridiculous.

SAINT-SIMON : I understand your plan.

MOLIERE : In that case it can be understood and does not dwell only in my imagination. (*He recites Oronte's sonnet with simplicity.*) What does the King think of it?

THE KING : That the sonnet is very good and appears in a new light.

MOLIERE : That is precisely the crux of the matter. I found it laughable at the time and today like Your Majesty I find it very good.

SAINT-SIMON : I had sometimes envisaged it from this angle and didn't dare believe in it, through this ridiculous fear of the ridiculous which prevents us from rectifying our aim.

MOLIERE : Let me confess that it was a sin of my youth and in that attributing it to Oronte I was turning my weapon against myself. It's certainly not a masterpiece, but many poems of the period are no more so. Especially among those whom it imitates.

THE KING (*to Molière*) : May I add that the little song which you put forward as reasonable in contrast to the unreasonable sonnet by your poor Oronte could also lend itself to revision and would lose the case on appeal. (*He recites*) :

If the King had given me
Paris, his big city.
And if I had to leave my love,
My love so dear to me.

There's a cheap proof of love that Alceste gives to his sweetheart, for let me tell you it's very unlikely that a king would have made a present of his city.

I would say to King Henry,
'Then keep Paris, your big city,
I'd rather have my love, my love,
I'd rather have my love.'

And do you think, moreover, that it is honourable to refuse such a gift from one's king, supposing that he thinks of making

it? Isn't it a skilful attempt to move the public? Between ourselves I can't see anything reasonable in that.

MOLIERE (*laughing*) : I confess I have played somewhat on people's
sensitivity . . .

SAINT-SIMON : And your sonnet will be successful.

MOLIERE : In what way?

SAINT-SIMON : The term 'precious' isn't necessarily pejorative. One
finds the influence of Oronte in an entire precious literature.
And, since the author is making us travel in time as the Comte
de Saint-Germain did, I shall quote a poet whom I admire
and who represents its furthest extreme : Stéphane Mallarmé.
If I've got it right and even if its syntax . . .

WOMAN SPECTATOR (*in the tones of a schoolmistress*) : If I remember
correctly and despite its syntax . . .

SAINT-SIMON : These mistakes are, alas, frequent today. They dis-
honour our beautiful language and I approve of the fact,
madam, that you're calling me to order, for in the past nobody
would have made them. . . . So, if I remember correctly and
despite its slightly confused syntax, I shall try to recite to you
a sonnet by Monsieur Mallarmé.

THE KING : Let's hear it. I hope he isn't one of Monsieur Fouquet's
protégés?

SAINT-SIMON : No, sire, nothing to fear.

### IDLE PETITION

Princess ! Jealous of some Hebe's destiny
Which dawns on this cup at the kiss of your lips,
Passion consumes me, achieving only
A minor role and even naked I'll not appear

On the Sèvres vase, since I'm not your bearded lapdog,
Or pastille, or rouge, or mawkish play
And I know your closed-in glance has fallen on me,
Girl whose hair was fashioned by heavenly goldsmiths.

Name us . . . you whose rosy-fruited laughter
Meets in a flock of tame young lambs
Cropping vows and bleating ecstasy
Name us . . . so that Love winged with a fan
Paints me there, my fingers to a flute, lulling this flock,
Princess, name us shepherd of your smiles.

THE KING (*to Molière*) : Heaven help me ! This sonnet is a thousand times more complicated than yours.

MOLIERE : Many things will become complicated after Your Majesty's reign; and many people will lose their heads as a result.

THE KING : Then it's better to remain in ignorance. Nature is a wild beast that Lenôtre tames for me, but I share his anxiety that one day it will want to take its revenge and contemplate some bad turn if man's knowledge progresses and upsets the obscure calculations of its equilibrium.

WOMAN SPECTATOR : Author ! Author !

SAINT-SIMON : Splendid ! Noted. Noted.

THE KING (*with a sudden change of tone*) : Saint-Simon !

SAINT-SIMON (*raising his head from what he was writing*) : Sire?

THE KING : Listen to me. Put your papers away. It's high time I cross-examined you and told you why I sent away the young gorgon and why I tolerated you among us. It amused me to set a trap for your note-taking fever. (*Saint-Simon, very embarrassed, pockets his papers.*) I've heard that you're drawing up your memoirs and that you're putting me in them, describing me just as you want to.

SAINT-SIMON : Sire !

THE KING : Take care, I still have some good rooms in the Bastille.

MOLIERE : Sire, if Monsieur de Saint-Simon accepts me as acting in his defence and if the King approves, I'll plead his case : it is in the prisons that the idea of liberty acquires the greatest power and perhaps those who imprison others inside them run the risk of imprisoning themselves outside.

THE KING : (*knitting his brows*) : Oh ho, that's a very disrespectful paradox.

MOLIERE : Sire, paradoxes are the clothes that truth puts on when it leaves the well and doesn't walk about among men in indecent fashion.

SAINT-SIMON : Shall I obtain from Your Majesty the favour that he will agree to forewarn me against the slanderous gossip who made himself capable of that lie?

(*The Duke entered a moment earlier through the door at the left. He is holding a dish of fruit, stops half-way towards the table and pricks up his ears.*)

THE KING : You dukes can sort this out between you.

SAINT-SIMON (*to the Duke*) : Ah ! ... Traitor. ... Take care that I don't return the ball to your court. (*Imitating Molière's style with a gesture of deference towards him*)

Sir, I feel my temper rising high
And I will spy against the man who is a spy.

THE DUKE (*aside*) : My God!
WOMAN SPECTATOR : Beware the reply! See the little cock Saint-
Simon astride the golden dung-heap of Versailles.
SAINT-SIMON (*standing up and rising on tiptoe*) : Ask him, when
he's no longer Duke and when you're no longer King, if he
keeps a journal of the smallest intrigues of the House of
Molière.
THE KING (*to the Duke*) : Is this true?
THE DUKE : Little notes, innocent little notes . . .
MOLIERE : My goodness, I've often been guilty of bringing grist to
his mill.
THE KING (*rising*) : This *Impromptu* is teaching me some fine
things! Leave, gentlemen! We shall not wash our dirty linen
in public, we shall wash it amongst ourselves and thoroughly,
tomorrow morning, between ten and eleven in the administrator's office.

(*The King sits down again. Saint-Simon and the Duke bow to
each other and go towards the doors, one to the left and one
to the right, the Duke first placing his dish of fruit on the
table.*)

THE DUKE (*before leaving*) : I'm quick to raise my fists. That viper
is lucky in being able to take refuge in the seventeenth century.

(*They go out, each one on his own side.*)

MOLIERE : I'm afraid the administrator's office won't be big enough
to contain all these fine people . . .
WOMAN SPECTATOR : It's the Marx Brothers' cabin.
THE KING : Good God! There's no end to it . . .
MOLIERE : I admit I would find this session entertaining.
THE KING : You'll be there. But since the young gorgon must enjoy
powers less effective than those of her sister Medusa, who
changes men into statues, you'll be there in the shape of a
bust. But now that I've given vent to my spleen and we have
at last attained some calm, I can tell you what our tête-à-tête
is all about and regale you with a surprise that I'm reserving
for you in exchange for your services and suitable for soothing
my remorse about the thunderbolts which threaten your
*Tartuffe*.

WOMAN SPECTATOR : Your *Tartuffe*! Happy Molière! Now he's got his *Tartuffe* back.

MOLIERE : Sire, I'm burning with impatience . . .

THE KING : But first . . .

*(The door at the right is opened violently, Monsieur, the King's brother, comes in. He is wearing a cloak of staggering magnificence.)*

THE KING : Well now, you were the only person still missing, my brother! What ill wind blows you in here? You're wearing a fantastic cloak, it seems to me.

MONSIEUR *(out of breath)* : This cloak is the cause of all the trouble! While the dresser was fastening it round my shoulders I reflected that Monsieur hadn't got the best of reputations and that some malicious critic wouldn't fail to allege that I was a suitable person to play the part. I've got a wife and children, sire, and I've just come down the stairs from the dressing-rooms four at a time to say I won't do it!

THE KING : The devil take your children and your wife! That doesn't interest the public. It's a matter between you and the author. Go and complain to him in the wings and don't wear me out any longer with your lamentations. You can proceed with them tomorrow morning.

MONSIEUR : Between ten and eleven in the administrator's office. I'll be there.

THE KING : What times we live in!

*(Monsieur rushes to the door at the right, stops, turns round and slowly comes back on to the stage.)*

MONSIEUR : Another thing. I'm amazed, sire, that you invite a mountebank to your table while you refuse to admit my friend the Chevalier de Lorraine to your ceremony of the bed-chamber.

*(Monsieur goes towards the door at the back, opens it roughly and goes out, pompously, escorted by the train of his cloak, without closing the door. The King and Molière burst out laughing.)*

THE KING : He couldn't resist either the cloak or the last lines of his part.

MOLIERE : Professional deformation is certainly stronger than anything else.

THE KING : Alone at last ! Close that door, Molière, since Monsieur does not find it worthy of his rank. One moment . . . (*he turns towards the audience*) I beg that lady to remain silent and not to interrupt my speech.

WOMAN SPECTATOR (*rising*) : I am the most humble of subjects and the most obedient of actresses. (*She sits down again.*)

THE KING (*to the prompter*) : What was I saying?

THE PROMPTER (*loudly*) : 'But first . . . '

THE KING (*to Molière*) : But first of all I must explain to you the meaning of this surprise which I have kept for you and explain to you my etiquette which the courtiers confuse with a variant of the old constraints of protocol. (*The minuet begins again very softly.*) Etiquette consists of rendering possible and harmonious a collection of individuals of unequal birth and intelligence and who make this collectivism into a machine which lives thanks to its internal strife and its contrasts. Otherwise, this collectivism would be an inert mass subjected to a despot : the King. I will tell you a great secret, Monsieur Molière : I believe that my artists, my ministers, my architects, my scientists, my philosophers, my princes of the Church, my dukes, my captains, my favourites, my pages, form a total of which the figures and the inequality of details guarantee the security of my throne. I need you, different or superior men, in order to embellish and transcend my priesthood. It is through all of you that I shine, that I avoid being merely the shepherd of a flock of sheep, that I justify my title of Sun King.

MOLIERE : I incline before Your Majesty's wisdom.

THE KING : This brilliance reaches me from you, I will reflect it like a mirror and return it to you in the end. One day, perhaps, my sun will embellish your tombs with flowers.

MOLIERE : I salute, sire, the grace with which Your Majesty lowers himself to share his fame with us and the excuses which he invents for the vanities of individualism by giving that of others the remarkable opportunity of becoming his.

WOMAN SPECTATOR : Don't throw any more bouquets, the place is full of them.

THE KING : The surprise I reserve for you arises from this policy. And since etiquette directs my court and regulates its conduct like a ballet, I'm now ordering a ballet from you.

MOLIERE : A ballet?

THE KING : Wait for my surprise. It's a big one : for I shall dance in it in person.

MOLIERE : You, sire?

THE KING : I, the King. You are not unaware, my dear Molière, of the ingratitude of men and you are too lucid not to understand that once your models are dead and the world still goes on nobody, alas, will pay any heed to your entertaining satires. While if I dance at Versailles, in one of your ballets, your name will remain linked to mine and I will have repaid my debt to you.

MOLIERE : Sire, I am speechless. Your Majesty is too kind.

WOMAN SPECTATOR : Big deal! (*Imitating the audience*) Hush!

THE KING : Take Racine, for example . . .

MOLIERE : Racine?

THE KING : Well, yes. . . . This week my censorship office opened a letter from a highly witty lady. This lady declares that 'Racine will pass, like coffee'. I agree with her. That is why I have appointed Racine historiographer of my battles. As a dramatist he will be forgotten. But, as historiographer of my reign, he will always be read. Now see . . .

(*We shall never know what the King was going to add, for the door at the right has opened and the stage manager appears. He comes up to the table casually, pulls back his cuff and taps the face of his wrist-watch. The King rises.*)

THE KING : It's true . . . we go on talking and time passes. I'd forgotten that we must return to our dressing-rooms, undress and dress again . . .

MOLIERE (*rising in his turn*) : To act . . . Racine . . .

THE KING (*bowing*) : And Molière.

(*They move away arm in arm towards the central door, while the stage manager disappears through the one on the right and the music of the minuet rises to full strength.*)

WOMAN SPECTATOR (*rising*) : The conclusion is good and my role as spectator obliges me to give the signal for applause.


CURTAIN

(*If there are any curtain-calls the stage-hands can be seen removing the three doors, the table and the chairs, and the artistes come to take their bows just as they happen to be, either in costume, everyday clothes, dressing-gowns or the costumes for the play which is being performed after* The Impromptu.)

Milly

Christmas 1961

# *Crucifixion*

Cocteau always regarded himself as a poet, and his bibliography is divided into six types of *Poésie* and then, finally, 'records'. The first section of the bibliography is simply *Poésie* on its own, and of the ten volumes of Complete Works two are devoted entirely to poetry. One day perhaps the whole corpus of his poetry will be studied on its own and at the same time linked to the rest of his work. It is unfortunate that to date so many of his admirers have not yet had the chance to study his poems in translation.

In 1946 Cocteau's friend Paul Morihien published the long poem *Crucifixion* which had been written during a period of illness. The poem is so densely written, so dramatic in treatment, that the impact made by a first reading is often unforgettable. Its compression, its use of dynamic rhythm, internal and half-rhymes are reminiscent of Gerard Manley Hopkins.

Cocteau authorized his friend Mary Hoeck to translate it and his one important directive to his translator was : *above all, no poetry*. The free translation here is adapted from Mary Hoeck's original version. The poem is about suffering and solitude, the suffering of Christ, of man in general and of one individual. If ever one piece of Cocteau's writing were quoted to dispel the image of the frivolous acrobat of twentieth-century literature, it should be this. There is no key to its obscurity; each reader must find his own way to its 'meaning'.

1

Most High Serene. Racks
lean on the tree. The ladder
leans upon the tree new dead.
The ladder leans upon the new dead
tree. And tears
enlarge the scene.
They saw then the barbed wire.
The dusk. They saw
then the chestnut burr
of nails. Veinings
of wood. Veinings of men.
Roads as they cross. The sheet
knotted the ways
road over road. The still wind
and torn-down blind.
They saw tied and untied
the racks. The dusk. The roof-tree.
The shutter. The groove. The husband
The scarecrow spiked with wings.
The wretched rose. The cooper's
ladder.

2

A rack. A hedge bristling
with thorns. The dregs
of sleep. Sunlight
through shred of shipwreck.
Oysters mussels and other shells
stick on struck trunks
of wreckage.
Who I ask you glues them
on windows?
Who? This white crust
of frost in the form
of a man flayed
alive.

### 3

Most High Serene. In place of mandrake spring
great coils of tripes.
Gruesome shapes. Fire-drakes
drenched in ooze.
Ooze-water. Through traps
of spume through fires lit
by fools through falling
metal shutters over shops.
Made of wax and needles.
Of cries thrust with hammer-blows
through the nervous
system of a
Judas-tree.

### 4

Sheets drenched in blood spread out
on traps of thorny hedge
with cruel spikes
of bramble-bush whose fruit
stains the bare boards with dreadful
stains. Stains the washing
that hangs on looped-up strands of
barbed wire. In sunshine
dry the clothes which draggle down
in muddy pools. Hang down
sheets haunted by the grinning
shadow-face
of a mock washerwoman
whose hands are real.

### 5

Tell me where does the shoe
pinch? I'll tend the wound
with its wide-open icy lips
crying its cry.
I shall hear the flute of the spine
so light its skeleton
it hangs by a thread

by bag of blood by bag
of spit by bag of bile
by bags ill-hung on wasp-waist
slashed in two
Tell me where does the shoe pinch?
I'll tend it with gauze and wadding
and the pink cross
stuck over it.


6


Tree angled and squared known
by its rare shape
extends two branches
where beat inviting
arteries within the pulse
so that the tunnels
of the bodies were
choked by the rush of a
crowd in terror.


7


It was washed and torn
worn undone befouled
savaged and split asunder
held up held down picked up
knotted nailed unnailed
joined and spread apart
moiled uncoiled spread out on high
spoiled embroiled
hated fated rated
slapped whipped
branded for all time
from the tortured scroll
to the boots of the sewer-men.


8


The tool of fate was moved

by reckoning
unknown to scene-shifters.
The wings were ladders
forbidden the chimney-sweeps
on pain of death. From all
eternity held in the heart
the plot ticked out its beat
with sickening skill
to regulate
the candelabra of the stars.


### 9

Were ever ladders seen so close?
Were ever on the topmost heights
of space so close so near so like
a screened rain-gauge
curiously twisted turning
amidst the scaffolding? Were
ever seen such spiders'
webs around the rafters?
How many ladders? A true
war machine
leaning on walls of ramparts.
This skyline disarray
of balconies eaves and gutters
parapets and other rails
for butchers and bakers
prisoners beckoning
girls. Black book
of Hebrew spells but I repeat :
ladders ladders leading
to nowhere leaping and nudging
knocking with elbows and wings
and shrill swallow cry.


### 10

Upon the scarlet ladder came
naked of foot bearers of unseen
firemen — these
disgustingly lacking discretion.

Coming going jostling
low and high high
and low and through
the spangled holly lacy
hate of nettles.
What am I saying? The solid sky
or so it seemed was space now is
a pinprick inserted *elsewhere* by hands
different and indifferent.
Here maybe here may be
(between ourselves) something to
laugh at.


11


There were thuds. Thuds
of iron on iron. Old rose
of the winds. Thuds. Rust
of thuds on the outspread fan of
foot-bones. On the mat
of toe-bones. On planks on
the exquisite illuminations of the missal
of nerves where pain runs swifter
than pain
in the coral-reef of tortures.
Echoed thuds. Medalled
thuds. Ears
of thuds. Soul of wood. The soul
of soulless thuds.
The cooper's thuds. The thuds
of the carpenter. Craters
of blue flesh. Signposts
like the hand's fate-lines.
Swan's neck.


12


Fine work. What strange
walking. What funeral
pomp. A hat
with eglantines. What heat. What barter
with loss and this to those

in barter skilled. What day
of dupes. I ask
a hearing but they say me nay.
They nail him. They
scourge him. They spit
upon him.
Oh ! the swine.

13

Upon the bridge in greatest
disarray the pirate victims
of a cunning spell
a meagre life of emigrants emplaced
in many-coloured sleep remembering
the riggings left
which now as gallows hold
a hurricane of shirts.
Big-toes at cyclone centre
point to point with
tips of standards touch. The attributes
illegible. Bull's
horns and horse's tails and he-goats
draggled eagles.

14

On the green notorious
gaming-table jolt about
small bones belonging to a skeleton
and neatly numbered with the specks
of flies. The soldiers
grouped for wrestling
the mounted statue stands
whose horse in sneezing sprays
with froth the carcass
of the fireworks in the suburb
where spent suns
are nailed.

## 15

The captain out of humour
because he missed his tryst
dominates
the group from a square-set horse whose limbs
reach to the ground.
He (using his whip) has chased away
the great green flies which now
beside themselves
have lost their heads.
Ritual like the drama set
in a butcher's shop where the raw meat hangs
with golden leaves and
rosettes.

## 16

Gordian. Such was the knot
of muscles of cords
of an old vulture dreaming only
of wounds and bruises
at the top of a kind
of greasy pole. He saw
ill he only glimpsed
a ladder made of hammerings
climbed by a horde
of white-clad scullions plucking geese.
A cock then sounded his clarion-call.
High was made low : *Down!*
*Down!* they cried to him
from the kitchens.

## 17

An accident happens so quickly.
The other scarecrow
too careful of his change to a tree-branch
a tree-knot a tree-bone to
peeling twisted bark of pine which bleeds
and cracks within a dream close to
mythology that frightened

the angels crying out : *Quick! Quick!*
*There's not a minute*
*to lose.* These simpletons
whirling round
screeching aloud and losing feathers
which blinded them and
clung to their wounds.


## 18


Most High Serene. The shield of
homicides.
The kneeling beasts who weep. Keys reach number
seven. The wheel
of miracles triangular.
The hand
which is no hand. The eye
which is no eye.
The death by disgust of dreaming
And – simply – how difficult to be.
The gypsy girl asleep. In chess
The castle piece. Its bishop
free.


## 19


On a black schoolroom desk
where she rears her giddy-geese
death bites her nails bites her pen
licks the inkstand's golden scarab –
the purple ink – and chews the ruler
chews the liquorice rubs out
draws straight lines then chews
some mottled blotting-paper
draws lines shoots out her tongue
squints licks the little scarab
under the master's eyes what cheek !
But how can he fail to see she's
cribbing?

## 20

The whole body numbed
exudes its moisture
fleeing the muddy roads
no longer passable.
Here it begins
under the arms takes tortuous ways
loses itself forms a river network
of anatomy.
Disintegration came from rusty nails
grinding the highly delicate machines
in a factory used to working at night in the dark.
Therefore all inner things
fled out
seeking some issue.
This anguish sweat clung on to corners
in the cornices which lived a little
wild drops of fear which fly
despairingly into the void.


## 21

That which cannot be said (and yet
what cannot I say
with my way of forcing words to be silent)
that which cannot
be said is the honey
dropped by the bees of agony. It
runs from the hive and binds
with a horrible giddy lattice
the contours lost at the root
of a caduceus. One guesses
what it is made of.


## 22

And now here an outline
full fronted but turned round and bound
to the vine-stock of legs by
drapery of blue dark-eyed like red
holds

balanced on its forehead a pillar
of salt. The other side
the outlines blur because
of tears which magnify the whole
and glue its cheek against
the ghastly resin.


## 23


Thunder of coaches beribboned
thunder of sprays of acacia
thunder of bridal beds
dragged upstairs
thunder of barricades
thunder of cannonades
thunder of crowds crying 'That way
that way'. Thunder
of buildings decked with flags proclaim
to heaven a jet
of blood turned to wine. Angel Cégeste
blew the trumpet. The shadow
of the object rearing up became
the object.


## 24


It tore from east to west
the stuff of silence. Heard was
the silence crying out aloud
unbearable
to hear within the heart. A
spray of ink certainly
full of masterpieces
spattered in black flight
compromising papers now burnt in haste.
Meanwhile a torrential rain
of bayonets
destroyed the victims savagely.

**25**

Kneeling to right
to left. Alone alas
of my kind (no cause
for pride) within a coat
of mail made of ciphers under
armour of uproar
kneeling alone to left
to right – snow with blind hands
laying the cloth – I close
kneeling alone of my kind
alas in this room where the crime
took place the yellow
lips of my wise
wound which could
pronounce some words.

PART THREE

*People and Places*

# *Satie*

The composer Erik Satie (1866–1925) was acknowledged by Cocteau to be one of his masters. Cocteau wrote about him with devotion in *La Difficulté d'Etre* and in various essays. Satie was a lone eccentric figure, his compositions were unlike those of anyone else, and it was he who composed the music for the ballet *Parade,* in which Cocteau and Picasso collaborated. This short tribute to Satie was written by Cocteau at the invitation of Rollo Myers who had been asked in 1952 to edit a special number of *La Revue Musicale,* the French periodical.

Satie can be cited as an example to every creative man. His lesson is not coming to an end. Never did he rely upon dubious charm or a striking effect. Never did he listen to the sirens, except his own inner ones. He always stopped up his ears with wax. He always, like the wise Ulysses, had himself tied to the mast.

In the midst of musical impressionism he preserved the line of his fingers, and without looking at himself in the mirror, the way women do when they are afraid of losing theirs.

This line emerged from his soul in a very simple and a very subtle form. He cared for it without pomposity, protected it and polished it as we saw him all his life interminably cleaning his hands with pumice-stone, believing that water was not adequate.

Like a cat he would lick himself, as it were, and shield himself with a very pure and very tender egoism. Like a cat he would unroll in light-pawed fashion this marvellously comical secret reel, on to which his thread was wound.

In *Socrate,* for example, there are moments when one wonders if the music has been written by a bird.

Too simple for ears accustomed to highly spiced sounds. That is the tragedy. Satie does not clothe his genius, never clutters it up with costume or jewel. His genius is unclad, and without the slightest modesty. To go naked, for Satie's music, was an act of modesty *par exellence.*

This admirable man made an impression on our youth, spared us much anxiety and many traps.

a mon cher Erik Satie
jean Cocteau
1920

It is true that no one among us was worthy of following to the point of invisibility (the height of elegance) this sage who admitted no compromise.

It will be to my honour that I venerated him, accepted the ups and downs of his mysterious character, and, as soon as I knew him, assigned him to his true place.

When people asked Rossini who was the greatest composer he would reply: 'Beethoven.' And when they said: 'What about Mozart?' he would reply: 'You asked me who was the greatest. You did not ask me which one was unique.'

If people were to ask me about our age, I would no doubt reply that the greatest are Debussy and Stravinsky. And I would add: 'But Satie is unique.'

# *Barbette*

It seems remarkable that an American acrobat who performed in women's clothes during the early 'twenties caused Cocteau to write an essay on aesthetics, but this in fact happened. Barbette's real name was Vander Clyde and the best account of his life is given in Appendix XIV to Francis Steegmuller's biography of Cocteau. The skill Barbette displayed in his *numéro*, or act, so impressed Cocteau that he regarded him as one of the world's most sensational exponents of 'professionalism'. Ever since he was very young Cocteau had admired acrobats and music-hall performers, he had told poets and other writers that they too should acquire the same degree of skill and live dangerously, otherwise they could never be true creators.

As already noted, this piece was originally published in 1928.

For two years now I've refused to write a few lines about Barbette's turn. I've followed the music-hall course too long : it's like the Sorbonne. I should add that the music-hall irritates me with its arrogant way of bringing our research into sharp focus and that air of moving faster than anyone else. But Barbette's turn is exceptional.

Genius is a gift from heaven. Our only duty is to create a vehicle for it since, until further orders, we must dispense our fluid gradually and hypnotize the world a little through the medium of art. This limits the role of the artist to that of workman. Life and its horrors take care of the rest. Encountering certain specialists, one is ashamed of knowing one's job so inadequately and I thought I could only allow myself to write a play (*Orphée*) after seven years of study, and on the strength of pantomimes and one adaptation. I was getting my hand in. This is to tell you how much I appreciate Barbette's performance, an extraordinary lesson in theatrical professionalism.

This paragraph will explain an enthusiasm that witty Parisians and dilettanti had to put down to fantasy, with which they always confuse our daredevil activities.

Barbette is a young American of twenty-four with the slightly hunchbacked look of a bird and a slightly unsteady walk (due no doubt to his very small hands and feet). A fall from a trapeze has left him with a scar which pulls back his upper lip from his irregular teeth. Only the astonishing arched eyebrows over his inhuman eyes draw attention to him, for offstage he is as anonymous as Nijinsky was.

Let us share the sandwich and hard-boiled egg which our acrobat eats at about six o'clock, and accompany him to his dressing-room where he arrives at eight (he goes on at eleven), with that conscientiousness unknown to actors in France and characteristic of clowns, Annamite mimes and Cambodian dancing-girls who are sewn into their golden costumes every evening.

Barbette gives meaning to the Greek legends about young men who were turned into trees or flowers. He displaces their easy magic.

We're going to follow, in slow-motion, with bright lighting, the stages in a metamorphosis of which Man Ray was good enough to perpetuate for me some significant moments; amongst others, the one when Barbette, his woman's head belied by his naked, leather-strapped torso, closely resembles the Apollo-like figures from the trussmaker's.

This dressing-room did not intimidate me now. I was smoking and chatting with a sportsman friend who washed and then spread cold cream thickly over his face. Some chorus-girls came along and chattered loudly until Barbette put on a towelling bathrobe, opened the door and exchanged a few words with them. Even when his make-up is finished and looks as precious as a brand new box of pastels, while his jaws are covered with a gleaming enamelled gum, and his body rubbed over with unreal-looking plaster, this strange diabolic youth, this dream of Saint-Just, this coachman of death, will remain a man, linked to his double by a hair. It is only when he puts on his blond wig, secured by a single piece of elastic round his ears, and sticks a bunch of hairpins in his mouth, that he assumes all the gestures of a woman doing her hair. He gets up, walks about and puts on his rings. The metamorphosis is complete. Jekyll is Hyde. Yes, Hyde. For I'm frightened. I turn away. I stub out my cigarette. I take off my hat. It's my turn to be intimidated. The door opens; the chorus-girls don't hesitate any longer. They go in and out as if they owned the place, sit down, powder their faces and chat about clothes.

The dresser puts on Barbette's gown for him, fluffs out the feathers and fastens up the bodice – tulle shoulder-straps which don't even conceal the absence of breasts. The procession – dresser, visitors and chorus-girls – goes down the stairs where Barbette becomes once more a boy disguised for a joke, hampered by his skirts and tempted to slide down the banisters.

He remains a man on the stage while he inspects his equipment, limbers up, blinks in the glare of the spotlights, hangs from the ropes and climbs the ladders. As soon as the possibility of danger has been eliminated, the woman reappears. A fashionable woman taking a last look at her drawing-room before the ball, patting the cushions, arranging vases and lamps.

The orchestra strikes up. Let us take our seats and watch Barbette's turn like any other member of the audience.

The curtain goes up on a functional set : a tightrope between two supports, a trapeze and rings hanging from the proscenium. Upstage there is a divan covered with a white bearskin on which, between his performances on the tightrope and the trapeze, Barbette will take off the gown impeding him and act a scandalous little scene, a real masterpiece of pantomime in which he parodies and recapitulates all the women he has studied, becoming the essence of woman, surpassing the most attractive creatures who come before and after him on the bill. For, don't forget, we are in the magic light of the theatre, in that magic box where reality no longer exists, where the natural no longer counts, where small people grow tall and tall ones grow shorter, where card tricks and sleight-of-hand, their difficulties unknown to the public, are the only things which succeed. Here Barbette will be as much woman as Guitry was Russian general. He will make me understand that great countries and great civilizations did not entrust women's roles to men simply because of decency. He will remind us of François Fratellini who explained to me why I could not get an English clown to play the bookmaker in *Le Boeuf sur le Toit* : an Englishman cannot act the part of an Englishman. And Réjane said : 'When I'm playing a mother, for example, I have to forget Jacques. Sometimes I have to pretend to be a man before I can get across the footlights.' What detachment! What concentration! What lessons in professionalism! By listening to these people, seeing Nijinsky or Pavlova gasping, after they had danced, like half-dead boxers, experiencing the atmosphere in the wings, like a ship lost at sea, while a charming ballet continues onstage, I learnt the secrets of the theatre.

When Barbette comes on, he throws dust in our eyes. He throws it all at once, so violently that he can then concentrate only on his work as an acrobat. From then on his male movements will serve him instead of giving him away. He will look like one of those Amazons who dazzle us on the publicity pages in American magazines. During the divan scene he again throws a handful of dust, for afterwards he will need complete freedom of movement in order to sway between the stage and the audience, hang by one foot, pretend to fall, show his crazy angel's face upside-down and link together the two shadows which grow longer when his trapeze carries him away.

When he comes onstage, when he is over our heads and when he comes down to earth again, even when he jumps up and down on the tightrope, he doesn't look very feminine.

One is reminded of those Florentine painters who employed young men to pose for women's portraits, and of Proust when he mingles the sexes with a cunning and clumsiness which endow his characters with a mysterious prestige.

Barbette's success is due to the fact that he appeals to the instinct of several audiences in one and in an odd way groups together contradictory enthusiasms. For he pleases those who see the woman in him, those who perceive the man in him, and others whose souls are stirred by the supernatural sex of beauty.

Barbette moves in silence. In spite of the orchestra which accompanies his act, his graceful poses and perilous exploits, his turn seems to be far away, taking place in the streets of dream, in a place where sounds cannot be heard, it seems to be summoned by the telescope or by sleep.

The cinema has supplanted realistic sculpture. Its marble figures, its large pallid heads, its shapes and shadows with splendid lighting replace what the eye previously demanded from statues. Barbette derives from these moving statues. Even when one knows him, he cannot lose his mystery. He remains a plaster model, a waxworks figure, the living bust which sang on a velvet-draped plinth at Robert Houdin's house.

His solitude is that of Oedipus, it resembles an egg painted by de Chirico in the foreground of a city on the day of an eclipse. Moreover, I leave to poets the task of comparing and imagining the ravishing creature. I represent the workman who seeks out the mechanism and takes it to pieces as Edgar Allan Poe dismantled Maelzel's chess-playing Turk.

After this unforgettable lie how upset people of a certain mentality would be if Barbette simply removed his wig. He does remove it, you tell me, after five encores, and people are upset. There is a murmur from the audience. Some look embarrassed, some blush. Understandably. For, after earning his success as a gymnast and making people almost collapse from shock, Barbette must earn his success as an actor. But observe the final *tour de force* : it is not enough to become a man again, running the film backwards is not enough. Truth must be translated and preserve an outline which can maintain itself on the same level as a lie. This is why Barbette, as soon as he has pulled off his wig, *plays the part of a man,* rolls his shoulders, spreads out his hands, flexes his muscles and exaggerates the sporting demeanour of a golfer.

And what skill he shows in perfecting this combination of enchantments, emotions and deceptions of mind and senses! When the curtain rises for the fifteenth time the former Barbette winks, moves from one foot to the other, begins a gesture of excusal, performs a street-urchin's dance in order to obliterate the memory of legend and the dying swan left behind by the turn, something that he knows well without having thought about it in advance and which seems a lapse of taste in the perfection of his craftsman-like modesty.

All minds which are disordered, sick, despairing, exhausted by the forces which threaten us from both shores of death, find repose in an outline. After years of vague Americanization when the capital of the U.S. hypnotized us, ordering 'hands up' as though producing a revolver, Barbette's turn shows me at last the real New York, with the ostrich plumes of its sea and its factories, its siren voice and its adornments, its aigrettes of electric lights.

# *In Japan*

All decades in Cocteau's life were busy, but during the 1930s his production shows perhaps more contrasts than in the years which preceded and followed. By 1930 Cocteau had recovered as far as he could from the death of Radiguet; he was able to form new friendships, first with Jean Desbordes, later with Marcel Khill, and his attitude was more extrovert than it had been for a long time.

In addition to three major plays, *La Machine Infernale, Les Chevaliers de la Table Ronde* and *Les Parents Terribles,* the 1930s saw the publication of the amusing reminiscences *Portraits-Souvenir,* first in the daily paper *Le Figaro* and later in book form. In the following year, 1936, came *Mon Premier Voyage. Portraits-Souvenir* had been dedicated to Marcel Khill, an attractive young man of half-Arab birth who had been given a small role in *La Machine Infernale.* Khill seems to have suggested the idea of the journey to the director of the evening paper *Paris-Soir,* who thought that this contemporary Jules Verne itinerary would amuse his readers and promptly supplied the financial backing. With Cocteau as Phileas Fogg and Khill as Passepartout the idea was to prove that it was now possible to achieve this journey in eighty days (29th March to 17th June), with only a minimum amount of flying. The route went through Rome, Cairo, Bombay, Rangoon, Toyko and Hollywood and was reported in the same type of 'indirect journalism' that Cocteau used again later in *Maalesh.*

Cocteau's version of his meeting with Charlie Chaplin, recorded below, is also included in *My Contemporaries.* I say 'version', for Chaplin apparently remembered the meeting quite differently. The following description of Japan, one of the most colourful parts of his travel-book, is taken from the English edition that appeared under the title *My Journey round the World.*

## 15th MAY

The sea becomes Japanese again. The waves and foam are snow-capped Fujis that rise up and melt away. Over there low coasts traversed by streaks of mist like agate. The boat crosses painted islets where five or six fishermen live in tiny gardens. They wish us good day as we sail by. These islands are so close and flat that you get the impression that the ship is passing between screens on which the sea, these people and their dwellings are painted.

*

## JAPAN, 16th MAY

Japan is still under the domination of martial law, and the young army chiefs are trying to introduce a fascist dictatorship. That is why, on the one hand, prospectuses of *Kashima-Maru* urge you to visit Japan and pour out appeals in attractive covers, and on the other, interrogations, threats to confiscate your camera, insolence from the police, discourage foreign visitors and render you suspect in your own eyes.

The impression of Japan that I am taking away with me is very different from the one I had formed before coming. It is true that mass may be a decorative ceremony and priests and congregation may participate in it without believing. But suicide, by which I mean the readiness of the individual to sacrifice himself to the community, or rather the Emperor, who sums it up, is at the basis of all the smiles and salutes here. The flowers familiar to us in Japanese prints plunge dark and twisted roots into the soil. This nation, condemned every sixty years to the ruin of its customs by earthquakes and cyclones, accepts the idea of building on ashes. Death winds up the play. The people bow patiently before this harsh destiny and offer their homes of precious woods, straw and rice-paper as a sacrifice in advance.

At Kobe the first sight which meets me is that of a little peasant girl playing hopscotch. This five-year-old is drawing on the pavement the ideal circle with which Hokusai signed his prints. After finishing her masterpiece, she hops off with her tongue out.

I should like to take this circle away with me. It reveals the secret of the Nippon soul. That calm which resembles the solemn calm of the park before the temple of the Emperor Meiji, the laborious patience, the sureness of eye and hand, that neatness, that precision which can give us this miraculous wood-carving or this piece of trumpery ware which swamps the European market.

Labour is cheaper here than anywhere else in the world, and the
soldier who used to be satisfied with one bowl of rice a day now
eats four. It constitutes his pay both on land and on sea. No possible
competition. If a chief disobeys or tries to follow the example of
European V.I.P.s it will not be long before he is falling on his
sword. In the recent affair of the army leaders' suicide, conquerors
and conquered vied with each other in their heroics.

The Imperial Palace of Tokyo, a town in the form of a wheel,
is the hub around which everything turns. Its grey walls and wide
moats of stagnant water never allow you to catch a glimpse of the
Mikado. If he travels between the palace and the station the crowd
fall on their knees and lower their eyes. Nowadays the police stop
the crowd from kneeling because it holds up the traffic. Everything
comes to a standstill. The shutters close, the inquisitive eye that
dares to look at the Mikado through a window risks being blinded.
No one cares to risk the experiment. The Imperial Palace is the
Vatican of such religious respect.

The Oriental Hotel of Kobe was to be a mere halting-place. We
decided to go back to Yokohama the next day by passing through
Kyoto, and once at Yokohama to travel to and fro between Yokohama and Tokyo. A journalist was to act as our interpreter.

At first sight the Japanese seem an anachronism. They look as if
they were in fancy dress for a carnival. The contrast between the
buildings and their kimonos is so striking that one is tempted to
put their facial expressions and meaningless laughter beneath their
flat sunshades down to embarrassment on going out dressed up.
Gradually you get used to it and notice that not a single Japanese
woman attires herself in European costume. The men who work
wear European suits of clothes, the others the kimono. Workmen
and delivery boys can be distinguished by their bare legs, enormous
calves, white gloves, a piece of towelling knotted round their heads
and a smock covered with monograms. They all, men and women
alike, wear white shoes which enclose all their toes except the big
toe. Through the slit in this satyr hoof passes a leather thong.
This strap and a reversed 'V' in velvet maintain in position pattens
like the Greek buskin which add to the wearer's stature, save him
splashing in the mud when it rains and clatter like castanets. When
it is fine they wear pattens that consist merely of wooden or straw
soles. They leave them outside on the doorsteps and the mats inside
are subjected only to the soft tread of satyrs in white canvas. Smart
people are distinguished by the way these white pattens fit the
feet with the strap hardly pressing between the toes at all.

Ceremony, I repeat, has pride of place. It is the rite that is all
important, and it is because a person has failed to observe some rite

or other that he commits suicide. Ceremonial and rank. From the Emperor (Number One) down to the poorest, each person keeps his relative place in the social scale and gives way to no one.

The actor has the right to a larger or smaller number of orchestral players according to his reputation. Lacquer hats tied under the chin with braid, head-dresses of black muslin, plaits, tassels, monograms, fans or fly-whisks, indicate the privileges of the bonze wrestler or courtesan.

Japan rises out of the sea. The sea threw it up like a shell of mother of pearl. The sea reserves the right to destroy it and take it back.

Since the pale fish, speckled with black and red, were the original source of the decorative idiom of Japanese art, they too appear to fall in with the national style. The Samurai, bristling with antennae and pincers, fought under the lacquer carapace of the crustaceans; shrubs imitate coral branches, and marine plants adorn the gardens of houses that look like frail fishing-craft.

The Japanese regale themselves on raw fish. The food is impregnated with a tang of the sea, and this perhaps throws light on the resemblance some Japanese types have to Eskimoes. It is all very confused and difficult to disentangle. I have to grope my way endeavouring to penetrate to the hearts of my hosts.

Photographers, photographers, photographers! That has now become the leitmotiv of our journey. At the Kyoto hotel, after we have been on a road that might be in the province of Lorraine, the servants recognize us and ask for our autographs. We escape so that we can dine in the Japanese style and go on afterwards to a geisha dance. The dinner, unpretentious and charming, in a small hall where we are served by a girl who looks like Igor Markevitch's sister, Tempera. After sukiyaki we have beef or chicken and vegetables which are cooked on a charcoal stove let into the centre of the table. Sukiyaki is the national dish of Japan. It comprises giant prawns, pimento and fried cucumber dipped in brown sauce. It is eaten with chopsticks. Saké – rice alcohol – poured out warm into tiny porcelain cups, replaces our wine and accompanies the meal.

We had eaten sukiyaki before, at the Japanese restaurant in Singapore. But the sukiyaki enchants us with its delicate perfumes at Kobe where we spent an evening. It must have been the hell-fire heat of the sun and Singapore curry that deprived it of its full savour. At the restaurant Miwa, which is built like a castle of cards, with wood, straw and paper, stuffed with armour, helmets, Samurai swords, kakemonos, rocks, bridges thrown over miniature rivers which seem to wind through the rooms themselves, we ate a first-class sukiyaki and drank saké. Vestal virgins of food on their knees served it to us.

At Tokyo the geishas, further priestesses of good manners, were to serve us food in a kneeling posture, bubbling with laughter and drinking from our cups. The geisha girls come from humble families. They are taken and educated at the age of twelve. When their training has taught them how to charm their guests, play musical instruments, sing, dance and converse with men, they qualify as geishas. They must not be mistaken for courtesans. Their role is limited to creating a pleasant atmosphere. They are, so to speak, perfumes for the guests to inhale. They respect order, and the rules of the game decree that they shall never go beyond certain prescribed limits. A central club of geishas has their addresses and sends them to order. Heavily powdered, made up with a mask in which their eyes move behind almond-shaped slits made with a penknife, crowned with shells, sombre coils and rolls of hair, built up in a monumental fashion, can we guess to what extent they accept without rebelling their slavelike existence and long evenings of decorative charm?

Exquisite actresses, automata whose make-up of white plaster stops short at the shoulder and elbows which mechanically execute a series of predetermined gestures, actresses whose gold-toothed smile is concealed like a yawn behind a fan and who sometimes put on learned spectacles with tortoise-shell frames.

They tender their names and addresses to us on cards, should I say rather, tongues of paper. *April Rain, Dynasty of Light, Gay Spring*.

*Dynasty of Light* is Utamaro's Japanese girl as one imagines her from the books. Her head is like an egg in equilibrium and it is crowned with a halo of black hair. Her body is a chrysalis, a larva in the act of metamorphosis, for multicoloured wings unfold on her round back. *April Rain*'s face is not so oval. It is a little ball of ivory, sugar and Indian ink. Her mouth is a crimson gash. Her coiffure is that which modern women adopted in 1870. Shells and volutes give way to plaits and fichus.

*Gay Spring* offers the distressing spectacle of the geisha in revolt. The geisha who is not content to let herself be one; who dreams of Hollywood. *Gay Spring*, a victim of the cinema, is no longer the young maiden driven mad by the lion of Kagami-Jishi, but the young maiden unhinged by the Metro-Goldwyn lion. She is ambitious. She adopts a fashionable hair-style. She speaks in a loud voice and swings her hips. She is unhappy. Her limitations are considerable and this makes her distress all the greater. She clings to what she considers the free and chivalrous element in us. Her job of charming this race of clean, impeccable, cold insects for whom woman is a vase of flowers, gives her the eyes of a crazy hen, and a miserable fixed grin does service for a smile. 'Oh, Mister Cocteau! Mister Cocteau!' She would like to talk to us, explain herself despite the glares from the others which keep her in her place. 'Mister Cocteau! Mister Cocteau!' She seizes my hand, kisses it and presses it to her breast and addresses me with a painful appeal, in execrable English. 'Since I saw your picture in the newspaper, I wanted to come near you, look at you, speak to you.' That was as far as it got. What could she do? And what can I do to remove a poor, struggling fly from this spider's web? The sounds of the gramophone replace chords from the instruments and songs in which the voice chokes in the throat, stylizing cries and tears. Mistinguett sings instead. I dance with *Gay Spring.* That is to say, I ferry round her paper prison a drowning woman clinging to a spar, one cheek glued to my shoulder, hands that clutch me. 'Oh, oh, Mister Cocteau!' Her wail rends my heart. Solemn, reproving eyes follow us round, inspect and pass judgment on us. The deeper she sinks down and the wilder she gets, the more I realize how impossible it is for me to come to her aid.

Two geishas are fighting for Passepartout. They are playing *mora* – guessing the number of fingers – for who is to have this dance. How far we have travelled away from Parisiennes for whom it is enough to be a woman. The weaker sex becomes the stronger sex. Women who eat or women whom you eat. Here the women serve us with things to eat and argue as to who shall have a young man as dancing partner. Mistinguett is still singing. Her pathetic voice reminds me of my own town where women triumph. Poor *Gay Spring,* she is becoming heavier and heavier. When the record has finished playing, she presses my hand to her lips and says 'Thankoo.' She would need a great deal of educating before she could shed this vanquished spirit. She literally drowns and sinks to the bottom before our eyes. La Fontaine says, 'I am not one of those who say, "It's nothing. It's only a woman drowning."' Our hosts are thinking, 'It's nothing, it's only a woman drowning,' and *Gay Spring* turns with all her remaining strength towards the perch that I would like to hold out for her. But what use is it to extend a bogus perch? I am leaving Japan and within nineteen days I shall be completing my tour of the world. I must take my place again on the mat between my hosts, eat a strawberry on the end of a stick, watch *Gay Spring* at the bottom of the water.

'Oh, Mister Cocteau!' The plaintive cry, continually repeated, haunts my ears. This morning, a double mirror that fits into a box was left at my hotel, a gift from *Gay Spring.* As I leave I haul a fishing-net in to my shoulder and in this net is *Gay Spring*, dead. She says nothing more; bewildered, on the doorstep, she gazes at the shoes that I am about to put on and which are to bear me far away from her island. Passepartout whispers in my ear, 'Nothing to be done, poor little creature.' And if he is plotting to carry her off as Aouda was carried off, he gives up the idea as he encounters the glance of the priests of national duty which geishas must also obey.

We climb into a car. *Gay Spring*'s face, less made up than any of the others, is pressed against the window. A few moments ago she was criticizing Japanese *danseuses* for never smiling and for dancing with a mask on. It is a mask without a smile that is now pressed against the window, jerked away as we suddenly start off and left behind there in the midst of the lanterns and poles.

I turn round. The little rear window frames a distressing scene. *Gay Spring*, her hands enveloped in the folds of her kimono, hobbling on her pattens, her mouth open as if shaping a cry, is trying to run after us.

Carried away by my emotions, I have reversed the order of events. Before this dinner which leaves this bitter memory we contemplated some spectacles which are well worth describing.

I left you high and dry at Kyoto. We were going to the theatre where the geishas dance. The theatre opens out at the bottom of a kind of cul-de-sac, illuminated by lanterns and chandeliers. Carriages advance and retreat; the compact throng enters by a kind of ramp where men cover our shoes with a blue and white protective linen overshoe.

Several of the bigwigs of Kyoto offered me cards and fans. They joined our group. First we go to a waiting-room. Then attendants lead us through a maze of staircases and corridors to a room furnished with chairs, set out behind each other as at amateur theatricals. We are present at the ceremony of tea-drinking. Two priestesses of tea (geishas), whose white make-up ends in three points at the nape of the neck, take turns in front of the holy table and prepare and stir the green tea with ritual gestures with a wooden spoon and whisk. After the ceremony they pour it into cups which diminutive geishas (fourteen-year-old girls who look no more than eight), painted up, wearing head-dresses and dressed like grown-up geishas, set down on lacquer tables in front of each of us. They bow and withdraw gravely into the wings.

The left hand curves to the shape of the cup, the right hand is placed flat against it. The tea, a brew of jade-coloured leaves, is drunk in one draught. The 'faithful' get up and go back to the waiting-room. A small door opens and, in accordance with the

ancient custom, the crowd rushes and crushes to gain the amphitheatre where the best places go to the strongest.

Our surprise of moving from these small rooms into this well-lit
edifice and seeing the public roll forward in great waves, crowd in
and pile up in silence, is the best part of the spectacle. The standard
of female choreography is pretty feeble and the oriental theatre has
gained by forbidding women access to the stage.

The men who take women's parts add an overtone which
enhances them and supplies the additional emphasis that the bigness
of a stage demands. Women playing men's parts weaken the effect.
The angles are rounded off, the lines get blurred. The ensemble
here, décor and costume, is derived to some extent from our music-
hall. Too much *brio*, too many lights. There is no question here of
stage-hands moving about on the stage, which is thirty yards wide.
The scenery flies up, descends or glides with fantastic precision. I
have seen a whole household of Fuji courtesans, who were trying to
entice two heroes through the bay-window, suddenly transformed
into the base of the same house, staircase and door. The women
walked down a few stairs. The illusion was complete. The only
difference from our music-hall – which adds a churchlike solemnity
to this programme – is that the women never smile. Neither the
actresses in the play *The Journey from Kobe to Tokyo* nor the
instrumentalists, ten on the left, ten on the right, seated on the floor
in long alcoves decorated with red fabrics and forming the sides of
the trapezium of which the stage is the base. On the left five
musicians beat cylindrical drums with wooden sticks or drums like
hour-glasses with a bronze wand. Five flautists bring up the rear of
this solemn show. On the right the orchestra is divided into five
players of those long mandolins which are played with an ivory
plectrum, and five singers, with the music placed before them on
lacquered music-stands. The players on the left are dressed in black
kimonos with white floral patterns. Those on the right in sky-blue
kimonos with purple patterns.

Sometimes the musicians are moved back by a mechanical device,
revealing a pit. A green curtain hides them from view and a new
row rises up from the pit like the Paramount cinema orchestra. And
all these drummers, flautists and singers proffer their livid, tortoise
faces and all the female dancers become a troupe of ghosts and
somnambulist Pierrots to this accompaniment torn out of the silence
note by note.

It was two days later in Tokyo at the Kabuki-Za Theatre that
I was to witness the amazing dumb-show of the Kagami-Jishi play.
A band of young painters and poets were awaiting me, and photo-
graphers galore. We arrived at eight o'clock in the evening; play

after play had already been performed and Kikugoro Onye VI was making himself up and expending every effort for the benefit of the vast public of which he is the idol. Kikugoro has to start purifying himself, preparing, bathing in the midst of his hairdressers, costumiers and general assistants. Auditorium crowded. Stage thirty yards wide, low ceiling; ideal proportions.

The unsatisfactory proportions of our narrow, overtowering stages would diminish a Kikugoro or a Mi Lang and cramp their acting.

Two bridges with illuminated boards pass over the seats and link the stage to the back of the auditorium; on the left, the evil road, on the right, the road of flowers.

The magnesium explodes and a young poetess offers me a bouquet on behalf of the President of the Society of Men of Letters. The audience stands up to watch this interlude. At exactly half past eight the famous dumb-show in one act by Ochi Fukuchi, accompanied by the music of Nagauta, begins.

The scene is set in a room in the palace on New Year's Day. The orchestra of fourteen male instrumentalists and singers, dressed in black and pale blue, occupy an open alcove back-stage. Dignitaries of the palace and aged ladies-in-waiting converse beside an altar covered with lion masks. These masks consecrate the residence on this solemn fête day. Ladies and gentlemen come out. The orchestra plays alone and the narrator relates that they will be returning with a young maid-of-honour, Yayoe. They will ask her to dance with one of the masks in order to bring good luck. The doors slide open on the court side, and Kikugoro makes his entry, acclaimed by the audience. He is playing the part of the young girl. The gentlemen and ladies-in-waiting thrust him into the middle of the stage despite his resistance. His nervousness proves too strong. He drags them into the wings, and a second time they push him forward and implore him to dance. He or she? It is 'she' we must say. Of this somewhat heavy, plump, fifty-year-old man nothing is left but a delicate young person turning his head on a slender neck and weaving round his gestures the décor of his stiff, mauve and sky-blue robes that terminate in a heavy train of red quilted folds.

This dance, long but not too long, repaid our journey. It was worth undertaking for this alone. Two supers on their knees, dressed in bistre robes, turn their backs and with formal gestures pass over the fans which he brings into play. In his hands these fans become razors that cut throats, sabres that sever heads, falling leaves, trays bearing poison-philtres, aeroplane propellers, the sceptres of kings. When he has finished he throws them behind with a brisk movement and the supers receive them as if they were arrows.

He approaches the altar and seizes one of the lion-masks. This mask is lengthened by a yellow silk scarf. Almost as soon as the mask is in his hands it comes to life. The jaw clatters. The scarf rolls and twines round. The young maiden dances. And in come two butterflies. Stage-hands dangle them on the end of poles. The lion leaps. The maiden becomes more and more excited. The mask subjugates and hypnotizes her. Finally the assistants retreat and the bewildered girl, compelled to follow the lion-mask, joins his retinue on the left-hand door.

At this point Kikugoro attains sublimity. He endeavours to conquer the spell. His head turns to one side. His hand makes his jaws crack and it seems to tear itself away from him. He hiccups, stumbles, falls, rises to his feet, in a series of spasms, crosses the room and leaves the stage amid a thunder of applause.

The orchestra divides into two parts and allows a platform to be passed over which supports two peonies. A tree of red and a tree of white peonies. In Japanese symbolism butterflies and peonies always escort the lion. The orchestra closes up again and accompanies the dance of the butterflies – two male dancers dressed in scarlet kimonos with sky-blue sashes and female wigs and little gold drums round their necks which they beat with fragile drumsticks. They execute symmetrical dance figures, beat their drums alternately and hop on one leg in front of the platform.

A repeated roar can be heard from the audience. The butterflies disappear. The orchestra is increased twofold by stage-hands who on the right- and left-hand sides of the proscenium beat the stage floor with drumsticks. And all at once with short rapid steps, his arms stiff under his gold sleeves, Kikugoro crosses the 'bad' road and comes on to the stage. He is wearing a white bristling mane which frames him and trails five yards behind. A red make-up gives him an angry mouth and eyebrows. His feet prance. His arms stretch out. His mane flutters, as though it was writing out the silent text of the play with an enormous brush. The maiden has become a lion.

Drunk with rage and fatigue the lion falls asleep among the peonies. The butterflies return and plague him. He wakes up and the curtain falls on his wrath and stupefaction.

Kikugoro is not only a mimic but a priest. This spectacle is liturgical; not in the sense of our mystery plays but in the strictly religious sense. I am not speaking of a religious theatre but of the religion of the theatre. Kikugoro and his orchestra are celebrating mass.

We are pulled along to his dressing-room. We cross foyers, court-yards, basements where you guess the mechanism of the revolving

stage to be concealed, corridors and different levels. We catch sight
of white rooms in which kneeling musicians are congratulating each
other. We go up, descend, mount again and finally make our way
to Kikugoro's dressing-room. We remove our shoes. We find ourselves face to face with the people's idol, a robust little man dressed
as a Samurai page who shows us the muscles which mask-dancing
develops on his arms and complains that they spoil him for playing
women's roles.

When the photographer asked me to shake hands with him I
realized that Kikugoro was afraid my hand might rub off the
make-up on his. I therefore made as if to shake hands with him,
keeping my hand at a slight distance away from his. He gave me
one of those inimitable glances such as fellow-actors exchange who
are aware of a situation and know something about theatrical
tradition. Next day I had hardly finished speaking about him on
the radio when he sent a messenger up to me on the hill as I was
coming away from the relay station, to express his gratitude.

Kikugoro Onoye, sixth of that name, and who wears the leonine
peruke that belonged to his ancestors in the play of Kagami-Jishi,
is to take the plays of the Dan Kiku Festival to the Paris Opera
House. But I feel nervous about the staging there. His acting
requires space, a perfect stage and a good audience. I am afraid
that our Opera House cannot fulfil any of these conditions.

Next day, after a somewhat sultry morning, Foujita and Nico,
my interpreter, take us along to the Kokugikan (Palace of Sports)
to see the Japanese wrestling matches which continue from dawn
onwards.

To reach one of the entrances you have to pass through a marshy
district where oranges, sugar-plums, souvenirs, postcards of popular
wrestlers are to be had at street-stalls. All the familiar hurly-burly
of Spanish arenas on bullfight days. Suddenly I find myself in a
gigantic amphitheatre, filled to the roof, and I stumble between
wooden cubicles into which cushions, empty bottles, orange-peel,
old shoes and felt hats have been thrown. A notable has invited us
into his box, one of those compartments where you sit down on the
ground itself.

In the centre of the amphitheatre stands the platform. A circular
mat under a pagoda roof supported by four pillars, white, black,
green and red respectively. A mauve canopy, surrounded by awnings of sea-blue, swells above the ring. Up there round the glass
partitions above the tiers of spectators, soldiers and schoolboys are
displayed colossal photographs of last year's victors.

In the ring itself under the supervision of referees in silver
kimonos who wear on their heads black lacquer helmets with

antennae and are armed with a kind of glassless mirror – the attribute of their office – the wrestlers eye each other. The bout itself will hardly last a second. It is the preliminaries which are responsible for these outbursts of cries, punctuated by silence. The wrestlers are pink, youthful Hercules who might have fallen from the roof of the Sistine Chapel and belong to a race of which only very rare specimens exist today. Some of them trained up in the old method display enormous bellies and women's breasts. But they are not the bellies and breasts of obesity. They derive from an ancient cult and bear witness to strength distributed in a different fashion. The others reveal the muscle development of our modern stadiums. A dark-coloured girdle is rolled round the waist, passes between the legs, dividing the buttocks and leaving a skirt of stiff wires draped over the hips. When the wrestlers stoop, these skirts erect themselves and lend them the appearance of cocks or porcupines.

Both categories possess charming feminine heads surmounted with a chignon. This is a thick lock of hair which they curl back, pin up to the top of their skull and spread out into a fan-shape.

After sprinkling salt on the platform to purify it, the opponents straddle their legs, place their hands on their hips, sway slowly and ponderously from one foot to the other. This bearlike motion makes them supple. They stoop down, face to face, waiting for a propitious moment, a miracle of equilibrium, an engagement of their wills. They are considering holds, calculating, they tense themselves and suddenly, as if by common consent, relax and abandon their stance and without even looking at each other turn back and leave the platform. The umpire allows them ten minutes of these fruitless trials. All at once the contact is made, their great bodies confront each other; they make a hold, slap each other, trample, snatch at the soil and in the storm of flashlight photographs a human tree rolls down to the edge of the platform, uprooted by the magnesium flash.

In the penultimate match a modern style athlete with a pleasant pug-face pits himself against the 'invincible' – a buddha whose paunch rests on his narrow boxer's hips. We were lucky enough to witness a rare spectacle. No sooner had they made up their minds and confronted each other than a perfect equilibrium of forces resulted in a clinch. If I half close my eyes I can see only one animal, one pink ox composed of these motionless bodies. This bridgelike immobility is prolonged to such an extent that no one breathes and you wonder if it will ever end and whether you are not witnessing a petrification of opposing forces. The deadlock becomes intolerable. The referee separates the bodies by giving a

sign with the attribute of office. People applaud. When they recom-
mence, the opponents find themselves in exactly the same posture,
but the distribution of forces may no longer cancel out, and when
they mount on to the platform and their bodies are interlocked it
is amid a respectful silence from the audience. And once more there
is a deadlock. Their limbs are planted apart, their fingers insinuate
themselves between their opponent's flesh and girdle, the stiff wires
bristle, their muscles swell and their feet take root in the mat; the
blood mounts to the surface of their flesh and colours it a bright
pink. Suddenly the 'invincible' discovers a flaw, exploits it and
breaks the clinch. The magnesium crackles and accompanies the
downfall of one of the pillars of the human bridge which gives way
and topples over backwards.

The victor sprinkles salt on the platform, the vanquished gets up,
goes back to the side, kneels and bows his head.

This year once more the athletes' idol will be awarded the
Ryogoky cup and his photograph will hang side by side with
Kikugoro's in prostitutes' rooms.

Our host opens the door of the wrestlers' quarters for us. A kind
of cloistered vault in which young divinities of rose marble with
women's eyes and chignons take their baths. Some of them splash
in a trough, others are strolling around in black kimonos with white
peonies; others again smile under their mops of hair which they
allow to grow until they can put it up, tie and pin it and spread it
in the form of a cockade.

I move forward to the victor who is squatting on a stone pedestal.
A hairdresser is combing and knotting his lacquered chignon. This
ingenuous monster is smooth and pink, and it is against a kind of
Easter egg that I am leaning for the photographers. This proof-
photograph of the victor being congratulated by Phileas Fogg and
Passepartout will be smiling at us tomorrow evening from the door
of the women in Tamanoï, one of the new quarters of Japanese
prostitution.

*

Tonight Foujita is acting as our guide. We cross a sombre park
and emerge in the middle of an avenue with cinemas; a beflagged
avenue, glaringly brilliant. The productive energy displayed completely bowls me over. I wonder how I could believe in the energy
of my own town without knowing this monstrous procession of
crowded halls, one on top of another, which shout at you with all
their hoardings, lanterns and flags. Not only does the avenue stretch
on interminably, one cinema theatre following another, but the

river is joined by tributaries and these adjacent streets pour out a
never-satisfied throng of Japanese and Chinese.

It is useless to try and reach the end of these streets and this
avenue. Tokyo, the destroyed and reconstructed, is an octopus with
rubber tentacles. But when the dream changes into a nightmare
you approach one of the five quarters which pile their closed houses
at the place where there are five ancient town gateways. Moats
surround each of these quarters, the most famous of which is called
Yoshiwara. Women are not allowed to leave the enclosure.

At the time of the cataclysm of 1922 the wooden brothels blazed
away merrily; the cyclone fanned the sheets of iron to a white heat
which decapitated some and roasted others. Women, their necks
crushed, were trapped between the beams and screamed beneath
the ruins; the boiling water in the moats boiled alive those who had
been seeking refuge from the collapsing earth. Corpses of women,
made up, decked out, hair styled, unrecognizable, stank in the
absence of a sanitary service. The Japanese believed Japan to be
destroyed and made no more effort.

The fact was that three-quarters of Tokyo were reduced to ruins,
the fire increased the tragedy and famine took charge of the rest.

To come back to our evening. Sombre avenues and waste ground
with fences round it ended in the labyrinth of Yoshiwara. A
labyrinth of streets that cross and ramify like the branches of a
genealogical tree.

All at once cinemas and garish film-posters. Then a succession of
brothels, display-photographs of prostitutes. Prior to the great
disaster they used to parade silently behind a show window and
display themselves in person as they stood up dressed in marvellous
robes. The demolished brothels were rebuilt on the same model and
differed only in decorative details. They look like very long, low
exchange offices in which shaven-headed, golden-toothed money-
changers occupy a little cash-desk at each end.

The first changer, supervisor of this suspect theatre, is nicknamed
'cow'. He stays in the stables. The second 'horse'. If the client
forgets his purse, 'horse' leaves the stable and accompanies him to
his home. There he collects the money. If it is lacking, he takes
away a walking-stick, a book or a hat.

On the right- and left-hand side four steps where the clients
remove their shoes. At the top of the stairs a curtain of embroidered
silk acts as a partition and you can feel a white face watching you.
Among the singular 'changers' who smile and call out to us as we
pass is a 'show window' containing photographs of the prostitutes
available and a niche housing ebony carvings, bronze goddesses or
sexual shells. Lanterns, dwarf cedars, signs in black lacquer

announcing side-show games, and little mottoes with their letters
cut out and picked out in white paint, gold-powdered screens, folds
of purple silk, views of rivers bordered with houses by moonlight
conscientiously painted in vernacular style. The brothels rival each
other in luxury and mystery.

Passepartout, hailed by the crapulous bonzes, intrigued by the
gaps in the crimson curtains and the shadow theatre on the wallpaper, declares that one ought to conquer one's European shyness
and see the rites of the Shogi priestesses of the cult *in situ*. He runs
off at top speed and disappears into one of the brothels. We pace
up and down, and then, as we are afraid of confusing the streets,
we go in after him and decide to wait on the first floor and drink
tea until he returns. An old female asks us to sit down on the mats
and goes off to find us some prostitutes to keep us company. These
seventeen- or eighteen-year-old girls, sold and exploited by their
families, get along without the aid of pimps. They sign contracts
for three, five or seven years and earn fifty yen a year (250 francs).
Passepartout's partner was astonished to receive a tip of more than
three yen paid in advance. She saw the patroness to ask whether
this tip was really for her, she cannot believe her eyes.

When Passepartout rejoins us he is still blushing with shame. It
is intolerable, criminal, he declares. All this ceremonial of tea-
pouring, mattress removal, slipping on of kimonos, masking of
lamps, to end up with this pallid child who kicks her legs about in
the darkness, swaddled in swansdown and linen. Take away this
padding and you are left with a creature the size of a half-drowned
angora cat.

And Passepartout drags his feet gloomily, congratulating himself
on his heroism and wishful about his adventure. He accuses me of
cowardice and I confess that I should never have succeeded in
conquering my shyness. So we cross the River Sounida weighed
down with melancholy, and the car takes us as far as Tamanoï, the
quarter of the cheap brothels.

At Tamanoï, where the photographs of us taken at the Kokugikan precede us, the women inhabit huts as closely crowded
together as the cubicles in public baths. A wicket-gate frames
ravishing faces of little peasant girls under red lighting which shows
these flower-market roses to advantage. They let out calls, laugh
and make eyes at us. Sometimes one of the poor girls dozes off.
Her poor head, cut off, swollen with fatigue, drops down at the
edge of the peep-hole window.

These love-cabins measure six feet by nine, the alleys ten. A
labyrinth in Hades and one which these girls never leave.

We hear plaintive notes from a pipe. Two monotonous notes. It is the blind masseur. Groping his way – which is not difficult since the house façades nearly meet – he offers his services and announces his arrival. The blind masseur and his pipe finish Passepartout off. He begs us to return to the hotel and we run a double gauntlet of dropping heads – a massacre of pretty, waxen faces.

*

I receive the delegation of young poets, young painters and that of the official painters. Passepartout's packing-case is filled with my books in Japanese, boxes containing boxes which contain boxes, full of escritoires, sticks of Indian ink, paint-brushes and sketch-books.

I open an exhibition of traditional kakemonos and an exhibition of young painters.

The kakemono-painters wear the costume of their ancestors. The young painters, caps and tweeds as worn in Montparnasse. A great deal of skill, power, grace, vivacity expended by both parties. At the base and the apex of the Empire.

The *President Coolidge* leaves Yokohama at six o'clock. At ten to six I pass down the gangplank preceded by photographers who walk backwards pointing their cameras at us. At five minutes to six I am still signing autographs. The ship's band – trumpet, saxophone, trombone and big drum – plays execrable leave-taking music. Paper-streamers link the ship to the quayside. The wind puffs them out, breaks and entangles them. Our newly made friends wave their handkerchiefs to us in the distance. Six o'clock. On the left a small car divided a knot of people. We catch sight of little Charlie Chaplin and little Paulette Goddard who are coming on board. Solemn sirens send out their appeal. Charlie Chaplin shakes himself free from the journalists. With his felt hat put on sideways – Napoleon Bonaparte style, one hand in his waistcoat, the other behind his back, this lonely figure who is too much at home everywhere to be at home anywhere, climbs up the gangway and gets away with a final pirouette. It is all over. The *Coolidge* glides off. The quayside moves away. The island leaves us. Our friends ashore grow smaller and smaller, almost disappear and continue their invisible farewell gestures. I let go my handkerchief. Passepartout does likewise. The two butterflies of Kagami-Jishi whirl round and alight on the waves.

## THE KUROYAKI

The oldest shop in Tokyo survived the cataclysm. It is a miracle of elegance in black and gold. Giant tortoises serve as a shop-sign. This herbalist stocks a love-philtre. It is the speciality which the proprietress sells without a hint of irony. A male and female lizard, roasted, face to face, preserve their delicate form in a small jar. Crush them to powder. Keep half the dose in your pocket and throw the rest over a girl whose love you desire without her noticing it. This philtre is making the fortune of this family which for five generations has been selling apples, ox-hearts, toads, tortoises, carp, bats, earth-worms and monkeys' heads in bowls in which at first you can only distinguish shining charcoal. It is the therapeutics of the Kuroyaki; the explanation of the witches' cauldrons in *Macbeth* and *Faust*. There is no legend which has not a definite source and whose origin cannot be discovered by the observant traveller. I bring away a charming monkey-head, a veritable Yorick in lightweight charcoal – a remedy for madness – and three small jars of the lizard-powder which can cause maidens to become infatuated.

*

## MICROBUS

An American lady in Tokyo offered me a cricket in a cage. Passepartout baptizes him Microbus. Microbus leaves his cage at night. He sleeps in the top of the thermos flask and plays the long green guitar that forms part of his body with great charm. Here is the story I made up to amuse Charlie Chaplin :

### THE MIKADO'S PRESENT

The Emperor of Japan wanted to send me a cricket named Microbus but he possessed only one cage, containing a little East wind. This little East wind captured in the autumn refreshed him in the summer. In short, he would have to take counsel, yet that was impossible, for no one in the world is allowed to address the Emperor. No one, that is, save the Duke O.K., Constable of the Cages, who is permitted to speak to the Emperor once every seven years, one Sunday between six and eight in the morning provided the sun is shining and the Empress mother has sneezed the night before.

He had hardly opened his mouth – for the stipulated conditions were fulfilled – than the Emperor commanded him to commit hari-kari. But after pointing to the sun, his watches and pretending to sneeze. But after pointing to the sun, his matches and pretending to the Emperor that he should put the East wind under a porcelain bowl and offer the cage to Microbus and that he should, above all, clean it well so the cricket should not catch a chill.

The Emperor was overjoyed. 'How wise I was,' he said, 'to allow my subjects to address me.'

The *Coolidge*, with her bronze and marble staircases shrouded in the mist, her floating dining-saloons, gold and crystal, her shops and unstable bathing-pools, is sailing through a thick fog, booming out her solemn siren calls. Sky-scrapers of grey water beat against the cabin walls. Everything creaks, groans, thunders. Balanced on the edge of seasickness.

*

## 26th MAY – MICROBUS SINGS

I have just received a cable on board from *Gay Spring*, 'Bon voyage'.

Tonight I wake up with a start. What is happening? Is it an alarm signal? The cabin is filled with a strange din. Passepartout, whom it would take more than a thunderbolt to wake up, is awakened and switches on the light. The noise emanates from Microbus, the Japanese grasshopper or cricket, that fake little tree-leaf, no bigger than a French bean, singing! His song is phenomenal, risks waking the *Coolidge*, prevents us from speaking, drowns the buffeting of the waves. It is like a sawmill in full swing, a thousand rattles turning. And when it stops it is only to slow down with the dull explosions and gaspings of an outboard motor. Then he tries to find his pitch again, chattering, stammering, soaring, he succeeds and begins his song. This amazing noise coming from the insect has something uncanny, almost frightening, about it. Passepartout wonders if he is not singing his dying song, for it is said that the Japanese cricket dies of exhaustion from singing, like the swan.

Passepartout unhooks the cage which hung from the thermos handle and places it on the table between our two bunks. I am going to find Charlie Chaplin. On his shoulder Microbus hasn't a care in the world. He just sings. He holds a high and endless trill without faltering. Is he going to give up the ghost? Is he calling a female? Is it a song of love, war or death? An infinity of kingdoms separates us. We shall never know the motive behind this song. An hour later the mysterious spring seizes up and Microbus is silent. We all look at each other. But he is not dead. He is in fine form. His death would have left a gap. We shall never forget this howling leaf; this Japanese tenor singing in the night.

# *Joan of Arc*

In his brief introduction to *Reines de la France* (Queens of France) Cocteau states that the essays it contains were originally written to accompany a book of etchings by Christian Bérard, published in 1949, and he feared that 'they might suffer from appearing without their costumes'. He goes on to say : 'But I have consulted so many volumes in order to write these short studies that they may have retained some life.'

The nineteen individuals and the one composite figure who make up the book are not all known outside France, but Cocteau was not writing to educate his readers and had no wish to repeat merely what history books had told him. He does not throw away history, but he succeeds in each case in illuminating an aspect of his heroine, which orthodox chroniclers and biographers had either forgotten, concealed or usually never even noticed.

He refers to Joan of Arc elsewhere as his favourite writer.

Of all French writers Joan of Arc is the one I admire most. She signed her name with a cross, since she did not know how to write. But I'm speaking of her language and her despatches which are sublime. Why does she write and express herself so well? Because she thinks well and this is the first requisite of style. She says what she wants to say in a few words. The replies at her trial are master-pieces.

These replies reflect her short and sensational life better than History can recount it to us.

Joan was not a little shepherdess from our countryside. She was a young girl from a great house who helped her family in the same way as other little girls of the penniless nobility.

Later she frequented the gilded youth of the Court. The King's gentlemen became her comrades. She adopted their ease and tact.

It is very probable that her purity and trustfulness met with no response from her entourage – who eventually found her irritating – and that her comrades, less naïve than she was, finally dragged her into some adventure less glorious than she had believed.

She let herself be caught in a commando-raid – to use a term from our era – whose aims were not hers. When she was captured nobody took the trouble to come to her assistance. She embarked on the career of setback and solitude to which all great figures must submit before they can shine in the sky of wonders.

Joan's life is too famous for us to set out the details. Let it suffice for us to write that this saint glitters in all her armour beside Antigone and those whose disobedience to dead rules perpetuates the dignity of living.

There is no doubt that, from the time of her first deed as a visionary, Joan became a plaything of silk and metal in the hands of politics. She was too ingenuous to understand it very clearly, too clean not to realize this and not to feel distress as a result. One has the impression that she sometimes threw herself at death and that it is because she escaped that the idea of witch took shape and brought about her downfall.

Nothing irritates great lords so much as acquired fame. Great lords and captains. Lyautey was the victim of this. Joan was not exiled but handed over, abandoned, burnt.

But neither Church nor great lords know that certain souls are salamanders. They move about magnificently within the fire. Burn someone like Joan! She is born again from her ashes, flies up and fills the horizon with an *arc-en-ciel*, a rainbow.

# Paul Verlaine, Place du Panthéon

Cocteau had his favourites among the writers and artists of the past but did not often write about any one of them specifically or at any length. An important exception is a long and refreshing essay about Jean-Jacques Rousseau which he dictated in 1939 and which was subsequently published in a literary history and later in the *Poésie Critique*, Volume I. Another exception is this brief article on Verlaine, sparked off by a hostile piece by André Gide. This article reveals Cocteau's remarkable talent for making us think he must have actually met the unhappy poet he describes. We are reminded of that famous remark from *La Difficulté d'Etre* : 'I love loving, I hate hatred.'

I was very surprised by one of Gide's articles in which he recounted a meeting with Paul Verlaine as though it were a thing to be ashamed of. There is something mistaken about rehabilitating Paul Verlaine and in condemning him. Both attitudes baffle me. Not least of a poet's metamorphoses is becoming a saint. And their fame is made up of a strange mixture of noisy visibility and of invisibility.

In short, Gide meets Verlaine, who is dead, behind the Panthéon. The admirable character is standing unsteadily, leaning on his stick, his top hat has fallen into the gutter and he is trying to keep at a distance some street-urchins who are insulting him. What a spectacle! And how surprised I am that Gide does not discover the greatness of it.

Imagine this hirsute man, wearing a topcoat, almost an animal, almost a tree, almost changed into a tree or an animal, this Marsyas, this savage God of poetry, forced to defend himself against a stupid gang who are more cruel than the Maenads. Imagine that stick, that vine-stock, that topcoat, that unkempt beard, that bald head, that lost hat, that tracked beast, that swaying tree, and tell me if the wall against which he seeks refuge should not open, save him, petrify him, metamorphose him into some fountain, spray water through his mouth over those wretched urchins, and an angel appear, a terrible angel who sounds the trumpet?

For my part, I find this Verlaine of the street, this Verlaine at grips with childish silliness, this Verlaine haunted by the great criminal opals of absinth and by the word love, this solitary Verlaine, lost in an almost deserted square in the Ecoles district, a suitable and definitive illustration of the mythology of poets. I would like those who marvel at him to see him like this : dirty, uprooted, drawn, incapable of furnishing some striking proof of the miracles which dwell within him. What would I not have given to have been present at this incomparable moment. And since nothing supernatural happened, alas, in that stone square, on that heartless pavement, I would have enjoyed cuffing those young idiots, picking up the dirty hat, wiping it on my sleeve and offering my arm to Verlaine as the Queen of Naples offered hers to the Baron de Charlus.

Why did Gide not allow himself this luxury? Must we see in this embarrassment, in his Protestant reserve, the defensive reflex of the Encyclopédistes when faced with the shameful behaviour of Rousseau? I wonder. Gide is an enigma. He freezes rapidly in front of the fire. Verlaine! This dog-man, this bearded lady, this adorable monster, possessed the privilege of swan feathers which don't get wet and don't get dirty. A child, that is what he was. For just as youth revolts me when it goes on too long, so in the same way does that childhood which accompanies a man until his death opens wide for him the gates of eternal fame. I even think that the guardian angel is none other than the symbol of this childhood which only leaves us when we do not know how to be worthy of it.

Through a curious phenomenon, it is difficult to give the same stature to Verlaine the vagabond (the Verlaine of London, Brussels, the Boulevard Saint-Michel, the hospitals) and the Paul Verlaine of the first period. It could be said that he never stops growing. It could be said that this bald little teacher who took his songs to Lemerre grows gradually from his shadow thrown by the gas lamps which put it out of shape. His topcoat and his opera hat and his streaming muffler and his stick enlarge his substance, extend it and succeed in making him into that magnificent scarecrow attacked by brainless birds. The storms and solitude of his Dionysian escort and the prayer and the pain and his deaths seem to inflict on him tortures of a mysterious growth until they create an astonishing statue which Gide deplored, in the Place du Panthéon, and which I put up alive opposite the ashen colossi which haunt that illustrious mausoleum.

# In Egypt

In 1949 a carefully selected group of twenty-two French actors and actresses made a tour of the Middle East, presenting a repertory of seven plays which included Racine's *Britannicus,* a farce by Feydeau, plays by Sartre and Anouilh and three plays by Cocteau – *La Machine Infernale, Les Monstres Sacrés* and *Les Parents Terribles.* Cocteau went with the actors, who included Jean Marais and Yvonne de Bray, as a kind of producer and ambassador. He kept a highly readable journal which included many notes about the production and reception of the plays, together with descriptions of sightseeing tours and visits to famous people, such as Pierre Loti, the French novelist who then lived in retirement inTurkey.

This description of what he discovered in Egypt, taken from *Maalesh,* is another example of Cocteau's 'indirect journalism'.

19th March, 1949

Had dinner with Wahid. Had arranged to go to see the Sphinx after dinner. Wahid did not seem enthusiastic. There is a ban on such excursions because the King has had a country house built at the foot of the Cheops Pyramid, of the type referred to in France as a 'folly'. Those who belong to the court are afraid that the King might see them if he suddenly turned up on a surprise visit there. I insisted, however, and Wahid gave in. So we are going to the Sphinx. Stopped at the police station beyond Mena House. Carullo gave Wahid's name. A detective got in and came with us. 'Miss Europe' had had dinner with us. Her lovely face showed disappointment when we came to the stony road. 'Where are we going?' 'To the Sphinx.' 'Oh! ... I misunderstood you.'

She thought the Sphinx was a night-club. She had imagined we were taking her to some place of ill-repute.

Last time I saw the Sphinx in 1936 she was surrounded by sand-hills. At the foot of the large vat of sand she lay, like a ship in dry-dock. At that time, I had said that we were walking on ancient temples. Excavations have since been undertaken and proved me right. Now the outer walls of the temple stand revealed, and it would appear likely that the dark-red Sphinx inhabited a niche, surrounded by ramparts and colonnades.

The car stumbles over large stones, slips, scarcely holds the road and goes down the curve which surrounds the huge, pumice-stone coloured mass. Her presence is felt rather than perceived, more grey and pale than the rest. The car comes to a standstill on the platform of sand, facing the walls of the Temple which hide the strange animal up to her breast. She is seen as Napoleon must have seen her.

The car turns and the headlamps light up her chest. The well-known body, gently sloping down, covered with stains as of leprosy, remains in the shadow. We come nearer, through corridors open to the sky. Four ill-shaped steps lead down to the fortress of the moulded Roman paws. The moon comes out, yellow and low. I suggest returning to Cairo to fetch Yvonne and Marais from the theatre and returning when the moon is high.

In Cairo we find that they have left the theatre already.

The car then takes us back to Mena House.

Same police station. Same detective who comes with us. Same joltings on the roadway, but the scene has changed.

From the moon, snow falls down. Her snow now covers the cornices of the terrifying 'machine'. I leave the rest of the party with Dermit, for we are struck dumb with a holy stupor.

In the sky lies the unharnessed Wain, shafts pointing upwards. Strange stopping-place! The Three Wise Men* have struck their tents of stone, stretched from base to point, one side in the shadow and the other three smoothed by the moon. They sleep while their dog lies awake. Their watchdog is the Sphinx. Still ... lying between the desert, the tents of the royal camping ground and the distant city, she stretches out her paws upon the sand and points her ears to catch the sound of dogs barking in farmyards and the prolonged screeching of vultures.

Kings camp as kings must. At some height. Near water which may be drunk. On the margin of silence.

I am glad this region is closed to tourists and couples. Mosques leave me completely unmoved, but here, where men wrapped in burnous prowl around like scene-shifters round the stage, I am integrated in the play which rises effortlessly before me.

This afternoon I had been to see the mosques with Felix R. There we saw the alabaster tombs of sleeping kings. They sleep: kings, with their wives, their sons and their daughters. And in the

*Translator's note: In English we refer to these three stars as 'Orion's belt' but that would spoil the whole word-picture.

porchway, so that their slumbers should in no way be disturbed, visitors take off their shoes, or if they will not, they slip their noisy soles into linen slippers.

Kings and princes sleep under mournful awnings made of alabaster, marble, turquoise, sapphires and gold. No doubt it is the time of the siesta in a country of fête-days, anniversaries and celebrations of this and that, of all the excuses for doing nothing, lying on the ground, sleeping. The palaces are empty. Empty are the great halls, where, from showers of useless flex, dead lamps hang limp.

Here I fail to feel any presence either divine or human. Emptiness alone is wedded to all the tiny ornamentations, the miniature pottery stalactites of these vaults which seem like Turkish baths of giants long dead. Under the milky light of the moon and stars, under the sky whose dark slate is pitted with calculations, I thought : What strange tackle, what warp and woof of unknown material, what harp-strings sensitive to who knows what wind, what spiders' webs did these men spin from one world to another, to catch secrets which are impenetrable?

There is proof enough here that they refused to be resigned, and that their insolent will forced the gods into dialogue.

20th March, 1949

Went this morning to the markets with Carullo and Dermit. We knew the markets, but I did not know this particular crumbling, dusty road, lined with hovels edged with golden jewels. At the same time the poorest and the richest part of Cairo. The district of drunkards and banks. Here men walk in couples, holding each other's little fingers. Here women are veiled and wear ornaments between their eyes. Here you can see the poise acquired through walking with large dishes or baskets balanced on top of the head. Here gold-dust sparkles in the air and at night the urchins scrape the dust together, put it through a sieve and sell what they can to the solderer. I bought two thick chains, because I like gold which is only partly refined and is heavy, dull and dusted as with pollen, but even more because I wanted to look at the work of soldering and cleaning. The solderer directs the flame on to the gold with a pipette. He blows on it and the flame throws out a thin tongue. The gold becomes an incandescent mass, after which it looks dirty. Then it is washed in a second booth, in a turquoise-blue liquid. After that it is dried in a charcoal fire which is fanned the while.

It changes colour and darkens. The workman goes on putting it through successive baths of the turquoise liquid, sand and ash, until it regains its original colour. It is weighed at the Government booth. Then you sign, pay and carry it off.

And now it is Sunday and I am in the theatre. Writing these words I hear the solemn swish of the curtains going up on the matinée of *Les Monstres*. The voice of Yvonne de Bray comes through the microphone as it does on the telephone, harsh, resonant, metallic, round, incisive and warm. In this theatre I now have little to do, but am held by it as a gambler by the gaming-table. If I leave it for a moment it seems to me like desertion. This frenzy for work has at length thrown me into a state of fatigue which has something in common with the condition of the athlete. If I rested I would die.

Waves of Sunday laughter, rather heavy but very living. Religious silence during the scene in which Yvonne de Bray does not speak. She is applauded.

I see by the articles in the Cairo papers that they criticize the acting much more minutely here than with us. In Paris they chop the actors heads off in three lines. If actors are considered good, nothing is said about them. In Cairo half the article is given to them. They are criticized or praised in detail.

Cairo sometimes breaks one's heart. Why? So many, many in rags, such heart-rending contrasts between the richness of the vehicles purring along and the poor who go barefoot. But it is a consolation to think that penury here does not produce as much suffering as it would in France, that there is an easy-going feeling, an ambiance of delight in which the people live and move and have their being – in a way, it gives the feeling produced by the accoutrements of wealth. Gide had warned me of the contrast. He simply could not stand it.

Arab dinner. Came back to the theatre at 9 p.m. The show is starting. The evening audience is highly strung, less sensitive than the afternoon one. One out of four goes home.

Tonight, after the curtain has gone down for the last time, the two first settings of *Léocadia* will be gone over.

The lighting of *Léocadia* is half-lighting, twilight. *In Camera* is a play of neon lighting. It is necessary to draw attention to the effect of the two types of lighting. Sartre has brought on to the stage the feeling and the appearance of the bars of Saint-Germain-des-Prés, where the tubes of neon light throw into relief both faces and souls. Jean Anouilh's characters walk about like slow-motion pictures in an aquarium or an iridescent soap bubble.

Night in the theatre. Beaurepaire's décors are not what they should be, they are not like the sketches which he made. Slovenly workmanship. We had to replace everything on the stage with bits and pieces from the Opéra. Out of this assemblage there emerges a Second Act décor which is almost wildly magnificent, in the style of Raymond Roussel.

20th March, 1949

Reception at the Amitiés Françaises. Crowded. Photographs and autographs. Grenier took the chair. I had not understood that the Amitiés Françaises was a group of people which included Egyptians friendly to France. I thought I was amongst Frenchmen and so the talk was addressed to my own people. I was afraid that I might have put my foot in it, but the Ambassador reassures me on this score. Tired to the very marrow. Many times I thought while speaking that I would neither be able to finish the sentence nor find my feet again, nor close the phrases in parentheses. Yvonne and Jeannot, who came in while I went up on the platform, noticed nothing. But it makes me afraid of what may happen at Alexandria where I have to give an unrehearsed speech for an hour.

I lunched today with Dr Drioton at the Doss's home, which is exquisite and only twenty minutes out of Cairo. He is not like those Egyptologists who love labels. Nor is he literal in his interpretations. He likes to decipher enigmas and is not inimical to our intuitional findings.

What curious language journalists put into the mouths of theatrical people. 'Little one', 'My children', etc. . . . Expressions which I never use; as far from the truth as a painter's interpretations of battle scenes. It probably comes from what Paris refers to as 'le boulevard'.

22nd March, 1949

Visited the museum with Dr Drioton, a jovial person who seems to infuse cheerful life into the necropolis. He slips from one century to another, spares us from looking at minor works and only stops before the masterpieces. The more I walk along, the more I listen, the more I move around the columns, the more do I experience the feeling of a dark world which fastens on to ours and which will not loosen the suckers through which it takes its life. Whatever it may cost, they find it necessary to confirm their existence, to perpetuate themselves, to incarnate, to reincarnate, to hypnotize nothingness and to vanquish it. Fists closed, eyes wide open and fixed, the pharoahs march against the void, put it to sleep, braving its powers. For this reason it does not seem a sacrilege to move them to a museum. They have exacted this nominal glory, a glory as of a tragedian in the limelight. They did not hide themselves in order to disappear, but in order to await the cue for their entry on the stage. They have not been dragged from the tomb. They have been brought from the limbo of the wings with masks and gloves made of gold.

Besides, I had proof of this in the room where the mummies lie. It is now closed to the public, but the Doctor opened it with his key. Here they lie side by side in their death, under the windows, in a kind of hospital, where the wounded are sorted out, a morgue where one bends down over the corpses in order to identify the victims. These prodigious men have to the end won the toss from Fate and have continued from effigy to effigy, sloughing and changing their skins. The mania for survival has sculptured the outlines of the leather and bronze faces which seem to threaten us with closed fists. In the waiting-room, where the great haughty family lives together, everyone escapes and finds again an honoured place in the museum where some gigantic form gives it permission to be at home, to put on a soul and to cry out 'It is I'.

Seti the First! How beautiful he is, with his little nose, his pointed teeth showing, his little face, like that of a human beast of prey, his little face which belongs to death, reduced to one require-ment alone – not to die. 'I! I! I!' This is the word which the rafters throw back. And the rich dignitary who, from his stela, repeats the attitude of the King, shouts it at the top of his voice. His double, facing him, echoes back the repeated image in which he contemplates himself, with or without a wig, with or without a loin-cloth. On the top of the coffer containing his entrails the four little faces of Tutankhamun look at each other as though the central one were reflected in a triptych mirror, and say 'I! I! I!'

Thanks to the Doctor we pass over the crude, uncouth period when women had men's faces, and over the subsequent long period of academic art, to the period influenced by the grace of Thebes when men had the faces of women. Thereafter King Amen-ophis IV changed the play and its setting. The sun became the only god (that which the sun foreshadows). By his order art became realist, then surrealist. Portrayal was carried to its limits, till a gran-diose folly was reached, when they decided that heads should be lengthened, until at last they hung down like pilgrims' gourds. But from one age to another distortion of effigies is always over-shadowed by the necessity of adopting the intra-uterine position and even the Queen's chaise carried by her flunkeys made her publicly contract herself like the foetus within the womb or within the egg.

Everywhere death protects itself against evil forces which might detract from its purpose of not being truly dead, of not being engulfed in slumber.

The Egypt which shows its flat road by means of living mile-stones is only the culmination of a neolithic Egypt lost to us because she had no writing, and because she carved her flintstones into weapons but into nothing else. We can only guess her outlines through those lay figures of ivory which blaze the trail for the future to follow. We have seen the costumes and stage setting, here now is the theatre and the stalls full of the accessories from which nothing is lacking : the Halls of Tutankhamun.

We shall be able to imagine the luxury surrounding this young invalid, born of what would now be deemed incest. Everything is there, almost untouched by time : seats, coffers, rings, earrings, false beards, gloves, beds, wagons, walking-sticks, clasps and little switches. Everything is new, shining, ready for use. The quality of this shining is held for us still, lambent in the alabaster lotus from which he drank. His chariot still holds for us the black horse caparisoned for his use, the make-up box seems ready to open, full of the kohl for his eyes, and his golden sandals await to shoe his royal feet, to take him where he would go.

This young king, be it said again, with his delicate lungs, has gained his point. Centuries have gone, but he holds his audience still.

The effigies of the pharoahs and the ritualistic nature of the sculpture-work presented difficulties to souls which wished to incarnate in them. Five sculptors all worked at the same time under the directions of a scribe. The master-sculptor did the left side, a pupil did the right. It seems that this made the full face look a little odd, as the left side is always more expressive than the other. It can be well understood that in this lopsided covering the soul feels somewhat ill at ease. (I can in no way vouch for this; I am only quoting the Abbé Drioton.)

To come back to the Prince. He fills with fear many superstitious Egyptians who touch wood whenever they hear his name.

He gives me no sense of fear. It is even he in person who leads us on and who helps us to understand the use of things in his reign: how he ate, how he slept without ruffling his head-dress, how he sat down on the throne, how he made up his face, and how he mounted his chariot.

With Tutankhamun, we are no longer guided by stelae and drawings. We walk about amongst his slaves, in his house.

Once out of the museum gateway Cairo people console us a little for living in a sordid age. A last breath of elegance hangs around them. No delicate fingers now work for any patron of the arts, but they still seem to hang the sumptuous folds of the materials which clothe this people. Two civilizations touch each other without even being conscious of each other – that of the people of Egypt and that of the American cars. This blind-man's-buff makes of each a ghost for the other. The whole problem of Egypt lies there.

# Diaghilev and Nijinsky

From his youthful hero-worship of actors, Cocteau progressed, by way of his early poems, to active work in the theatre, and he was lucky enough to be a young man in Paris at the time of Serge Diaghilev's Russian invasion of 1908. Beginning with an exhibition of Russian painters it continued with visits by singers and finally the dancers, who first appeared there in 1909. Cocteau was at once drawn into this magic circle, and Diaghilev's famous remark 'Surprise me' was the most exciting challenge Cocteau ever received. From that moment until his death he was to surprise a great number of people, sometimes even himself. Through Diaghilev he met dancers, painters, composers, forming lifelong relationships with many of them, and if Cocteau himself has often been described as an impresario and an *animateur* he might never have developed the way he did without his acquaintanceship with the imaginative Russian contact-man of genius who created nothing except creativity.

Cocteau's debt to Diaghilev and Nijinsky was great, and he acknowledged it on many occasions. He has written and talked about them both as in fact hundreds of other people have done. Historians of the ballet, famous dancers and choreographers have all given their versions of these two extraordinary Russians, but Cocteau's telling and staccato description is not easily forgotten. It is astonishing that this detailed double portrait (from *La Difficulté d'Etre*) amounts to less than a thousand words. It shows how the bravura technique used in *Portraits-Souvenir* became, years later, more concentrated, less obviously polished; the mode is minor, the rhythms more intense, the reader is left to fill in a good deal of empty space, and he obediently, if unconsciously, does so.

The handling of details is as intriguing as Nijinsky's technique as a dancer. Without saying so, Cocteau compares the two men's hats and overcoats, superimposing a caricature on his rapid but intensely serious character-sketch in both cases. With Nijinsky everything is action, with Diaghilev it is contemplation, rumination or the presentation of other people.

□□□□□

DIAGHILEV AND NIJINSKY

In a book where I give evidence in the Socratic trial brought against us by society, I must express my appreciation of two free men who lived to cry their cries.

Nijinsky was below average height. Body and soul, he was pure professional deformity.

His Mongolian-type face was linked to his body by a very long and very thick neck. The muscles in his thighs and calves stretched the fabric of his trousers and made his legs look as though they curved outwards at the back. His fingers were short and seemed to have been cut off at the knuckles. In fact nobody would ever have believed that this little monkey-like man with thinning hair, a full-skirted overcoat and a hat balanced on top of his head, was the idol of the public.

But he was, and deservedly so. Everything about him was designed to be seen from a distance, in the limelight. On the stage his overdeveloped muscle formation became slender. He grew taller (his heels never touched the ground), his hands became the foliage of his gestures, and his face was radiant.

Such a metamorphosis is almost unimaginable for those who never saw it.

After 1913 he danced *Le Spectre de la Rose*, in which he expressed his entire self, with a bad grace : this was because the choreography of *Le Sacre du Printemps* shocked people and he could not bear to hear the former ballet applauded and the latter booed. The force of gravity dwells within us. He searched continually for some trick that would do away with it.

He had noticed that half the final leap of *Le Spectre de la Rose* could not be seen from the auditorium. He invented a double leap, a way of tying himself in a knot in the air while offstage and then falling headlong into the wings. He was treated like a boxer when he came down, with hot towels and slaps, while his servant Dmitri spat water into his face.

Before the première of *L'Après-midi d'un Faune* he astonished us all for several days while having supper at Larue's by moving his head as though he had a crick in his neck. Diaghilev and Bakst became anxious, questioned him and received no answer. We learnt later that he was training himself to carry the weight of the horns on his head. I could quote hundreds of examples of this constant studying which made him gloomy and withdrawn.

At the Hôtel Crillon (Diaghilev and Nijinsky used to emigrate from one hotel to another, driven out by the fear that their belongings would be seized), he used to put on a towelling bathrobe, pull the hood over his head and note down his choreography.

I saw him create all his roles. His deaths were heart-rending. In *Petrouchka* the puppet grew so human that we shed tears; in *Schéhérazade* he used to leap up and down on the boards like a fish at the bottom of a boat.

Serge Diaghilev wore what seemed to be the smallest hat in the world. If anyone else put it on it came down to their ears. For his head was so big that any headgear was too small for him.

His dancers nicknamed him 'chinchilla', because of a single white strand in his hair which otherwise had been dyed jet black. He used to bundle himself into a pelisse with an opossum collar and sometimes fastened it with safety-pins. He had a face like a bulldog, and he smiled like a very young crocodile, with one tooth jutting outside his mouth. When he sucked this tooth it meant that he was either pleased, or worried, or angry. He would sit in the depths of theatre-boxes, watching his artists, in whom he let nothing pass, chewing his lip, which was surmounted by a little moustache. And his moist, downward curving eyes were like Portuguese oysters. He took round the world a troupe of dancers as confused and multi-coloured as the Nijni-Novgorod Fair. His only luxury was to discover a star. He brought us out of the Russian ghetto the tall, thin, glaucous Madame Rubinstein. She didn't dance; she came onstage, exhibited herself, mimed, walked, went off and sometimes (as in *Schéhérazade*) she would risk movements that hinted at dancing.

One of Diaghilev's triumphs was to present her to the Paris public in the role of Cleopatra. In other words, he presented her to Antony. A bundle of fabric was brought on, put down in the middle of the stage, unrolled and untied. Ida Rubinstein appeared, her legs so thin that she looked like an ibis from the Nile.

I am sketching these figures on the programmes of the great celebrations which played a decisive role in my love of the theatre. One mention of Vestris or Talma gives me an appetite. I should like to read more about them.

# The Myth of El Greco

On various occasions Cocteau wrote about painters, usually his contemporaries, such as Picasso, de Chirico, Christian Bérard, Bernard Buffet and others. He was well versed in the history of art and architecture but he preferred to allude to the past rather than write about it. In the whole of his work there is no essay about a classical painter or writer so dramatic and perceptive as this piece about El Greco, published in 1943.

Although he is not writing as an art critic Cocteau tells us more about El Greco's vision than any analytical monograph can do. He has looked at El Greco with the eye of a poet, and there is no better proof as to why he chose to classify writing of this kind as *poésie critique*. After reading such a piece one cannot think of El Greco in the same terms as before. More 'facts' may be discovered about the painter and his technique, but such 'facts' would be subsidiary to this imaginative interpretation.

Under the name of El Greco, Domenico Theotocopoulos passed live into mythology.

Was he not born in Crete, place of myth, where the man with the bull's torso beat his curly head against the walls of the labyrinth? And since the painter's mythology permits all audacities, should we not like to imagine him as born in the labyrinth and growing longer until he incarnates his shadow, in order to flee his geometric jail for a sky peopled with a chaos of wings and clothes which twist and tear, and rays of light.

From the labyrinth of Crete, a real prefiguration of the plan of Toledo, he went to the labyrinth of Venice where outlines elongated and tormented in the water no doubt enriched him more than the school of Titian and Tintoretto.

For violent minds, like that of El Greco, draw their strength from sights upon which the glances of others do not dwell. It can even happen that they find help from those they laugh at and I wonder if Michelangelo, whom he despised, did not deliver him from the torment of following his masters and if he did not discover in him a world where transparent painting yielded to bas-relief.

From 1575 in Rome he became the incomparable El Greco, haunted by ghosts of Byzantium and Egypt, ready to take root in Toledo, to select a hard soil into which he sank like a knife and from where he was to open out the twisted branches of a tree struck by lightning.

From then on he was a prey to the secret universe of the drowned, the hanged, the dead, frozen statue-like in their last pose by the magnesium of catastrophes. All the faces, hands, torsos and legs that will emerge from the feverishly shaped tube which they resemble, will stretch out, knot and unknot, turn upside-down, rise up and suffer from the sublime cramps of those who perish on earth. Through the intermediary of a storm of clattering standards, they will aspire to rejoin the pools of light where angels and gods swim upside-down in a swirl of skirts and echoing waves. This 'written cry' by El Greco cannot be subjected to the methods attributed to him by the specialists. I was brought up by such people, who would cover his paintings with tracing paper and try to discover the hidden geometry which dictated his outlines to him. And they made discoveries and rejoiced and dissected an enigma. Now the enigma remains an enigma. Nothing explains it. The geometric ideas which they believe to be at the origin of a piece of work exist, but they arise from the mysterious equilibrium which an artist expresses, from which he creates his way of walking and without which this terrible somnambulist would fall from above.

It is possible that our painter, in spite of his lucid sleep, resembling the somnambulists who go along the edge of precipices, knew in some marvellous way where to place one foot after the other, that he became profoundly conscious of his rhythm, organized like the meanderings of the Cretan labyrinth lines which mingle or oppose each other, used the interior curve of an arm to indicate the exterior angle of an elbow, placed one figure on a leg which does not belong to him, folded up a flag in the shape of a stormy sky traversed by signs of the apocalypse. Possible and probable. It is none the less true that the vehicle of his hand was at the command of the fluids which passed through it and emerged from a nocturnal zone whose analysis would lead to death.

El Greco, more than anyone else, raises the problem of the conscious and the unconscious, of voluntary and involuntary poetry. For my part, I believe that the obscure mingling of these contradictory motives produces the lyrical caduceus of the stake and the bramble. In El Greco the caduceus succeeds in becoming visible and the figures in the *Martyrdom of Saint Maurice*, by means of tangling up towards heaven a burning bush, an organism of the vegetable kingdom, amount finally to the monster made of man and plant : I mean the mandragora.

We know the origins of this root with its human outline, the child of the earth and a hanged man. We know through what horrible process the semen of the hanged man fertilizes the green mud.

I would not wish to associate the genius of El Greco with these sacrilegious legends. But one legend includes them all. That of El Greco forces us to question the unknown.

From the unknown, from the marriages which are consummated within it and have produced masterpieces for us, El Greco draws the divine decay of his colours. And his yellow and his red, unique to him. He uses them like the angels' trump. The yellow and the red awake the dead who gesticulate and tear up their winding sheets. They stand up in these colours in the broken folds of linen rocks. They live again, open wide their nostrils, mouths, eyes and hands, and hoist themselves up towards the judgment of a wide-open heaven.

There has been much talk, recently, about the poetry of decay. I would like someone to quote me any poetry which isn't. Poetry, whether written or painted, whether seen or heard, composes its chords from an exquisite type of decomposition. It could be defined like this : Poetry forms on the surface of the world like iridescence on the surface of a marsh. The world should not complain. It comes from the depths.

That is what I meant when I wrote 'divine decay'. That which, from the depths of the human soul, seeks its response in the brilliant watered silk of God.

El Greco is an appeal, El Greco is a prayer, El Greco is a cry, El Greco is a prisoner's glance towards the air-vent, El Greco is the diver who brings up the pearl and, if his elongated faces bend down, in the stone dahlia of the Spanish fraise, towards the corpse of the Comte d'Orgaz, they will not be long in reassuming their pose and raising their heads like sunflowers towards the sun.

'I shall make the celestial faces elongated.' El Greco's terrestrial faces grow longer in their turn. The maelstrom from on high draws them up. It looks as though they want to link the visible to the invisible and that a virgin forest of limbs in ecstasy fills the no-man's-land of inextricable lianas. Only a thunderbolt goes through them.

People cite astonishing tricks played by thunderbolts. Sometimes the blast of bombs emulates them, and after a bombardment one discovers phenomena similar to those created by storms. The fires of heaven sometimes undress their victims and carry off their clothes far away.

Mightn't it often occur to one that El Greco's creatures have been undressed by a thunderbolt? They remain naked where they stand, motionless, in the attitude in which they were surprised by death.

And their clothes fly away, twisting and tearing apart in the distance, resembling the clouds to which one cannot fail to return as soon as one talks about El Greco.

Clouds, egg-white, egg crammed with living convolutions, mother's womb, man's stomach, meandering labyrinth of entrails, guts entangled together, sexual organs which stand up or part, veins curling round each other, arteries pulsating, shoulders hunched, biceps bulging, backs arched, swallows nesting under the arms of chiefs with cuirasses painted on their bodies, pages whose wiry hair bristles beneath the armpits of that naked general who is reflected three times from three angles as happens with the subtle play of mirrors, there, once and for all, and we shan't mention it again, is that erotic sensibility which links our man, whatever he may say about it, to that of Michelangelo and which distinguishes him from painters of total stillness.

One day we will see this mud carved from the earth become Cézanne's bathers and from one cross-breeding to another end in the terrifying race of grasshopper-men, dog-men, lion-men, skinny ogres and women with bunches of flowers for heads with whom Salvador Dali peoples his solitudes. Rimbaud's 'mound-of-entrails' woman and the man who lays bare the last secrets of his anatomy: these are the furthermost point of the headland which El Greco projects into the estuary where the angels appear. And one wonders why Dali has not yet painted a man walking without the shape of a shadow and the shadow of this shadow becoming the man himself flattened on the sand and, in the same way as Dali's watches, assuming the outlines of the ground.

One can imagine what 'tortil' can twist the voluntary and the involuntary so that El Greco succeeds in putting on a single canvas the world which, if unfolded in space, would be as astonishing as the interminable procession of our organs. The brain, the lungs, the system of veins, arteries and intestines accumulate within us. They coil themselves up with a surprising economy.

In El Greco's egg (for his cosmos is concave and ovoid), illuminated through the shell by the light from beyond, bunches of bodies lie curled up, conjoined limbs, clouds and draperies which seek to become creatures. We find there the yolk and the little red speck of blood. But let us make no mistake. It would be naïve to confuse the genius of El Greco with the stupid genius of nature. Free will plays its part in the latter. It engages in battle with fatality.

This struggle and the constraints among which an artist worthy of the name moves are made evident in the *Martyrdom of Saint Maurice* which belongs to the painter J.-M. Sert.

At first sight this picture looks as rough as the signs on a fairground booth or in the Musée Dupuytren. After this initial shock it plunges us into ecstasy. There indeed is the open city from where groups of the martyrdom spill out like entrails from the picador's horse, there indeed is the sky rent like the veil of the temple and the angels beating it clear with their spirals, there indeed is the raised mound and the three figures who are all the same and the little page who carries the helmet. But take care. The three figures have limbs like the dead frogs we saw in pools when we were children, the upturned face of the hirsute page nestles like swallows beneath the legionary on the left, whose gesture limits that of the legionary in the centre. And the page is clad in white. His costume is that of a page at the court of Philip II. You will observe for yourself, in comparing the two works, the one owned by J.-M. Sert and the one owned by the Prado, what bitter road the painter was forced to climb before insults were silenced and the attitude of the court allowed the King to let him enter the Escurial.

According to Bermudez the canvas which intrigues us was in the parish of San Torquato where El Greco had been buried. It disappeared when the church was destroyed.

Philip II wanted to keep his promise (the *Martyrdom of Saint Maurice* had been commissioned), but he could not tolerate the impact of a masterpiece whose daring represented for him the insolent acts of a madman. It is probable that Pompeo Leoni, the King's sculptor, came to El Greco's assistance in order to untwist the limbs, strip the ivy from their veins, make the legionaries fatter, dress the page in classical costume, remove his hair from an indecent place, calm the excitement of the angels and reduce the tip of the standard whose dark side, pierced with gulfs of light, became the celestial regions. El Greco defended himself in secret, as is proved by the leg of the legionary on the right, elegantly bent by Leoni and skilfully prolonged by our painter, with the help of a leg close by.

In spite of everything he succeeded in creating a masterpiece which unreservedly astonished us until the shattering appearance of the first canvas.

The skill of the poet is not inadequate, in the sense that he cannot be mistaken about the life of his lines and distinguishes instantaneously those which are alive (and are in danger of death) at every point along their length, and those which are not alive and are dead even though they achieve the representation of a living figure and through this subterfuge seem to be alive.

My expertise is carried out by stethoscope. I listen to myself and the canvas. If my heart beats faster there is every chance that I hear the canvas produce a similar beat.

*

This is what happened to a relative of Paul Eluard, who told me about it. She has a small house at Bécon-les-Bruyères and this house is at the corner of a street. Inside, in a corner, she had hung up a blue kitchen apron. During the last bombardment the explosion of a bomb blew the walls apart, the apron flew into the air, the walls closed again and the apron was caught in the stone in such a way that no trace of a crack could be seen, except for this apron hanging from its nail inside, and a corner of it hanging outside.

This phenomenon achieved by the fire of heaven rapidly represented for me El Greco's draperies immured within the lofty citadels in the sky over Toledo.

A thunderbolt leaves similar signs in its wake, but we do not recognize it. We discover it with surprise. El Greco's life is a thunderbolt. It is famous and unknown. I imagine that like all the occult forces of art he must have enjoyed great prestige and total incomprehension.

A letter from Giulio Clovio shows us El Greco in Rome. It is a valuable photograph :

> I went yesterday to El Greco's house in order to take a walk with him in the town. The weather was very fine with delightful spring sunshine which made everyone happy. The town seemed to be *en fête*. I was astonished on entering El Greco's studio to find the curtains drawn so tightly that one could hardly see anything. El Greco was sitting on a chair neither working nor sleeping.
>
> He did not want to come out with me, for the daylight disturbed his inner light.

This letter allows us to imagine El Greco. No portrait of him exists. Perhaps he painted himself in one of the figures in the *Burial of the Comte d'Orgaz*. Perhaps his severed head is shown to us on the platter in the Spanish frieze, as the head of St John the Baptist. I imagine him in the darkness described by Clovio. He is thin. His beard is pointed. His eyes blaze. He must be all muscle and bone. His veins stand out a great deal and nourish his marvellously thoroughbred body with a kind of fever. His hands, you may be sure, are splendid. Made in order to join together or hold the brush which Gongora tells us about : 'Which gave soul to wood and life to linen.'

These hands must certainly be used to capture celestial waves. I would not attribute any others to St Theresa or St John of the Cross. It is normal for such lightning-conductors to stand up together and assume attitudes of ecstasy, at the same period, in the same shadowy cells.

But the thing that caused Giulio Clovio's astonishment would cause him none in the East or in Spain. There men protect themselves against the sun. They go out in the evening and shut themselves up in the daytime. In this artificial night souls on fire are at ease. They receive other lights. El Greco meditates. He wants to remain alone. He does not want to take a walk. He sends his guest to take one, he sends him away.

It matters little to him that the 'delightful spring sunshine' makes everyone feel happy. He wants to take out of the cupboard the little wax figures that he sculpts and which serve him as models, and like a spellbinder he wants to endow them with life. In Toledo his palette has been reduced to five colours : white, ivory black, vermilion, yellow ochre, crimson lake. With darkness, solitude, his canvas, his five colours, his wax figures, the fires of his soul and the fire of heaven, he is going to enter the struggle and will only find relaxation for eating his meals to music and for sleeping after opening breaches in the Unknown.

These holes, rents and lock-gates through which the fauna, flora and searchlights of heaven pour a torrent, these are the only windows which El Greco condescends to open in his many closed rooms.

And what splendour there must have been where El Greco lived! But not what people are accustomed to call splendour. In 1943 Picasso shows us an example of that royal magnificence in which those beings move who oblige objects and shapes to obey them. Everything they touch, everything they break, everything they destroy, everything they mend, everything they buy, everything people give them, everything they couple together, everything they mark, all the order and disorder they pile up, and dust itself, assumes superhuman dignity. Nothing becomes neutral. Nothing accepts insignificance. Significance is the major preoccupation of a world where the somnolent and noisy platitude of current events does not penetrate.

Picasso rescues a bicycle saddle and a set of rusty handlebars. In his hands they become a bull's head and horns. He has them cast in bronze. It is then that he advises them to rejoin the street, so that some tramp, seeing this minotaur's head, will break it and find again a bicycle saddle and handlebars.

I am certain the vast rooms of the Transito, in the group of houses belonging to the Marquis de Villena, presented this unusual aspect.

El Greco must have starched, plastered and bunched up draperies there, he must have piled up Greek books, Arab objects, Spanish furniture made of tortoise-shell and silver. He must have disguised a servant-girl with a tablecloth, thrown back her head and illuminated her with candles, from below. He must have searched amongst his models for those who had the most delicate wrists and ankles and the biggest muscles; he must have attempted the impossible in order to encounter his dream and conquer inertia. He must have lit big fires and seen the victims of accursed towns twisting within the flames.

> It was then that the fire
> Broke out, like a thousand angels in fury.
> They thrust hair and clenched fists into the air.
> All shouting with dark mouths : I told you so !
>
> 'I told you so,' cried the cruel tulips,
> Moving their heads unevenly,
> And below the disgusting organ of guts
> Plunged down to the gutter-tomb from each open belly.
> ............................................................................
> The distraught angels were wringing their hands.
> Cries reached them : abandon your faces !
> (For most of them no longer had human faces)
> But mistook the ladders for a cage.
>
> And the holly, the angels, the flames,
> Formed one whole only, traversed by sprays. . . .

I was writing these lines from the book *Allégories* in 1938. In 1943, in the midst of our great misery and the planes which catch fire and explode in the night sky, I feel that these lines were in praise of El Greco. I feel that everything exalting fire, death and prayer belongs by right to this painter.

On 31st March, 1614, he dictated his will and signed it with an illegible signature, the last zigzag of his lightning. On 7th April,

1614, he returned to the only lightning he knew, adored and searched for and whose mystical blaze elongated his deformed shadow on earth.

\*

On re-reading these lines it appears to me that I have been caught by the exalted rhythm of El Greco and have not expatiated sufficiently on the painter he was as such, as well as being a great figure of mystical initiation.

The case is so exceptional that it would be unjust not to take it into account. In fact it often happens that an artist preoccupied with problems of an occult order expresses himself more through the spirit than through matter and that the artist preoccupied with matter often neglects the spirit and only seeks to resolve problems of a pictorial nature. With El Greco we witness this miracle : a painter who 'fingers matter' like Velasquez and puts his strength as an artisan in the service of the mind.

It is because of the good fortune linking in one perfect knot different forces which are so rarely found together in one man that El Greco disapproved of the painter in Michelangelo and did not like Raphael. Those great architects of dream disappoint him. He wants to paint and concerns himself only with painting and wants that painting which usually limits itself to portraits and still-lifes to be placed in the service of divine inspiration. This is why El Greco's figures belong to heaven and earth. This is why the tubes of colours, the canvas, the wood, the secret concoctions, the little figures (alas, if only we had them!) which he carved from wax, plaster and mud, become more effective in the hands of this monk than fasts and hairshirts.

# The Lesson of the Cathedrals

Cocteau was eighteen years younger than Marcel Proust, yet they had many friends in common over a number of years. They admired each other's work and exchanged letters about it. Proust used some aspects of Cocteau's characters in describing Octave in *Albertine disparue*. Now and then the two writers showed a certain coolness towards each other, but these periods were short. Cocteau wrote about Proust in at least three memorable passages, once in *Opium* and twice in literary magazines. I have chosen *The Lesson of the Cathedrals* (La Leçon des Cathédrales) for this anthology because it is less anecdotal than his other pieces and anticipates Proust's elevation to classic status.

I have just written this title and the empty sheet of white paper draws me irresistibly into the room of that friend who loved those pages best and is still preoccupied with them. But this time there was no question of my going to see Marcel Proust as I used to do at the time when only four or five intimate friends knew his work and regarded him, through the prestige of this work and his own self, as a character from fairyland. In fact nobody suspected that this nocturnal spectre was constructing a world, and yet, from the first contact, we acquired the respectful habit of considering him from the viewpoint of fame and death.

This visit which I am telling you about was the last, the visit to our poor Marcel who had just died, depriving us of an uninterrupted relationship of affection and quarrels. That was his way. With his illegible handwriting, which resembled exactly the tracks of some drunken insect, with some spiritualist table, with some confused thread from the night, or with his voice which he would crack or lengthen with laughter and spread over his face with a white-gloved hand, Marcel Proust would sometimes pay you compliments until you felt embarrassed and sometimes produce a list of complaints, imaginary in our world and no doubt real in the magical world of his mind. For just as Proust suffered from the failure of his models to read him, a fact which makes one think of

Fabre's displeasure at the indifference of insects towards his books, in the same way he reproached his intimate friends for intrigues of such Machiavellian subtlety, for acts of impoliteness so complex, that it was impossible to feel guilty of anything whatsoever. One had to pretend to be, to join in the game, follow the downward path he was taking, and even go up it again step by step and prove to him that one was not guilty in any way, at the same time endowing one's proofs with the labyrinth of oriental haggling. Haggling without which an oriental would refuse to sell his merchandise; labyrinth without which friendship, for Marcel, would have had no charm.

But that fatal morning it was no longer a question, alas, of going to Marcel Proust's with one's head high or one's tail between one's legs, of coming up against the door, of breaking the rules and going through, in spite of Céleste who wanted to be sure that the previous day you had not 'touched the hand of a person who might have touched a rose', which risked provoking an attack of hay fever. Had not Marcel said to me one day that he no longer wanted to hear Pelléas, for a certain phrase about the wind of spring passing over the sea was enough to bring on an attack?

What did Marcel Proust die of? Of an attempt to be healthy, of a break in his habits, a window open on the sealed chamber of his alchemy. So that day Lucien Daudet and I had to go into a room which was familiar to us, with all the shutters closed and all the lamps extinguished, but one which would become strange to us, unknown and frightening, through the fact that we were going there in the morning, at a time when Marcel Proust usually received no one.

From the hall door itself we entered the house of a stranger. Death received us in his stead. The shutters of this Nautilus where naphthalene glimmered like stars in the darkness and cracked beneath our feet, where Proust would prowl among the lustrine chair covers, wearing beards, wigs, gloves and capes, the shutters, I say, were open, illuminating a kind of burgled villa. Friends stood there looking as though they had been struck by lightning, and it was indeed lightning, this mourning that struck the whole of literature and a few individual hearts.

Céleste led us to her master. The room was empty. Over it lay that silence which resembled silence as darkness resembles ink. Something definitive, light, solemn. The absence of anti-asthmatic powder and eucalyptus revealed it to us without disguise. Proust, flanked by his cork hood on his child-size bed, revealed the admirable profile of a vizir. He wore that beard which he would alternately remove and grow again, and one never knew, after a period of absence, whether one would see him with it or without it. This beard which during his lifetime seemed almost a joke, a postiche as worn by the dead Carnot in the Musée Grévin, concealing the curves of the young dandyish face as painted by Jacques-Emile Blanche, that beard behind which he would choke with laughter as behind a woman's fan, this beard, on his corpse, became the attribute of a magus and a king.

And suddenly, as our eyes moved away from this upsetting spectacle, we saw to his left, right in the corner of the chimney-piece covered with dust as though draped in grey fur, a high uneven pile of school exercise books. This pile leant over towards the darkness that was faintly illuminated as though by a white porcelain night-light, by the pale profile; and we remembered that it was his exercise books which Marcel confused and muddled if he wanted to read some chapter to us. This high uneven pile of school exercise books was, whether lovers of catastrophe like it or not, the complete work, or to be grammatical, the final work of our friend.

This pile of paper, on his left, continued to live like wrist-watches worn by dead soldiers.

I could not take my eyes off it. Gradually the room faded away, only the disturbing pile of paper grew and grew, its uneven edges, its angles, its corners, became an indescribable lacework of walls, arches, rose windows, vaults, niches, spires and roofs.

A cathedral of paper (and I remembered having seen the cathedral of Rheims sinking, thundering, blazing, crowning the dead cathedral with a phantom cathedral of smoke) from where the search for time lost rose and built in the air a nave where Albertine would be the angel with the mutilated smile, and the others, the saints, the damned and the gargoyles.

# Corrida of 1st May

Many French writers, including Théophile Gautier and Victor Hugo, have been fascinated by Spain. Cocteau did not go there until he was over sixty, and he too was impressed by all the country embodied, by its drama and ritual.

The *Corrida* (La Corrida du Ier Mai) is no journalistic piece about bullfighting; it is part of the *Poésie Critique*, a poet's analysis of the origins of bullfighting and the symbolism it unconsciously expresses. It is not an attempt to explain, for any such attempt would be prose.

As Cocteau himself states, he assembled these notes after an illness and made no attempt to edit them or clarify their obscurities. There is a long lead-in relating his personal 'philosophy' to the background of tauromachy. The text is allusive and colourful, full of images and details which bring Spain to life in a way no guide-book could achieve.

This long piece, translated here in entirety for the first time, was published in France in 1957 and with it were three poems dedicated to the great toreador Manolete, a *Lettre d'Adieu à Federico* (Garcia Lorca), earlier notes about a first visit to Spain, and the text of the extempore talk about Picasso given in Rome in 1953. The latter was included in the anthology *My Contemporaries*.

It would be utterly ridiculous to consider Spain as a poetic and picturesque place. It is neither one nor the other. It is more. It is a poet. And shall I quote Max Jacob's remark which is no mere quip, 'The traveller fell dead, stricken by the picturesque'? Let us leave the tourist to the blows of the picturesque and venerate that Spain which, from one age to another, sets fire to what it loves, that phoenix which burns itself in order to survive.

By driving across so many green and red lights I pretended not to see, I have encountered a real red light. A heart-attack has left me still unable to move and I find the draft of a text brought back from Spain after a long interruption, a long period when reading

and writing were forbidden. I wonder if the arenas in Seville and the dangerous races at which we were present do not derive from the crisis which I have just suffered, and if the blood I was reproaching the spectators for failing to sweat out was not coagulating within me as a result of an emotional collaboration between my nerve-centres.

In short, it is possible that I am paying for the eternal shocks which enabled me to make these notes. I group them together without taking advantage of convalescence to put them in order. I should risk removing from them that clumsy second sight characteristic of those who are threatened by a serious illness without knowing it.

The origin of this text lies in an incident from the Feria of Seville. On 1st May, 1954, the last day of the races, during which no bull had been dedicated, Damasco Gomez accorded me the homage of his. I was to learn the next day that Domingo Ortega had planned, the day before, to dedicate one of his animals to me, but had not done so because he did not consider the bull worthy of it. That is the Spanish way. And, moreover, Gomez was paying homage not to a famous foreigner but to a poet, and instinctively placed in the hands of a poet, along with his montera, his lucky or unlucky star. An alarming responsibility which I had not been aware of when two other bulls were dedicated to me in Barcelona, and one which was to overwhelm me with uncustomary feelings.

In order to make intelligible to the few readers who are good enough to read what happened to me on 1st May, 1954, in the arena of Seville, it is essential not to boast of some privilege, but, on the contrary, to emphasize a faculty of non-self that I possess, an aptitude for becoming the performance at which I am present, to the point of no longer existing except in relation to this performance, how can I put it, through the total abolition of a self that only deceives (simulating presence) through the phenomenon of automism which one observes in animals decapitated in the slaughter-houses.

During the corrida, that suggested to me confused ideas which I am in no way trying to clarify, I was as little in place on the stone seats as was the black hat on my knees – it belonged to the dramatic group and linked me to it like the testifying object by means of which mediums travel.

At first I only realized my embarrassment by discovering the sudden silence of a tribunal of forty thousand judges, in whose eyes a young priest, badly informed about the meaning of the attributes of his ministry, caused to pass into foreign hands the sign of a cult as deeply rooted in the soil of Spain as a mandragora.

In short, Gomez's hat became a dangerous blade flying over people's heads, and I must have looked like the spectator called on to the platform to serve as a target and who does not look too happy when his face is suddenly framed by knives.

Man is a schizophrenic, either normally or artificially by means of a toxin, and he never cuts the last thread, still seeking the refuge of a symbol or of aestheticism even when he imagines he is free at last and despising the masquerades of Art. For example, Baudelaire and hashish making a kiosk divine, Huxley and mescalin making armchairs divine (splendid feet and apotheosis of the Last Judgment), or myself finding that the opium addict becomes a social masterpiece, without feeling the slightest need to inform anyone outside his kingdom.

This giving of information or attainment of equality is one of the loftiest forms of the distress-cry in man, a despairing signal from a shore towards some ship, a supreme hope of communication between one solitude and another, of making contact with other people.

It is rare for a passenger on the ship to notice this, or for him to take it into account, and it is therefore important to consider our vain fraternal attempts, like a silent cry of despair coming from a world which our own tries to take for creaking furniture, the gnawing of an insect or the moan of autumn wind – in short, for some realistic phantasmagoria which allows a sleeper who has been suddenly wakened to go to sleep again without keeping one ear open and without having to give help.

My book of poems *Clair-Obscur* could have been entitled *Faire-Part*. It is in fact a last attempt to give information or issue an invitation, and neither *L'Ange Heurtebise* nor *La Crucifixion*, which are accepted solitudes, born and dead in advance in their islands, could be related to it.

*Clair-Obscur* could be divided into various phases : (1) The author tries to make do on the desert island; (2) The author waves his shirt; (3) The author calls for help; (4) The author utters his appeals precisely in morse; (5) The author falls down on the sand again with his face between his hands.

The notes which will follow are not caused by that strange madness which drives men to hoist themselves up desperately to the extremity of themselves and then let go and break their necks, because they find around their signals nothing but emptiness. It was a question of pinning down the modifications of consciousness produced in a Frenchman by that drug of the Spanish people : the Corrida – pinning them down at the door of some Spanish friends who call me the *banderillero* – 'then man who says clearly what he means'.

Well, yes, it is true that my intention, in publishing this text, was not to tell people about a particular event and to leap over the fence which separates each one of us from other people. Certainly I believed myself to be a very long way from that idolatrous and naïve breed of men who, as soon as they are faced with an unusual phenomenon, even if it is provoked by the organic disorder of absorbing a drug, are made divine, plunged into the state of savages looking at fireworks or a mere electric light. Certainly I did not suppose that the powerful Spanish drug of the arena, and the visions that it produces, would reveal anything of the hallucinatory phenomena which those who experience them have rapidly taken to be a flattering grace rather than the first symptoms of schizophrenia, every poet worthy of the name being a miniature schizophrenic.

But on re-reading what I have just written I perceive that I have been unable to prevent myself from following the tendency and relating it to some cult, to one of those beliefs through which men have tried for centuries to transcend their carcasses and give a superior meaning to the most mediocre, to the most hazardous of adventures, to this tragedy of being and of being nothing, against which their pride rebels.

We live in a relatively calm period of the system, sitting between two cataclysms, with a moon which the romantics do not suspect of being destined to destroy us, while its approach pumps the seas dry and destroys our cycle as it pulverizes itself against us. It is because we are so far from the beginning that we see its mechanism as a theatrical spectacle, without understanding anything about the implacable reality.

Renan's phrase, which should serve as an exergue to all books of science fiction, 'It is possible that truth may be sad', is the type of pessimistic remark that it is important for frightened people to misunderstand. It destroys our religions of hope and the one that Nietzsche puts in their place. Moreover, it will be easy to reverse the meaning of the word 'truth' into a human meaning which removes the terror from it. Unfortunately the Jules Vernism of our era threatens to restore its true perspectives.

How right I was, ever since childhood, before I knew the theories of Hoerbiger, to be wary of the moon, to feel afraid of it and not to associate myself with those who celebrate it. It had always frightened me even before I looked at it through a telescope and learnt how it bombards us from cycle to cycle – cycles whose duration seems incalculable to us and which, assuming that a few superior microscopes observe our wretched system, must occur at high speed and form only an integrating part of the universal atomic bombardment.

Hoerbiger informs me that the moon is not a likeable star, but an engine of destruction, and that my turn of mind never allows me to envisage a show as an entertainment, since every show for me is a ritual, or what remains of it, in a universe which Bergson describes as 'a machine for manufacturing gods' and which manufactures fewer and fewer of them, due to lack of workers.

The longer I live, the more convinced I am that the human race has invented a whole tragedy for itself and has allotted the leading role.

But sometimes a period of decadence removes from the tragedian the power of persuasion that he experienced and communicated to others. It is therefore up to us, we poor men, to try by means of psychism to return to the periods when entertainments resembled divine enterprises more than theatre. Men took part in them body and soul, linked to the Eternal by dreams.

In addition I find more and more, among my scientific friends, an instinctive urge for self-preservation which would tend to counteract, with a wave of psychic knowledge, an excess of physical science that is hurrying man towards self-destruction.

In short, they seek in Paracelsus a refuge against Descartes. Now, if what are called the occult sciences – that is to say sciences lying fallow (so suspect in France, Gabriel Marcel finds them regarded as 'the shameful parts of knowledge') and so feared that Claude Bernard's *Cahiers Rouges* cannot be found in scientific libraries today – if, I say, these courageous and modest sciences preserve us from destructive Cartesianism, the mind may be able to take wing.

It is this conspiracy of silence that must be overcome. It is important that we should not consider as suspect any of those who, like me, possess neither the pathos nor the trappings demanded by such profound studies, but who, lacking these trappings and this pathos, enjoy a kind of prescience, possibly unhealthy, that scientists rejected in the past with horror in the same way as they rejected the exceptional and monstrous subjects from which they turned away in fear lest they brought them more trouble than help and cause them to be burnt alive (or else burnt gradually, as the Cardinal in my play *Bacchus* discovers when he speaks of the moderate anarchism of France).

In our age burning is carried out gradually and if a science is already suspect because it puts two-plus-two in doubt, what would people think of a paramystic and a paramoralist, any writer in fact worthy of being called a poet and whose entire protection, like that of Tristan when he was mad, is that he will be taken for a *jongleur* and an eccentric.

In 1954 I find in scientific knowledge so many breaches, drawers that are empty and false-bottomed, that I feel endowed with the audacity to look at the science of tauromachy with a somewhat unorthodox eye.

Perhaps the *aficionados* will regard me with the indulgence of the philosophers, mathematicians, physicists and paraphysicists of our country when they find I am concerning myself with something that in the past only concerned the specialists – and if they are astonished by my intuition (which is perhaps, after all, only a still unknown form of memory) they will laugh neither at it nor at me. Am I not a virtuoso player of the *violon d'Ingres*?

To sum up what I have been saying, as a result of the kind of state of grace into which my sense of responsibility puts me, that bullfight in the Seville arena became for me the reverse of an entertainment : a series of objects similar to those which lead the detective through devious ways that nothing could have predicted. Since my journey is probably starting here, I think of that black toque, that *montera* : the visual interest of the show caused me to forget their primordial roles as testifying objects.

All this has given me the courage to talk about the science of tauromachy, which is no better protected than the others against the *hole that leads to something* which Nietzsche mentions.


It is depressing to know that all those spaces which make Pascal feel dizzy are well and truly solid and that every solid is made up of spaces inhabited by people, similar to those spaces which break our hearts at night.

It is through a kind of disgust caused by the inhuman problems which disturb us that I find relaxation in a show invented by men and which, in spite of its roots which go down into myth, does not leave the human level. (People will no doubt wonder why I am wrapping up my Spanish text in so much cellophane. I shall reply that it is in order to warn the reader against the spitefulness which consists in labelling as fanciful any man who moves above the norm. Cellophane, a number of boxes one inside the other, constitute the Japanese method whereby, going from one box to another, you finally discover a small accessory, the purpose of which is enigmatic.)

Sometimes invisible duchess and nun playing *River Tagus* on the organ, sometimes Pastora, sometimes appearing at the foot of my bed in nurse's uniform, the White Lady in the quicksands of sleep draws me away towards your fake Mont Saint-Michel, Toledo, with its halo of pale lightning.

My Castile has a black eye, and an iridescent mark above it, beneath the dark catafalque on top of which a pious and poverty-stricken hand has lain all the flowers from the dustbins of dawn, and she nurses a crow against her heart. This young old woman, with one hand on her hip, provided the arm is not undulating and executing over her head the gesture of refurbishing an old dream – and that flat-iron Escurial handled by a ghastly washerwoman. She has replaced her hand on her hip and through the Venetian blinds of her eyelashes she looks at this glassy Tagus and this bold Castile that was once covered with a thick fleece.

Faced with this high and arrogant ruined wall, covered with posters for the Fiesta and painted and repainted and spattered with blood beneath a mourning veil, any pen would recoil, whether it were an eagle's quill or held like a golden spoon against the boiled egg-shells of the Spanish grandees' skulls.

I am very much afraid that I must seize this mule's head by the hair, and receive full in my face its four hooves that were once planted in the dust of a road where water-jugs poured out a star of blood near a strange young man who lay stretched out and pale, as though lit by the neon lights of Orgaz's page in the dahlia-shape of his ruff. This makes me think of that terrace, one evening at the fine hotel in Algeciras. Down below I could see the street-children making up their faces with the neon lights from the lamps and playing at funerals – carrying a corpse on their shoulders.

I saw this and many other surprising things after escaping, not without difficulty, from that plum pudding of Gibraltar in which heavy guns are the currants. In short, I have seen things of all colours apart from yellow and red, and mainly that of a gracefully filthy sticking-plaster gagging the mouth of your wound, Spain, with a pink cross.

I dared not search through this dustbin of still damp dead leaves, mussel-shells and ripped-open tins of food – to use my feet and a fork and make a horse get up, a one-eyed, medieval horse caparisoned with the rugs from a sordid hotel.

And yet the Prado is reassuring, it is a café *terrasse* where one greets masterpieces as one greets famous people having a drink, from table to table, with its painters who caused no stir while mediocrities did so in France. And the Madrid night, full of children singing. And Barcelona caught in the *art-nouveau* hair of

Gaudi and the casks of Jerez where sleeps the ferruginous blood of kings. The Escurial, a deep hive of dead queens, and the bearded woman and the catafalque or balloon of the infantas. Malaga looking at us with the Egyptian eye of its boats. Pale Granada drying its linen in the moonlight, like a cut-open pomegranate, bleeding and weeping for its poet (through the mouth of its wound).

And the linen and mandragoras of this Theotocopoulos garden, which takes its siesta lying on the armlike shape of its road. And Carmen's Customs officials with boiled leather hats shaped like pen-boxes. And again the way that Toledo looks like Christ outraged – like a kneeling bull. And its telegraph-poles simulating a Calvary – and the blood from the jugs and the twist of lemon-peel that uncurls against their cool cheeks and the funereal sleep of a Castile that is only half asleep above the meanderings of that river in whose metal they dip swords.

And the Queen of all the Spains, she whose arms are swan's necks, Pastora Imperio, kneeling beside my sick-bed, tying up charms in a handkerchief that she slips under my pillows – one eye on me, the other on the toreros standing, in silence, with their black felt hats in their hands, against my bedroom walls.

And the handsome Alberto Puig pushing away with an affectionate tap on the chin the bunch of little gypsy girls hanging round his neck. And the cake for my birthday blazing with sixty candles, brought on his orders by the gypsies to the Barcelona sailing-club and the club floors beaten by drumming feet until dawn like fish dying in the depths of boats.

Shall I leave you, Spain, after merely approaching you?

No, I'll stay.


Seville offers two aspects of such contrast that you wonder, as you go into the old quarter, whether this change of place is not a change of time, if space-time is not inventing a new joke and if some sort of Pompeii has not withstood the fire of earth and heaven, the flow of lava and the grey ash which covers us.

It is true that during the Feria a huge area of the new town seethes with all the costumes, riders and equipages which correspond to the old town. You meet there proud centaurs with inflexible torsos, wearing pearl-grey or black sombreros, and those young girls riding behind them, clinging to the upright rider, whose haughty splendour embodies a cascade of roses (a cascade of roses against the wall of grave men's backs, men with one hand on their hip). And with their right hands on their hip also the women side-saddle riders with their round hats which carry flying scarves, and the six mules with nets and multicoloured plumes and all those thoroughbreds dancing, and the seguidillas round about, and the little gypsies begging and carrying babies heavier than themselves – babies which seem to be attached to their bodies by the membrane of fairground monsters.

Outside the fairground area cars move at high speed and transport on their roofs those hampers of flowers which are young girls. But in the old town nothing moves, cars don't go into it, a few fiacres drive round, except in the streets which are too narrow.

The Santa Cruz district is strange in the sense that it is not a dead city and that the orange trees do not scent the ruins. Its invisible gardens overflow from the windows on façades so clean, elegant and perfect that one feels slightly ashamed. Through what fatal evil spell has man lost this grace and poise? It is probable that the old town, small, lively and embalmed (in the double sense of the term), reflects souls that were as well constructed as itself and that the incoherence of our modern towns condemns the disorder of which we are victims. This fidelity to the style of the Infidels, this reserve of the Musulman courts, this uninhabited air of Arab dwellings full of people, here only a fountain seems to be alive. A house which is veiled like Moorish women, allowing only the eyes of windows to be seen. And these flowers emerging from the windows and these tongues of fire and shoulders of young women calling for help form such a contrast to the indifference of the façade that I cannot help thinking again of those girls from the Feria, running round the streets at night at high speed, as I said, on the roofs of cars. You might think they had fallen from another era – without hurting ourselves.

And, I reflect, if I turned my attention to the origin of the bullfights, to the Minoan enigmas of Knossos and to old Seville, is it not through a reaction similar to the phenomenon of memory which unwinds the long strip of old recollections at the second when a fatal accident threatens us?

I cannot prevent myself from knowing that our living, thinking and active earth is trying to get rid of an excess of human livestock. It wants to kill off its fleas. If man becomes afraid of the means of self-destruction (which the earth indicates to him and for which he considers himself responsible), if he avoids them, it will take action itself through some geological catastrophe.

Men feel the uneasiness of this blind alley: like old age, the modern world goes back to the past. There has never been such interest in the age of caves, the discoveries of archaeologists and speleologists, while, on a lower level, the radio broadcasts the little songs of 1900. So perhaps I don't escape the norm anyway.

When riders and carriages leave the Feria and the castanets cease their night-time cicada chattering, one seeks a refuge. There are two : the old town where Spain hides its intensity, and the arena, where this intensity shows itself : the bowl of shade and sunshine where the Castilian wine and the Arabic wine ferment. In the arena, despite an unfortunate tendency among young people to lose their identity and prefer football grounds, the public fan a yellow and red flame, a smouldering fire. It is at the Fiesta de Toros that the Spanish breath blows on the embers and an incendiary people, who sometimes rest between two fires, is aroused.

Spain ! Vulgarity, so far as I know, has never set foot on your soil and, if you are poor, you are incalculably rich.

The Spanish use an untranslatable word in order to say that a thing, a man, a woman, an action, a style, is the reverse of elegant. This word is *curci*. I don't know of any equivalent term in French. From Perpignan to Gibraltar one is either *curci* or flamenco. Perhaps Don Juan de Maraña deserved the inscription which adorns his tomb in Seville : '*Aqui yace el peor hombre que fué en el mundo*' – Here lies the worst man who ever lived. Possibly he was, but he was certainly not *curci* and he was certainly flamenco. The same thing is true of Don Juan Tenorio, whose sacrilegious acts delight the Spanish crowds because there is nothing *curci* about them and his audacity remains flamenco to the end – no more, it seems, than the arrogance of the captain of a Flemish regiment inviting to dinner not a stone statue, but Don Tancredo, or even one of the white companions of El Cid – .

Spain, I hang up on my prison wall your superb beribboned panoply of torches, horns, castanets rattling like bones, ropes which sever the neck and combs which bite. And death seated with her little crown of flowers on top of her skull, and the sun which sleeps in the shade, with one eye bandaged and the other wide open.

Perhaps one can add nothing to the severe, honest book (1952) by Don Enrique for the use of people staying in the Casa Valesquez. This book, which is written in French, gives more information than any in Spanish. After reading this remarkable guide one finds that through the attendance and obedience it demands the Fiesta de

Toros seems to follow the same curve as the theatre. Some people want an intellectual theatre and some a theatre of action. Nobody recognizes the style whose distinguishing feature is the marriage between word and deed. (Confused period when museums become churches and churches museums.) But what is strange about the Fiesta is that people reproach it for becoming intellectual, whereas in the past it demanded an effort of the mind and no longer does so, for it is entirely subjected to effect and show. Further, the use of the muleta, as an end and not a means, adds to the risk taken by the matador, gives the bull time to think and to understand vaguely that he is being taken in. By tortuous means therefore the Fiesta rediscovers a tragic strength that strict rules were making it lose and restores its prerogatives to death, to the White Lady, seated like a Don Tancredo, motionless in the centre of the ring. But this time her immobile whiteness does not only deceive the bull. (Dali possesses a remarkable documentation about political Don Tancredism, about leaders who endure through immobility, and invisibility.)

The numerous accidents I saw in Seville were caused by a type of romanticism which the aficionado criticizes, but they are suitable for satisfying a crowd enamoured of sensations and theatricality.

(In the boxing-ring Al Brown was booed when he brought the fight to an end too soon. He obeyed the rules of the noble art. When he abandoned boxing he told me that the public preferred a massacre to skill and that only skill saved his fragility from being reduced to pulp. I have to observe my opponent, he would say, take advantage of an opening which I decide upon by a trick, and knock him down. If I waited *he would understand me* and would knock me down.)

In the modern Fiesta, unless the bull reaches the last act, crippled and diminished by the lance, he has more chance of sensing the strange mechanism of perspectives to which he falls victim.

My point of view could not be that of the aficionado. It can only be that of a devotee who seeks out the continuity of the drama as expressed by the different schools and in spite of the decadence which the specialists deplore.

Death, always present, I repeat, whatever the behaviour surrounding the ring and in the ring, whatever the interests of the manager, the race of bulls, or the tips of the horns, death remains the central point of the show. It loses or recovers its rights according to whether man respects or not the architecture of the temple, the strange, moving geometry assigning one piece of ground to the bull and one to the man (neither should ever confuse them); rules broken by an act of disobedience without which nothing amounting to genius exists.

Mihoura's play, *The Man in the Purple Costume*, a satire on the intellectual torero, could have been written by one of those clever bulls whose name the author has more or less taken, and I doubt very much whether an intellectual torero remains so when the man has to think like the animal and the animal has to try and think like the man.

One could dream of a play in which the author would approach the problem of Crete, would show Theseus, at the entrance to the labyrinth, receiving from Ariadne not a thread but a complete matador's panoply. It is at Knossos that the play begins, and perhaps even earlier, since Minoan frescoes show acrobats resembling those in the circus as we see it in the sanguines of Goya, in countless anonymous canvases and posters where Turks, Indians, bulldogs and carriages join in the dance.

Perhaps, in that marvellous decadence of Crete, there was also a decadence of the bullfighting ritual and we must search very far back for the sources of this mysterious encounter between intelligence and strength.

My own point of view therefore will consist of forgetting the rules and the aristocratic anarchy, thanks to which they are transformed and can live, it will envisage only tragedy which the Fiesta seems to resemble by becoming simpler and observing Aristotelian rules similar to those of the unities of time and place.

The Fiesta today seems to obey and disobey these rules and to mingle classical simplification with the spectacular effects of romanticism. It presents the spectacular with a very curious amalgam of antagonistic styles from which there emerge intact only fear, audacity and the kingdom of death. (Even if this kingdom is limited – all the more, I repeat, because these nuances cause the torero to run new risks.)

The only time Don Enrique seems to me to be mistaken is when he regards disorder as decadence. A tradition could not live if it did not evolve, and if it did not become disordered. It would be forced to go down to the end of the curve, and I hope for all the arts that the disorder of today is only the preamble to other rules which will have other starting-points. One could not therefore speak of who is responsible, or accuse anyone, but find that everything moves and observes the law of knots and waves. And no doubt we shall one day see breeders crossing and rearing bulls suitable for restoring the noble outline to the unexpected directives that the public and the young matadors are giving to bullfighting.

I have often pointed out to my friends in Athens how mistaken they are in thinking that respect for Greek tragedy should force people to reject any renewal of myths. I would see no sacrilege in performing *Oedipe-Roi* or *La Machine Infernale* at the foot of the Acropolis. Far from being sacrilege this is an act of homage that poets pay to the origin of the great Hellenic fables, when they perpetuate them by means of a new angle, when they adapt them to our modern rhythm.

The life of forms has nothing to do with the forms of life. As Antigone said, 'They belong to all times' – and I doubt whether our anarchist saint would agree that the Greek theatre 'should keep to the old laws'. Creon's method leads simply to the exhaustion of the forms of life, which are only prevented from dying or at least from developing sclerosis in the long run by the life of forms.

And I cannot offer adequate congratulations to Jean Marais and Gérard Philipe, young toreros of the boards, for having acted *Britannicus* and *Le Cid* differently from their illustrious predecessors. It is, moreover, fair to point out that in order to conquer the public (that wild animal) they used their capes less than Edouard de Max and Mounet Sully. The theatrical curve is therefore the reverse of the bullfighting curve. Art can only rise from its ashes through the phoenixology (a Dalian skill) of which the driving force can only be, in the circumstances, the instinctive spirit of contradiction.

In fact, everything changes and nothing changes. Whatever we might say about it, the black heart of a corrida remains unchangeable. The corrida carries out its manoeuvres round the throne of the White Lady. Salvador Dali was no doubt right to imagine a surrealist bullfight, so was Picasso to paint one embellished with crape and women spectators in mourning. These obsequies could renew the ritual, change habits and act as a balance between two eras (just as Belmonte represents the dividing line between what the Fiesta used to be and what it is).

It must not be forgotten that discoveries which alter a habit threaten to be regarded as mistakes before imitators classify them and establish their dogma. The bullfighting public is unfair. Each person seated up there knows better than the matador what it would be best to do down in the ring. Moreover, as with every type of public, criticism proves intelligence and enthusiasm is ascribed to credulity, naïveté and stupidity. There is more whistling than applause and it can happen that people applaud against something, as I found on the last day of the Feria 1954, at the triumph of the young Pepe Ordonez, who was applauded against the presidential box which refused to lend him its ears. He did not have the bull's ear, but this injustice earned him that of the public, which is better and from which he should draw many advantages.

After having taken upon himself four deaths through the dramatic elimination of his comrades, after having missed three *estocadas*, he was totally successful with the fourth and we owed him this spectacle : the bull, with the sword plunged into him up to the hilt, slowly crossed the entire ring before going to lie down and die near the gate. He was followed by the toreros walking slowly in procession, pages trailing their capes. They followed a hearse beflowered with banderillas. The spectators were silent. They did not applaud until the bull fell and I no longer knew if they were applauding the bull, the man, or the magnificence of this funeral march.

All this speculation about the sacrilege of the modern Fiesta does not, however, touch upon the heart of the matter, that is the role of death, which remains, whatever happens, the heroine of the tragedy where the matador is the hero to whom she delegates an ambassador extraordinary, this animal which is sacrificed in advance, charged with negotiating their nuptials (the strangest and most obscure nuptials which exist).

If I had to make a film in the Madrid bullring, I would end it with the White Lady seated on the croup of the general's statue, the croup that the toreros see as they come out of the ring and which seems to them to be the greatest masterpiece of equestrian statuary. I would show her, like those young girls at the Feria of Seville, seated behind the rider, for the torero's relief is temporary, since in the end none of us will emerge alive from the bullring of the world which deceives us and whose illusory perspectives lead us towards death.

Is it not enough to read Montherlant, to leaf through the fine books of Popelin and Laffont, to which one could not add a single line – is it not enough to look at the pictures in them in order to realize that styles may change but the tragedy remains and even finds resources in the diversities of the spectacle demanded by the public? And if one wishes to find proof of the sacrament and the sacrifice whose hieroglyphics I am attempting to decipher, one has only to look at the famous photograph of Belmonte on his knees before the bull. His face expresses ecstasy.

There must in fact be some sacrament concealed here. In Spain attempted suicide is punished like attempted murder. And if there is no sacrament it is astonishing that the Church agrees to take under its holy protection men who, in touching the sand in the bullring, walk *a priori* towards suicide.

The bull should therefore be considered as an ambassador extraordinary from death – from the princess – he will or will not conclude the marriage. It is of the White Lady that I speak when I speak of the bull, since she delegates her powers to him and will only marry the torero whom the bull kills.

These countless suitors who present themselves are drawn by the redoubtable honour of being admitted and know very well that the bull is only a double, an animal who represents a woman (at least in certain languages, since in the German and English languages death changes sex). The torero attempts to emerge unharmed from an ordeal whose prestige is greater than the fear he feels for it.

It will be a question therefore of being conquered, which represents for the public the act of being the conqueror. But the torero is not deceived and, while admitting that he is lying to himself, he knows very well that the true victory is in losing. Without the perfect nuptials of Linares, Manolete would grow old before a public which would become cold and unfair during the wait for the sacrament.

For it is certainly a question of funereal nuptials and is not the death of Manolete an example of one of those country weddings 'without the slightest ceremony' where great ladies amuse themselves taking virtuoso artists, the artists of genius with whom they are in love?

The torero should put on wedding clothes when he is told that the moment is near. From that minute candles will be lit in front of the Madonna, those present will be silent, feeling an insurmountable uneasiness, and the torero will find himself prey to a sacred fear, that of a royal fiancé who is travelling to meet a powerful wife whom he can imagine without knowing her and whom etiquette forces upon him.

This fear of finding oneself face to face with the ambassador of the White Lady, hope mingled with fear that this lady will refuse to give herself, the attraction that she exercises and the fear of pleasing her, accompany the torero up to the time which it would be impossible to delay by one second, for the slightest pause would cause the overspill of this anguish which he dissimulates and which fills him to the brim.

Starting with the procession, preceded by the Alguazils, old crows in collars and tassels, there will come a series of scenes in which the nuptial act unfurls its rites outside all mediocre intrigue. Sometimes I astonish businessmen in explaining to them that the prestige of one among them stems much more from a secret poetry that expresses itself in figures rather than from a skill for taking in his fellows. And it is true, moreover, that there are poets of business as there are of sport. This is what distinguishes a Carpentier, an Al Brown, a Cochet or a Pélissier from a simple sportsman and this is what renders their prestige inexplicable in the eyes of a world for whom the grace that dwells within them remains a dead letter. In this way circus acrobats were astonished by the success of Barbette who knew less than they did but presented it with genius.

What then is this ambassador? A heavy mass which presents itself suddenly, always the same and different through its dress, its heaving shape and that of its frontal weapons, some wide open, others curved. Weapons of a breadth which one had difficulty in imagining from a distance and which seems astonishing whenever one approaches those stuffed heads adorning the balustrades of inns. This dark heaving mass of entrails which one does not know how to reach, except through a keyhole which the Spaniards call the eye of a needle, this male who asserts his rights with a long lance and a double bag of testicles, this battle tank, moves on slender legs and the Devil's hooves. Sometimes it looks as though his legs cannot support him. He slips and kneels down. The crowd become indignant or at least insult the school that trains naïve and sombre diplomats. To the beast-fighters of the past they sent great brutes of ambassadors. To modern fiancés they send ambassadors who are less massive, less incapable of trickery. And sometimes the problem becomes complicated. Go and see this for yourselves when today Concita Cintron for example takes part in things and the bridegroom becomes a bride, changes into a horse and flouts the Devil's hooves with other little teasing sabots.

When the race of Miuras occupy the post, their reputation as killers, the long list of their victims, their grey cloaks and the vast array of the weapons they possess endow the ceremony with a macabre atmosphere. They simplify in a dangerous fashion the imaginary labyrinth of straight lines cut from its architecture, and Theseus runs a greater risk of coming unexpectedly face to face with what he seeks and fears, with the marriage envoy of Ariadne and Phaedra.

Is not the singularity of the corrida due to the fact that its very principle is inconceivable? Good heavens! One demands of an animal that he defends a lost cause on the pretext that he doesn't know it is lost in advance. He is brought up to be duped. As soon as he comes into the ring the light blinds him and he wonders quite rightly where he is. The torero has already removed his sumptuous chasuble on one of the balconies of shade in the plaza, but, stripped of this sacerdotal embellishment, he still looks like a

flower and our dreary fashions have not succeeded in removing the
flowers from his costume. (I saw Manolete's last white chasuble
with its crimson roses at the home of the famous *rejoneador*, the
Mayor of Jerez, Alvaro Domecq.)

Then, a long way away, men wave capes and the bull rushes
towards them. These puppets already tease him by disappearing
and sometimes intriguing him with the tip of a cape showing
outside the hiding-place, proving the presence of humanity. I
wasn't dreaming then, thinks the bull, and he turns away, when he
catches sight of another cape waving in the distance. (Let us note
that the colour of this cape is of no importance. It has only to be
waved, and the British Royal Society for the Prevention of Cruelty
to Animals was extremely naïve in insisting that at bullfights a
green muleta should be substituted for the red one. It can be seen,
moreover, that the bullring attendants, wearing red shirts, circle
invisibly round the manoeuvres of the picador.) The bull is going
to come up against a second joke. The third and fourth deceive
him even more, for the adversary remains visible, but the recollection of the phantom curtains hurls him against an empty piece of
fabric behind which he supposes that a man is hiding as he hides
behind the planks. Woe to the man who does not get out of the
way quickly enough. In Seville I have seen Miguel Angel kneeling
down and then gored full in the mouth through being over-hasty to
brave fate. This time the bull is no longer deceived. He is presented
with a horse, a real horse. Here is some living flesh covered with
old quilts. Here is a fine Rosinante. Here is something to gore. But
the lance becomes more serious. While the bull attacks the covers
and cracks the innocent ribs, the picador drives nine centimetres of
lance into him, making a wound from which his strength flows out
and of which a lady will say : 'It's a hole for putting banderillas in'
(*sic*). Flowers in a vase, in fact.

The banderilla joke would be less painful, but the targets of satin
and gold which dance in front of the bull disappear after having
decorated him with a ferocious bouquet of hollyhocks (unless the
man does not climb the fence quickly enough, for the adversary
begins to suspect that he is being deceived).

I observe what looks like a hunched-up piano, like the phantasm
emerging from some hallucinatory substance, a grand piano with
candelabra and the atrocious keyboard of the blind horse with his
guts ripped out, an image completed not only by the horns of a
desk shaped like a lyre and the little feet of the pedals, but also by
the wild hair of some Abbé Liszt planting the furious banderillas
of his fingers in a gleaming spine to appalling horsy laughter
emerging from an old ivory denture.

Horror. After so much disorder I take a grip of myself and cling to the remnants of a hardly more assuring reality that I seek on the absent-minded faces of my neighbours. Our period of radio, television and magazines is a school of inattentiveness. They teach people to look without seeing, to listen without hearing.

His body arched back, chest thrust forward, slippers dragging on the sand, the muleta low down like a court train, the torero now proudly defies the ambassador : 'Ho, ho, toro!' The bull, motionless and as though hypnotized, listens. He watches the stranger who provokes him. Then there appears the leader who charms, commands, speaks and sometimes imagines he can hear a reply (this happened to Joselito and made him beat a retreat), the liturgical gestures of a priest. He begins the *faena* – the series of passes during which the circle of the arena shrinks round the couple until it is no bigger than a wedding-ring. The poor dupe will understand the deception and submit to it like a victim demanded by the Greek oracle.

Why does this Iphigenian destiny shock no one? Why do our nerves accept it and a whole nation subscribe to it? It could only happen if, to use a common and opportune expression, the poor beast hadn't had enough. It could only happen if some secret consecrates a crime as a rite, and transcends it, a secret which the corrida of 1st May whispered in my ear.

In reality there is no struggle, no duel between the man and the beast, but the creation of a couple isolated by the silence of a double hypnosis, unified by the operation of an ancestral sacrament over which rules no longer have any sway.

A woman unhappily in love once confided to me, 'When I'm too much in pain I go and see my dentist,' meaning that the physical pain soothed her emotional suffering. If the picador slows the bull down too much he increases the risk to the matador, instead of reducing it. Pain can rouse the bull from the hypnosis of love just as a shout from the spectators can rouse the man. A deathly silence should precede this sacrifice in which the hypnosis is achieved by an extraordinary effort, I repeat, the effort of the man to think like the beast, the effort of the beast to think like the man, an effort which makes the couple deaf and blind to everything outside themselves. The danger does not lie in the murder of one of the duellers, but in the possibility of this murder cutting the thread linking them and destroying what death expects of them, either because the torero kills the ambassador or the ambassador kills the torero, or they perish together as happened at Linares, or because the ambassador proves ineffectual, when a harmless *manso* comes for him and leads him away to be executed outside the ring, or because the bull takes advantage of the pause when the torero exchanges his make-believe sword for a real one and rashly slackens the thread of the hypnosis.

Moreover, whether they marry or not, the White Lady grants no pardon to any of her ambassadors. The confiding of the secret costs them their life and the Lady's equipage carries them away, once she is certain of their silence. I think of that ear that is offered to the matador, a bleeding ear filled with the sound of the crowd as a shell is filled with the sound of the sea. I think of that hairy conch brought to Manolete, which he kisses and which receives his last sigh.

Hatred is absent from the corrida. Only fear and love rule there. I admit that a woman in love with a torero can become, without realizing it, jealous of the bull, that is of the White Lady, and ascribe this feeling to the demands of a milieu which preoccupy the torero and undermine her influence. We must not forget that in this dream which he incarnates the torero is open to obsessions which cut him off from the rest of the world. I have referred to Joselito who heard a bull speak to him and I refer to Dominguin who constantly saw, in the same place in the arena, a man in black who stood up and accused him of being a murderer when he was due to appear as a torero in Linares after the tragedy there.

We shall see, moreover, with what strange voluptuousness the couple – beast and man – coil round each other, touch and caress. One might say that the successive curves of a long *faena* owe their perfect round pebble shapes to the dark encircling movements of a wave engaged in polishing a masterpiece.

For one moment the nuptial phenomenon no longer functions. The bull stands respectfully aside in order to leave the great tragic actor Belmonte alone on the stage. No part of his black body now plays the slightest part. He effaces himself like someone playing a minor role as a confidant – he is obliged to be there but tries to be present as little as possible.


Let us limit ourselves to the ignorance of a spectator similar to that of the *espontaneo* who jumps blindly into the arena and affronts the creature anywhere, even in the middle of the ring and on the ground the man assigns him. I have seen men who do this holding their guts and their trousers together with both hands. Let us imagine we are jumping into the arena. Let us approach the couple and watch what is going on, regardless of bullfighting customs. Here the only law operating is that of the insects, when the female couples with the male and devours him. But which one is the male? Apparently there are two males face to face with each other, no erotic contact links them together and yet some toreros have admitted that the *estocada* provokes ejaculation. The great mystery of the Fiesta lies precisely in this paradox of adversaries who alternately become feminine and resume the prerogatives of virility.

This is how a little girl in Seville described the corrida : 'They killed the cow because it tried to eat the lady's dress.' Just as that horned beast represented a cow for her, in the same way the matador with his chignon, his sequins, his satin, his bright pink stockings, his red train, represented a beautiful lady. This was not as silly as it sounds. For if the torero wears the brilliant colours of the male and the bull the modest dress of the female in the animal kingdom, when the act of love is over the male has to change his sex and, through his grace and his dancer's costume, become once more the female who kills. The bull must also recover his male prerogatives and this must be done while he is being stripped of them by the lance and the banderillas. This is the great enigma. The bull is therefore adorned with a bouquet of hollyhocks and a mantle of blood, as though he were exhibiting his pride at the moment of accepting death at the hand of a creature so feeble that he could overcome it by one last little charge. But no. The nuptials continue in accordance with an immemorial code and, since the ambassador has not killed, he must die at the hand of the husband who has become the wife, thanks to a spell cast by the White Lady. Is not the gesture of Luis Miguel Dominguin, as he leans his elbow against the wild beast's forehead, a proof of the quasi-feminine domination exercised by the matador?

The bull is Hercules vanquished by Omphale and we come to understand the woman's dress that Omphale inflicted on Hercules and why she reduced him to spinning and arming himself with a distaff while she disguises herself with his lion's skin. Dominguin would never dare to rest his elbow between the horns if he were not sure of his hypnotic power, of his complete domination. At that moment the exchange of sexes is clear. It is the beautiful lady, for whom the little girl in Seville mistook the matador, who rules over a great submissive brute beast.

So it is truly the male's brilliant costume that the torero wears during the feminine predominance. But he wears it from derision, one could say, facing a male deprived of sequins, embroidery and colours in spite of the shirt of Nessus and the painful multi-coloured distaffs with which his colleagues rig him out.

(If you tell me that the wild beast is only a beast and rejects the slightest emotional contact with the man, I will reply with the example of that young peasant Isidoro Alvarez who in 1936 won the favour of the bull whom he fed and caressed at the farm of Juan Cobaleda in the province of Salamanca. He jumped into the ring, called him and exchanged caresses with him at the moment when Civilon, who was being hunted down, seemed to be disposed towards feeling but the slightest gratitude for human beings.)

From this long rise and fall between agreed strengths and weaknesses, from this geometry of bullfighting, which runs counter to that of Euclid, from this profound and invisible metamorphosis, comes the uneasiness which disturbs the men and women spectators at the Fiesta, uneasiness which they feel without analysing, and which they confuse with straightforward anxiety experienced by the witnesses of a duel.

Olé. This slow 'olé' which escapes from the mouths of the Spanish is like a smoke-ring from a cigar. It accompanies, stimulates and emphasizes a handsome matador's or flamenco dancer's face. You might think you heard it coming from the skull of the guitars. It affects the Andalusian nonchalance of a fan. It never rises to a shout. It alternates with the insulting shouts aimed at the unfortunate picadors. Olé! My neighbours are certainly accustomed to the hereditary spectacle which fascinates me. The only excuse, nevertheless, for knowing that we are safe would be that our visceral emotions express themselves through stigmata, obliging the blood to piss out from our skin like the crimson thread from water-coolers.

I know, moreover, to what shocked reaction I am exposing myself by describing in this way the last act of what is usually taken for a duel. No matter. This is what it was granted to me to understand while I was holding Gomez's montera on my knees. My body, I said, no longer existed. My mind became the couple and penetrated secrets that I would have been incapable of surprising without the phenomenon which metamorphosed me into an action.

At this moment nothing appeared more comic to me than my neighbours and their certainty of being the golden calf – an ideal measure, made in 'the image of God' to the extent that instead of saying that something is bigger than they are and something else smaller, they will say that the smallest is minute and the largest gigantic.

None the less, these mysterious changes of sex represented for me the sexual hesitation preceding the chaos of the Cosmos and the two sexes linked together in the body of the pre-Adamites. 'These evil and shattered worlds had differed from our own especially through sexual life. In any case, so far as the latter was concerned, the men reproduced themselves without women.' (The Cabbala) From this arose the legend of Sodom destroyed by the fire of heaven. The (giant) angels came to reproach little men for imitating the sterile customs to which the giants had condemned themselves through fear of giving birth to ogres.

In this way a ceremony is performed where we must see, in spite of our distaste for the literary, an attempt, either by the horn or the *estocada*, to imitate that penetration through which our solitudes try to delude themselves and to obtain, through the assistance of an act deflected from all procreative aim, a kind of fleeting triumph – a victory over the figure 2, which is the sign of death.

As soon as the mechanism of thought is set in motion we never cease to destroy ourselves. It can happen that the testifying object informs us that, in spite of the acceptance of the sacrifice, the beautiful insect, gilded and feminized, implants its sting and, to its amazement, at that moment experiences the orgasm of love which emits an arrow of sperm without any bending of the bow, or to put it more clearly, without any masculine erection.

I saw then the gigantic insects and the giants who fought them, Hercules killing a monster with *three bodies superimposed on each other and with long wings* and those giants who perpetuate, in spite of decadence, the dogma of those insects so highly placed in the scale of antediluvian creatures, so that in every cult, and noticeably in our own, one encounters again the symbol and ritual of sacrifice and resurrection.

I describe all this inadequately because of an ailing body. Only, in the bullring, I understand it wonderfully well and I knew that I would cease to understand it when I woke up, as happens in the sudden vertiginous adventures into which nitrous oxide plunges us and from which awakening snatches us, leaving us with only the memory of a memory and the astonishment of losing the ease of multiplicity.

But unlike the dream which is dreamt all of a piece and which is 'developed' and 'projected' into the human order – I knew that this waking dream and this order would be transformed after the corrida into a tight, indivisible knot which I would try as hard as I could to unravel.

And I saw clearly the links between the phenomena which the scientists who discover them cannot relate to each other, enclosed as they are in their circle of study and in marginal economy, which is indispensable in bringing things to completion.

The *estocada* is interminably prolonged. The matador traverses a hundred years on earth out of time, and then returns to human time, like the aviator for whom distance annihilates his house, which does not prevent this house from living, for if he comes closer to it, the perspective of space-time recreates it and he finds it intact after destroying it.

I have had car accidents. A skid against a wall was interminable – interminable and swifter than lightning. The wall would come up to me majestically and slowly, as tender as a mother's cheek, and I would see my absent-minded mother as she put her cheek close to mine in the past and say to me : 'You must want to ask me for something.' And I could see every pore in this maternal cheek as though through a magnifying-glass.

The hotel-keeper by the road-turning adorned with a painted skull is used to accidents. When my car is in pieces, with the eye of one headlamp still blinking at the end of a wire, the lady who lives behind the wall appears, displeased that I have survived and accept the brandy that is always offered. And the torero sees approaching slowly the vast array of horns with the only place between them where he can drive in the blade. And this deceptive slowness worked for me as I participated in the sacrifice.

Damasco Gomez made the kill.

It was all over. He became once again a moon-prince dressed in fine colours. He was a young man safe and sound who climbed up the fence and asked me to return his black toque. And it wasn't his *montera* that I threw him from my bench but a paving-stone that was crushing my chest without my realizing it and of which I only became conscious as I awoke. (I learnt later that certain people to whom bulls had been dedicated, among others the son of the Mayor of Madrid, were obsessed by the fact that toreros were killed during the fight, and they felt responsible. A dangerous honour from which I am glad to have emerged unscathed.)

The fact remains that I shall never forget that 1st May of 1954 and the considerations that have resulted from it. I hope the experts will forgive me and find in what I write only the unbridled bravery of the *espontaneo* who leaps into hell like an angel and gives himself up afterwards to the police. I am not unaware that if I encroach upon the ground of classicism I shall soon be gored, especially if I don the red waistcoat Théophile Gauthier wore for the première of *Hernani*, the corrida of romanticism.

Don Enrique will say that the modern torero 'composes his face' and clings to the bull behind the horns. He will talk of the 'mawkish graces' and will regret the beast-handlers whose place, according to him, has been taken by dancers.

If he sets eyes on this text he will no doubt consider that I am letting myself be caught up in the dance. This is not true. But a skilful butcher matters little to me. Perhaps he will find in my clumsiness an excuse for the new bullfighting technique in which ends have become means and start from a basis too serious to allow a descent into the tricks of sport. Does not the phenomenon which transforms a flower of Seville into a wasp of Toledo belong, whatever the cost, to the secret arcana of nature?

The corrida and flamenco dancing are a language that is spoken by the body. I am aware, unfortunately, of my contradictions and repetitions, my grammatical mistakes. I do not change them in any way. They are only waiting for the clapping of hands in order to acquire style. And I want this text to resemble those night-time discussions when a few toreros agree to be interested in my point of view, round a table. When I was very young Bombita became my friend. It was at Saint-Jean-de-Luz. I was fascinated by his little plait, by that postiche coleta that his colleagues wear, by that word 'toreador' which is a rhyme from *opéra comique* that one would like to use, it fits in so well with 'matador' and 'picador' and expresses its meaning clearly. I knew nothing about these bullfights and do not pride myself on knowing more. May some secrets be heard murmuring within this text, as happens in Santa Cruz where houses full of people seem empty and only inhabited by a fountain. After all, a non-specialist should no more have free entry to the Spanish arenas than to the Indian ones where only vultures penetrate.


A young poet from Arles, Jean-Marie Magnan, has been able to establish this text from illegible notes, some taken on my knee during a corrida, others on my two invalid knees in bed; as I finished reading it I was listening to Toscanini, who had died the day before, conducting Beethoven's Fifth Symphony.

So much lofty pomp reminded me of the astonishing encounter between Beethoven and Goethe described by Nietzsche. 'The peasant and the aristocrat'. And suddenly I wondered if Nietzsche's 'Alas for me, I am subtle' did not lose its power (did not change its meaning) before this deaf man in whom there were no subtleties, and if Beethoven does not give us an example of genius in its primitive state, in short if the text that I have rediscovered thanks to the noble patience of a young Arlesian, did not condemn me once more to chew over subtleties far from triumphal marches and apotheoses. And a sentence from *Le Potomak*, written in my youth, comes back to me : 'I could have written *La Marseillaise* or *Plaisir d'Amour*. I am writing this text.'

Nothing changes. A vast curve passing through the vaults of a romanesque church, sorrows and struggles and ruins and the empty spaces which are my glorious scars, shows every danger of completing the terrible zero of a serpent of pride biting its tail, the zero of the bullring, in the centre of which, sitting in wait for us all, terrifying in its immobility, there sits in majesty this bisexual insect with white wings : death (male or female, according to the language).

# PART FOUR

*Ideas and Experiences*

# Cock and Harlequin

In 1918 Cocteau and his writer friend Blaise Cendrars set up a small publishing firm, which they called Les Editions de la Sirène. One of the titles that appeared under its imprint the same year was *Cock and Harlequin* (Le Coq et l'Arleqin), a slim volume which included two monograms and a portrait of the author (in uniform) by Picasso. It was reprinted in *Le Rappel à l'Ordre* and in Rollo Myers' translation, *A Call to Order*, both of which appeared in 1926. *A Call to Order*, from which the following version is taken, was the first work by Cocteau to appear in English. A critic reviewing the book in *The Times* wrote: 'The question remains whether ... M. Cocteau and his friends are not so far ahead of their epoch that they postulate human organisms that are still non-existent for their audiences.'

At least one French critic has chosen the term 'staccato' to describe the essay, which was subtitled 'notes around music'. Its themes and expression are youthful and uncompromising; while attacking Wagner and Debussy it praises Erik Satie and demands that France should produce French music. At the same time it enunciates various ethical and artistic principles which were to recur in Cocteau's work during the rest of his life.

Stravinsky quarrelled with Cocteau after reading this text and the additional pages at the end which implied criticism of him and of his music. However, the two men were reconciled later and a further piece about Stravinsky, expressing Cocteau's admiration for him, was added to the 1926 edition.

Le groupe des Six

AURIC, DUREY, HONEGGER, MILHAUD, POULENC, TAILLEFERRE

# DEDICATION TO
# GEORGES AURIC

My dear friend,

I admire the Harlequins of Cézanne and Picasso, but I do not like Harlequin. He wears a black mask and a costume of all the colours. After denying the cock's crow, he goes away to hide. He is a cock of the night.

On the other hand, I like the real cock, who is profoundly variegated. The cock says Cocteau twice and lives on his *own* farm.

Had I not dedicated *Le Cap de Bonne-Espérance* to Garros in captivity, I should dedicate these notes to Garros escaped from Germany. But you are the second friend of mine who has *escaped from Germany*.

I offer them to you because a musician of your age proclaims the richness and grace of a generation which no longer grimaces, or wears a mask, or hides, or shirks, and is not afraid to admire or to stand up for what it admires. It hates paradox and eclecticism. It despises their *smile* and faded elegance. It also shuns the colossal. That is what I call *escaping from Germany*.

Long live the Cock! Down with Harlequin!

19th March, 1918                                                      J. C.

N.B. Harlequin also means : 'A dish composed of various scraps.' (Larousse)

At the beginning of every book it would be a good plan to draw up a special glossary by means of which, in assigning to each term its exact value, many misunderstandings of vocabulary would be avoided.

Almost all misunderstandings arise from the *quid pro quos* of vocabulary.

The word SIMPLICITY, which occurs often in the course of these notes, calls for some definition.

Simplicity must not be taken to be the synonym of 'poverty', or to mean a retrogression.

Simplicity progresses in the same way as refinement, and the simplicity of our modern musicians is not the same as that of our clavecinists.

The simplicity due to a reaction from refinement benefits from that very refinement – it detaches and condenses the richness acquired.

This book is not concerned with any existing school but with a school to whose existence nothing points – were it not for the first-fruits of a few young artists, the efforts of the painters, and the tiredness of our ears.\*

\* I add here the 'Socrates' of Satie which was unknown to me at the moment of writing these lines.

Art is science in the flesh.

The musician opens the cage-door to arithmetic; the draughts-man gives geometry its freedom.

A work of art must satisfy all the muses – that is what I call 'proof by nine'.

A masterpiece is a game of chess won 'checkmate'.

A YOUNG MAN MUST NOT INVEST IN SAFE SECURITIES.

TACT IN AUDACITY CONSISTS IN KNOWING HOW FAR WE MAY GO TOO FAR.

We must get rid of a Baudelairean prejudice; Baudelaire is bourgeois. The 'Bourgeoisie' is the bed-rock of France from which all our artists emerge. They may possible get clear of it, but it allows them to build dangerously on substantial foundations.

With us, there is a house, a lamp, a plate of soup, a fire, wine and pipes at the back of every important work of art.

Instinct needs to be trained by method; but instinct alone helps us to discover a method which will suit us, and thanks to which our instinct may be trained.

The nightingale sings badly.

In the world of comedians there are conjurors, and they amuse us, but only on condition that their tricks come off. To put a rabbit into a hat and bring out a cage is all right; but to put in a rabbit and take out a rabbit – would this bad conjuror expect to be taken for a poet?

In feeling his way an artist may open a secret door and never discover that behind this door a whole world lay concealed.

Hence, if he who passes for the high-priest of a school because he founded it should one day shrug his shoulders and disown it, the school is in no way discredited thereby.

The course of a river is almost always disapproved of by the source.

It is the artist who is really rich. He rides in a motor-car. The public follows in a bus. How can we be surprised if it follows at a distance?

THE SPEED OF A RUNAWAY HORSE COUNTS FOR NOTHING.

Be suspicious of M. Prudhomme walking on his hands.

WHEN A WORK OF ART APPEARS TO BE IN ADVANCE OF ITS PERIOD, IT IS REALLY THE PERIOD THAT HAS LAGGED BEHIND THE WORK OF ART.

An artist does not jump upstairs. If he does it is a waste of time, because he will have to walk up afterwards.

An artist who goes backwards betrays nobody. He only betrays himself.

Emotion resulting from a work of art is only of value when it is not obtained by sentimental blackmail.

In art every value which can be proved is vulgar.

WE SHOULD BE MEN DURING OUR LIFETIME AND ARTISTS FOR POSTERITY.

Truth is too naked; she does not inflame men.

A sentimental scruple, which prevents us from speaking the whole truth, makes us represent Venus hiding her sex with her hand. But truth points to her sex with her hand.

Satie said : 'I want to write a play for dogs, and I have got my scenery. The curtain goes up on a bone.' Poor dogs! It is their first play. Afterwards they will be shown more difficult ones, but it will always come back to the bone in the end.

Every 'Long live So-and-So' involves a 'Down with So-and-So'. One must have the courage to say this 'Down with So-and-So' or be convicted of eclecticism.

Eclecticism is fatal to admiration as well as to injustice. But in art, it is a kind of injustice to be just.

It is hard to deny anything, above all a noble work of art. But every sincere affirmation involves a sincere negation.

Beethoven is irksome in his developments, but not Bach, because Beethoven develops the form and Bach the idea. Most people think the opposite.

Beethoven says : 'This penholder contains a new pen; there is a new pen in this penholder; the pen in this penholder is new' – or 'Marquise, vos beaux yeux. . . .'

Bach says : 'This penholder contains a new pen in order that I may dip it in the ink and write', etc., or 'Marquise, vos beaux yeux me font mourir d'amour, et cet amour. . . .'

There lies the difference.

One is sometimes bound to defend those of whom one does not approve. For example, how can one help defending Strauss against those who attack him from pure Germanophobism or in favour of Puccini?

A revival of the mysteries of Eleusis would free art from prostitution. The worst tragedy for a poet is to be admired through being misunderstood.

There is a moment when every work in the process of being created benefits from the glamour attaching to uncompleted sketches. 'Don't touch it any more!' cries the amateur. IT IS

THEN THAT THE TRUE ARTIST TAKES HIS CHANCE.

We all have a skin that is sensitive to tziganes and military marches.

*SENSES.* The ear repudiates, but can tolerate, certain kinds of music which, if transferred to the sphere of the nose, would oblige us to run away.

The bad music which superior folk despise is agreeable enough. What is disagreeable is their good music.

Beware of the paint, say certain placards. I add : Beware of music.

Look out ! Be on your guard, because alone of all the arts, music moves all around you.

Musicians ought to cure music of its convolutions, its dodges and its tricks, and force it as far as possible to keep *in front of the hearer.*

A POET ALWAYS HAS TOO MANY WORDS IN HIS VOCABULARY, A PAINTER TOO MANY COLOURS ON HIS PALETTE, AND A MUSICIAN TOO MANY NOTES ON HIS KEYBOARD.

ONE MUST SIT DOWN FIRST; ONE THINKS AFTERWARDS.

This axiom must not serve as an excuse to those who are always sitting down. A true artist is always on the move.

Picturesqueness, and especially exoticism, are a handicap to musicians, and cause them to be misunderstood.

Sculpture, so neglected on account of the current contempt for form and mass in favour of the fluid, is undoubtedly one of the noblest arts. To begin with, it is the only one which obliges us to move round it.

That bird-catcher and scarecrow over there is a conductor.

The creative artist must always be partly man and partly woman, and the woman part is almost always unbearable.

THE BEAUTIFUL LOOKS EASY. THAT IS WHAT THE PUBLIC SCORNS.

Even when you blame, only be concerned with what is first class.

A sound opinion is always taken for a literary opinion.

What makes optimists of pessimists like ourselves is the intuition that a work of art tends to maintain a supernatural equilibrium.

I am working at my wooden table, seated on my wooden chair with my wooden penholder in my hand, but this does not prevent me from being in some degree responsible for the courses of the stars.

A dreamer is always a bad poet.

If you are going to shave your head, don't keep a curl for Sundays.

You tell me you have come from Right to Left owing to a passionate conviction, and you have only changed your clothes. You ought to have changed your skin as well.

The important thing is not to swim lightly on the surface, but to disappear heavily and leave only a ripple.

The eyes of the dead are closed gently; we also have to open gently the eyes of the living.

Let us read again Nietzche's *The Case of Wagner*.

Never have shallower or profounder things been said. When Nietzsche praises *Carmen*, he praises the crudity that our generation seeks in the music-hall. It is to be regretted that he compares to Wagner an 'artistic' work and one which is inferior in artistry to Wagner's work.

Impressionist music is outdone, for example, by a certain American dance which I saw at the Casino de Paris.*

Wagner is played in London; in Paris Wagner is secretly regretted.

To defend Wagner merely because Saint-Saëns attacks him is too simple. We must cry 'Down with Wagner!' together with Saint-Saëns. That requires real courage.

Nietzsche was afraid of certain 'ands' – Goethe *and* Schiller, for example, or worse still, Schiller *and* Goethe. What would he say at seeing the spread of the cult of Nietzsche *and* Wagner or rather Wagner *and* Nietzsche!

There are certain long works which are short.

Wagner's works are long works which are long, and *long-drawn-out*, because this old sorcerer looked upon boredom as a useful drug for the stupefaction of the faithful.

It is the same with mesmerists who hypnotize in public. The

* This was what the dance was like:
The American band accompanied it on banjos and thick nickel tubes. On the right of the little black-coated group there was a barman of noises under a gilt pergola loaded with bells, triangles, boards, and motor-cycle horns. With these he fabricated cocktails, adding from time to time a dash of cymbals, all the while rising from his seat, posturing and smiling vacuously.
Mr Pilcer, in evening dress, thin and rouged, and Mlle Gaby Deslys, like a big ventriloquist's doll, with a china complexion, flaxen hair, and a gown of ostrich feathers, danced to this hurricane of rhythm and beating of drums a sort of tame catastrophe which left them quite intoxicated and blinded under the glare of six anti-aircraft searchlights. The house was on its feet to applaud, roused from its inertia by this extraordinary turn, which, compared to the madness of Offenbach, is what a tank would be beside an 1870 state-carriage.

genuine 'pass' which puts to sleep is usually very short and very simple, but they accompany it with a score of sham passes which impress the crowd. The crowd is won by lies; it is deceived by the truth, which is too simple, too naked, and not sufficiently shocking.

Schoenberg is a master; all our musicians, as well as Stravinsky, owe something to him, but Schoenberg is essentially a blackboard musician.

Socrates said : 'Who is that man who eats bread as if it were rich food and rich food as if it were bread?' Answer : The German musical enthusiast.

The opposition of the masses to the élite stimulates individual genius. This is the case in France. Modern Germany is dying of approbation, carefulness, application and a scholastic vulgarization of aristocratic culture.

With us a young musician from the beginning meets with opposition; in other words, a stimulant. In Germany he finds ears. The longer they are the more they listen. He is taken up and academized, and that is the end of him.

*SATIE VERSUS SATIE.* The cult of Satie is difficult because one of Satie's charms is that he offers so little encouragement to deification.

One often wonders why Satie saddles his finest works with grotesque titles which mislead the least hostile sections of the public. Apart from the fact that these titles protect his works from persons obsessed by the sublime, and provide an excuse for the laughter of those who do not realize their value, they can be explained by the Debussy-ist abuse of 'precious' titles. No doubt they are meant as a good-humoured piece of ill-humour, and maliciously directed against 'Lunes descendant sur le temple qui fut', 'Terrasses des audiences du Clair de lune' and 'Cathédrales englouties'.

The public is shocked at the charming absurdity of Satie's titles and system of notation, but respects the ponderous absurdity of the libretto of *Parsifal*.

The same public accepts the most ridiculous titles of François Couperin 'Le tic-toc choc ou les Maillotins', 'Les Culbutes Ixcxbxnxs', 'Les coucous bénévoles', 'Les Calotins et Calotines ou la pièce à trétous', 'Les vieux galants et les Trésorières surannées'.

The impressionist composers cut a pear into twelve pieces and gave each piece the title of a poem. Then Satie composed twelve poems and entitled the whole 'Morceaux en forme de poire'.

Satie acquired a distaste for Wagner in Wagnerian circles, in the very heart of the *Rose-Croix*. He warned Debussy against Wagner. 'Be on your guard,' he said. 'A scenery tree is not upset because somebody comes on to the stage.' That is the whole aesthetic of *Pelléas*.

Debussy missed his way because he fell from the German frying-pan into the Russian fire. Once again the pedal blurs rhythm and creates a kind of fluid atmosphere congenial to *short-sighted ears*. Satie remains intact. Hear his 'Gymnopédies', so clear in their form and melancholy feeling. Debussy orchestrates them, confuses them, and wraps their exquisite architecture in a cloud. Debussy moves further and further away from Satie's starting-point and makes everybody follow in his steps. The thick lightning-pierced fog of Bayreuth becomes a thin snowy mist flecked with impressionist sunshine. Satie speaks of Ingres : Debussy transposes Claude Monet 'à la Russe'.

However, while Debussy was delicately bringing to flower his feminine grace and parading Stéphane Mallarmé in 'Le Jardin de l'Infante' (Albert Samain), Satie continued to follow his little classical path. He reaches us today as young as any of the 'younger' men, having at last found his place after twenty years of modest labour.

When I speak of the 'Russian trap' or 'Russian influence', I do not mean by that that I despise Russian music. Russian music is admirable because it is Russian music. Russian-French music or German-French music is necessarily bastard, even if it be inspired by a Moussorgsky, a Stravinsky, a Wagner, or a Schoenberg. The music I want must be French, of France.

*SMALL WORKS.* There are certain small works of art whose whole importance lies in their depth; the size of their orifice is of small account.

In music, line is melody. The return to design will necessarily involve a return to melody. The profound originality of a Satie provides young musicians with a teaching that does not imply the desertion of their own originality. Wagner, Stravinsky, and even Debussy are first-rate octopuses. Whoever goes near them is sore put to it to escape from their tentacles; Satie leaves a clear road open upon which everyone is free to leave his own imprint.

Satie does not pay much attention to painters, and does not read the poets, but he likes to live where life ferments; he has a flair for good inns.

Debussy established once for all the Debussy atmosphere. Satie evolves. Each of his works, intimately connected with its predecessor, is, nevertheless, distinct, and lives a life of its own. They are a surprise – and a deception for those who expect one always to keep on treading the same piece of ground.

Satie is the opposite of an improviser. His works might be said to have been completed beforehand, while he meticulously unpicks them, note by note.

Satie teaches what, in our age, is the greatest audacity, simplicity. Has he not proved that he could refine better than anyone? But he clears, simplifies, and strips rhythm naked. Is this once more the music on which, as Nietzsche said, 'the spirit dances', as compared with the music 'in which the spirit swims'?

Not music one swims in, nor music one dances on; MUSIC ON WHICH ONE WALKS.

> De la musique avant toute chose
> Et pour cela préfère le pair,
> Plus lourd et moins soluble dans l'air
> Avec tout en lui qui pèse et qui pose.
>
> Il faut surtout que tu n'ailles point
> Choisir tes mots avec quelque méprise,
> Rien de moins cher que la chanson grise
> Où l'imprécis au précis se joint.

The Impressionists feared bareness, emptiness, silence. Silence is not necessarily a hole; you must use silence and not a stopgap of vague noises.

*BLACK SHADOW.* Black silence. Not *violet* silence, interspersed with *violet shadows.*

*YOUTHFULNESS.* Nothing is so enervating as to lie and soak for a long time in a warm bath. Enough of music in which one lies and soaks.

Enough of clouds, waves, aquariums, water-sprites, and nocturnal scents; what we need is a music of the earth, everyday music.

Enough of hammocks, garlands and gondolas; I want someone to build me music I can live in, like a house.

A friend tells me that, after New York, Paris houses seem as if you could take them in your hands. 'Your Paris,' he added 'is beautiful because she is built to fit men.' Our music must also be built to fit men.

Music is not all the time a gondola, or a racehorse, or a tight-rope. It is sometimes a chair as well.

A Holy Family is not necessarily a holy family; it may also consist of a pipe, a pint of beer, a pack of cards and a pouch of tobacco.

In the midst of the perturbations of French taste and exoticism, the café-concert remains intact in spite of Anglo-American influence. It preserves a certain tradition which, however crapulous, is none the less racial. It is here, no doubt, that a young musician might pick up the lost thread.

THE CAFE-CONCERT IS OFTEN PURE; THE THEATRE IS ALWAYS CORRUPT.

Certain masterpieces of the theatre are not strictly speaking 'theatrical', but are rather scenic symphonies which allow nothing to be sacrificed to decoration. For example : *Boris Godounov*.

Let us keep clear of the theatre. I regret to have felt its temptation and to have introduced to it two great artists. (Naturally, I do not regret it because of the scandal : the full realization of my idea would have created the same scandal. But here we are moving in a sphere where the public, a hundred years behind the times, cannot possibly be taken into consideration.) 'Well, then, why do you write for the theatre?' That is precisely the weak point about the theatre; it is forced to depend for its very existence upon immediate successes.

When I say that I prefer certain circus or music-hall turns to anything given in the theatre, I do not mean that I prefer them to anything that might be given in the theatre.

The music-hall, the circus, and American Negro bands, all these things fertilize an artist just as life does. To turn to one's own account the emotions aroused by this sort of entertainment is not to derive art from art. These entertainments are not art. They stimulate in the same way as machinery, animals, natural scenery, or danger.

This life-force which is expressed on the music-hall stage makes, at first sight, all our audacities appear old-fashioned. This is because art is slow and circumspect in its blindest revolutions. There, there are no scruples; you jump upstairs.

*A LIGHT STEP PRODUCED BY HEAVY FEEDING.* Much fun has been made of an aphorism of mine quoted in an article in the *Mercure de France* : 'An artist must swallow a locomotive and bring up a pipe.' I meant by this that neither painter nor musician should make use of the spectacle afforded by machinery in order to render their art mechanical, but should make use of the measured exaltation aroused in them by that spectacle in order to express other things of a more intimate kind.

Machinery and American buildings resemble Greek art in so far as their utility endows them with an aridity and a grandeur devoid of any superfluity.

But they are not art. The function of art consists in seizing the spirit of the age and extracting from the contemplation of this practical aridity an antidote to the beauty of the Useless, which encourages superfluity.

We may soon hope for an orchestra where there will be no caressing strings. Only a rich choir of wood, brass and percussion.

I should not be averse from substituting for the cult of St Cecilia that of St Polycarpe.

It would be a fine thing for a musician to compose for a mechanical organ, a veritable sound-machine. We should then hear, properly employed, the rich resources of this apparatus which are now lavished, haphazard, upon hackneyed tunes.

I should like this composer to imagine a steam roundabout with Louis XIV Pegasus-chargers, done in ripolin, pirouetting in a coach royally bedecked with mirrors, lights, and cloth of gold.

*CONCERNING A CERTAIN ACROBATIC TENDENCY.* Our musicians have avoided the Wagnerian torrent on a tightrope, but a tightrope cannot be considered, any more than a torrent, as a respectable mode of locomotion.

MUSICAL BREAD is what we want.

For the last ten years Chardin, Ingres, Manet and Cézanne have dominated European painting, and the foreigner comes to us to put his racial gifts to school with them. Now I declare that French music is going to influence the world.

In *Parade* I attempted to do good work, but whatever comes into contact with the theatre is corrupted. The luxurious setting characteristic of the only European impresario who was sufficiently courageous and sufficiently interested to accept our work, circumstances in general, and fatigue, made me unable to realize my piece which remains, as it stands, in my opinion, an open window through which may be had a glimpse of what the modern theatre ought to be.

The score of *Parade* was meant to supply a musical background to suggestive noises, e.g. of sirens, typewriters, aeroplanes and dynamos, placed there like what Georges Braque so aptly calls 'facts'. Material difficulties and hurried rehearsals prevented these noises from materializing. We suppressed them nearly all. In other words, the piece was played incomplete and without its principal *clou*.

Our *Parade* was so far from being what I could have wished that I never went to see it from the 'front', confining myself to adjusting with my own hands, from the wings, the notice-boards bearing the number of each 'turn'. The managers' step-dance, amongst others, rehearsed without Picasso's 'carcasses', lost all its lyric force as soon as the 'carcasses' were put on the dancers.

One day I was looking at the children's puppet show in the Champs Elysées when a dog came on the stage, or rather a dog's head, as big in itself as two of the other actors put together. 'Look at the monster,' said a mother. 'It is not a monster, it is a dog,' said the little boy.

In the theatre men rediscover the ferocity of children, but they have lost their clairvoyance.

Sick to death of flabbiness, fluidity, superfluity, frills, and all the modern sleight-of-hand, though often tempted by a technique of which he knows the ultimate resources, Satie voluntarily abstained, in order to 'model in the block' and remain simple, clear and luminous. But the public hates candour.

Each of Satie's works is an example of renunciation.

The opposition put forward by Erik Satie consists in a return to simplicity. Moreover, that is the only possible kind of opposition in an age of extreme refinement. The good faith of the critics of *Parade*, who thought that the orchestral part was a mere din, can only be explained by the phenomenon of *suggestion*. The word 'cubism', wrongly applied, *suggested* an orchestra to them.

The Impressionist musicians thought the orchestra in *Parade* poor, because it had no sauce.

The arrangement of *Parade* for four hands is from beginning to end an architectural masterpiece; that is what ears accustomed to vagueness and thrills are unable to understand. A fugue comes bustling along and gives birth to the actual melancholy rhythm of the fair. Then come the three dances. Their numerous themes each distinct from the other, like separate objects, succeed one another, without being developed, and do not get entangled. A metronomical unity governs each of these enumerations which are superimposed upon the simple outlines of each character and upon the imaginative ideas evoked by them.

The Chinaman, the little American girl, and the acrobats, represent varieties of nostalgia hitherto unknown, so great is the degree of verisimilitude with which they are expressed. No humbug, no repetition, no underhand caresses, no feverishness or miasma. Satie never 'stirs up the bog'. His is the poetical imagination of childhood moulded by a master technician.

In *Parade* the public thought that the transposition of the music-hall was a bad kind of music-hall.

The public, so accustomed to the incongruous graces of opera ballets, mistook the dances based on the familiar gestures of life for mere grimacing.

Nothing is more comic than prejudice about the sublime.

One recalls the picture of Balestrieri. For the majority of artists a work cannot be beautiful without an intrigue of mysticism, love or boredom. Brevity, gaiety, and unromantic melancholy are suspect. The hypocritical elegance of the Chinaman, the melancholy of the Little Girl's steamboats, the touching simplicity of the Acrobats – all those things which remained a 'dead letter' for the public who saw *Parade*, would have pleased them if the acrobat had loved the Little Girl and had been killed by the jealous Chinaman, who had then been killed in his turn by the acrobat's wife – or any other of the thirty-six dramatic combinations.

TRADITION APPEARS AT EVERY EPOCH UNDER A DIFFERENT DISGUISE, BUT THE PUBLIC DOES NOT RECOGNIZE IT EASILY AND NEVER DISCOVERS IT UNDERNEATH ITS MASKS.

The 'useful' and the 'useless' exist in art. The majority of the public does not realize this, since it looks upon art as an amusement.

One ought not to say 'panem et circenses', but 'circenses panis sunt', or rather 'quidam circenses panis sunt'.

That which makes the public laugh is not inevitably beautiful or new, but that which is beautiful and new inevitably makes the public laugh.

'Cultivate those qualities in you for which the public blames you : they are Thyself.' Get this idea well into your head. This advice ought to be written up everywhere like an advertisement. As a matter of fact, the public likes to 'recognize' what is familiar. It hates to be disturbed. It is shocked by surprises. The worst that can happen to a work of art is to have no fault found with it so that its author is not obliged to take up an attitude of opposition.

When Baudelaire defended Wagner, it was a case of *aristocratic opposition*. There was no other possible attitude to adopt. All that one can say is that it is a pity that certain epochs can put their great men into a false position.

*MISDEAL*. Ingres, the revolutionary *par excellence*; Delacroix, the typical 'rapin'; Ingres, the hand; Delacroix, 'la patte'. Lapse of time brings more clearly into relief the rich bazaar of Delacroix, the architecture of Ingres. The scorn of some of the younger school for Satie's classicism and his respect for the 'Schola Cantorum' reminds one of this strange misdeal. Beware of music *à la Delacroix*; never forget that Ingres did not have his own public. He saw his own public running after Delacroix, and remained at the height of his fame, a great innovator, but unrecognized.

The public, accustomed to redundancy, disregards works that are terse.

To the musical public terseness signifies emptiness, and stuffing prodigality.

The longer an artistic expression is destined to last, the fuller and denser it will be, compact like an egg, and the more it will facilitate surface-trickery.

The public does not like dangerous profundities; it prefers surfaces. That is why, when an artistic expression appears to it to be suspect, it leans towards a belief in trickery.

THE PUBLIC ONLY TAKES UP YESTERDAY AS A STICK TO BEAT TODAY.

The indolence of the public : its armchair and its stomach. The public is ready to take up no matter what new game so long as you don't change it, when once it has learned the rules. Hatred of the creator is hatred of *him who alters the rules of the game.*

PUBLICS. Those who defend today by making use of yesterday, and who anticipate tomorrow (1 per cent).

Those who defend today by destroying yesterday, and who will deny tomorrow (4 per cent).

Those who deny today in order to defend yesterday (which is their today) (10 per cent).

Those who imagine that today is a mistake, and make an appointment for the day after tomorrow (12 per cent).

Those of the day-before-yesterday who defend yesterday in order to prove that today exceeds legitimate bounds (20 per cent).

Those who have not yet learnt that art is continuous and believe that art stopped yesterday in order to go on again, perhaps, tomorrow (60 per cent).

Those who are equally oblivious of the day-before-yesterday, yesterday, and today (100 per cent).

There are people who are considered quite intelligent but who do nothing but lean towards good things. Their heads get near, but the rest of them remains rooted.

An unfinished work flatters the public because it finds it can make something out of it. It detests a finished work against which it bruises itself, and from which it feels itself pitiably excluded.

Superior folk have discovered the word 'stylization' to describe everything which is lacking in style.

THE EXTREME LIMIT OF WISDOM IS WHAT THE PUBLIC CALLS MADNESS.

In Paris everyone wants to be an actor; no one is content to be a spectator. People jostle each other on the stage, and the auditorium remains empty.

'Why do you do these things?' asks the public.

'Because you would not do them,' answers the creator.

*TO PLEASE, AND TO RETAIN ONE'S MERIT.* If an artist yields to the public's overtures of peace, he is beaten.

The danger of the *Case of Wagner* lies in the fact that it is an idiot who flings it in your face. There are truths which can only be said after one has acquired the right to say them.

'Look' – said a lady to her husband, in front of one of Claude Monet's cathedrals – 'that's futurism.' And she added : 'It looks like a melting ice-cream.' In this case the lady spoke the truth, but she had not acquired the right to do so.

There are profound fashions as well as frivolous ones. A musician must submit to these fashions or else create one according to his taste. Every masterpiece having once been in fashion goes out of fashion, and long afterwards finds an everlasting equilibrium. Generally it is when it is out of fashion that a masterpiece appeals to the public.

In art anecdote is nothing, *except for the artist.* 'Shall we buy a Venice or a pot of flowers?' asked a couple once. This tale makes you laugh, but nearly everybody thinks like that.

A favourite phrase of the public is : 'I don't see what that's meant to be.'

The public wants to understand first and feel afterwards.

'Show me a fine work of your school and I shall be convinced.' Thus speaks M. de la Palisse.

A fall makes people laugh. The mechanism of falling plays an important part in causing the laughter which greets a new work. The public, not having followed the curve which leads up to this work, stumbles suddenly from where it was standing down on to the work which it is now seeing or hearing. The result is a fall, and laughter.

If it has to choose who is to be crucified, the crowd will always save Barabbas.

To listen with all her skin is what a timid hind does; I prefer to listen with all my ears.

*REAL SENSITIVENESS.* Music threw St Douceline into extraordinary ecstasies. One day when out for a walk : 'How beautifully that bullfinch sings !' she said, and fainted away.

Resemblance is an objective force which resists all subjective transmutations. Do not confound resemblance with analogy.

An artist who has the sense of reality must never be afraid of being lyrical. The objective world preserves its force in his works, no matter how it may have been transformed by the lyrical element.

Our intelligence digests well. An object profoundly assimilated exercises a strong motive force and results in a realism which is superior to a mere unfaithful copy. Do not confound a canvas by Picasso with a mere decorative arrangement, or mistake *Parade* for an improvisation.

An original artist *cannot* copy. So he has only to copy in order to be original.

If birds know grapes when they see them, then there are two

sorts of bunches. The good bunch which is eaten, and the bad which
is left uneaten.

DO NOT DERIVE ART FROM ART.

Music is the only art which the masses will allow not to be like
something else. And yet good music is music which has some
resemblance.

All good music resembles something. Good music arouses emotion owing to its mysterious resemblance to the objects and feelings
which have occasioned it.

Resemblance in music does not consist in representation, but in
the strength of a dissembled truth.

*ARCHITECTS.* One may find fault with the colour of the
rooms, but what does that matter if the house is solidly built and
lacks nothing from top to bottom?

One has been accustomed too long to the charm of mere
scaffolding. We architects demolish the scaffolding as soon as the
house is built.

Impressionism has fired its last fine fireworks at the end of a
long fête. It is up to us to set the rockets for another fête.

One does not blame an epoch; one congratulates oneself on not
having belonged to it.

To be on one's guard against a decadent movement is not to
deny the individual value of its artists.

Impressionism is a reaction from Wagner. The last reverberation
of the storm.

The impressionist school substitutes sunshine for light, and
sonority for rhythm.

Debussy played in French, but used the Russian pedal.

'What a crowd of false disciples there is around a Picasso, a
Braque, a Stravinsky or a Satie, who discredit them!' Such is the
opinion of the Impressionist. No doubt he forgets the Salon
d'Automne, and Melisande's hair-splitting.

*Pelléas* is another example of music to be listened to with one's
face in one's hands. All music which has to be listened to through
the hands is suspect. Wagner is typically music which is listened
to through the hands.

One cannot get lost in a Debussy mist as one can in a Wagner fog,
but it is not good for one.

The theatre corrupts everything, even a Stravinsky.

I should not like this paragraph to affect our faithful friendship,
but it is useful to put our young compatriots on their guard against
the caryatids of the Opéra – these stout gold sirens who caused
even so formidable a ship to change its course. I consider the *Sacre
du Printemps* a masterpiece, but I discern in the atmosphere

created by its production a religious complicity existing amongst the initiated, like the hypnotism of Bayreuth. Wagner wanted the theatre; Stravinsky finds himself involved in it by circumstances. There is a difference. But even though he composes *in spite of* the theatre, the theatre has none the less infected him with its microbes. Stravinsky gets at us by other means than Wagner; he does not try to hypnotize us or plunge us in a semi-darkness; he hits us deliberately over the head and in the heart.

How can we defend ourselves? We set out teeth. We feel cramps like those of a tree which grows in jerks *with all its branches*. There is even in the very speed of this sublime growth something theatrical. I do not know if I make myself clear; Wagner cooks us slowly; Stravinsky does not give us time to say 'Ouf!'; but both of them upset our nerves. This is music which comes from the bowels; an octopus from which you must flee or else it will devour you. It is the fault of the theatre. There is theatrical mysticism in *Le Sacre*. Is not this music which one listens to through the hands?

When I wrote *Le Potomak*, I could not see clearly owing to my disordered state. Stravinsky helped me to shake this off as a charge of cheddite liberates the ore. Now that I have emerged from my black mood, I look at it like everything else.

Stravinsky will get a man out of a quicksand, but he still does not belong to the race of architects. His work is not based on scaffolding – it grows.*

*CONCERNING A CERTAIN FRIVOLOUS ATTITUDE.* If you feel you have a missionary's vocation, don't hide your head like an ostrich; go amongst the Negroes and fill your pockets with worthless bric-à-brac.

*NEGROES.* It is only by distributing lots of bric-à-brac and by much imitation of the phonograph that you will succeed in taming the Negroes and making yourself understood.

Then substitute gradually your own voice for the phonograph and raw metal for the trinkets.

Too many miracles are expected of us; I consider myself very fortunate if I have been able to make a blind man hear.

WE HAVE IN OUR KEEPING AN ANGEL WHOM WE ARE CONTINUALLY SHOCKING. WE MUST BE THIS ANGEL'S GUARDIAN.

Take care to conceal your capacity to work miracles, for 'if they

---

* This unjust remark is, of course, annulled by *L'Histoire du Soldat*, with which I was then unacquainted, as well as by all Stravinsky's later works. See 'Stravinsky – Stop Press', pp. 330-2.

knew you were a missionary they would tear out your tongue and nails'.

What are the thoughts of the canvas on which a masterpiece is being painted? 'I am being soiled, brutally treated and concealed from view.' Thus men grumble at their destiny, however fair.

# APPENDIX

### FRAGMENTS FROM 'IGOR STRAVINSKY AND THE RUSSIAN BALLET' (*La Noce Massacrée*)

I prefer, myself, a talented childhood which grows up in bad surroundings, takes wrong turnings, spends itself futilely and at length suddenly discovers its error in time to escape the consequences, to a childhood which makes its first 'faux pas' on the right paths, and which progresses normally, holding out no hope of startling developments. I except the early flame of genius, which dies down again unless the prodigy, combining wisdom with genius, retires in time under some pretext or other. The indiscipline and bad taste, proper to youth, preserve the pre-existent gift which is delivered in due course painfully, delicately, gradually, by spade-work, like a buried Venus.

For this reason, do not regret your mistakes, even public and notorious ones, heavy drags though they be, and which do not alleviate the fatigues of the journey towards the Left. One turns round, takes a sponge-down, looks to see where one has come from, and is astonished. The chief stumbling-block people put in the way of this Herculean task is ingratitude. One passes through many milieux in order to attain a relative solitude, and these milieux reproach one with having shared their table and with having cleared out 'on the quiet'. The result is the heart suffers much from a pilgrimage which the world commonly attributes to egoism, disorder and versatility.

\*

And the Flower-Maidens! Amongst the most recent Flower-Maidens, the most maidenly and most flowery, I class the Russian Ballet.

\*

I had a presentiment that I should have to find an excuse for my enthusiasm– a last scruple before clearing out 'on the quiet'.

It was in 1910. Nijinsky was dancing the *Spectre de la Rose.* Instead of going to see the piece, I went to wait for him in the wings. *There it was really very good.* After embracing the young girl the spectre of the rose hurls himself out of the window ... and comes to earth amongst the stage-hands who throw water in his face and rub him down like a boxer. What a combination of grace and brutality! I shall always hear that thunder of applause; I shall always see that young man, smeared with grease-paint, gasping and sweating, pressing his heart with one hand and holding on with the other to the scenery, or else fainting on a chair. Afterwards, having been smacked and douched and shaken he would return to the stage, and smile his acknowledgements.

It was in this semi-obscurity, under the moonlight of the lime-lights, that I met Stravinsky.

\*

Stravinsky was then finishing *Petrouchka.* He described it to me in the Casino at Monte Carlo.

\*

*Petrouchka* was given in Paris on 13th June, 1911. I remember the private rehearsal at the Châtelet. The work which, today, gives off its whole aroma, at that time withheld it, so much so that it displeased the public.

The dilettanti, used to clichés, were unable to follow a synthesis of the soul of the Russian people whose melancholy is not expressed in a whine, and which goes straight from beginning to end, like a drum-roll.

One or two specialists recognized the master-hand, and gradually the concert-halls consecrated *Petrouchka. Petrouchka,* then, was recognized; firstly on account of the folk-lore it contained; secondly, as a defence against still newer things.

For it is the public's way to hobble from one work to another, always one behind, adopting what precedes, in order to use it to blame what is going to follow, and 'never keeping to the page', as the expression goes.

We saw very little of Stravinsky until the famous première of the *Sacre du Printemps.*

## LE SACRE DU PRINTEMPS

The *Sacre du Printemps* was given in May 1913, in a new theatre, untarnished by time, too comfortable and too cold for a public used to emotions at close quarters in the warmth of red velvet and gold. I do not for a moment think that the *Sacre* would have met with a more polite reception on a less pretentious stage; but this luxurious theatre seemed, at first glance, symbolic of the misunderstanding which was confronting a decadent public with a work full of strength and youth. A tired public, reposing amidst Louis XVI garlands, Venetian gondolas, luxurious divans and cushions of an orientalism for which the Russian Ballet must be held responsible. Under such conditions one digests, as it were, in a hammock, dozing; the really New is driven away like a fly; it is disturbing.

*

The natural trend of bad taste is already marked; but since 1912 a false audacity, tempting some, and mistaken by others (hating both alike) for true audacity, has taken possession of innumerable categories of fashionable æsthetes. Dilettanti and 'precious' women thought themselves The Thing, and a class made its appearance in the world belonging to no class – neither to that of respectable bad taste, for which it was most fitted, nor to the one of new ideas, happily out of its reach. The provinces outprovincialized in the very heart of Paris.

*

It would, perhaps, be of interest to trace the part played by each of the collaborators in the 'ensemble' of this work : Stravinsky, musician; Roerich, painter; and Nijinsky, choreographer. We were then, musically, in the heyday of impressionism. . . . Then suddenly in the midst of these charming ruins grew up the Stravinsky tree. When all is said and done, the *Sacre* is still a 'Fauvist' work, an organized 'Fauvist' work. Gauguin and Matisse pay homage to it. But if the backwardness of music as compared to painting, prevented the *Sacre*, of necessity, from coinciding exactly with other disturbing elements, it none the less contributed an indispensable explosive force. Moreover, it must not be forgotten that Stravinsky's unbroken collaboration with Diaghilev's company, and his attentiveness to his wife in Switzerland, kept him at a distance from the centre of things. His audacity was, therefore, quite gratuitous. In brief, the work, as it stands, was, and is, a masterpiece; a symphony, impregnated with a wild sadness, of primitive earth, camp and farmyard noises, fragments of melodies emerging from the depths of time, animal paintings, profound upheavals, the Georgics of a prehistoric age.

Certainly Stravinsky had studied Gauguin's canvases, but, in the process of transformation, the weak decorative register became a colossus. At that time I was not familiar with all the variations in the scale of values adopted by the Left, and thanks to my ignorance I was able to enjoy the *Sacre* to the full, away from the petty schisms and narrow formulæ which condemn free values and too often serve to mask a lack of spontaneity.

Roerich is a mediocre painter. On the one hand he designed costumes and scenery for the *Sacre* which were in keeping with the work; on the other hand, he enfeebled it by the softness of his accents. There remains Vaslav Nijinsky. . . .

When he is at home – that is to say in the Palace Hotels where he bivouacks – this young Ariel frowningly examines folios, and revolutionizes the grammar of gesture. Badly informed, his modern models are not of the best; he makes use of the Salon d'Automne. Too familiar with the triumph of grace, he rejects it. He seeks systematically the opposite to that to which he owes his fame; in order to escape from old formulæ, he hems himself in with new ones. But Nijinsky is a moujik, a Rasputin; he carries in him that fluid which stirs crowds, and he despises the public (whom, however, he does not refuse to gratify). Like Stravinsky, he metamorphoses into strength the weakness of whatever he derives his inspiration from; by means of these atavisms, this absence of culture, this meanness, this *humanity*, he escapes the German danger, the system which desiccates a Reinhart.

I have heard the *Sacre* again without the dances; I ask to see them again. In my recollection, impulse and order are as equally balanced in them as in the orchestra. The fault lies in the parallelism of music and movement, in their want of 'play', of counterpoint. We had the proof that the same chord repeated often tires the ear less than the frequent repetition of the same gesture tires the eye. Laughter was caused by a monotony, as of automata, rather than by the abruptness of the attitudes, and by the abruptness of the attitudes rather than by the polyphony.

The choreographer's work may be divided into two parts. One part dead (e.g. keeping the feet motionless, merely with the idea of contradicting the traditional pose of the 'danseuse' 'toes out') and one part alive (e.g. the Storm and that dance of the Chosen One, foolish and naïve, the dance of an insect, of a hind fascinated by a

Boa, of a factory explosion – in fact, the most stupefying spectacle
I ever remember having seen in the theatre).

\*

These different elements formed, then, an 'ensemble' which was
both homogeneous and heterogeneous, and what shortcomings there
may have been as regards detail were volatilized and eradicated by
sheer force of temperament.

Thus we made the acquaintance of this historic work in the
midst of such an uproar that the dancers could no longer hear the
orchestra and had to keep time to the rhythm which Nijinsky,
stamping and shouting, was beating in the wings.

After this sketch of what was going to happen on the stage, let us
pass through the little iron door to the auditorium. It is packed. A
practised eye could discern there all the material for a scandal : a
fashionable public, décolleté, decked with pearls, aigrettes and
ostrich feathers; and, rubbing shoulders with tulle gowns and tail-
coats, the jackets and headbands and conspicuous garments of that
species of æsthete who acclaims no matter what novelty in season
and out of season through detestation of the 'dress-circle' (the
unintelligent applause of the former being more insufferable than
the sincere hisses of the latter). Add to these the musicians of the
'feverish' school, a handful of 'moutons de Panurge', hesitating
between public opinion and the admiration one ought to entertain
for the Russian Ballets. And, without insisting further, mention
ought to be made of the thousand varieties of snobbism, super-
snobbism, anti-snobbism, which would require a whole chapter to
themselves. A feature of our audience ought to be recorded –
namely, the absence, with one or two exceptions, of the young
painters and their masters. An absence due, as I afterwards learnt,
in the case of the former, to their ignorance of these functions to
which Diaghilev, to whom they were as yet unknown, did not
invite them; in the case of the latter, to social prejudices.

This condemnation of luxury, which Picasso professes like a cult,
has its merits and demerits. I fling myself upon this cult as upon an
antidote, but it may be that it restricts the horizon of certain artists
who avoid contact with luxury from motives of envious hatred
rather than conviction. In any case, Montparnasse is still ignorant
of the *Sacre du Printemps,* and the *Sacre du Printemps*, played on
the orchestra at the Concerts Monteux, had the same bad reputation amongst artists of the Left as the Russian Ballets; and Picasso
heard Stravinsky for the first time with me in Rome in 1917.

\*

Let us now return to the theatre in the Avenue Montaigne, while we wait for the conductor to rap his desk and the curtain to go up on one of the noblest events in the annals of art. The audience behaved as it ought to; it revolted straight away. People laughed, booed, hissed, imitated animal noises, and possibly would have tired themselves out before long, had not the crowd of æsthetes and a handful of musicians, carried away by excessive zeal, insulted and even roughly handled the public in the loges. The uproar degenerated into a free-fight.

Standing up in her loge, her tiara awry, the old Comtesse de P flourished her fan and shouted, scarlet in the face, 'It's the first time for sixty years that anyone's dared to make a fool of me.' The good lady was sincere; she thought there was some mystification.

*

At two o'clock in the morning Stravinsky, Nijinsky, Diaghilev and I piled into a taxi and drove to the Bois de Boulogne. No one spoke; the night was fresh and agreeable. We recognized the first trees by the smell of the acacias. When we had reached the Lakes, Diaghilev, enveloped in opossum furs, began to mutter in Russian; I felt Stravinsky and Nijinsky listening, and when the driver lit the lamps I saw that there were tears on the impresario's face. He went on muttering, slowly and indefatigably. 'What is it?' I asked. 'Pushkin.' Again there was a long silence; then Diaghilev stammered out a short sentence, and the emotion of my two companions seemed so acute that I could not refrain from interrupting in order to know the reason. 'It is hard to translate,' said Stravinsky, 'really very hard; too Russian . . . too Russian. It means, roughly, "Veux-tu faire un tour aux îles" – Yes, that's it; it is a very Russian expression, because, you know, in our country one goes to the islands in the same way as we are going to the Bois de Boulogne tonight, and it was in going to the islands that we conceived the *Sacre du Printemps*.'

It was the first time the scandal had been alluded to. We came back at dawn. You cannot imagine the state of softness and nostalgia of these men, and whatever Diaghilev may have done since, I shall never forget his great wet face, in the cab, reciting Pushkin in the Bois de Boulogne.

It is from this meeting in the cab that our real friendship with Stravinsky dates. He went back to Switzerland. We corresponded. I had the idea of 'David', and went to join him at Leysin.

*

An acrobat was to do the parade for 'David', a big spectacle which was supposed to be taking place inside; a clown, who subsequently became a box, a theatrical version of the phonograph at a fair, a modern equivalent of the mask of the ancients, was to sing through a megaphone the prowess of David and implore the public to enter to see the piece inside.

It was, in a sense, the first sketch of *Parade*, but uselessly complicated by the Bible and a text.

It contained good and bad features; the idea was too fresh, too 'reactive', and I congratulate myself that circumstances saved us from committing a half-blunder, worse than a blunder.

For me, it was a time of transformations. I was moulting, I was in a state of growth. It was natural that frivolity, lack of concentration and talkativeness should have been followed by an excessive desire for sobriety, method and silence. Moreover, without knowing what the painters' opinion was, I realized thoroughly the antagonism between the genius of Igor and the 'chèvre et chou' atmosphere of the Russian Ballets, and also the difficulty for an artist to concentrate within the limits of a frame so vast and encumbered with such elaborate accessories.

But the idea was not ripe.

\*

THE COLLABORATION OF 'PARADE'

*Letter to Paul Dermée, Editor of the review* Nord-Sud

My dear friend,

You ask me for some details about *Parade*. Here are some too hastily jotted down. Excuse the style.

Every morning fresh insults reach me, some from a long distance, for critics assail us without having seen or heard the work; and since abysses cannot be bridged, and it would be necessary to start with Adam and Eve, I considered it more dignified never to reply. I therefore peruse with equal surprise articles which are insulting or contemptuous, articles in which amusement is mingled with indulgence, and congratulatory articles which are based on misunderstanding.

Before this pile of shortsightedness, crudeness, and insensibility, I think of those admirable months during which Satie, Picasso and I lovingly invented, sketched and gradually put together this pregnant little work, whose modesty consists precisely in not being aggressive.

\*

I first had the idea of it during a period of leave in April 1915 (I was then in the army), on hearing Satie play his 'Morceaux en forme de poire' for four hands, with Viñes.

A kind of telepathy inspired us simultaneously with a desire to collaborate. A week later I returned to the front, leaving with Satie a bundle of notes and sketches which were to provide him with the theme of the Chinaman, the little American girl and the acrobat (there was then only one acrobat). These indications were not in the least humorous. They emphasized, on the contrary, the prolongation of these characters on the other side of our showman's booth. The Chinaman could there torture missionaries, the little girl go down with the *Titanic*, and the acrobat win the confidences of the angels.

Gradually there came to birth a score in which Satie seems to have discovered an unknown dimension, thanks to which one can listen simultaneously both to the *Parade* and the show going on inside.

In the first version the managers did not exist. After each music-hall turn an anonymous voice, issuing from a kind of megaphone, sang a type-phrase, summing up the different aspects of each character. When Picasso showed us his sketches, we realized how interesting it would be to introduce, in contrast to the three chromos, un-human or superhuman characters who would finally assume a false reality on the stage and reduce the real dancers to the stature of puppets.

I then conceived the 'managers', wild, uncultured, vulgar and noisy, who would injure whatever they praised and arouse (as actually happened) the hatred, laughter and scorn of the crowd by the strangeness of their looks and manners. During this phase of *Parade* three actors, seated in the orchestra, announced through speaking-trumpets, as loudly as posters, the names of advertisements such as Pears Soap, etc., while the orchestra was settling down.

Subsequently in Rome, where I went with Picasso to join Leonide Massine, in order to unite scenery, costumes and choreography, I perceived that one voice alone, to represent each of Picasso's 'managers', even though reinforced, jarred and constituted an intolerable error of equilibrium. We should have had to have three timbres for each manager, and that would have led us far from our principle of simplicity. It was then that I substituted for the voices the rhythm of footsteps in the silence. Nothing satisfied me so much as this silence and these stampings. Our mannikins quickly resembled those insects whose ferocious habits are exposed on the film. Their dance was an organized accident, false steps which are prolonged and interchanged with the strictness of a fugue. The awkwardness of movement underneath those wooden frames, far from hampering the choreographer, obliged him to break with ancient formulæ and to seek his inspiration, not in things that move, but in things round which we move, and which move according to the rhythm of our steps.

At the last rehearsals the thundering and languorous horse, when the stage-carpenters had finished his badly made carcass, was metamorphosed into the cab-horse of Fantomas. Our wild laughter and that of the stage-hands decided Picasso to let him keep this fortuitous silhouette. We could not have supposed that the public would receive with such bad grace one of the only concessions made to it.

We now come to the three characters of *Parade,* or rather four, since I altered the one acrobat to two.

Contrary to the belief of the public, these characters are more Cubist than our 'managers'. The managers are a sort of human scenery, animated pictures by Picasso, and their very structure necessitates a certain choreographic formula. In the case of these four characters, the problem was to take a series of natural gestures and to metamorphose them into a dance without depriving them of their realistic force, as a modern painter seeks his inspiration in natural objects in order to metamorphose them into pure painting, but without losing sight of the force of their volume, substance, colour and shade.

FOR REALITY ALONE, EVEN WHEN WELL CON-CEALED, HAS POWER TO AROUSE EMOTION.

The Chinaman pulls out an egg from his pigtail, eats and digests it, finds it again in the toe of his shoe, spits fire, burns himself, stamps to put out the sparks, etc. . . .

The little girl mounts a racehorse, rides a bicycle, quivers like pictures on the screen, imitates Charlie Chaplin, chases a thief with a revolver, boxes, dances a ragtime, goes to sleep, is shipwrecked, rolls on the grass, buys a Kodak, etc. . . .

As for the acrobats (shall I confess that the horse was ridden by a manager, and that when this manager fell off we suppressed him for good and all at the very last moment?), the poor, stupid, agile acrobats – we tried to invest them with the melancholy of a Sunday evening after the circus when the sounding of 'lights out' obliges the children to put on their overcoats again, while casting a last glance at the ring.

Erik Satie's orchestra charms without the use of pedals. It is like an inspired village band.

It will open a door to those young composers who are a little weary of fine impressionist polyphonies.

Listen to it emerging from a fugue and rejoining it again with a classic freedom.

I composed, said Satie modestly, a background for certain noises which Cocteau considers indispensable in order to fix the atmosphere of his characters.

Satie exaggerates, but the noises certainly played an important part in *Parade*. Material difficulties, however (amongst others the suppression of the compressed air), deprived us of those 'ear-deceivers' – dynamo, Morse apparatus, sirens, express-train, aeroplane – which I employed with the same object as the 'eye-deceivers' – newspapers, cornices, imitation woodwork, which the painters use.

We could hardly enable the typewriting machines to be heard.

And this is the history, though superficial and lacking in form, of a disinterested collaboration which, in spite of universal indignation, was crowned with success, the truth being that for centuries one generation has handed down a torch to another over the heads of the public, whose breath has never succeeded in extinguishing it.

PICASSO AND STRAVINSKY

## APPENDIX 1924

S T R A V I N S K Y – S T O P   P R E S S

During an interview which I had recently with the Russian poet Mayakovsky, Stravinsky acted as interpreter.

The conversation took an unfortunate turn. It was not only a question of running from one language to another, but from one epoch to another.

In a country in which everything has been completely turned upside-down, literature gets mixed up with the rest. Ideas predominate; poets become politicians.

In our country, after a similar crisis, speeches are succeeded by conundrums – as a reaction. Finally the conundrums disappear and the struggle is waged over points of extreme subtlety which escape the notice of inattentive persons or foreigners.

This economy and dynamic reserve remind one of certain machines which are used for the retouching of zinc clichés : a complicated monster controls an insignificant little tool.

It is for this reason that our best periods produce upon foreigners an impression of smallness. You can imagine how the giant Mayakovsky looked at my little sling !

All this time Stravinsky went on translating. I could learn nothing from the expression on Mayakovsky's face, which resembled that of a prodigious baby. The real sight was our interpreter, who was engaged upon a strange sort of smuggling adventure, travelling all alone from one tongue to the other, and only letting through what he chose to let through.

Here stands revealed Stravinsky as he is today. In vain did he try to enrich the Russian's remarks, and impoverish my own; when Mayakovsky had gone we felt we were compatriots.

For it is the first time I have ever observed this miracle – the miracle of a thunderstorm entirely engrossed in searching for an apparatus which will give it an outline. A case of oriental romanticism (with its uneasiness and savage upheavals) submitting to the discipline of Latin order.

*

Genius cannot be analysed any more than electricity. You either have or don't have it. Stravinsky has it, and so never bothers about it at all. He never allows himself to be hypnotized by it, nor does he allow it to make him giddy. He does not expose himself to the danger of his own emotions, or of trying to beautify himself, or the reverse. He canalizes an elemental force, and, in order to make it serviceable, provides it with appliances ranging from factories to pocket-lamps.

To perfect and vary these appliances is the problem by which the old one of inspiration has to be replaced.

This is a full-face portrait of Stravinsky in 1923. Now let us examine him in profile.

Charm demands perfect tact. It means standing on the brink of an abyss. Nearly all the 'graceful' artists fall into it. Rossini, Tchaikovsky, Weber, Gounod, Chabrier, and, today, Francis Poulenc, lean over but do not fall. A very deep root enables them to lean a very long way.

*Mavra* is an acrobatic turn on the edge of a precipice. One is reminded of those clowns who play the mandoline perched on the top of a pile of chairs. The pile sways about, and hesitates for a long time at the critical point.

How is it possible to describe Stravinsky without following him in this, his latest, phase? Rings, spats, scarves, waist-belts, neckties, tie-pins, wrist-watches, mufflers, fetishes, glasses, eye-glasses, pince-nez, watch-chains – all these things would fail to describe him. They merely prove, by superficial tokens, that Stravinsky does not put himself out for anybody. He composes, dresses, and talks as he pleases. When he plays the piano, the piano and he are merged into one; when he conducts his Octet he turns on us an astronomer-like back in order to solve this magnificent instrumental problem, written in silver figures.

He inherits from N. A. Rimsky-Korsakov orderly habits, which he upsets for his own purposes. On Rimsky's table the ink-bottles, penholders and rulers revealed the bureaucrat. Stravinsky's order is terrifying. It recalls the surgeon's instrument-case.

This composer, in the midst of his work, wearing it like a garment, harnessed into it like a man with an orchestra on his back, stripping off and piling up round him pieces of musical bark, is all of a piece with his room. To see Stravinsky at Morges, or Leysin, or in Paris in his rooms over Pleyel's, where he lodges, is to see an animal in its shell. Pianos, drums, metronomes, cymbals, American pencil-sharpeners, desks, drums of all descriptions seem to prolong his person. They are like the air pilot's rig, or the arms with which an insect is bedecked when we see it in the cinema, magnified a thousand times, at pairing time.

*

Certainly the *Sacre du Printemps* uproots me, while *Noces* carries me away at top speed, like a racing car, but even in *Noces*, where the spirit of the *Sacre* finds its definite orchestral formula, the appeal of its beauty is still to the entrails. How can I forget that my neighbours in the stalls who are applauding it showed no interest in *Mavra*, which was written later? Their approval embarrasses me. It seems as if I am watching the musician being applauded on his own cheeks.

What could be more admirable than the spectacle of this hard man being begged by an amorous public to be brutal to them and deal still more blows – and then offering them lace. So graceful a gift perplexes them. They understood the blows better.

## BEAUTY ONCE AGAIN COMPROMISES HERSELF WITH US

Hazard arranges things well. On 6th and 19th January, 1924, it invited Francis Poulenc and Georges Auric to come and triumph at its own headquarters. For Serge de Diaghilev was giving his festival of French music at the Casino at Monte Carlo.

Of course everyone knows that Monte Carlo is a very ugly town, Venice a very beautiful one, and Lourdes a very impressive one. But Lourdes may shock, and Venice disappoint you, and I confess that I like Monte Carlo. There you see the sun shining on gold, and the Café de Paris resembles St Mark's. The sky-blue façades stimulate our appetite for life, and the pigeons which the shooters have missed come and settle on Massenet's head. There is one thing wanting, however, and that is a bust of Pascal, to whom we owe Roulette, in the middle of the Terrace.

The tourist in Greece turns to his Homer. Here I am guided by Fantomas. The systems are in full swing, and the pilgrims enter their losses on registers. There they are, licking their pencils while the roulette is still slowly turning under its coat of many colours, reminding one of racehorses coming back to the paddock. Moving about between the tables are a few of the fairies who bring good and ill luck : charming, mad old Englishwomen, who sleep standing up, and walk about without ever having undressed since the reign of Queen Victoria. It was in this illustrious spot that I was to win what I had staked upon the two young musicians, with whom my friendship is well known.

I LES BICHES

I think, to begin with, in order to emphasize the significance of what I am going to say, I had better confess that I do not like the choreography of *Noces*. I admire it, however, without liking it, for although I may blame the form of a piece of furniture I can respect the skill of the cabinet-maker.

Perhaps my severity is due to a too whole-hearted admiration of the purely musical part of this ballet. It is an oratorio, any addition to which I should find disturbing.

In the music of *Noces* I discern a very important feature : in it Stravinsky de-ridiculizes the sublime, just as you are going to hear Poulenc de-ridiculize grace. The spirit of the *Sacre* here finds its orchestral formula.

The *Sacre* still preserved some shadow; in *Noces* the mystery takes place in full daylight and at full speed. I consider that the conscious striving after grandeur and mystery in the choreography is ill adapted to the spontaneous mystery and grandeur of the bare orchestra that has no drapery, and never raises its eyes to heaven. It wears its grandeur underneath, and to emphasize it on the stage is almost like making it seem to be worn outside.

But after all, in order to find fault we have to start from a very high level. This work is a masterpiece of its kind, but I should have preferred the music to have been only a pretext for them, and to have watched the heads being piled one upon another, and the groups being built up and dissolved, in silence.

In *Les Biches* Mme Nijinska has succeeded in attaining grandeur without premeditation. This was made possible by the absence of subject and the apparent levity of the musical style. For the beauty and melancholy of *Les Biches* are not the product of any artifice. I doubt whether this music knows it hurts. I suspect it of being as hard-hearted as Youth, which spatters passers-by with impertinent scorn. Its rhythms have a sporting distinction. They are like splendid girls going by, covered with sweat and a racquet under their arms, who throw a shadow over us as they pass. After it is over, I go home feeling humiliated. I want to impart emotion to a contemptuous body. I recall my solitude when I was twelve and used to visit the Palais de Glace. I measured the distance that separated me from the celebrated *cocottes*. They would be limping round the warm passages, and then, suddenly, out there on the rink in the cold (reminding one of the ice in a surprise omelette), I would see them bowing and gliding about like ships in full sail.

Yes, Poulenc's music is distant. It is haughty, exhibiting itself half-naked, and by failing to understand itself, producing the same effect as perversion.

It only wanted Marie Laurencin. Her scenery and dresses are as apt as can be. They frankly underline the point of everything. This painter's pictures always make us feel sad at the thought that plants and animals do not like us, and are not interested in us. Perhaps a kiss would be enough to break the spell. But who would dare place one upon those muzzles?

Think what a combination of naïve luxury and cruel freshness we get from such a painter as this and such a musician! Look at that bouquet, and those ribbons in the florist's shop! We flatten our noses against the window; we dare not even go in and ask the price.

With an instinct, surprising in a Slav, Mme Nijinska slips into her place without striking a false note. What Poulenc – like a young animal awkwardly trying to make love and – Laurencin – girl-flower or girl-beast – needed, was just this kind of saint.

Mme Nijinska lives shut up in her work. She never stops. Scarcely does she pause to do her hair or fasten her dress. By dint of jumping, and pirouetting, and working her muscles, she ceases to be a worker and becomes a tool. Looking at her sturdy legs, her hair, and her angel's eyes, one admires her as one would a pickaxe or a carpenter's plane.

How will she hold a fragile fan, or proffer beribboned hoops for poodles to jump through? But her brother's blood runs in her veins – a blood that has wings. She does not try to discover what there is at the back of Poulenc or Laurencin. She is guided by intuition. Without the slightest calculation, and by simply obeying the rhythm, and the exigencies of the frame she has to fill, she is about to create a masterpiece : the Fêtes Galantes of her time.

To have thought about Fêtes Galantes, to have thought about the hidden audacities which specialists discover in a Watteau tree, to have thought about the authors' names – so redolent of the Ile-de-France – to have thought about art – in short, to have thought at all, would have meant losing the game.

The poetry of these dances was not expressly written down. The dances in *Noces* oblige us to recognize a Russian poem about sacrifice, maternity, birth, marriage, and death. Here nothing forces us. We are free. There is no poetry except the poetry that resides in figures and clear outlines.

I shall not attempt to describe *Les Biches*. When the curtain goes up you would think you were at the photographer's. A carping critic will think the frocks are too pink. That is the result of the fever brought on by playing hide-and-seek. A sofa plays the part of star dancer and tenor. One can hear, in imagination, its celestial voice. It is rolled about and jumped on, and when everybody is tired out they collapse upon its cushions. The characters come on and go off. Here we have an up-to-date park, and a tea party that might have come straight out of the *Bibliothèque Rose* – a flesh-coloured rose.

I recommend to you the following : the laughing women near the footlights, and then the entry of the men down the steps. What are these wild creatures, these champion swimmers, these Sports Club prize-winners, these heavenly bullies? They speak along the ground. Their voices come out of the orchestra. Their stout, naked legs leave the young ladies quite unmoved. The latter belong to an age in which couples dance on the beach in bathing costume, and their wreaths are woven on the football field.

Look! There are our fine fellows locked together for an Apotheosis tableau : the Wrestling Match. The ladies unlock them, follow them about, and whisper mocking words into their ears. And I can assure you our heroes are not lacking in self-confidence! The way they swagger about is positively preposterous.

These garden parties, cotillions, and plastic poses prepare us for the entry of Mlle Nemtchinova.

How right Stendhal is in his use of the word 'sublime'! The entry of Nemtchinova is, in the true sense of the word, sublime (no Wagnerite will be able to understand what I mean). When this little lady issues forth from the wings on her toes, in an excessively short jerkin, with her long legs, and her right hand in its white glove raised to her cheek as if in a military salute, my heart beats faster, or stops beating altogether. And then, with unfailing taste, she presents us with a combination of classical steps and quite new gestures. The most difficult sums solve themselves all alone on this slate, with the aid of the pupils' coloured chalks – white, blue, and pink.

\*

Next the two pigeons make their appearance. Two young girls in grey, side by side, but facing one another. One holds the other by the neck; the other places her companion's hand on her own heart. They are profoundly actuated by a singular friendship. They perform their disdainful dance. To the accompaniment of a stormy roll of drums and swallow-like twitterings, the dance increases in intensity, and finally leaves them crossed one behind the other, like a pair of steel scissors, and then they part – but not without exchanging, as they go off, one on the left and one on the right, a brief glance – proud, full of complicity, and unforgettable; the glance of the young girls in Proust.

\*

Marie Laurencin, were you looking for a horse? Here is one : it is Mme Nijinska. A circus horse with a plume on its head, or, if you prefer, a champagne-coloured person who has been drinking champagne, and who plunges on the stage alone, with her cigarette and her pearls, to the rhythm of a Rag-Mazurka. Poulenc's music jumps round her like a poodle.

You must look with all your eyes, for this is a sight you will never see again. Mme Nijinska accomplishes a *tour de force* : she escapes from the domain of the dance and its judges; when she enters, it is the theatre itself which enters; and as for her dance, which looks so easy, so sketchy, and so nonchalant, she could never teach it to anyone. For here a single look, the teeth pressed on the lower lip, a gesture of the shoulder or elbow are just as important as an *entrechat* No. 5, or as her brother's famous leap.

See how she maintains her balance on the brink of caricature without ever falling into it, just as the musician, in spite of his easy manner, never lapses into mere facility. Watch her sit down, stretch out her hands towards the dancers, lead them by a movement of her eyelashes and shoulders towards the screen, and bring the work to an end on a note of confusion provided by three persons whom the fall of the curtain has taken by surprise.

In conclusion, what do you think this ballet reminds us of?

From the house opposite a most mischievous, cunning, and skilful hand is flashing a ray of sunlight from a pocket mirror on a woman's face.

## II  LES FACHEUX

With Poulenc we were being intoxicated with strong honey – a honey which we often had to gather from the paw of a very young bear. The orchestra of the *Fâcheux* gives us a change of scene. Handfuls of salt are being thrown on the slippery, frozen streets; coaches are colliding, whips cracking, horses are restive, and the sound of a military band comes round the street corner.

Or are we in the country? A hailstorm is in progress; hailstones are dancing round the flowers, and the wasps are clustering on the fruit trees on the wall.

*

Good music resembles something. It resembles the composer. It is not Spain that I look for in *España,* but Chabrier. *Les Biches* is a portrait of Francis Poulenc, *Les Fâcheux* a portrait of Georges Auric. Poulenc's eye sings a tune, half-covered by its drooping eyelid. Auric fires his black eye at us point-blank.

Occasionally the influence of a master is apparent. As we perceive it, we are profoundly touched. For, when thoroughly assimilated, it is a sign of love. It is a mother's voice, step, and manner reappearing in her son.

\*

We are too apt to vent our bad humour on Wagner. But we ought to have the courage to go back as far as Beethoven. It is there that the drama, or rather the melodrama, begins.

Pascal, with his remark about Cleopatra's nose, has taught us how to play the barren game of 'ifs'. If Mozart had lived longer the face of music would have been changed. Since his death it has been one long theatrical procession which prevents me from crossing the street and going home.

The director of the casino, in entrusting me with a card that opens all doors did not know he was conferring upon me a magic pass. It is true that Stravinsky had several times already cleared the way, but now, seated in this theatre, I feel myself once again, after a century of waiting, really at home.

\*

As long as I am talking about music I avoid what does not concern me. I skip details, and deny myself all marks of expression and the use of pedals. I am accused of being crude. I can't help that; I haven't a moment to lose. I am obliged to go quickly, and clear the way, and do spade-work. I leave it to the critics to count the colours in each pearl, while I pass quickly from one to another – unjust, perhaps, but sincere.

I have not told you that I have thrown in the fire Wagner, or Beethoven, or any of the composers who inspired them, or who derive from them. I have not said that *Les Biches* were like *Cosi fan Tutte*, or *Les Fâcheux* like *Don Juan*. I have only said, roughly, and I repeat it, that, apart from Debussy and Stravinsky, whose greatness cannot, of course, be called in question, no musicians since Mozart have given me as much satisfaction on the orchestra as Georges Auric and Francis Poulenc.

I know that Poulenc's goose-quill traces the initials of love, while Auric's stylo stabs holes in the paper, and that the flourishes, up-strokes and down-strokes of the former are very different from the almost passionate handwriting in which the latter records even the tenderest things; but in thus bracketing them together I merely prove how free every member of our group is to dispose of his forces as he chooses, after the spiritual meal eaten in common.

The score of the *Fâcheux* bristled with broken bottles and stinging nettles. Here was a difficult obstacle to be overcome. It was also Georges Braque's début in the theatre. He is a great painter, but would he be a good scene-painter?

From the moment the curtain goes up, Braque, in one stride, and without effort, 'gets over' the footlights, hand-in-hand with Molière. His fawn-coloured, lionlike elegance is dangerous, as is proved by the fact that he devours the choreography without making the slightest movement. There is too much bustling about, but Braque gets the better of it, like a very calm man having an argument with a very talkative one.

His décor, when the stage is empty, is intriguing. It renders the peculiar aspect of a town in which you walk about at night. The entry of one of the characters completely alters it; such an entry has the effect of dawn breaking. The houses grow bigger; the windows come to life; the trees begin to breathe. Such a décor is the height of good taste; it restores its full value to this demonetized expression. The painter in making his début avoids making a cheap theatrical sensation. He is well aware of the popularity of any sort of scandal, and knows that certain forms of audacity signify, in 1924, merely a desire to please. He has no wish to please, or displease. He does not even avail himself of any of the advantages which the theatre offers. He makes his entry naked, like an athlete confident in his beauty, after twelve years of training. He conceals his calculations under the freshness of his skin.

\*

I said that Braque got the better of the choreography; I ought to have said that he was the real choreographer and Mme Nijinska could only follow him. All the real dancing in the *Fâcheux* is done by the colours – beiges, yellows, browns, and greys. The girls who play at battledore and shuttlecock, whose faces, thanks to certain shades of yellow and mauve, seem abnormally pink, fill our field of vision without the aid of any artifice other than that of having a wall or tree as a background.

Orphise, handsome in a flat sort of way under her hat, which is too big for the window from which she watches Eraste, if she wants to express herself, merely has to turn her back in order to disappear like those insects which know how to assume the colour and shape of a dead leaf. If she turns round, why bother to run on her toes? If she stands on them it will be enough. Her costume affords us a

surprise equivalent to that of an ingenious step. The entry of the
bowls-players is enough to change the whole lighting, and plunge
the scene in moonlight.

When they all run away the décor rocks like a boat. Eraste
becomes half as big again, and the houses come nearer. These
strange stage effects accompany a pantomime which ought to have
been discreetly outlined. No doubt Mme Nijinska, on account of
the restraint imposed upon her by the fact of having such an artist
as collaborator, will be blamed for the tactful way in which her
dancers hesitate between the Russian Ballet and the Comédie
Française.

In my opinion, there are few scenes as noble as the massing of
colours at the end, merging together, as Renan would say, like
those on a dove's neck, while a military call on the trumpets, torn
from the orchestra, announces the fall of the curtain.

## THE EXAMPLE OF ERIK SATIE (1925)

I have admired, loved, and helped Erik Satie devotedly. And now
his loss goes to swell the list of bereavements which embitter my life.
The day after his death the 'Douanier' Rousseau entered the
Louvre, as if to celebrate their meeting in heaven.

At a time when everything is done in haste and by machinery,
what strikes me most is the solid elegance of the work of these two
artists – *entirely made by hand.*

Another feature is common to them both : neither the composer
nor the painter ever exploited himself, or spoilt his natural beauty
by that fatal preoccupation with Beauty by which so many great
things are disfigured.

A love for reflections in water is a French failing; it is this that
makes the French neglect authentic form. Now my old master,
fearing to benefit from that accidental charm which appertains to
narcissism, made grimaces at himself. An excellent system, which
serves to protect him from inattentive admirers.

I can imagine no truer or nobler nature than his. When Satie
sulked with me, or played me some of his tricks which sooner or
later caused his friends to quarrel with him, I examined myself
and would discover growing within me a weed which was the real
cause of his seeming caprice. As soon as I had pulled up the weed,
Satie came back again.

He taught me the perspective of time, and the absurdity of
attaching the slightest importance to either praise or insults. Inten-
tionally to seek to give pleasure, or the reverse, seemed to him an

incomprehensive attitude. Without hesitation he would take up an untenable position.

His patience was angelic. And so from 1917 to 1924 we were treated to the spectacle of what horticulturists call 'tardy flowering'. Satie, who was supposed to have dried up, blossomed out with flowers and fruit; his candid branches scented and nourished a younger generation wearied with too much artificiality.

Raymond Radiguet, from fifteen to twenty, and Erik Satie, from fifty-four to fifty-nine, were of the same age, and followed the same road. Indeed, the works of Radiguet, together with Hans Andersen's *Tales*, were, in the end, the only books which the solitary old man of Arcueil would read.

Would that I might soon rejoin my old collaborators there where they are waiting for me.

# Professional Secrets

Written in 1921 in the company of Raymond Radiguet who was working on *Le Diable au Corps*, the short but important essay *Professional Secrets* (Le Secret Professionnel), was first published in 1922. In it Cocteau makes his personal statement – which he often repeated – as to how a poet should behave and work. For the first time he defines the 'Angel', who had previously appeared in his poems, notably in *Le Cap de Bonne-Espérance*, his first collection published in 1919. He defines the role of the poet and describes how, by means of all the arts, including the art of the cinema, men endeavour to 'capture' poetry for their own use.

This piece was republished in *Le Rappel à l'Ordre* and is now available in the first volume of *Poésie Critique*.

The translation here is taken from *A Call to Order*.

□□□□□

### TO THE STUDENTS OF BELLES-LETTRES IN GENEVA AND LAUSANNE IN GRATEFUL REMEMBRANCE

'It is therefore not right to impose the same limitations on all kinds of natures, or to esteem without reflection bad that which is merely extraordinary. To do so were to act like that poor native of Norway on seeing roses for the first time; for it is said that he durst not approach them for fear of burning his fingers, marvelling that fire in this wise did grow on trees.'

GUEZ DE BALZAC (1594-1654)

It would be a great mistake to consider the tone of the judgments passed by the author, both on himself and on works which are universally held to be masterpieces, as being a sign of his own conceit. And yet, if the author pleads his case before he is accused, he must clearly be somewhat apprehensive of appearances. The

truth is that, by taking up a high standpoint so as to gain a better view of the subject as a whole, it may appear as though one were merely seeking to draw attention to oneself.

On the other hand, the reflections of one who holds himself aloof are always tinged with an aristocratic flavour, which annoys other people exceedingly. Nothing is more disconcerting than aristocracy in any form. A book like *La Princesse de Clèves*, from a social point of view, is a masterpiece of its kind. This fairy-tale – at once so divine, so human, and so inhuman – makes novels dealing with what Tolstoy calls 'the higher spheres' seem terribly vulgar. Compared with Mme de La Fayette's book, the 'monde' portrayed in the best novels seems no better than the 'demi-monde'.

Similarly, from an intellectual point of view, Nietzsche's *Ecce Homo* makes any other book look stupid in comparison.

At the same time, an intelligent reader will see in the naïvetés it contains the proof of an aristocracy bred of solitude. There is no one so simple as your Prince, whom everything astonishes.

Nietzsche writes in *Ecce Homo* : ' . . . France, which possesses psychologists like Mme Gyp, Guy de Maupassant, Jules Lemaître. . . .'

Jules Lemaître was most helpful to me. One day, when I quoted this sentence to him, and expressed surprise at this heterogeneous list of names : 'But, my dear child,' he said, 'Nietzsche is talking about what you find on the station bookstalls at Sils-Maria.' This happy remark illustrates the dangers of solitude.

I am not comparing myself to any of the princes of this earth, and only quote these big names as an example. But solitude is solitude, and the following notes were written in solitude; a circumstance which has influenced them both for good and bad. If they have gained in frankness, they are lacking in those qualities of prudence and politeness which we acquire by living in great cities, and without which our authority is no better than a boor's.

Moreover, it is my custom, as soon as my flock has come back to the fold, to scatter them again. In this way I shall gradually acquire a very sparse, but very reliable, following. I am therefore used to being alone, or almost alone, and to this agreeable state of literary solitude must be added the solitude of a country holiday, to which I referred just now.

Living alone, especially by the sea, restores something primitive and childlike to one's character.

I know a small boy who used to ask old ladies their age. Sometimes it was seventy, sometimes eighty. 'Oh,' said he with an icy stare, 'then you haven't much longer to live.'

An enormity of this kind, which leaves all the fragile conventions of civilization far behind, does not astonish one who is used to solitude. For he thinks to himself, no less ingenuously, 'My works will live.'

\*

The classics and the romantics. Racine versus Shakespeare. Here we have the simplest of wars : Greeks and Trojans face to face. Progress has involved us in wars more complicated than this. So let us imitate the diver, and plunge, haphazard, into the mêlée – taking with us no Ariadne's thread but a few antidotes against poison.

\*

Style can never be a starting-point; it is a result. What is style? Many people think it is a complicated way of saying something very simple. According to us, it is a very simple way of saying something complicated. A Stendhal, even a Balzac (the Balzac of *Le Père Goriot*, or *La Cousine Bette*) are chiefly concerned to hit the bull's-eye. Nine times out of ten they succeed, without minding how they do it. It is just this 'not minding how', a sort of quickly improvised method of their own which they adopt according to the results obtained – this way of shouldering the rifle, aiming, and shooting quick and true, which I call style.\*

A Flaubert only thinks about shouldering his arm; the target doesn't interest him; he lavishes all his attention on the weapon. The lady of the shooting-gallery, who has her back turned to the targets, is watching him. What a handsome fellow he is! What a sportsman! What style! Little she cares whether the marksman hits the 'bull', provided he takes a long aim, has a graceful style, and most important of all, takes plenty of time over the job.

The target? The target is ten yards away – an infinite distance for short-sighted people and those who refuse to look further than the end of their own noses – in other words, the élite.† So many of the so-called 'realistic' scenes of Flaubert have very little to do with reality. *Madame Bovary*, for example, every page of which reveals the writer's concern to 'shoulder' effectively, is a mass of unreality – a series of Salon pictures. The painter turns to his colleague with

* To go into finer distinctions would mean writing another book. This one is made up of extremes – black and white. We are now leaving out of consideration the 'perfect mean', Class I, comprising the marksmen who both shoulder their rifles correctly *and* shoot straight.

† 'Rapid firing' should not be taken to mean brevity, or only to apply to short works. Marcel Proust hits the bull's-eye a thousand times while you think he's only aiming.

a wink, and says : 'You'll see, I've got a surprise for you.' The picture 'with a story' represents a country wedding, a ride on horse-back, an operation for club-foot in the village, adultery in a cab, a blind beggar, and the priest and the free-thinker drinking together at the bedside of a dead woman dressed in her wedding garments.

It would be fatiguing to quote examples of all the shots gone astray through a desire to hold the weapon gracefully. A typical one would be the hollow scene at the Bovarys' house, to the accom-paniment of Hippolyte's cries, serving as a pretext for an atrocious genre picture, or the scene where Bovary meets his wife in the Rue Renelle des Maroquiniers.

Only once in the book do we seem to catch sight of something like the target at which our favourite novelists would aim, and that is when Léon lets himself be carried away by Homais – a moment of sheer maudlin weakness, and a prodigious 'Yes' on the part of Homais.

What charges had to be trumped up in order to get the book condemned ! Ernest Pinard would have caused general surprise if, amongst others, he had attacked the passage about the club-foot, which is much more immoral than the rest, just as at the fair the anatomical museum shocks us far more than the naked ladies painted on the switchbacks.

There is much difference of opinion as to what constitutes a 'sense of reality'. Almost always those who do not possess this sense take up arms on its behalf against those who do. Photography is unreal; it alters values and perspective. Its cowlike eye stupidly registers everything that our eye first has to correct, and then dis-tribute according to the needs of the case. Among our painters, Degas is one of photography's victims, just as the Futurists were victims of the cinematograph. I have seen photographs of his, which he enlarged himself, and then worked on directly in pastel, full of admiration at the grouping, foreshortening, and deformation of the foregrounds.

Similarly, in view of the meticulous care with which Flaubert will analyse a motive, it is all the more surprising to see how casually he conducts his narrative, skipping whole periods, and laboriously fluttering from detail to detail.

The real marksmen (those who shoot at a target) do not incur the same reproach. Wasting no time over superfluities, they can really flutter; then, suddenly swooping down on the flower, they extract its honey at one stroke.*

---

* When Balzac seems to be wasting time over superfluities, it is because he was paid by the line, and he has our sympathy.

To make your style your starting-point is a sign of great weakness.

This weakness is characteristic of epochs, during which it is of no avail to throw oneself into the water, relying on one's instinct of self-preservation to teach one how to swim.*

After the storm, and the necessary return to tranquillity and good order, we get the phenomenon of art being monopolized by marksmen who go in for 'stunts'. They exhibit every sign of the worst disorder. They manage to shoot straight, but they are chiefly concerned with the way they hold their weapons. We then get what may be described (since we are now exploring a maze) as a sort of classical romanticism, with its pretence of conciseness, speed, and an anxiety to hit the mark. Hence (to push our metaphor to its conclusion) these writers resemble those marksmen who take their aim in a mirror, or from between their legs, head downwards, as Robert, the acrobatic rifleman, used to do, until one day a general with a sense of humour suggested to our friend Garros that he should have him as his partner. Garros was amused at the idea, and decided to test him; but Robert missed everything. He pretended that not having his false beard put him off. He was allowed his beard, but still missed every time. Finally he confessed to having employed an accomplice, being a very bad shot himself, but hadn't dared to say so before, as his papers were not in order.

A mannerism, no matter how distinguished, can never constitute style. To cultivate one's thought – to learn to shape and handle it – is to cultivate one's style. Looked at from any other point of view, style merely makes for obscurity and acts as a drag.

Your true writer is all bone and muscle. The others are either fat or lean. Those who go in for 'stunts' (and are always in the fashion) exhibit a dreadful mixture of fat *and* lean.

*

Youth, in its simplicity, believes that certain injustices will never be repeated. For example : a Rimbaud, or a Cézanne, would never again find themselves without a public and an international body-guard.† If they or what they stood for were to come to life again, no doubt this would be true. The injustice will be made up to their children and grandchildren. But the new Rimbaud, or the new

---

* Stylization in the plastic arts. Sculpture : last period of Egyptian art; a great deal of Negro statuary; under the Empire, Canova, at the present day, Bourdelle.

† Rimbaud and Mallarmé have become a sort of Adam and Eve. The apple is Cézanne's. We shall always bear the burden of Original Sin.

Cézanne (or whoever *contradicts*), will be treated in the same way, and will experience the same solitude. Nothing changes. His very audacity, too different from theirs, will cause the 'advanced' circles to smile and shrug their shoulders. (You will remember the story of the 'serious customer' who first of all drank half his coffee, then added brandy, then water, and finished up with sugar and water alone. That is the point we have now reached as regards the 'poètes maudits'.)

The 'academic' or conventional artists are not where they are commonly supposed to be; that is to say, it is no use looking for them on any planet but our own. How could a Bonnat, a Saint-Saëns – so very talented both of them – possibly be 'academic'? Those whom *we* ought to consider so are Rimbaud, Mallarmé, Cézanne, and before very long, ourselves.

People often wonder why Rimbaud abandoned literature. There can be no doubt on this point. Alone as he was, avoided even by those anxious to make up for past injustices but who were unjust in their turn to others, sick of cafés, and judging that this fine world of ours was not worth committing suicide for (and that, in any case, suicide is slightly ridiculous), he chose the only possible solution.

Writing, especially writing poetry, is like perspiring. The poem, or book, is a kind of sweat. It would be unhealthy to walk, or run, or play games, or practise athletics without sweating. The only things that interest me are the man himself, and the kind of exercise he takes. That is why most works by living artists leave me cold. What I look for in the work of a dead artist – in the fragrance, as it were, of his sweat – is a proof of activity. The Louvre is like the Morgue; one goes there to identify one's friends. We like to show off, and sell our own sweat. Both the masses and the fastidious like nothing better than to intoxicate themselves with sweat; but they take no interest in the exercise, or sport, itself.

Rimbaud, when he was at Harrar, is an example of a poetical athlete who does not sweat. But then he had ceased to run about. If one is going to run about (granted that one agrees to put up with the inconvenience), then one ought to sweat as little as possible, and so to speak, sweat dry.

(PS. When I speak of 'exercise' or 'sport' I do not mean that way of living which Wilde used to say was his masterpiece. I refer to the life of the intellect.)

\*

My friend Francis Picabia, who has the most supple mind of anyone I know, finds it more amusing to shoot at the proprietress of the shooting-gallery than at the egg. But does he do so? No, for fear of the gendarmes.

When we argue together I feel at a disadvantage. Neither of us plays to the gallery; we enjoy the game, but whereas I force myself to play within certain limits, and according to the rules, he, on the other hand, jumps about, plays anyhow and anywhere, and makes a virtue of cheating, although he knows the rules of the game better than anyone. Tired of being beaten, I copy him, and finally we find ourselves playing back to back, each for himself, in complete agreement.

Ah! Narcissus! How strange a pair art thou!

Words have no sense. All right. Granted. Then have they any when you explain to me at length why I do wrong to use them? Accept the game, master it, arrange it as you please, but let there be a chance of give and take, so that you may find a partner worthy of you.

Clearly, you won't find many people to play with you. But can anything be more exclusive than certain clubs? In any case, you will chiefly play either with the dead, or with very young people.

(PS. One day Picabia said to me : 'You are resigned. You have the same desires as I have, but you take into account the question of feasibility. You are quite right. It is better to go in a two-seater than on foot, and have a racer in one's head. I, who am both a nigger and a Spaniard, carry a limousine in my head.'

I replied : 'I have also a limousine in my head, but I sit in my two-seater.'

Picabia also said : 'We each have an equally sensitive pair of scales, with a special contrivance to give everything the same weight. I put on this contrivance in public, and take it off at home; you put it on at home, and take it off in public.')

*

The 'modern style', 'modern poet' and 'modern spirit' have all been invented. There is no more sense in saying 'I am modern' than there is in the expression 'We medieval knights'. (Allusion to a well-known farce.) The confusion arises because man, like the primitive nigger he is, is dazzled by 'progress' – in the form of aeroplanes, the telephone and the cinematograph. He can't get over them. He talks about them in the same way as M. Jourdain telling everybody that he expressed himself in prose.

This is what simple people, mistaking words for a state of mind, call 'modern poetry'. They give the first place to mere accessories.

The part played by the things of everyday life should neither be ignored, nor given undue prominence. The poet should make the same use of them as he does of anything else.

As for the man who will have modernism at any price, and startles the public by offering them an orgy of colour and sensations grafted on to the old material, instead of weaving a new tissue altogether – he will soon be left behind by progress.

Everything goes out of fashion sooner or later, you tell me. That is another question. A masterpiece is not hailed as such, but it transforms everything. It is profoundly in the fashion. Everybody follows it without knowing it. It is bound to go out of fashion: another masterpiece drives it out. Finally, it begins by being picturesque, and then, having ceased to be just an old-fashioned gown, it takes its place in the costumes museum.

Certain poets of today, being ill-disposed towards our times, and disconcerted by their multiple variety, hark back to things that were young long ago, and copy them, adding just a dash of 'today' in order to justify themselves in our eyes. Hence they are not really dressed, but merely disguised in fancy dress, producing the effect of maniacs going about in Louis XIV costumes, and wearing stiff collars and bowler hats to make themselves look modern.

This kind of artist (some of whom have real merit), and the undiscerning multitude, believe that an epoch can make a mistake, or that they somehow belong to the wrong one; whereas had they lived during the period which they love so much now, on account of its remoteness, they would have hankered after some other still remoter one.

\*

The age in which we live might fitly be called the age of *quid pro quos*. One of the reasons for this is the abundance of books and of facilities for publishing them. It is true there have never been any undiscovered masterpieces, and those which are exhumed from time to time are false ones. Whatever is destined to grow and flower, grows and flowers. But never has it been so easy for young writers to get published. They all talk, air their opinions, make the game more and more complicated, put more on to Arthur Rimbaud and Stéphane Mallarmé than they can carry, and generally reek with worn-out anarchical theories.

Rimbaud's night enhances the brilliancy of his stellar system; Mallarmé, through the medium of night and pure carbon, produces a diamond. Ever since, their discovery has simply been exploited by what is known as 'modern poetry'. All that remains is coal and darkness.*

             *

I had been tempted to write a few pages on children and lunatics, considered in relation to poets. But the subject is one that is now in vogue, and I do not feel sufficiently alone in it to please myself.

However, I will state my opinion in a few words, as follows :

To cut the Gordian knot is not the same as to untie it. Children and lunatics cut what the poet patiently spends his life in trying to untie. The cord will be used again by others, who must make another knot, and so on to the end of time. But in the hands of lunatics, or even the most wonderful children, nothing remains but loose ends.

             *

The influence of Mallarmé is considerable, and may be taken as the type of those occult influences which, in France, are more far-reaching than that of a Hugo. And yet! In 1921, in collaboration with R. Radiguet and Francis Poulenc, I wrote, for a joke, a critical farce in one act, in which we placed the *Ecclésiastique,* out of *Divagations,* in the mouth of a policeman, supposed to be drawing up a summons.

The piece was performed, but no one, neither the public nor the critics, recognized this famous text, or even detected any allusion to the style of its author. M. Banès, in *Le Figaro,* talked about the 'palinodies de ce pandore stupide'. I will refrain from quoting the others; I do not wish to be unkind.

             *

The present reign of the *quid pro quo* is also largely due to the fact that we are apt to confuse two planets, two separate universes, two distinct breeds of writers, who are constrained to journey together, but at different speeds and different altitudes.† The apparent connection between them is due to a strange error of perspective, against which we have no remedy.

Arthur Rimbaud is taken to see Victor Hugo. They belong, none

* If we look into ourselves, we see that one half of us is in shadow, as the planets are. The element of night is already so active in the human body that we need not seek to darken our light half as well.

† I say 'two' for the sake of simplicity.

the less, to different epochs. This kind of epoch is nameless; it must be felt.

We can respect and pay homage to glorious reputations, and weigh their merits, but what counts in our eyes is another kind of glory, undiluted and intact, which penetrates certain souls, and never troubles others.

You know the names of the men who possess this glory, but have you ever seen their statues? I can count seven of Musset, not one of Baudelaire, who, in spite of his countless editions, will never 'mix'.

Erik Satie, an old native of Honfleur, told me the following story:

'One day, in 1869, Alphonse Allais's father thought it would be a creditable thing for Honfleur to put up a small bust of Baudelaire in the house of General Aupick. After waiting two months, the Municipal Council considered this proposal. "Baudelaire? Mme Aupick's son? Wait a minute ... Mme Aupick.... Ah, yes.... M. Bahon's neighbour? Ah, yes. Such a good fellow, M. Bahon ... etc. etc." "Well, gentlemen," said M. Allais, "to come back to our bust...." "That's all very well," cried the Chairman, "but after all, we can't put up busts of all Mme Aupick's sons!"'

\*

The 'accursed' attitude (in literature) has made the 'accursed' one a privileged and favoured person – now that this title is so much sought after. It is, however, awarded to few. The young generation does not realize that the public has no discrimination, and that it is not only in its eyes, but in those of the 'advanced', that one ought to be held accursed.

Young man, you crave for this sombre fame. You have my approval, but take care!\* If the younger schools receive you, and make much of you, you will never attain it. You cannot live on the same level with what is vital in your epoch. Not that the true poet is ahead of his epoch, or above it. He *is* it. It is the epoch which lags behind and is beneath him.

\*

The taste for 'tics' of style, which are mistaken for real style and expression, is so prevalent in literary circles that only writers with whom this 'tic' has become a grimace are looked upon with favour. But a grimace, if kept up for a long time, soon produces wrinkles.

---

\* Beware of the poets who are too quick in winning the esteem of the young. Nothing evaporates so quickly as a too hasty success, even though it may be of a promising kind.

The only way to avoid these dangerous 'tics', and the only method of making oneself unpopular, and thereby preserving one's youth, is to let oneself be guided strictly by all the contradictions of one's individuality.

Your literary bigwig is like a fly-paper. He catches more and more flies. Soon he is so covered with them that he can no longer be seen. What one ought to be is a whisk to drive flies away.

So much the worse for those who only recognize a poet from external signs. The shape of his thought, a limited number of problems, the angle of his vision (which is what style really is), these are the qualities which distinguish him from the others, and this is his way of saying : This is what I am. The rest – what commonly passes for style – must be made to follow unobtrusively the outline of this individual silhouette. Show a connoisseur ten quite dissimilar pieces of tapestry. He looks at the back and pronounces them all to have been woven in the same factory.

A good writer always strikes in the same place, but each time with a hammer of a different size and substance. The sound varies; he treats the nail with care. If he always used the same hammer, he would end by smashing the nail-head, driving nothing in, and merely making an empty noise. That is the noise our bigwigs make. But be careful! He who upsets expectations gives offence. The public was not prepared for what the true poet offers it. It is disappointed. It considers that he has not kept his promise.

What have I promised you? When will you learn that a good book is never what it is expected to be? It should never come up to your expectations; it should cause you to bristle with interrogation marks.

\*

To return to the question of the 'tic', which consists in saying no matter what in a certain way.

Take Barrès. You will find that his chief mannerism is the voluptuous phrase, predestined to celebrity, and the rare, but fitting, epithet. The death of Jules Tellier leaves him with an 'intolerable' souvenir. Toledo is one of the 'saddest and most ardent things in the world'; Granada 'the softest pillow in the world', and so on. A chain of roses threaded on a wire, and pressed one against the other. Barrès' style, monotonous and ineffective, since there is an effect in every line – this style so highly flavoured and yet so dead – the style of a melancholy 'gourmet' – reminds us of the corpses stuffed with honey, of the Greek embalmers.

On him glory acts as a drug.

On the other hand (as we are now on the subject of drugs), notice how Baudelaire's style in the *Paradis Artificiels* – a book which might easily have been so eccentric – gains in richness and relief from being made to adapt itself so closely to the subject. It aims at being as convincing as possible. Whereas certain passages of the *Fleurs du Mal* give an uncomfortable impression of being spoilt prose, and appear old-fashioned owing to the style, in which, *a priori*, the verses had to be written, the *Paradis Artificiels* are devoid of any of those trimmings which characterize fashions and make them look ridiculous to another age, the reason being that Baudelaire was not trying to clothe a body elaborately, but rather to emphasize its outline.

But this, you will object, is an apology for prose and an attack on all poetry. Not at all. Strip it of the epithets and images by which the world is accustomed to recognize it, and then poetry, more concise, and possessing more structure and line than prose (with its power, too, of turning the very restrictions of rhyme and rhythm into an unlimited source of surprises which are just as fresh and mysterious to the poet as they are to the reader) will at last cease to be prose in evening dress.

*

Ours is an age infected with literature. Not only that, but following on a recent attack of convulsions, and by dint of running down literature, an anti-literary literature has been engendered by this very attitude of romantic disgust.

A destructive spirit is romantic, and betrays a taste for ruins, and a pessimism which I condemn.

The antidote for intelligence is stupidity. But stupidity is not as common as you would think – still less madness. Here again we see the unhappy muse with her dishevelled hair. . . .

Now I endeavour to be as un-literary as possible – and that, to the littérateur, is an unforgivable sin. But a littérateur will flirt with Dadaism, which is literature *par excellence*. He is tickled, intrigued, excited, and a good deal troubled by it.

'What do you mean by literature?' asks some carping person.

'Mannerisms, style treated as a starting-point, and everything that constitutes "genre".'

'Then you are for the poetry of ideas?'

Not at all – and here we see how the secret, inner forms of poetry are unlike anything which can be explained. I remarked elsewhere* that what I ask of the musician is that he should see

* See *Cock and Harlequin.*—Translator's note

that his work *resembles* something – it should resemble the original movements which urged him to develop them thematically, even if it is only a simple case of musical mathematics.

The same thing is true of painting. When Picasso has finished a picture its beauty is due to the intensity of its resemblance, even if our eyes are unable to distinguish each separate object which called it into being. The reason is that Picasso, saturated in the methods and technique of the great masters of painting, and for ever turning up new ground, is conscious of the inferiority of arabesques and 'spots', which he leaves to mere decorators.

When he looks at a group of objects, he digests them, and gradually transports them into a world of his own, of which he is the ruler, he never embroiders, and never loses sight of their objective force. In this way he does away with slavish imitation, but maintains the resemblance between these objects – a resemblance conceived on another plane, but forming the same sum-total. Instead of deceiving the eye he deceives the mind. His picture is a picture; it has an independent existence; it tells you nothing about anything else.

A poem should be like this too. Its form will be determined by this same desire to express the truth (alas! so far from the reader's idea of truth!), and by this preoccupation with a reality which is yet unreal. This form of truth, however, which is apparent to certain superior intelligences, would be as difficult to explain to the others as the Trinity.

In the *Mariés de la Tour Eiffel* I claim to have at last succeeded in producing something of this kind. The author gives the public twenty years before they feel the poetry it contains. Until then the piece will rank simply as a rather feeble and more or less comic dialogue. His aim was too true, his weapon too perfect. The bullet goes clean through; in spite of his groans the adversary feels nothing.

\*

Strongly sensitive people have their weak moments in which they desire to spread contagion. They weary of being always the only sick ones on board; and it is not much consolation for them to know that after their death all the passengers will catch their complaint more or less, and that it will have a name and a notice in the dictionary. But this very solitude, and the certainty that his illness cannot be either diagnosed or cured, turns the patient into an aristocrat. He soon pulls himself together. He regrets nothing. He contemplates without envy those whose colds everyone catches.

He writes with sympathetic ink. And does not this ink become
visible one day, especially when exposed in the open air? And that,
in my opinion, is the most sympathetic kind of all.

\*

What is commonly called genius is rarely accompanied by intelligence. But there is no harm in intelligence, as far as I can see.
Stendhal and Nietzsche are types of intelligent geniuses. True,
Zarathustra is often no better than an old guide turned phrase-
maker through leading a lonely life in the Alps. None the less,
there is nothing that his diamond does not cut. Nietzsche
denounced, saw, and foretold everything. He sensed the approach
of a Dionysian pessimism; and that describes our present state.
Who is aware of it?
The optimist is blind, and the pessimist bitter. But Dionysian
pessimism is neither blind nor bitter. There you see yourself, O
modern young man, not as you are, but as you should be – or,
rather, as you are, but as you try not to be. We are not blind, and
are therefore fully alive to the folly of writing; but neither are we
bitter, and therefore do not remain silent.

\*

I have often amused myself by signing letters and articles 'Le
Parisien', perhaps as a result of the teasing I received from friends.
It was Francis Picabia, the 'European' (and a very poor European,
since he can only live in Paris), who maliciously dubbed me with
this nickname.
I have a habit (no doubt a detestable one) of using certain
expressions in a special sense, which I attribute to them without any
explanation. In this way I called *Parade* a 'realistic ballet', by
which I meant 'more real than reality', relying, in order to make
myself understood, on the gulf which, in the eyes of the spectator,
separates this ballet from another, and on the word 'realist', combined with the unreal appearance of the spectacle.
Shortly afterwards Apollinaire described his *Mamelles de Tirésias*
as a 'super-realist' drama. He was quite right to emphasize it in
this way, but he was cultivating the 'bizarre' – a jewel that he alone
can wear with extraordinary grace, but which is so unbecoming to
others.
And so, when I call myself Parisian instead of super-Parisian, I
am not thinking of the Boulevards, or the Green Room, or of
hawkers or their wares. I merely localize myself. And I think it is

my luck to be a Parisian, just as your genuine Negro thinks it's his to be a Negro, your genuine Jew to be a Jew, and your genuine German to be a German. I may add that two genuine Germans (in spite of all they said) – Nietzsche and Heine – ranked Paris above all other capitals. That is enough to make my head turn for five minutes. . . .

There is no such thing as either literature or poetry for the masses. Picabia, who is a mocker, has Spanish blood. Only a Spaniard takes pleasure in blasphemy, and is always talking about the Virgin.

The more a poet sings in his genealogical tree, the truer his accent will be. The more he concentrates the more useful he is.

Stéphane Mallarmé has an influence now on the style of the daily papers without their suspecting it.

It is simple enough; all you have to do is to give up when you die a flask of attar of roses. Its odour is overpowering; it contains enough to form a stock of scent for a long time. If people hold their noses when you pass and avoid your neighbourhood, you may now and again pour out a drop yourself in a little water. What a surprise! This is your worst scent, and people find it sweet, and are surprised that it could have emanated from you. If you publish a very simple essay dealing with a subject with which the public are familiar, they are almost sure to praise it and to confess that, judging by your poetry, they would never have thought you capable of having written it.

*

A friend said to me once : 'I am going to take you to see the Puy de Dôme. You always go to the sea, and hypnotize yourself with the sea, which is bad for your nerves. Try mountains for a change.'

Now I dislike the Puy de Dôme. 'There is no doubt about it,' said my friends, 'you certainly don't care for mountains.'

Don't let there be any misunderstanding. Open your eyes. Look at those soft, undecided curves, those badly distributed masses, that switchback conformation. Are those mountains? No. The Cantal is perhaps a mountainous region; the Puy de Dôme is merely hump-backed.

Be careful. By confusing breasts and humps you dull your intelligence and make it not only lose its faculty of seeing clearly (except in the case of certain details) but even calmly acquiesce in the most flagrant errors.

Certainly I prefer the sea to mountains. Real mountains impose on me forms which are ready-made. They advise and restrict me. They put my spirit into a mould, from which it has the greatest difficulty in escaping. The sea puts no pressure on me of any kind. It does not shut me up. Its mass has no opinions. It is a dictionary, not a selection, or a monument.

Mountains, I do homage to your majesty, as I do to works which I respect, but do not choose to live with.

But do not ask me to bow down before pretence mountains. Real or pretence, it is all one to the public, who love the Sublime. Quantity is what astonishes them. Alas! they are easily pleased. Poor tourists! Puy de Dôme or the Sierras! The guide-book mentions mountains, and, guide-book in hand, they admire. There are also people who, with camels in their mind's eye, declare that the desert is hilly.

It is not our object here to complain, or to point out how the masses (true Wagnerites, though they know nothing of, or even repudiate Wagner) love whatever is quick to tickle their sensibilities. And Wagner is a magician whose poisons are unique. The deformities of such a cripple as this naturally arouse our suspicions. Even an angel's shadow is the same as a hunchback's.

But what can be said of a Rodin, for example, whose work is not like a house, solidly built from top to bottom, a definite habitation for the spirit, but only like part of a staircase, a balcony, or a fragment of a door.

Here we have the well-known type, consecrated by official guide-books, of the hump mistaken for a mountain. Michelangelo, Delacroix, Goethe, Hugo, Shakespeare and Balzac are mountainous countries.

In every age the humps always conceal everything else. Behind the humps nobody can see anything at all. Nothing astonishes or annoys people more than to see that we take no notice of the humps, but salute the mountains from afar, and embark on a voyage of discovery across the sea.

*

There are certain names that a self-respecting pen cannot bring itself to write. Alas! These names are either the only ones which mean anything to the critics or the general public, or else those which are indiscriminately praised in the 'advanced' reviews.

As a proof how far this blindness exists, not only in official circles but in others as well, I may mention that when I was writing my Monday articles in *Paris-Midi* (Carte Blanche), a poet ( a real one) reproached me for only dealing with famous artists. Now, apart from the fact that I was writing these articles for the information of a public as remote as possible from our set, and which I could not possibly have initiated into all the mysteries of all the coteries, I only mentioned those names which came most naturally into my mind, and hardly one of those which one is accustomed to see in the advanced reviews.

He failed to realize how little known to the public are artists like Derain, Braque, Picasso, Apollinaire, Max Jacob, Erik Satie, and our own group of writers and composers. *He thought I was too prudent.**

Would you believe that, in 1920, a well-informed dilettante said to me (he was trying to recall the name of a painter, with all the grimaces a man makes when he has a name at the tip of his tongue) : 'You know whom I mean, that Spanish fellow who belongs to the Russian Ballet.' He was referring to Picasso.

In 1919 a pretty American asked me to take her to Picasso's studio. She was taking lessons of all sorts – boxing, dancing, gymnastic, singing, book-binding and history. She even went to a professor of Mallarmé. Had she chosen me as a professor of cubism? I refused, knowing how much Picasso dreads such visitors and the kind of reception he gives them – outwardly amiable enough, but fraught with hatred. Knowing that explanations are useless, he acquiesces without hesitation in all the insults which our elegant young women never fail to proffer to artists.

One fine day my pretty American told me triumphantly that she had been taken to see Picasso by the painter Zuloaga. 'Well?' 'Well, Zuloaga is one of his oldest chums, and old friends don't stand on ceremony with each other – he confessed everything.' 'What did he confess?' 'Why, that his cubism is only a farce. I asked him if it wasn't, and he said he didn't want to amuse himself any longer at the expense of a person as beautiful and intelligent as myself.'

The discovery of this inability of ours to introduce certain names into our works is a great source of strength to our enemies.

---

* One ought to be able to deal boldly with a great artist, and blame him too, because one ought never to bother about the others, like a sultan, who, being always surrounded by fifty women chosen for their beauty, ends by discovering their ugly features. A critic was shocked because I made certain reservations with regard to the latest work of Matisse, on account of its high intrinsic value. No doubt it would be very misguided of a critic, in discussing Matisse together with second-rate painters, to make reservations with regard to the works of Matisse, but a poet-critic is not in the same position. His handbook only deals with first-class purveyors, and consequently he has no scruples whatever in expressing a detailed opinion on the goods. I like the obstinacy of Ingres, who refuesd to paint Shakespeare among the other dramatists in his apotheosis of Homer.

They know we cannot answer them. Among the names which count today, can we tell which will fall out of the running? As a proof of this, take an article by Baudelaire or Stendhal. But could any collection be more amusing than the one which, a century hence, will furnish a proof of our own clairvoyance? This is my way of buying canvases which 'will be worth a lot of money one day'. A hundred years after my death I shall retire, having made my fortune.

\*

Again, by virtue of that luxury of ours which consists in employing without commentary certain terms that clearly do not mean the same thing to the reader as to ourselves, poets often speak of angels. According to them, and to us, an angel is midway between the human and the inhuman. An angel is a brilliant young animal, full of vigour and charm, plunging from the seen to the unseen with the powerful gestures of a diver, and the thunder of a myriad wild pigeons' wings. The radiant swiftness of its movements hides it from our view. Were it to slow down, doubtless we should perceive it. Now is the time for Jacob, that fine wrestler, to throw himself upon it. Death has no meaning for this magnificent specimen of a sporting monster. It strangles mortals, and impassively tears out their souls. I imagine it to be something between a boxer and a sailing ship. . . .

All this is very far removed from a sort of hermaphrodite in sugar, with folded hands, wings of gold and lilies, and a crown of stars. Behold an angel of fury, 'swooping from the skies like an eagle', Delacroix's angel, or those angels which brought upon El Greco the condemnation of the Church, because he had failed to fit them with the regulation wings.

We all of us regret the loss of those pages which are missing from the Scriptures, and which dealt with the Fall of the Angels, the birth of the Giants, their offspring, and the crimes of Lucifer – a complete Christian mythology.

With regard to these matters, Mme Bessonet-Fabre, who is both profound, and, I may say, a most sensible Hebrew scholar, gives me enthralling information. Angel and angle, she tells me, are synonymous in Hebrew. The Bible, which only reveals to the profane its surface, consisting of coarse imagery, and anecdotes sometimes naïve, sometimes altogether obscure, is in reality made up of several layers of meanings which have to be decoded before they can be understood. It was in this way that the Jews were able to hide their secrets from the eyes of the curious when they were obliged to deliver the Bible into sacrilegious hands. Once this code is deciphered you may see revealed the complete economic and erotic systems, and all the science and chemistry of Israel.

The fall of the angels may also be interpreted as : the fall of the angles. The sphere is made up of an accumulation of angles. Angles and points liberate force. This is the explanation of the architecture of the Pyramids. The fall of the angles therefore signifies : the ideal sphere, that is to say, disappearance of the divine force, apparition of the human, the conventional.

All these facts do not inspire a poet, but they stimulate him. And so, when you hear it said of an artist or of a woman that they are angelic, do not expect to see them looking like the pictures you had when you made your first Communion.

Disinterested, selfish, tender, pitying, cruel, shrinking from contacts, pure in the midst of debauchery, taking a violent delight in, and at the same time despising, earthly pleasures, naïvely a-moral – make no mistake, these are the signs of that state which we call angelic – signs by which you may recognize all true poets, be they writers, painters, sculptors or musicians. Few people will admit this, because few are sensitive to poetry.

Up to the present Arthur Rimbaud represents the type of the angel on earth. I am one of those who possess a certain photograph of him, which shows him full-face, in schoolboy's dress, and wearing a little necktie tied in a bow. The principal features have been obliterated by time. What remains is a face with a phosphorescent glow. If you look too long at this portrait, turning it about, holding it first at a distance, then near to, all at once it seems to turn into a kind of meteor, or Milky Way.

Once, when I was speaking of the 'angelicalness' of Verlaine, a certain eminent critic burst out laughing. 'It is obvious that you never knew him,' he said. He was thinking of the faun, the cab-driver, the drunkard, and nothing else. And yet, in addition to his life and works, another photograph, which I possess, reveals him as he was : Verlaine is standing up, wearing a furry top hat, a scarf thrown over one shoulder, with stars in his eyes – adorable.

Another poet, whom the angels guide, cherish, and torment, Erik Satie, who walks every night from Montmartre or Montparnasse to his home at Arcueil-Cachan (a miracle which cannot be explained unless the angels carry him) – Satie told me once of a truly angelic encounter of which he was a witness. It was at the Auberge du Clou. Mallarmé came in to buy snails; Verlaine was drinking at a table. They did not know each other but exchanged greetings. It is impossible to reproduce the timbre of Satie's voice, or the expression on his face when he tells this story.

I am not going to draw up here a list of the angelic ones. But they are the only ones that count for me, or touch me in any way; and while I recognize the worth of others, they alone, in my opinion, deserve the name of poet.

It is unnecessary to add that being in this state makes a man universally suspect. He escapes all classification or registration. It is as though he had run away, without his papers or military identification card. In fact, he hardly has a right to live. There are certain blessed evenings, at the beginning of spring, in his own town for example, when such a one will realize that he is nothing but a parasite, and even while he is enjoying the spectacle of the green world all round him, will be conscious that he carries no papers entitling him to do so.

This composite status, which it is so difficult for an onlooker – even for a father or a mother – to understand, and so trying to the sufferer himself, leads to both scandal and disaster. Scandal, on account of the conflict between such a state and a society which has no place for it; disaster, due, it would seem, to a mysterious recuperating influence which the Other World exercises upon these feeble beings. One will commit suicide, another mope and pine away, others you may see plunging into battle like cheery bathers in the sea. The Other World will see that they are either drowned or have their legs cut off. Murder, hospitals, love or opium – it will employ any means to finish them off, and so recover its lost children. If their names are mentioned at all in dictionaries, or in literary handbooks, it will only be in the most guarded terms.

\*

A poet cannot have one style only, or, rather, cannot always season every dish with the same sauce. Owing to a modern prejudice, a poet who, in a critical article, for example, ceases to be esoteric, and does not confuse the catalogue with the objects it describes, is looked upon with disfavour. And yet literary work, like fine architecture, ought to present here and there a resting-place for the eye, a flat surface, or a simple scheme of decoration alternating with passages which bear the stamp of the architect's individuality.

Mallarmé's *Divagations*, which are written on the same level as his poems, only serve, by their inferiority, to enhance the value of the latter. There is no relief, or contrast, to be got by turning from one to the other.

We, who can unravel this prose as easily as an Oxford undergraduate translates Greek, see in it nothing but frills and furbelows. We seem to be listening to a very beautiful *précieuse*.

Let us make a stupid division of literary work into three classes, the prospectus type, the distillery type, and those which are pure liqueur.

These three classes are necessarily dissimilar in appearance. As an example of the first, let us take a manifesto, or a preface; of the second, a critical work; of the third, poetry and fiction.

Today, at a time when what is most urgently needed is simplicity – and colours turn so quickly that they all become white, thereby confusing eyes which have hitherto delighted in dazzle effects – today it is the form 'prospectus' which suits everyone's taste the best.

The reader adopts it because he interprets the words : simplicity, design, line, outline, and directness of expression, according to his own ideas, and applies them to all the ugly things he loves best. He touches at arm's length the herbs and stills, of which he is a little afraid, and spits out the liqueur in disgust. It is not a bit like what the prospectus had announced. He has been deceived, made fun of, cheated. There has been a misdeal. Moreover, he has been robbed of seven francs. . . .

\*

In each of my books I have the impression that it is only the continuation of an original drawing which my friends, who are looking over my shoulder, see my pen tracing, without understanding what it is meant to represent. You only have to begin a figure by drawing the feet first, and everybody's calculations will be upset. When it is finished, you put in an eye, and the mannikin suddenly appears. To do this, no doubt, will be the function of our last book.

It astonishes me to see how our modern authors, instead of fitting every detail into its place with a view to creating an ensemble, make do with a succession of detached figures of all sizes and scales, regardless of any considerations of balance.

Naturally every drawing of this kind, complete in its way, and easy to define, procures for lazy people the same sort of satisfaction as for a class doing dictation, the words : Full stop; The End. All they have to do is to choose one, and hang it on the wall. The straight lines, curves, and all the strokes and shadings in a drawing which seems, as it were, to arrive from every direction simultaneously, merely look to them like sketchy and incomplete forms, not without a certain charm, but not to be compared with a figure completely finished from head to foot.

This is due simply to an imperfectly educated sense of perspective.

Even a complete and solid piece of work, if looked at from directly underneath and from too near, appears badly constructed, as for example the Eiffel Tower, if we stand at its foot and look up at it with our nose in the air. Try to do this, and you will find that nothing remains of that graceful spire but a confused medley of club-feet, leaning towers of Pisa, and the debris of a railway accident.

As it is, perspective is a regular booby-trap for our eyes, but force of habit helps us to correct its worst deceptions. What can we say about the perspective of the mind? It is possible that we once possessed a corrective for this too, but, alas! it exists no longer.

I figure to myself the critic, comfortably seated in front of any of our theatrical productions, in which the complaint from which he suffers prevents him from seeing anything but disorder. Occasionally, if he is inclined to be good-humoured, he will detect, here and there, what seemed to him to be an amusing bit of colour, line, or expression.

This he loyally records. 'And now,' he adds, 'we await a serious *work*.' That is the consecrated expression. Doubtless after one or two poems from the *Fleurs du Mal*, Sainte-Beuve, finding they showed promise, was waiting for Baudelaire to produce some 'serious work'.

'We await a *work*. Give us *works*.' What a shock our loyal critic would get if his atrophied eye were to open, and, transforming the picture, restoring colours and perspective to their proper places, were suddenly to reveal to him the realization of the 'promise' which he imagined so absurdly he had been able to detect.

Critics are always waiting for poets to produce a 'work' until the day of their death. Let them wait. Apart from the fact that the word 'work', which we are obliged to use, has now become exceedingly distasteful, I can imagine nothing more deplorable than a poet who fulfils his promises.

The life of a poet who fulfils his promises is a perpetual autumn. But every year of a poet's life should have its autumn, and every year his unripe fruit ought to make those who thought that all they had to do now was to enjoy his ripe fruit, pull faces and be seriously upset. What the public likes best is fruit that is overripe. The first sign of this is a little red spot : the rosette of the Légion d'Honneur.

I do not mean to say that the Légion d'Honneur is incompatible with real talent. That would merely be a repetition of the silly old pretence that if a work is hissed it must necessarily be good, whereas the fact is that hisses prove nothing at all, nor does applause, the deliberate solicitation of either being equally ridiculous.

Last year, in his speech at the ceremony to celebrate the removal of Gambetta's heart to the Panthéon, M. Millerand did a bold thing. Having occasion to mention the artists who are an honour to France, he ignored those who have received official recognition, and cited Renoir, Cézanne, Claude Debussy. The scandal can be imagined.

The next day, when I was expressing to M. Arthur Meyer my surprise and pleasure at this – 'Good heavens!' he replied, 'how innocent you are! Millerand is in the pay of the dealers.'

And he believed it. He was sorry for me. He preferred to accuse the President of the Republic of corruption, rather than find him guilty of a palpable absurdity.

*

An inferior taste is attracted by the reverse side of a piece of rich material.

There are certain Chinese stuffs the reverse side of which is worked entirely in gold in order to show the embroidery on the right side on a background of dull silk, of an inky blackness. Almost invariably women wear them wrong side out.

The romantic stands in a similar relation to true poetry.

Its pseudo-luxury often exhibits quite real riches, but, while it may deceive the vulgar, a practised eye is shocked by its inappropriateness.

Poetry must have an air of poverty in the eyes of those who have no experience of real luxury. A poem is the height of luxury – that is to say, of a form of reserve which is the very opposite to avarice. An expert can judge the value of a book at first glance – I was almost going to say, from its mere smell and weight.

A true poet does not bother to be poetical. Nor does a nursery gardener scent his roses. What he does is to subject them to treatment which ensures their having the finest colour and the sweetest scent. Paul Valéry takes a pride in being a versifier and in exercising himself in this art. It is lucky for us he is a poet. But this mystery does not concern him.

If, however, you may observe, all a poet has to do is to play a sort of game of chess with himself, it will still be necessary to have rules. Valéry writes in verse. What can you claim on behalf of this game of yours, which we don't understand at all? To begin with, the more I realize the prestige of the commonplace, the more inclined I am to think that the mind is the more readily stimulated when the means at its disposal are most limited, and so I am increasingly attracted by verse, which is like an old uniform, always the same, but which each one of us wears in a different way.

Friends often imagine our poems to be just notes, jotted down haphazard, which we have been prevented by laziness from carrying any further. Now, in spite of all their invisible architecture, the effort of concentration, and the sacrifices that the writing of these poems entailed, I admit that it is impossible for even the most enlightened reader to be penetrated by the same rhythm as the writer, or be conscious of all his smallest reactions.

Since, therefore, everyone works for himself and creates his own rules, I am unable to believe in the advent of any one new rule, and can only see in this state of general disorder, which is made up of individual order, the signs of an intellectual quickening, and emancipation. After impressionism, *vers libre*; it is impossible for the mind to dispense altogether with so valuable an asset. And so everyone prunes and models and disciplines it in his own way. It is thus that our age, anarchist in appearance, is escaping from anarchy, and returning, in a new spirit, to the path of the law.

\*

In our opinion the poet should not derive his art from art. He should have recourse to genuine realism, that is to say, he should accumulate within himself a stock of visions and sensations (including his pre-natal equipment), and, instead of immediately turning them to account, as a brilliant journalist would do, in the hope of appealing to the emotions by means of a sort of sentimental blackmail, he should leave them undisturbed. In this way, without his knowing anything about it, there will gradually be formed within him an accumulation, a regular storehouse of unfamiliar associations of ideas and objects. For too long, poetry has been spoilt by the use of imagery for its own sake. A book of poetry was a book of images, a string of comparisons, enabling everyone to satisfy that apelike love of imitation, which is even now, alas! so alive in men.

A poet who relies on imagery may amuse us in the same way that a commercial traveller amuses the *table d'hôte* by making a rabbit out of some matches and an almond, but he will never touch our feelings. *He is out to write poetry.* He scents his roses. If the roses are false, he deceives the ignorant; if they are genuine, he

spoils them. It might be said of almost all our official great poets
that they spoil their roses.*

\*

It is not pathetic passages that make us shed our best tears, but
the miracle of a word in the right place. Few people are worthy to
shed such tears. And it is very likely that few are sensitive to poetry.
Have I not already said that poetry is the height of luxury?† A
poem should be made to cast off, one by one, all the ropes attaching it to whatever was the source, or motive, of its creation. Each
time the poet cuts a rope his heart beats. When he has cut the last
one, the poem detaches itself, and rises, unaided, like a balloon,
carrying its own beauty with it, having severed all connection with
the earth.

Is it necessary to point out in addition that strange words,
epithets, emphasis, and a cult of the picturesque prevent it from
rising?

Here you have in a few lines a picture of our poetical mentality
as it is today. That is to say, as it will be in twenty years.

\*

Having renounced rhyme and turned our backs on the pleasing
disorder of *vers libre*, we had naturally to adopt something else in
their place. That 'something' was not unlike those forms of cerebral
'tic' from which children nearly always suffer, and which have to
do with preserving a certain mysterious equilibrium, and encumber-
ing one's life privately with rites, such as making one's age, or the
day of the month, or the numbers on the houses in the street a basis
for calculations, relieving one's feelings by acts of cruelty, or by
repeated touchings of table utensils or doorknobs, counting the
number of steps from one tree or one lamp-post to another, raising
the left shoulder when passing anyone on the right, and vice versa,
praying for what one does not desire in order to deceive one's
destiny, or even for what one does desire, in order to confuse it
still more, letting oneself be tyrannized by the relations between
names and faces, seeing the days in colour, and a thousand other

---

\* On the other hand, there are some born writers who aspire to write
academic works and obtain official recognition. They fail to do so. To this
failure they owe their salvation and their rare charm.

† A good thing cannot succeed because it is good, but it always contains
enough bad to enable it to appeal to certain natures, and thus gradually to
acquire a footing.

deep-rooted grimaces which come to the surface as soon as we lose control of our nerves, and which, if we allow any one of them to gain too firm a hold on us, lead to madness.

Putting the verb in its right place, arranging for masculine and feminine terminations, establishing the rhythmic beat, submitting to a discipline of incredible severity (which the reader mistakes for laziness) – all these processes take place slowly and painfully, straining the nervous system to breaking-point. It is absolutely essential that one's thoughts should beat as one's heart beats, with its systole, diastole, and syncopes which prove that it is not a machine.

Even while the poet is in the act of creation, his poem runs a thousand mortal risks.

A bather in danger of drowning, and not knowing how to swim, invents the art of swimming. A poet, in order to save his poem, reinvents all the old familiar devices. He remembers how to work them, and begins again. He is possessed by a thousand devils whom he must obey. These mysterious laws stand in the same relation to the old laws of versification as do ten games of chess played simultaneously to a game of dominoes. But our player involves himself in increasingly subtle combinations where no one can follow him, and amongst which he is himself in danger of getting lost one day. He develops various systems; either he gets intrigued, finds an artificial stimulant in the rewriting of a text, and endeavours to re-create or destroy its inner proportions, or else he refines curiously on the game of acrostics.

Some think he is playing the fool, others that he is ill, but there are some who feel the tragic beauty of the game and take pleasure in it without wanting to know why.

Here we have a case of what Jean Epstein calls 'grammatical suicide'.

\*

Let us go back to rhyme again, that old and well-known stimulant. After tasting other more elaborate drugs, we take to it again with pleasure. In my own case I have often made use of it even where it was least suited to my purpose, and especially in a certain passage of the *Cap de Bonne-Espérance*. A great number of rhymes are here distributed at intervals which enable the ear to perceive them as it might perceive the distant murmur of machinery.

May I recall a phrase of H. Poincaré's which I quoted in *Le Potomak* without saying from where I had taken it : 'Poets have the advantage of us. A chance rhyme, and a whole system, hitherto obscure, stands revealed.'

This saying is too masterly to need any comment. For if we search the earth for one pebble which must be like another and yet different, the chances are that we discover a treasure.

I was forgetting the 'cheville'.*

This, of course, attracts the attention of the experienced poetical amateur. But, if it be true that poetry often changes her clothes and underclothes, she changes her 'ankles' ('chevilles') as well. We detect the old ones immediately, but the new ones are not so obvious. In the last resort they are all alike. Rimbaud did not attempt to 'camouflage' them; on the contrary, he gives them great prominence, and obtains from their use incredibly rich effects. But even when treated thus, they still exist, and will be recognized for what they are. There can be no poetry without 'chevilles'.

*

It is the custom to represent poetry as a languid lady, veiled, and reclining on a cloud. This lady has a musical voice, and everything she says is a lie.

And now, have you ever experienced the surprise of being brought suddenly face to face with your own name as if it belonged to someone else – seeing, as it were, its shape, and hearing the sound of its syllables, with eyes and ears undulled by long familiarity? The thought that a tradesman, for example, does not know a word which seems so familiar to us, opens our eyes and unblocks our ears. A wave of the wand restores the commonplace to life.

The same phenomenon may occur in the case of a thing or animal. All of a sudden we *see* a dog, a cab, a house, *for the first time.* We are overpowered by the unique, the crazy, the ridiculous, the beautiful features of each object. The next moment habit, with its eraser, has rubbed out this vivid picture. We stroke the dog, hail the cab, and live in the house. We do not see them any more.

This is the role that poetry performs. It *unveils* in the fullest sense of the word. It reveals naked, and lit by a light which arouses the mind from its torpor, all the surprising things by which we are surrounded, and which our senses registered mechanically.

It is useless to go far in order to seek bizarre objects and sensations with which to surprise the now awakened sleeper. This is the bad poet's method, and it leads to exoticism.†

* 'Cheville' is the technical word for a line of poetry inserted for the sake of the rhyme. Its ordinary meaning, of course, is 'ankle'. The play on words in this paragraph is untranslatable.—Translator's note

† The exoticism of a Blaise Cendrars is legitimate. Cendrars has travelled; he uses natural material.

What we have to do is to show him the things which his mind and eye pass over every day, but from such an angle, and at such a speed that he seems to be seeing them and experiencing them emotionally for the first time.

This is the only kind of creation permitted to the created. For, if it be true that statues acquire their patina from being looked at by innumerable eyes, commonplaces, those eternal masterpieces, are covered by a patina so thick that it makes them invisible and hides their beauties.

Take a commonplace, clean it, polish it, and light it so that it produces the same effect with its youth and freshness and spontaneity as it did originally, and you will have done a poet's work.

All the rest is literature.

\*

We have now indicated a few recipes for the benefit of the model versifier without, however, expatiating upon the numerous ways in which it is possible to adapt the rhythm, vary the cadences, and prevent the mind, by the erection, as it were, of a system of sluices, from flowing too rapidly over the lines, each one of which will be henceforward of equal importance, since we are not here concerned with merely getting under way, or preparing to lead up to the main subject; on the contrary, there is nothing at all to lead up to, the subject being, not a mere anecdote put into verse but the poem itself, complete from beginning to end.\*

But what we have to examine now (as far as it is possible to analyse the un-analysable) is that miraculous fluid in which the poet is immersed – a fluid which is latent in him and around him like a sort of electricity, a veritable element in suspense, the force of which is proved by the history of humanity every time an artist succeeds in concentrating it and building a vehicle for it. And when we come in contact with one of the best constructed of these vehicles – a picture, a piece of sculpture or music, a poem – do we not feel a poetical shock as if we were holding the handles of an electrical apparatus?

The recipes we have given only refer to the fabrication of a vehicle of still greater perfection and better adapted to the present age, in which a stumpy little auto takes the place of a hundred horses.

\* I am reminded of an evening party at which a fashionable actress, having announced the title, recited a sonnet by Baudelaire. At the last verse the women, having arranged their dresses, put their diadems straight and opened their fans, were just getting ready to listen.

For while poetry itself does not 'progress' any more than electricity, which was just as accessible to the ancient Greeks as it is to us, the methods of transmitting it are nevertheless susceptible to progress. It is this fact that makes certain poets of the day before yesterday, Vigny for example, appear strange, in the same way as old railway engines do. After a century the old-fashioned vehicle becomes an artistic curiosity, at which we no longer smile.

The Comtesse de Noailles (of whom one would like to be the Eckermann, for her wit and intelligence never miss their mark, whether she tries to bring down an eagle or smash an old clay pipe) – the Comtesse de Noailles remarked once that an electric-lamp afforded her the satisfaction of feeling that at last she could control the forces of the thunderstorm. Her girlish senses had always been tormented by their mystery. Now they are useful in the house. The gods obey.

Do you remember also the picture in the books for children, of Franklin, armed with a whip, chasing the lightning out of his room, like a dog?

But neither the lightning-conductor nor the electric-lamp tell us anything about the soul of electricity.

And, of course, it is no longer a question of inspiration. Inspiration will be a matter of more or less electric current, or of a strong or weak discharge.

We do not pretend to be able to analyse an occult power which permeates the universe, and does not only reveal itself through the medium of artists. This power may move us to tears through the medium of phenomena quite unconnected with art. For example, a certain firework display a few days before the war, a wounded seagull falling from the sky, my first sight of the moon through a telescope, the disaster of the *Titanic* read in a newspaper, a crowd trying to catch a thief in the Rue de la Bourse, a steam roundabout on the Place du Trône, the gallop of a horse slowed down on the film, or, on the other hand, the accelerated blossoming of a rose – I mention here a few things I happen to remember which seemed charged with an accumulation of poetic fluid like a gathering storm, filling me with feelings of uneasiness, presentiment, and poetry.

Let us, then, for the sake of simplicity, call this fluid poetry; and let us call the more or less successful methods we employ to domesticate it art. Herein lies the function of the artist. But 'if Heaven did not make a poet of him at his birth', in the words of the excellent Boileau, it will be no good his laying the necessary wires – his lamp will never light.

Poetry in its raw state is a source of life to those in whom it arouses a feeling of nausea. This sort of moral nausea is caused by death. Death is at the back of life. That is why we cannot imagine what it is like, but we are always obsessed with the idea that it forms the lining of the tissue that is ourselves. We may even some-times establish a sort of contact with our dead, but in a way which precludes any kind of communication. Imagine a text of which we can never get to know the continuation, because it is printed at the back of a page of which we can only read the front. Now, although the words 'back' and 'front', useful though they may be for the purposes of human expression, probably mean nothing at all where the superhuman is concerned, the idea of this mysterious 'under-neath' makes every one of our actions, words, even our slightest gestures, seem as though they were suspended in a void, which makes the soul as dizzy as looking over a precipice may make the head.

Poetry aggravates this uneasiness, and mixes it with the emotions aroused in us by scenery, love, sleep, and our pleasures in general.

The poet does not dream; he counts. But he is walking on a quicksand, and from time to time plunges his leg into the jaws of death.

He gets used to this, however, and soon looks upon it as quite normal – just as people with heart disease are not alarmed by the severest attack of palpitations.

Poetry, then, implies a predisposition to the supernatural. The hypersensitive atmosphere in which it envelops us sharpens our secret sensibilities, and causes us to put out feelers which probe into depths which our official senses ignore. The scents which rise from these forbidden regions make our official senses jealous. They rise in revolt, exhaust themselves, attempt to do work which is beyond their power, and the individual is overcome by a marvellous confusion. Beware! Whoever finds himself in such a state may see miracles in everything.

Poets live on miracles. They happen on the slightest pretext apropos of anything, great or small. Objects, desires, sympathies place themselves spontaneously under their hands. For their sake the incoherencies of fate take on a rhythm of their own. They live for a time like kings. But let a miracle fail to happen, and their nervous tension relaxes, their senses calm down again. It is as if the magic ring had fallen from their suddenly shrunken finger. These are painful periods. Poetry, like a drug, continues to act, but turns against the poet and torments him with a series of misadventures. The consciousness of death, which was to him what the pleasure of giddiness is to speed, sickens him with the spasm of a sudden fall.

One day the finger grows fat again, the ring returns to its place, and miracles happen once more.

We are here in the presence of phenomena of a quite special character over which we have no control, and which stand in the same relation to tame poetry as occultism does to science.

Poetry, though it may form part of the mechanism of dreams, is in no sense a cause of dreams, or of a dreamy state of mind. What it does sometimes is to invest dreams with a certain relief, combined with a critical intensity and the super-position of one background on another, recollections of which, added to memories of what are known as 'waking dreams', increase that feeling of moral nausea which poetry always brings.

Dreaming and dreaminess may be left to the poet who has no poetry in him. For poetry in no way excludes liveliness, childish pranks, penny toys, practical jokes, and the wild laughter in which poets indulge in the most incredibly melancholy way.

As you will perceive, we are not very far from the spirit of religion, or from what Charles Péguy called 'the missionary's laugh'.*

\*

Religion is something different again. I have no means of knowing in what way poetry may bring us nearer to God or the reverse. I refer the reader to Paul Claudel's preface to the Complete Works of Arthur Rimbaud – despite the fact that his love for both the Church and the poet oblige him to reconcile them at all costs.

Far be it from us to accuse Claudel of interpreting to his own advantage the delirium of a dying man as recorded by a very pious sister. But such a confusion would be quite justifiable precisely on account of this poetical spirit reaching its highest possible pitch of development at such a supreme moment. The spirit of poetry equals the spirit of religion – as distinct from any given religious system – which is no doubt what Paul Claudel means when he says so justly that Rimbaud was 'a mystic in the raw' ('un mystique à l'état sauvage').

The poet is a believer. In what? In everything.

Hence Renan, who is saturated with our fluid, is undoubtedly a religious nature, unlike Voltaire, whom poetry shuns, just as a silken thread is shunned by electricity.

* The primary importance which people like ourselves attach to the lyrical element (although it might be supposed that we should be the first to despise it) forces us to see in it a touch of the divine. It has the power to transform the most insignificant object into an idol, and to make it seem to us to be living in a state of surprising isolation; the painter, G. de Chirico, can do this with a dry biscuit.

Scepticism is a bad conductor of poetry. That is why poetry has no great hold in France, a country which is much too knowing.

(PS. The spirit of poetry with its accompanying spirit of death, is not only to be found in works of a sad, but also in those of a most frivolous nature.)

We may leave on one side poetry proper, which abounds in examples of this. Ronsard's sorrow wears a crown of wild roses, and Heinrich Heine dies of *amourettes*.

But with perfect poets you will find both moods are intertwined like initials carved in the bark of a tree.

We may mention straight away the name of the master of a genre, the very name of which is a diminutive : Offenbach. Words gradually lose their exact meaning. We cannot help giving very high rank to certain 'operettas' when we think of those *amourettes* of Heine, and of the title which the second edition of *La Princesse de Clèves* was to have borne : *Les Amourettes du Duc de Nemours et de la Princesse de Clèves*.

Offenbach's poetry is of so perfidious a kind that some people feel in it the power of the 'evil eye', and protect themselves by signs as soon as they hear his music.

Poetry in this form is all the more effective in that it is totally unexpected. We thought we were going to laugh, and we laugh. Then the fluid takes effect. The orchestra is convulsed by mournfully catchy strains. After hearing the letter to Metella, and the passage 'ce que c'est pourtant que la vie', the mysterious impression it makes upon us is unforgettable.

Read again Baudelaire's 'Danse Macabre', and you will be startled by its resemblance to the music of Offenbach :

> Cette coquette maigre aux airs extravagants . . .
> Avec son gros bouquet, son mouchoir et ses gants . . .
> Aucuns t'appelleront une caricature . . .
> O charme d'un néant follement attifé !

This last line might serve as a heading to the quadrille in *Orphée aux Enfers*, the faded brilliance of which may appeal to a bad conductor of poetry; whereas a good conductor will feel as if he were having old wounds reopened.

In 1914 there were plenty of sour-minded people who thought the tango was an invention of the German devil, designed for the undoing of our race. They thought wrong. But then what about Offenbach? Looked at from this point of view, does he not appear to have fulfilled a special role in 1869? Dancing on the edge of the abyss.

I have related elsewhere how Mme Wagner was found weeping in the recesses of a box during a recent revival of *La Belle Hélène*. She could have borne without crying the 'Procession of the Gods' at Bayreuth, but in Paris, giving way to memories, and under the influence of the fluid, she wept at the 'Marche des Rois'.

\*

In the old days the priests commanded and the artisan obeyed. Was the latter a real artist? His work in those days had the double merit of being both outwardly beautiful and at the same time full of profound meaning. Thus the Jews were Egypt's true sculptors. At the present day, art vegetates exclusively in the hands of artisans. The artisan-priest is extremely rare. It is to him we are looking today. The public is content to admire doors which lead nowhere. But, like the game of chess which, it appears, derives its distorted rules from the itinerary of the Ark of the Covenant, is there anything into which the ancient game of art does not plunge its roots? The most insignificant player sets more mystery afoot than appears on the surface. This is another of the reasons why this game intrigues us, and is a source of so much uneasiness, surprise, sorrow and consolations.

It is none the less a game which is essentially human, earthly and, in a sense, humble. It is dangerous in the same way as was the Holy Ark – that mighty electrical machine around which surged a people ignorant of electricity. The cowherd who brushes against it while driving his cattle on the road to Jerusalem falls dead, struck down by the hand of God, perhaps, but above all a victim of his own imprudence. Depend upon it, the priests never touched it before cutting off the current. Similarly, the secrets of art are also man's concern.

Moreover, man is entitled to play this game. This is not the case, however, as regards science and metaphysics, to which it almost always leads. The poet, whose range is unlimited, sometimes brings back a pearl from depths into which the man of science *proves* it is impossible to descend. Metaphysics and primary causes are intently engaged in a leisurely game of hide-and-seek. The poet goes for a stroll and discovers their hiding-place. But though he is always the first to discover things, the poet never exploits his discovery. He sees and passes on. He does not worry or chase after the unknown.

And yet it is precisely owing to this faculty of being able to penetrate to the core of things, more deeply than any science, that art seems to be enveloped in an atmosphere of punishment. Science, who moves slowly and counts her steps, makes mistakes. She does not appear to be a cause of much inconvenience to the Unknown. And the Unknown leaves her pretty well alone. She is sometimes useful to man, and never disturbs the gods.

The Unknown is a sea which 'we are forbidden to explore'. Science, philosophy and spiritualism bathe in it, and paddle on its shores.

The artist builds a ship, or a villa on the beach.

He who plays the game of art is doing something which concerns him, but with the risk of opening a breach on to something which is not his concern at all. The discoveries of an Einstein outstrip our limited capacities, but do not reach the feet of the gods. He exhausts himself in empty space.

An Einstein proves the existence of errors, and opens the door to fresh ones. If you want to expose errors without appearing ridiculous, you ought to place yourself at such an altitude that you are out of all human earshot. The fact of remaining within limits accessible to a mass of good medium intelligences is enough to invalidate any theory.

Let us imagine a fable. Some insects are living and thriving shut up in a round bottle lying on a table. After a time one of the insects discovers that their universe is flat. Presently another discovers that it is cubic, and after that another that it is triangular, and then that they are living in freedom, but confined to a rounded surface, and so on and so forth. One of the insects, who is a poet, writes, merely for the sake of rhyming with 'onde' :

'Moi, pauvre prisonnier d'une bouteille ronde.'

He has discovered everything, but no one is any the wiser.

I am looking at a solid object, say an old nail. Its matter is made up of molecules, which have no connection with each other, and which are whirling about at wild speeds. Imagine one of these molecules to be inhabited by rational beings like ourselves, gravitating, living and dreaming, surrounded by empty space, and seeing at varying distances in this pseudo-space other molecules from which they derive warmth and light, and which are gravitating like themselves. Is it likely that their pride will allow them to believe that they are merely an infinitesimal fraction of an enormous nail-head?

The metals contained in our atmosphere lead me to believe that our eyes and our ether form one of those spaces which separate the molecules of a solid object.

I attain the conviction that the earth, sun, moon, and stars are fractions of a nail-head on an earth which again is itself, etc. . . .

A lot of good that does me !
  What discomfort, what loneliness !
  I go back to the games which console me.
  It is therefore for disciplinary reasons that I advise artists not to
mix up art, and science, and philosophy, and occultism. Such
mixtures lead either to laziness, or to the kind of pedantry peculiar
to learned women. The art of Picasso, so simple and so instructive,
and the lessons which may be learnt from it are obscured, not only
by the term 'cubist', but also by futile discussions in which, instead
of talking about painting, people talk about Poincaré, Bergson, the
Fourth Dimension, and the pineal gland.

*

M. Marnold, the musical critic of the *Mercure*, blames me for
always employing metaphors in speaking about music. For me it is
the only language possible. With the help of musicians I might be
able to dazzle credulous readers. But, apart from the fact that
musicians find articles written by technicians incomprehensible, I
am not a technician, and wish above all things to make myself
understood.
  'It is impossible to like a piece of music without having a
thorough knowledge of counterpoint and harmony' – so M.
Marnold tells me. You might as well say it is impossible to enjoy a
tree without knowing the nature of its fibres, or a dish unless one is
a cook. This is our bone of contention with a man whom we find
most sympathetic, since he does not hesitate to stand up for the
younger school.
  But although it is fatal for art to imagine that it has anything to
learn from science, there is nothing to prevent the artist from
'opening the cage-door for arithmetic'. Art is science in the flesh.
For example, the scientific theory showing why it is possible to
review the whole of one's past life at the moment when death alters
the speed of one's molecules has had great charm for me ever since
a friend of mine expressed it in the following way : when a gun is
fired, the sound and the flash form one single commotion; but if
the flash were to turn back, on the way it would hear the sound.
  Where fifteen chapters threaten to lead me out of my depth, I
prefer to have them broadly, but intelligently, translated into my
own language.
  It is this feeling of delicacy that makes us treat lightly our most
deep-seated anxieties. It is this delicacy which prevents others from
listening to us, or from taking us seriously. The drama underlying
*Le Potomak* I concealed under a thousand jokes just as one sings
in the dark to keep one's spirits up.

The reproach of wanting to 'get there' at all costs is levelled at whatever grows with an irresistible force. The theatre, above all, which attracts more attention than books, brings down this reproach upon anyone amongst us who has anything to do with it. This always astonishes me.

'Getting there.'. . . Where? And with what object?

As far as we are concerned – we who are uninfluenced by any considerations relating to rewards or place-seeking – this expression has no more sense than a wad of bank-notes would have in the hands of a savage. It is doubtless this complete indifference to publicity that attracts a certain amount of publicity to theatrical enterprises of a special character.

For my part, in spite of the fact that I make a rule of never reading articles about myself, good or bad, unless I am forced to, I have always noticed that a great deal of quite gratuitous fuss is made over my own theatrical enterprises.

And the critics are all convinced that our group either spends a fortune over the production of a show, or else makes one out of it.

My friends cite me the most extraordinary articles. Hence, although I had read neither the *Mercure de France* nor *l'Action Française*, I was nevertheless extremely gratified to learn that in 1921 the critic of the former thought that Auric, Honegger, Durey, Milhaud, Poulenc, Germaine Tailleferre and myself were millionaires, quoting Cézanne and Chabrier as examples of the 'penniless artist', and sincerely believing that we paid to be performed; while the other expressed the opinion that 'I would do anything to see my name in print'.

It is astounding that a review and a newspaper of such standing can open their columns to naïve rubbish of this kind, and still more so that there are men, even devoid of all culture, capable of writing it.

A question I often asked myself is why spectacles like *Parade, Le Boeuf sur le Toit,* or *Les Mariés de la Tour Eiffel* are so revolting to professionals, and give rise to such sustained animosity, when there is no question of their competing with anything else.

These spectacles are not in the market. They are seldom given. They have nothing to do with the Boulevards. The path they follow is quite outside so-called 'contemporary production'.

An article by my friend, Lugné-Poë, opens my eyes. He is alarmed. And yet he is surely the last person who need be. He points to a danger. He remarks on the atmospheric importance of this special form of theatrical undertaking which is growing up outside the theatre proper and causing it to appear old-fashioned; while at the same time it offers the public no substitute for the other kind, but merely makes them feel vaguely bored with it.

The circus, the music-hall, the cinema, and those other enterprises which, since the advent of Serge de Diaghilev, have provided our younger men with great opportunities, are so many forces conspiring together, in an unconscious alliance, against the present-day theatre, which is now nothing but an old photograph album.

The Boulevard-type play fills everyone with hope. If such and such an author, thinks the knowing public, can rise to such lofty heights, and if this ancient actress is able to look so young, then after all there is still a chance for me. Roughly speaking, this is the kind of feeling that pervades a successful dress-rehearsal.

I have seen a fashionable dramatist endeavouring to make us share his mediocre triumph. Near me were four women, of the kind one only meets at the theatre, yellow-haired, and covered with pearls, who were drying the tears in their eyes with the corner of a handkerchief to prevent them from running down and spoiling their make-up.

A mere chance observation, you will say. Not at all. That is how an audience composed of the 'élite' behaves. The others just herd behind.

But if this public consent to bestow a glance on, and lend a distracted ear, just for fun, to one of our entertainments, it will leave a mysterious mark upon them, making them feel uneasy, as if they had a fly up their nose. They were asleep; now they shake themselves, and rush about. For the theatre is a powerful conveyor of poetry.

Alas! it calls for immediate success. Therefore the only way to arrive at any result is to treat it in an equivocal way so as to cater for several kinds of public simultaneously (cf. Shakespeare and Molière). On this delicate subject I will take the liberty of referring the reader to the preface of *Les Mariés de la Tour Eiffel*.

To return to the subject of 'getting there'. Even when it is a question of place-seeking, who ever does? Did Victor Hugo? I doubt it. The landlady of the inn where I am staying has never heard his name. The young generation does not read his books. Baudelaire has swarms of readers, but has he 'arrived'? Can a piece of meat be said to have 'arrived' because it ends by attracting flies? That is rather a sign of staleness.

Nothing ever gets anywhere. The earth keeps turning round and gets nowhere. The moment is the only thing that counts. Certain fortunate works flourish like those seeds which were discovered by excavators in Egypt on the mummy of a young girl, and when they were put into the ground five thousand years later, in Baltimore, blossomed into roses. That was the moment for those roses.

Youthful beauty is despised over here. When it grows old we kill it, and when it is dead we embalm it. But then Youth shrinks away from it in sorrow.

\*

If I must now make a résumé of, and cast a comprehensive glance backwards over what I have said, these are my conclusions:

That form should be understood as meaning mental form. Not a way of saying things, but a way of *thinking* them;

That the need to express oneself in public is a form of secretion which cannot be excused, unless one is born with it and finds it incurable;

That one must either coincide, or commit suicide – the state of mind of a spectator who finds a play absurd, but stays in the theatre to warm himself and then makes a disturbance, whistling and preventing other people from hearing, being inadmissible;

That there are always very few people who really belong to their own epoch, seeing that there is no such thing as a precursor – one such so-called precursor – that is to say, the only man who really expresses his epoch, whether it likes it or not – being capable of making a whole epoch, although quite unaware of the fact, seem to be lagging behind him;

That stupidity, insensitiveness and spiritual scepticism protect a country's finest individuals by failing to recognize their true value. They act as a kind of refrigerator for the preservation of our finest fruit. A too curious, or a too serious, or a too amiable, or a too indulgent attitude results in the fruit being passed from hand to hand, and finally losing its bloom;

That fighting stimulates us, whereas a kindly disposed public sends us to sleep;

That we continually need a wall, as in the game of 'pelota', in order to carry on our game, either alone, or with or against others. It is this that brings down on us the reproach, now of arrogance if the wall we have selected is a masterpiece univeraslly respected – now of maliciousness if our wall is a 'master'.

But in no case is either masterpiece or master a target. The wall in the game of 'pelota' is not a target. We are not playing with arrows which stick in, but with balls which bounce off. No one in the Basque country ever thinks of feeling sorry for the wall. It is precisely in order not to have to feel sorry for the wall, or spoil it, or make holes in it, or split it, that we choose strong ones, upon which even the hardest balls leave no mark.

Let me confess that, when under the comprehensive title of *La Noce Massacrée* (the farcical victims of which are invulnerable, and recover their upright position immediately) I chose Maurice Barrès, it was in the capacity of a pelota wall that I meant him to serve. I needed a wall that was very high, very solid, very sunny, and very much in the public eye. A wall that even my best drives would leave unperturbed, but one which would be of the greatest service to me and to my game.

The same thing applies to *Madame Bovary*, dealt with at the beginning of *Le Secret Professionnel*. I do no harm to the book, so there is no need to blame me, or to cry out in indignation. Let me run, and jump about, and take my exercise. On weekdays at Saint-Jean-de-Luz, Hendaye, or Bayonne, any amateur may use the 'Fronton' as much as he likes, and may practise there. (Barrès, to whom in his capacity of a wall my balls cannot be either agreeable or disagreeable, will not feel hurt, now, at being compared to a wall. I know some in several villages which are Frontons on one side, and on the other are covered with peaches, grapes and roses.)

We also concluded that :

A man who is quite independent, and who does not seek rewards of any kind, must inevitably appear to be something of a megalomaniac;

That the poet resembles the dead, inasmuch as he walks about invisibly amongst the living who only vaguely perceive him after he is dead – that is to say, when they speak of the dead as ghosts;

That poems, poetical forms and poetry are quite different things, and the fact that there are excellent lightning-conductors which never attract lightning in no way discredits storms;

That it is when poetry assumes a confused – as we see it – and as it were a stormy shape, that it becomes capable of producing a collective effect on a great many different kinds of people;

That this cattle-like herding together under the storm gives rise to artificial caresses, which are a source of misunderstanding and friction;

That shipwrecks, and occasions when one's country or one's purse are in danger, are fertile in poetry of this description;

That poetry ceases to be obvious to all as soon as it begins to mean something to a few;

That the fact of abandoning rhyme and fixed rules in favour of other intuitive rules brings us back to fixed rules and to rhyme with renewed respect;

That, for example, a poet who has been brought back in this way concentrates in a single line what he would have previously spread out over four stanzas;

That when an infidelity brings us back to our first love it binds us thereto so strongly that it is rendered indestructible; whereas in a love exempt from the slightest kind of infidelity all the germs of infidelity are latent;

That 'grace' exists in the sense that there are inventors of new vehicles, or simple drivers of old ones who never manage to get hold of the 'fluid', but that 'grace' is a mystery which does not concern mankind, from whom we need not demand any mystical activity outside the sphere of religion;

That music, painting, sculpture, architecture, dancing, poetry, the drama, and that muse I call 'Cinema, tenth Muse', are all so many traps in which man endeavours to capture poetry for our use;

That few of these traps work, and few are lamps which can be made to light; and all the time the majority of mankind go strutting about in the dark and imagine that their houses are magnificently illuminated.

# Order Considered as Anarchy

In May 1923 Cocteau gave a talk to the students of the Collège de France and it was published three years later under the title *Order Considered as Anarchy* (D'un Ordre Considéré comme une Anarchie), in the collection *Le Rappel à l'Ordre*.

Cocteau had composed the talk partly during a visit to England with Radiguet and he spoke much about his young friend, now famous at the age of twenty through his recently published novel *Le Diable au Corps*. Cocteau also acknowledged his other 'master', the composer Erik Satie, and expressed his admiration for Picasso. During the talk Cocteau also read passages from his own work and attempted in his own way to explain the various misunderstandings about himself and his writing.

Gentlemen,

After thanking the Collège de France for the extraordinary honour which it is doing me, allow me first of all to tell you how deeply it moves me that we should be meeting here in the gravest place in the world. This confession is in itself significant. You may see in it the first proof of the formation of an absolutely new spiritual state. Yesterday, this morning even, emotions were not fashionable.

Each time that art is on the way towards that profound form of elegance known as classicism, emotions disappear. It is the ungrateful stage. The icy serpent is sloughing his mottled skin.

But after a good deal of discomfort and solitude, art, now stark naked, recovers its equilibrium, and replaces the richness of its garments by a wealth of soul.

This is a great moment. The lesson of economy has been learnt. The heart does not overflow and merely exchange an excess of colour for a cataclysm of moonlight. It expresses itself with reserve, and adds to a sense of proportion that slight deviation from the straight without which architecture seems dead.

Here I pause. I am afraid of slipping into a lecture. The sound of my voice worries me. I give it up. I am simply going to chat with you.

Each of us has a spring inside him. We must not break it, but we must none the less wind it up as far as it will go. Then we shall go on living, thanks to the mechanism set in motion by this spring as it unwinds. Everything depends on the last turn of the key. It is absolutely necessary to have an instinctive feeling for this. You must understand that I am speaking of a system of ideas which governs us and ensures a connection between our actions, however incoherent. Winding up the spring as far as it will go involves a certain amount of repetition. This is indispensable. Winding a little too far results in mere babbling. A little further still, and everything is smashed.

After *Le Secret Professionel*, I had promised myself to keep silent. For I do not call writing poems or novels talking. I felt I had come to the end of a certain number of notice-boards which I display, now in a preface, now in a pamphlet, the results of which, daily becoming more and more numerous (to which I hope you will allow me to add your present invitation) encourage me to allow them to produce their effect by themselves.

Doing detective work would soon make me ill. Tenacity sends out far-reaching waves. Near at hand these waves irritate, and when they clash, their crackling prevents the neighbours from sleeping. One has no idea of the misunderstandings which one of those simple phrases – one of those homely truths which the public call paradoxes – may give rise to. Here is an example :

In *Le Coq et l'Arlequin* I remarked that there was no such thing as a precursor, but only latecomers. This is a fact. But I stated it in 1917, when puzzles were all the rage. Instead of realizing that genius, whatever surprises it may bring, always arrives at its appointed time, and that, when its hour strikes, immediately all the other clocks in the world go slow, people thought I was accusing one lot of being behind the times, while not allowing the others to be considered as precursors. A strange confusion, which has crept into people's minds owing to the obscurity of Rimbaud, Mallarmé and Ducasse – a false obscurity, moreover, since their darkness is always so concentrated that it finally approaches the brightness of a diamond. . . .

It was my luck, no doubt, to realize that it was essential to appear idiotic, and to be bold enough to cry, like the child in the Andersen story : 'Why, look ! The Emperor has no clothes !'

A cry like this pleases no one – neither the Emperor, nor the people, nor the swindlers who, you will remember, pretended to have woven a tissue which fools could not see.

Alas! the misunderstanding that approves is often just as bad.
One has only to write : 'No hair should be allowed to appear on
the head in future', and immediately the bald triumph.

Gentlemen, the simplicity of today is not the same as that of
yesterday. Nowadays it is not by singing 'J'aime mieux ma mie', but
by reciting the Sonnet of Orontes that Alceste would reveal his
conservatism.

Read *Les Précieuses* again. No stranger exercise exists. It is the
ridiculous language of the women and of Mascarille which is going
to fertilize literature. Do not forget that Cathos and Madelon give
a pretty bad imitation of the correct style, while Mascarille is the
clown. Thus we may guess that the language which Molière made
fun of was doubtless the predecessor of the style of a Mallarmé, a
Marcel Proust, an André Gide, a Max Jacob, a Giraudoux, or a
Jacques Rivière. He made fun of what was new, just like our
revue writers.

I conclude that Molière must have been a type of that peculiar
French mentality which is so disconcerting in its combination of
transparency and thickness.

Hence our kind of simplicity will astonish the shade of Molière by
its complication, and puzzle the avant-garde by its childishness.
You see the position. The shade of Molière is the public. Youth
also revolts. And so you alone are walking on a tightrope, with
everybody hoping you will break your neck. Could one be in a
finer position? Frequently my lower self grumbles and demands
to be on firm ground. But it soon becomes resigned. Moreover, while I am talking to you now I am not dreaming. *Cave
somniasti*, the Latins say. I would add : a dreamer is always a bad
poet.

Since I am unable to attach myself to any school, or to form
one myself, public opinion, in its passion for labels, sticks them all
on to me. It is thus that abroad I represented Dada, whereas I was
really the Dadaists' *bête noire*.

None the less I salute them in passing, for I confess I have
occasionally found their material astonishingly rich in poetry,
though not approving the form in which they presented it.

To return to that bad metaphor of the tightrope. You will tell
me : Solitude never lasts long. You will soon have a school of
solitude, or a school of tightrope. That is possible. But since it is a
dangerous one it does not attract many people.

Moreover, one of the secrets of a *tour de force* consists in
deceiving one's followers, if one has any. Deceive? In what way?

Ah! gentlemen, let us turn up our sleeves, and turn out our
pockets, and show what we have in the wings. One risks nothing

by divulging professional secrets. Nobody knows how to put them into practice.

In short, this is what I propose : an absence of style. To have style, instead of having *a* style; and, since no writer can avoid having a certain quality which enables a sensitive observer to establish a relationship between his works, to wear one's style underneath, instead of on the surface, and pay more attention to the quality of the material than to painting it over with arabesques.

It is this which enables one to turn one's back on the preceding work, and with each new one to enjoy all the risks of a début. My method is not a good one as far as fame is concerned. Fame is an absent-minded lady. She likes to be able to recognize her own folk at first glance. But even if the artist who adopts it only presents a questionable sort of picture on the upper side, on the under he constructs a foundation which will always be superior to mere ornamentation.

Will you permit me to read you some pages I wrote at different periods? You will see where they are alike and where they differ. If I allow myself to perform that ungraceful action which consists in thrusting oneself forward, it is not so much from a desire to 'show off', as from a fear of being like a strategist who never exposes himself. I should feel I was merely using empty words if I did not prove what I put forward.

[Here followed a reading of fragments of *Le Cap de Bonne-Espérance, Vocabulaire,* and *Plain-Chant.*]

Let me name my masters : Erik Satie and Picasso. I owe more to them than to any writer. The influence of a writer may easily infect one with 'tics', but the astonishingly disciplined freedom of this musician and this painter rules out all weakness. Now, in this case, it would be weakness not to know when to run away.

How many times have I heard the reproach against Satie and Picasso that they do not know where they are going. One day it is Picasso who gives up cubism. The next, it is Satie who starts going backwards. The miracle is that they are treated as if they were débutants.

Satie once said to me : All great artists are amateurs. This *mot* calls up a vision of the whole crowd of illustrious bureaucrats, who have been so scornful of the 'bourgeoisie' and thrift, sitting bent over their writing-desks until the day of their death.

I grant you that, seen at a distance, the homogeneity of a man's work is what strikes us most, and that it is extremely difficult for us to grasp the sudden volte-face by which a man of genius renews himself. But it is none the less true that our own epoch affords some obvious examples of this, and that homage is due to an Igor

Stravinsky when, after having completely upset the musicologues by the surprise of the *Sacre du Printemps*, he turns his back on them and addresses himself elsewhere.

But, gentlemen, I am digressing. Shall I confess that that has been my intention? I dread lectures, and would have been incapable of giving you one. It would seem to me ridiculous to address you as pupils. As comrades, it is quite a different matter. I am more accustomed to friendship than to teaching.

Baudelaire, when describing his visit to Victor Hugo in Brussels, says that 'Hugo plunged into one of those monologues which he called conversation'.

It is rather cowardly of me to propose a conversation now, but I am going to ask you to interrupt me if I startle you, and I will try to explain myself better, although I improvise very badly.

I wrote the notes I am now reading to you at Oxford and at Harrow. Harrow was like an empty shell, on account of the holidays. From the window of The King's Head I could not see the boys going by on bicycles in their black clothes, wearing those fantastic straw biscuits on their heads, but it seemed to me to be quite normal to be writing for students in a paradise of studies. Oxford confirmed me in my intention not to give you a lecture. It bores me to visit its cloisters and its parks with their Burne-Jones flowers. The wonder of Oxford is its shops. There the dead languages come to life. Each shop-window responds to a youthful desire. They are dressed and lit up in order to tempt youth. I am not ashamed to confess that the Ashmolean gives me cramp, while the streets take the stiffness out of my legs. While admiring those piles of cigarette boxes, pipes, flowers, eatables, neckties, gloves, and knitted garments of many hues, and the houses with their porches supported on columns, each one like a miniature family temple, I reflected that the museums were full of old hats belonging to the pharaohs, and that it was far more worthwhile to look at the shops. It was this walk which, by an easy transition, suggested to me to take a stroll with you, instead of assuming the lecturer's desk.

A period only seems confused to a mind which is confused. The one we are living in now, on account of its very richness, is counted a puzzle. Some flounder about in it, others withdraw, and take refuge in the past, others again fish in its troubled waters. Few know where they are going. And yet it is easy to take a bird's-eye view of the map.

Did not Guillaume Apollinaire speak of a light so soft that one could see right through it? He died before he could enjoy it. This exile from the eighteenth century lived in a small flat on the

Boulevard Saint-Germain stuffed with Negro sculpture and barbarous knick-knacks.

I never knew a man more uncomfortably situated at the extreme end of his epoch. He endured it, made a mystery of it, and decorated it delightfully. He foresaw a reaction. One day, while we were walking near the Ministry for the Colonies, where he was working, he confided to me his ill-humour. It was on account of that modernism of which he wished to be the apostle, and which caused him much annoyance. After having opened the flood-gates, he even went so far as to abuse the flood, on the grounds that he had opened the gates for a joke. His charm was due to the contrast between his duties as an anarchist and a little blue flower. See the drop of ink trembling at the tip of his pen. It falls, and makes a starlike blot. All this great poet's work is made up of a series of exquisite blots.

Hence, in spite of a vague desire for order, Apollinaire amused himself with chance, Negro bric-à-brac and New York advertisement posters. He was a cosmopolitan. I am not.

Soon after this I was deeply grieved to see a snow spreading colder than death. The object was to mock and destroy literature. This strange suicide attracted me with its blue eyes. But frenzied littérateurs were employed on the job, who, with the avowed object of spreading demoralization, merely continued the nonsense of Alfred Jarry.

I had just written *Le Cap de Bonne-Espérance*. This poem, which is of an epic nature, might be compared to an aeroplane propeller, or a cable strand; it is an attempt to break away from Mallarmé's fan, Arthur Rimbaud's angelic hair, and the still-life school. I felt very much alone. The only possible group would have been the Dada Suicide Club. But I did not feel fitted for that sort of job. Music had already supplied me with one of another sort – I had just written *Le Coq et l'Arlequin*.

I have described in the *Revue de Genève* the formation of the new French music group.

After *Le Coq et l'Arlequin* we ran the risk of being taken seriously – a sign of approaching death. One morning when I was brooding over this, Darius Milhaud said : 'Would you like me to give you a bar !' It was the Bar Gaya, in the Rue Duphot, and was always empty. Jean Wiéner, a fellow-student of Darius' at the Conservatoire, was giving prodigious performances there of American music, and had asked Milhaud to get me to adopt this bar as my headquarters. I did not hesitate a minute. The bar belonged to Louis Moysès, the present proprietor of the 'Boeuf sur le Toit', Rue Boissy d'Anglas.

I am very good at jazz, and am proud of it. That and drawing are my 'violon d'Ingres'. With Wiéner at the piano, and the Negro Vance playing the saxophone, I found the jazz more intoxicating than alcohol, which does not agree with me. When playing jazz, you grow a score of arms, and become a god of din.

In the twinkling of an eye the bar was packed. We had been threatened with a kind of musical chauvinism; now we were like people who contradict themselves – buffoons and clowns. It was said – and still is said of me with regard to the 'Boeuf' – that I ran a dancing place. I was irrevocably done for, compromised. We were saved!

It would take too long to enter into the details of the wonderful history of the young musicians. You know their merits and their success. Well, this was largely due to that bar.

From blues to sonatas, from foxtrots to melodies, from the *Boeuf sur le Toit* to *Les Mariés de la Tour Eiffel*, a new movement made itself felt. After the rain fine weather. This blossoming intrigues the snobs, stimulates youth, and spreads consternation among the critics. The latter ought, however, to realize that, far from being lost, their cause is really won. That it is precisely because it is won that fresh battles begin. No; instead of smiling (as it was their turn to do) the members of this clan rose in revolt. Did not M. Vuillermoz write, after the apotheosis of Satie in the packed theatre of the Champs-Elysées: 'I denounce Wiéner's concerts; they are really Cocteau's concerts; it was Cocteau who had filled the hall.'

Quite true, Monsieur Vuillermoz; only it took me five years to do it.

You see the turn of affairs. The critics and dilettanti had been taught with much difficulty an extremely complicated game of bezique. They were just beginning to be very proud of having got fairly good at it, when everything is changed; a game of leap-frog is now announced.

Since I am mixing up different epochs, and trying to disentangle a skein of thread by fingering it lightly, I will not bore you with describing all the discomforts of the moulting stage. There is nothing less simple, or less clear than the origin of a simple and clear state of mind. But one can gradually distinguish a thread here and there disentangling itself.

Max Jacob suggested founding an Anti-Modern League. I invented the disappearance of the sky-scraper, and the reappearance of the rose. This was misunderstood as meaning a return to the rose. Exactly the opposite.

There is a time to drink cocktails, and a time to bring them up. We had drunk too much, and were feeling sick, and so we started writing poems in strict form, banishing rare words, anything smacking of the bizarre, exoticism, telegrams, posters and other American accessories. Your friend Aron has observed that, like a Berlitz School teacher, I was constrained to call things by their names, since they were so covered up with metaphors and adjectives that it was no longer possible to see them.

Then Raymond Radiguet appeared. He was fifteen years old, and passed for eighteen – a fact that has confused his biographers. He never had his hair cut, was short-sighted, almost blind, and rarely opened his mouth.

The first time he came to see me (sent by Max Jacob) they came and told me : There is a child with a walking-stick in the hall.

As he lived at Parc-Saint-Maur, on the borders of the Marne, we called him The Miracle of the Marne. He seldom went home, slept anywhere – on the ground, on tables, or with painters at Montparnasse or Montmartre. Occasionally he would take out of his pocket a dirty little piece of crumpled paper. When the paper had been ironed smooth you could read a poem as fresh as a sea-shell, or a bunch of fruit.

I dedicated to him my *Visites à Barrès*.

This meant I was staking my fortune on the number Radiguet, as in my preface to *Le Coq et l'Arlequin* I had staked on the number Auric.

Shall I confess to not risking any more than a player who cheats? There are feelers which tell me which numbers will come up.

Georges Auric has great surprises in store for you. With *Le Diable au Corps* I considered I backed a winner.

If I talk a lot to you about Radiguet and his book, it is because he seems to me to be one of the best examples of that mentality which I prefer to discuss with you in a roundabout way, rather than extinguish with a definition.

A position of mystery is too favourable a one for a well-trained mind to occupy for long. I admire the kind of pride that is on good terms with the world more than the scornful kind. There is a phrase of Jacques Rivière's which expresses this perfectly : 'There is a time for mocking and a time for being mocked at.' Here you have the hand-to-hand struggle, as between Jacob and the angel. Before writing his novel Radiguet had done a play. I never saw a soap-bubble extended so far without bursting. Pierre Bertin mounted and performed the piece at a performance of 'bouffe' plays before a bewildered audience. After the performance, its terrifying author walked about the theatre in order to embarrass the pundits, who did not know what to say to him. From this little piece, with its impertinence bred of solitude, to *Le Diable au Corps,* you see the ground that has been covered.

This progress is not, however, the result of a manoeuvre; for what is striking about the book is its spontaneity, comparable to that of an Auric, or a Poulenc.

Think how tedious a work would be which was deliberately intended to be direct, and comprehensible, and colourless, and sober, and normal.

But the mentality of which I am speaking was not determined by me, or by anyone else. We might say that it induced a certain number of musicians, painters, and writers to form something which is the opposite of a doctrine – a friendly group.

Perhaps I shall be asked : Who is the *we* that you often refer to instead of *I*? Is it a ruse? Or are you trying to attribute to your own individual efforts a collective sense? I will explain.

Every time I say 'we', I have at the back of my mind the Saturday dinner. This weekly dinner took place in 1919–20–21, either at Montmartre, or Place de la Madeleine. We organized it, I and the musicians, in order to meet at fixed times. Later, these dinners developed into a wider kind of reunion. We never talked about art. We used to go, after dinner, to Milhaud's rooms, who at that time was composing *Le Boeuf sur le Toit,* and would play it with Auric and Arthur Rubinstein, arranged for six hands. Paul Morand and Lucien Daudet were the barmen. Morand carried ice about in a napkin, and it used to melt and numb our hands. When there was no more left, he would shake up the last drinks with the help of snow scraped up from the window-sill. We disguised ourselves, and rode a bicycle round the tiny dining-room – in short, did everything which sounds appalling when talked about afterwards, but which at the time is far more stimulating to everyone in his own sphere than the literary café.

Perhaps I can give you an idea of the fertile encounters and contrasts of these picnics when I tell you that *Ouvert la Nuit, Fermé la Nuit,* and *Le Diable au Corps* were the works which they gave birth to.

You will wonder what is the connection between them. For the public, a want of heart. For me, the 'heart' itself, and the spirit of those admirable dinners.

There are certain works which affect us emotionally, and others which uproot us. Others, again, oblige us to leave home – the pleasures of travel are what they provide. The *Sacre du Printemps* uprooted me; so did *Phèdre,* as played by Mme Coonen with Tairoff, at the Théâtre des Champs-Elysées. Paul Morand forces me to leave my room. His stories disturb, fatigue, and enchant me.

No doubt amongst his pickle jars, red pepper, cauliflowers and onions in mustard all mixed up together I detect again the flavour of those Saturday cocktails.

I shall be told that Morand is a chameleon walking on Harlequin's shoulder, and the prototype of everything I am bound to dislike. That may be. But, underneath the colours of his baroque style observe how legibly he writes, how he shapes his letters, and how clear and swift and sober he is, as rich as Croesus, and as simple as good morning.

Here I open a parenthesis within a parenthesis in order to tell you a significant story about Morand. When he was a child, a lady who was a palm-reader told his mother that he had no line of luck. Well he went off to the kitchen, and made himself one with a knife; he shows the scar to this day, and you all know that it has served its purpose.

'We', then, means him and a whole troop of first-line writers, amongst whom I perceive a mysterious family likeness. To these I add Drieu La Rochelle, Jacques de Lacretelle, and François Mauriac, who were not Saturdayites, but ought to have been.

The Saturday dinners came to an end for several reasons. There were two chief ones – one sad : the death of Fauconnet; the other amusing : the dinners began to take themselves seriously. Morand had christened them the 'S.A.M.' (Mutual Admiration Society). We talked about our respective sales : Goldschmann organized his concerts there; and Maurice Martin du Gard and Marcel Raval used to steal from each other contributors to their respective reviews. I began to feel possessed with the spirit of my grandfather – a great stickler where family dinners were concerned. I frowned at the slightest defection. Our friendly dinner was becoming an irksome duty. So we broke it up without further ado.

Let us cultivate a hatred of family dinners and systems. Picasso is not a cubist. He charms objects, and transports them wherever he likes, imposing on the disorder of nature a human order which is called 'cubist', and exploited as such, without his having any hand in the matter at all. Mallarmé, so far as I know, was not a Mallarméist, nor Debussy a Debussyist.

The musicologues think they are very clever in representing me as a detractor of Claude Debussy. They cannot understand that doing so is one thing, and venerating another; and that the whole scheme of *Le Coq et l'Arlequin* obliges me to ignore everything that is second class, and be unkind to whatever is first class. It is understood that I admire all the works I blame, and that what disgusts me is not the works themselves, but the process of prolonging them, splitting them into halves and quarters and eighths, serving them up with sauces, and chewing them over and over again to the point of exhaustion.

A great man is contagious. His victims herd together. His 'school' is a hospital, which does not interest me.

A failure to understand the rules of a royal game, as played by crowned heads between themselves, embarrasses the players. My *Visites à Barrès* was so miserably misunderstood that I burnt the portraits I was intending to collect and publish under the title of *La Noce Massacrée*. I was considered malicious. What could be more foolish. I used Barrès as a kind of searchlight to throw light on certain things. Rough play is low play. That is to say, the play becomes rough as soon as ill-bred players join it.

We are living in a gloomy epoch of great personages. People have forgotten how to play. I was only playing. I am too familiar with Barrès' mentality not to know that I have his approval.

It was natural for Barrès to reply to a journalist: 'My war correspondence is what I shall live by', and equally natural that I should reply: 'That is a lie, Barrès. War is a bad preservative. Mme Astiné Aravian embalms better.' Natural, too, that I should add: 'But, after all, patriotism is his "violon d'Ingres", and he naturally would say he preferred it to everything.' It was also natural that Barrés was angry about it in public, while saying to himself in his study, over a cigar: 'These insults are very mild; anyway, I prefer them to the handshakes of my electors.'

I left the subject of Radiguet too soon. His book is useful to me in order to illuminate a victory. How dramatic is the entry of this silent book, preceded by a formidable clashing of cymbals.

Everything about his adventure is fresh, and everything in it amuses me. First of all, there was the publisher's advertising, which was enough to kill any début. Grasset did not calculate at all; he was madly in love with the book. It was he who had 'le diable au corps'. Here we have the first novelty. Without knowing it, he substitutes the anathema of noisy advertising in place of the anathema of silence. Every strong work is accursed, but from one generation to another the hate which it arouses changes its character. *Le Diable au Corps*, of which the scandal consisted in not seeking to cause a scandal, was in danger of coming to birth too easily. An Americanized publicity put it in its place and obliged it to struggle for its life, and begin all over again from the beginning.

The novelty of this affair lies in the fact that, in spite of universal grumbling, the book should be in everybody's hand, thus demolishing the superstition that masterpieces have to wait a century before they are acknowledged.

I had the good fortune to watch Radiguet writing his book, as if it were an imposition, during the summer holidays of 1921, when he was between seventeen and eighteen years old. All the rest is inexact. I insist on this, because the astonishing thing about this infant prodigy is his lack of abnormality. Rimbaud can be explained to a certain degree by the nightmares and fairy-tales of childhood. One wonders where this starry conjuror puts his hands. Radiguet works in full daylight, with his sleeves rolled up.

Rimbaud corresponds completely to the dramatically dazzling and summary notion which most people have of genius. Radiguet had the good luck to be born after the epoch in which lightning was at the beck and call of too much insipid daylight. He may therefore cause surprise by his platitude and by the calm of a genius which resembles the best kind of talent.

You will have guessed what it is I am praising in the course of this encomium : a straight line, which I am surrounding with zigzag praise.

Do you see it, this lovely straight line which hypnotizes hens, but which wakes me up? The martyrs of the 'accursed' literature, described by Verlaine, are going to enable us to loop the loop, and, like Charlie Chaplin in the cinema, to reach several different kinds of publics simultaneously for different reasons. *Le Diable au Corps* gives me pleasure, without any reservations at all, and also appeals to typists. Therefore I hail it, along with the heavy sales of *Ouvert la Nuit*, as being one of the first true signs of a reconciliation.

Do not imagine that those who think like us are numerous. The conventions of scandal (Rimbaud would call it that 'old itch') still prevent people from admitting that, in the age in which we live, anarchy may reveal itself in the form of a dove.

Here you find me again on my tightrope. Already I hear even the friendliest voices saying : 'Take care. Radiguet is young, you will turn his head. Remember that the little chess champion, when playing at the "Rotonde", lost his tenth game owing to the photographers' magnesium flare.' There is no danger. Our young champion will not allow his head to be turned by photographers, for the muses have struck him with an inverted madness which is wisdom itself.

A future consisting entirely of colonnades would be depressing from an architectural point of view; but a goddess inhabits the temple. I mean poetry. And within this temple I should like my cosmopolitan friends to put up to her a painted statue, with great enamel eyes – something as terrible in its way as the war-god, with red feathers, in the British Museum. For poetry, as I (and here

I think I may say *we*) understand her, is not what the neo-classics imagine her to be. She authorizes me to praise with impunity, and simultaneously, the Comtesse de Noailles and Tristan Tzara. Poetry is an electric fluid, which both these writers transmit to me. The shape of the lamps and the shades is quite another question.

*

Do not imagine that I neglect either the lamp or the shade. The time has come for me to see to this. It alarms me to see that the shape of an apparatus which works, and that of one which does not, are both equally admired. Here we have a fresh aspect of novelty.

Unfortunately, 'La fille de Minos et de Pasiphaé' of Racine will always appear more beautiful than 'La servante au grand coeur dont vous étiez jalouse' of Baudelaire.

But, while I dislike verse expressing 'an idea' ('à idée') (as an example of this kind of verse take Hugo's 'J'ai mis un bonnet rouge au vieux dictionnaire'; I do not say Baudelaire's verse is of this kind, as there the sense is wedded to the form), nothing could be worse than melodious verse. The public likes melodious verse and melodious prose. If a newspaper opens an inquiry as to which is Renan's finest phrase, all the answers quote the most melodious ones. If I had a voice in a plebiscite of this sort I should say: 'When Renan's thought moves me, it is then that his phrase is a fine one.'

The beautiful French language does not unwind itself, or flow like Italian. It dovetails into itself. Whether it be the language of Benjamin Constant, Stendhal, Mme de La Fayette, Montaigne, Pascal, Montesquieu, Rimbaud or Mallarmé, it is always light, compact, starlike, and tightly packed like a snowball.

All ready-made notions about poetry, its music and its images, are grotesque. Poetry is a card-trick performed by the soul. It dwells in unstable equilibria and divine puns. In certain poems by Max Jacob I can touch it, as if it were an animal which had never allowed anyone to come near it before.

In *Les Mariés de la Tour Eiffel* I provided poetry with a powerful transmitter, adapted to theatrical presentation. In this piece I claim to have shown for the first time – in spite of an absolute and universal failure, even on the part of my admirers, to grasp what I was aiming at – a true poetry in terms of the theatre; for poetry merely transferred to the theatre is a mistake; it is like a piece of fine lace seen from a distance. My rope-lace was incomprehensible. People saw in it, and applauded, a farce, a satire, but nothing which I had intended. For I suppress all imagery and subtleties of language. Nothing remains but poetry – that is to say, to modern ears, nothing at all. Anglo-Saxons think *Les Mariés* is nonsense.

Why should we be unduly surprised if new beauty is invisible? Max Jacob wrote to me this summer : 'You complain of the difficulty of your work, and congratulate yourself on having an angel who has been helping you these last four days. Take care. Be suspicious of angels; they are often devils in disguise.'

This is very true. I, who have so much difficulty in writing, felt then I was inspired. My work, however, was just fit for the fire.

We are worried when we cannot make comparisons. Our whole system of pleasures is based on comparisons. If we are satisfied with our own work, it is probable that it bears some resemblance to other works with which we are preoccupied. But if we produce something really new, as this novelty is not based on any definite recollection, it leaves us as it were, with one leg in the air, alone in the world. We are as much disconcerted and disappointed by it as the reader will be.

According to the period, it will seem either barbarous or insipid. Our eye judges severely this bald baby which is not at all our ideal of what offspring should be. It is extremely difficult to approve oneself against one's own inclination.

Listen to the picture dealers selling a picture : 'This Picasso might be a Giotto. This Giotto might be a Picasso. This Renoir might be a Watteau. This Watteau might be a Renoir. This Cézanne a Greco. This Greco a Cézanne. This Goya a Manet. This Manet a Goya.'

For the critics, a masterpiece is a work which can be compared to something else, and which has an air of being a masterpiece. Now a masterpiece can never look like a masterpiece. It must necessarily be bandy-legged, incomplete and full of defects, since it is the triumph of its errors and the consecration of its faults that make it a masterpiece. It is not because of its family likeness to *Adolphe* that I admire *Le Diable au Corps*, but for just those reasons for which it is blamed by the critics.

Picasso will enter the Louvre with a cubist picture. All of us, however, like the sailor in the story, have a parrot on our left shoulder and a monkey on our right. When Picasso reminds us of Ingres or Corot, our parrot sings. But the features in which he is furthest removed from them make our monkey angry. Kill the brutes.

Here I will ask you to let me tell you a story about some motorists in China. The car has broken down in a Chinese village, with a small hole in the petrol-tank. An artist is discovered who cannot repair the tank, but who will copy it in a couple of hours. The motorists start off again with a superb new tank. In the middle of the night another breakdown. The Chinaman had copied the hole as well!

Gentlemen, do not imagine that I advocate going backwards, or that I advise copying the hole. The purity which I proclaim will appear, alas! sadly impure, the peace I proclaim, sadly lame, and my Parthenon sadly awry.

But the face of the world changes, and Cleopatra's nose with it.

# Letter to Americans

The *Letter to Americans* (Lettre aux Américains) was written in 1949 in the plane that brought Cocteau back to France after a short stay in New York. Apart from his surface flattery, Cocteau makes a serious plea to the Americans to play their part in the world of culture, to concern themselves with the freedom of the mind rather than with material success.

The interesting aspect of this essay is that Cocteau spent time and thought in his analysis of the American way of life. In contrast, his brief visits to Britain produced little comment about the British character. The Americans seem to have given him more scope to indulge his love of paradox.

□□□□□

Americans,

I'm writing to you from the plane taking me back to France. I've spent twenty days in New York and I've done so much and seen so many people that I can hardly calculate whether the time I spent with you was twenty days or twenty years. You'll tell me that you can't judge a country by one town, the United States by New York, and that my stay was too short for me to dare do so. But sometimes our first glance at a face can tell us more about it than a prolonged study. Sometimes in the long run we become confused about a person, we revise the first impression and the second impression deceives us. The third impression and what follows imply living completely with the person and as a result becoming a bad judge, for one can only judge well from the outside. If you live with people a confused substance forms, one in which the shapes of two personalities are mingled. Sometimes, too, a town that believes it gives a poor reflection of others can reflect even vast regions, with time variations, in such a way that night for some is day for others, and some are awake while others sleep. I mean that some are occupied with the absurd magnificence of dreams while others are in action and not dreaming. This induces, without anyone realizing it, the circulation of contrary waves which the soul records while the mind does not decipher them. It is none the less true that these waves circulate and work in an obscure way. It is possible that the New Yorkers' taste for a world that removes them from their own comes from this considerable tide of dreams and that the perpetual interrogation with which they counter it represents the defensive weapon, the wall, the dam which prevents them from being submerged.

For this attraction exercised by enigmas and this horror of enigmas are the big problem of the American mind.

In New York all is paradox. People demand something new and want nothing to change. The temporary failure with which all big enterprises start off remains incomprehensible to you and only appears in its final aspect. Success is essential for you – and this is the tragedy of the motion-picture industry, since all the muses know how to wait, must be painted and represented in waiting attitudes, grow younger in the end instead of ageing, and while painting, sculpture, music and poetry can wait and triumph belatedly after the death of the person who transmits them, a film cannot wait, costs too much to wait, and must be an instant mammoth success.

I shall mention these things again. For the moment I am relaxing to the rhythm of the propellers and that strange kingdom of the memories which inhabit us. They move like grasses under the sea and each time they touch each other they take other directions.

New York is not a city that sits down. It's not a city that lies down. New York's a city that stands up, and not because of the sky-scrapers where figures (which devour New York) have established their ant-hill. I'm speaking of a city that stands up, because if it sat down it would rest and reflect, and because, if it lay down it would sleep and dream, and it doesn't want either to reflect or dream, but to divide itself, standing up, between its mother's two breasts, one giving it alcohol and the other milk. It wants to remain standing, forget (what?), forget itself, exhaust itself, escape, through fatigue and the imperceptible swaying of the people who drink and the sky-scrapers with their motionless bases and undulating tops, escape, I say, the interrogation you are afraid to conduct on yourselves and to which you continually subject other people.

Man is inhabited by a darkness, by monsters from the depths. He cannot go down into them, but occasionally night-time despatches somewhat terrifying ambassadors, through poets. These ambassadors intrigue you. They attract you and repel you. You try to understand their language and, since you don't understand it, you ask poets to translate it for you. Alas, poets don't understand it either and content themselves with being the humble servants of these ambassadors, the mediums and individual phantoms which haunt you, disturb you and which you would love to organize.

New York detests *secrecy*. It concerns itself with that of others!

It no longer calls its own anything but *Boredom* and exorcizes it by a means of optimism.

New York is an open, wide-open city. Arms are open there, faces are open, hearts are open, open are the streets, the doors, the windows. The result is euphoria for the visitor and a draught in which ideas cannot mature, and whirl about like dead leaves.*

I say it again. You refuse to wait and to keep people waiting. In New York everyone arrives for appointments ahead of time. Tradition revolts you and so does novelty. Your ideal would be *an instant tradition*. Novelty is studied immediately. From that moment it ceases to be novel. You classify it, you label it and, since you don't admit that an artist should make experiments, you demand of him to repeat himself and you replace him when he tires you.

In this way at the Museum of Modern Art I saw an unforgettable sight. In a nice clean nursery fifty little girls were painting on tables covered with brushes, inks, tubes and gouache. As they painted they were looking somewhere else, sticking their tongues out like clever animals striking bells, their tongues protruding and their gaze remote. Nurses were supervising these young creators of abstract art, and would tap them on the hand if by misfortune their painting inclined dangerously towards realism. Mothers (who had remained at the Picasso stage) were not allowed in. In the galleries, alongside masterpieces by Rousseau, Matisse, Picasso, Braque, Bonnard and Vuillard, they hang our young people's dirty linen, our ink blots and wine stains on the old tablecloths from La Rotonde and Le Dôme. For New York is a tall giraffe, spotted with windows, laden with relics.

How can one convey to this youthful note-taking crowd that audacity does not necessarily wear the attributes of audacity, that it is only a spirit of revolt and that we must now contradict ourselves and sidetrack youth once more by new audacities, which youth regards as retrograde steps.

I look at a lady on my right who is dozing, her face held in a beard of orchids. *Life* Magazine is open on her knees. I think it is one of the largest circulation publications in the United States. And as I close my eyes in my turn I see again my Sunday and Sunday night. *Life* Magazine had asked if they could take eccentric photographs of me. When I told the journalists that neither my age nor my job as poet (that is to say workman) allowed me to let people take eccentric photographs of me, they said it was usual and

* No trees in New York. Trees look suspiciously as though they are dreaming.

that their readers were only interested in that kind of photograph. Since I was the guest of New York I therefore yielded to their request and suggested some themes likely to satisfy them and only likely to compromise me so far as I allow myself to be compromised.

We worked from three in the afternoon to seven. I dined with Jacques Maritain. We worked again from eleven o'clock until five in the morning. About two o'clock there was a break. Sandwiches and ginger ale. It was then that the journalists from *Life* said this surprising thing to me : 'What will a man at the barber's, looking at *Life* Magazine in the far reaches of Massachusetts, make of these photographs? Don't you think they'll disconcert him?' 'But,' I replied, 'these eccentricities don't come from me. They come from you.' Anxiety alternated with the conviction that photographs of this sort were the only ones valid. They then raised the serious problem of the text, asking me how one could explain the inexplicable. I suggested they should say the photographs they had taken were very normal, that the camera had played a trick on them, that they apologize to the public for this, that machines were becoming dangerous in the same way as men. Add, I told them, some publicity for Rolliflex. For example : Rolliflex thinks.

This anecdote is typical of the American paradox. In your country one continually finds oneself face to face with audacity and the fear of audacity. It reaches such a point that in your theatres passion must be sick, curable or, if not, should appear with an excuse and be finally punished. Passion must result from disorder provoked by madness or alcohol. In films, imagination should be put down to dream. And if a man goes to sleep at the start of the film and wakes up at the end, the film-maker can let himself go to any lengths anywhere.

If you need excuses, are you then guilty? Do you recognize yourselves as guilty? Your censorship is subject to the strange psychosis of the *bed* as a shameful piece of furniture, representing love and dream, the two things that haunt you, the two things that frighten you; this censorship reproaches me over the scene between the son and the mother in my film *Les Parents Terribles*; aren't you ashamed, you, noble people, of an unworthy thought, don't you feel the repression that forces you to interpret kindness and innocence so badly?

You deify Van Gogh and I approve of you.

But wasn't Van Gogh the typical example of the artist dying in poverty? What New York despises most.

In that you follow the rest of the globe, for if Joan of Arc had not been burnt she wouldn't be a heroine and people couldn't make films about her.

I write 'you', and it's not you, American people, that I'm
talking about. I'm talking about those who have money, fear risk
and lose face because in the long run only risk is worthwhile. I'm
talking about the world of money and immediate returns. I'm
talking about the gold curtain which is as hard as the iron curtain,
the curtain of gold which separates the United States from the
United States, the United States from Europe.

The New York public is the best in the world. I've seen them
eager, attentive, laughing, enthusiastic, not going at the end and
acclaiming the artists who please them. But the producer despises
this public. He declares them incapable of understanding lofty
works and believes it is essential to present them with base ones.
If the work he is presenting to the public is lofty he cuts it,
improves it, upsets it, lowers it, he tries to bring it down to the
level of a public whom he judges at his own level and which
doesn't exist. True, the public can sometimes be wrong. They have
been taken in for a long time and have their excuses. No attempt
is made to educate them. But this public, relying on instinct, may
not be wrong and the producer pays dearly for his extremely
malicious behaviour.

In Hollywood, after interminable discussions and in spite of his
repugnance about composing music for a film, Stravinsky was
about to reach agreement with Mr G.... Mr G... declared that
he would also have to pay the arranger. 'What arranger?' asked
Stravinsky. 'The one who will arrange your music.'

This habit of arranging everything is your method. On no
account should a work remain what it is. Hollywood is the origin
of this phenomenon. A phenomenon which is explained by the
thin blood of a film aristocracy (technicians and artists) whose
kingdom no longer communicates with the outside world and
whose line is dying out.

This aristocracy whose blood is becoming very thin drives out
those heads whose crowns are too mysterious. Greta Garbo and
Charles Chaplin were the admirable victims of this imperialist
beehive.

Americans, human dignity is at stake. Be what you are. A nation
which has preserved its childhood. A young and honest nation. A
nation where the sap runs. Relax. Question others less and yourselves more. Entrust yourselves to your friends. Don't be satisfied
with those meetings where you exchange alcoholic drinks without
saying anything to each other. Don't exhaust yourself in fruitless
activities. Don't abandon yourself to the deadly bewilderment of

radio and television. Television helps the mind to stop chewing, to swallow soft, predigested food. The mind has strong teeth. Chew things with those strong teeth. Don't let them be merely ornaments for the smiles of the stars.

I know what you're going to reply: 'What business is it of yours, man of old Europe?' I know that it's ridiculous to preach when I deserve to be preached to. I know my own faults better than I know yours. But in our country there's still a kind of disorder which makes birth and surprises possible, a compost-heap in which our cock sinks its claws; this must not be confused with a rubbish-heap – a fatal misapprehension, of which our government has almost always been guilty.

I realize that we live in a farmyard and you live in a bathroom. But tell me, isn't it pleasant for the man who lives in a farmyard to see a bathroom, and for the man who lives in a bathroom to see a farmyard? There is one basis for exchange. That is what I dream of, I, the man from the old French farmyard, I, the artisan who manufactures his object with his hands and carries it, under his arm, into your city.

And tell me, shouldn't you despecialize yourselves a little and teach us your specialist methods? Shouldn't you entrust us with your machines to see if we could humanize them, and humanize yourselves by reducing the prerogatives of your machines, in short tame our individualism and stir up yours, in order to make us all rebel against false moralities and bad habits, marching hand in hand?

Richard Wright spoke to the French a few days ago, and the things he said aren't pleasant for anyone to hear. I know that Bible trumpet, that trumpet dear to black people. When Louis Armstrong puts it to his lips the sound rises into an angel's cry. What does this cry mean? What I'm trying to tell you. What emerges from my visit to New York. A cry of anguish and love.

And in my words there is possibly a selfish fear and something resembling an instinct of self-preservation. For the fate of us French people is linked to yours, and if the values which threaten you triumph, we're lost along with you.

Americans, neither the confessors nor the psychiatrists of New York can suffice to give us a clear conscience. The man who confesses and sins and confesses, and the man who tells everything to the psychiatrist and feels secure in his freedom and then lumbers himself with complexes again and goes to tell everything again, each forces himself into a world which drives him out.

Neither confession nor psychoanalysis should be looked upon as a form of comfort. It's an insult to the priests and psychiatrists and a waste of their time. I pity those countless people who have treatment for the sake of treatment and refuse to get better.

I don't have much faith in your statistics. Did anyone among you expect to see President Truman re-elected, the day before it happened? And aren't the Kinsey Report interviewers the poor man's psychiatrists, to whom you can all tell everything, vaunt yourselves, invent yourselves, invent a free self, decked out with imaginary vices, as happens when there is a crime in New York, Chicago or San Francisco and a thousand people confess to it?

Americans,

Admit that superfluity lightens the mind. Luxury is a noble virtue which must not be confused with comfort. You have comfort. You need luxury. And don't tell me that money has anything to do with it. The luxury I'm talking about has nothing to do with money. It can't be bought. It is the reward of those who are not afraid of discomfort. It commits us vis-à-vis ourselves. It is the nourishment of the soul. It makes a young man wake up in the morning with a profound malaise and without a shadow of bitterness or disgust.

Americans,

I must now express my gratitude to you. New York has received me better than a guest, it has received me like a friend. The moment I set foot in the city I felt that lightness of air where the sky-scrapers drape their tulle, set up their beehives from which flows the golden honey. I repeat, everything is wide-open in New York. Don't tell me it's because New York hasn't 'suffered' (that's a polite remark). Suffering never made anyone more beautiful. The French have not been beautified by it, and since our wounds are ugly they will grow scars. No. Your graciousness comes naturally. Never, in my contacts with the most diverse kinds of milieux, have I heard a man speak ill of his neighbour. Slander does not exist in New York, and if it exists, it does not parade itself.

By day, the sky of New York is maritime. Wind, snow, sunshine and blue sky alternate at full speed. You die of cold or heat. At night Broadway is like a woman covered with jewellery and racked by nervous tics. Your street is blocked with yellow taxis and their electric diadems follow each other so closely they almost touch and form a slow cortège, bathed in the mysterious vapours which rise like incense from the ground. The other evening I was contemplating your nocturnal city as I drove, inch by inch, to the cinema where I was presenting my film *L'Aigle à Deux Têtes*. I was hoping that the hold-ups along the road would increase. You had reasons for disliking me. The play, adapted in England, transformed in the U.S., staged hastily and badly, cut by actors who were trying to save the production and do not know that if you cut something you lengthen it, had failed in New York.

My English is too poor to express the difficult nuances forced upon me by my profession. I therefore had to go on to the stage and speak French. I invited Jean-Pierre Aumont to help me by coming along and translating for me. From the first moment I no longer felt any scrap of embarrassment. The audience carried me and carried me away. They guessed the meaning of the sentences in such a curious fashion that their applause rendered the translator useless. Sometimes I asked Jean-Pierre to translate me. He replied, 'It's not necessary.' The audience laughed. An American shouted 'Yes, yes, translate!' and a Frenchwoman translated from her seat. The atmosphere was one we would always like to have in France where the élite among the audience remains on its guard and is afraid of being laughed at.

*

Americans,

You are within an inch of understanding what Europe understands no longer. Everything predisposes you to it and my visit to New York proves to me that you are walking endlessly up and down in front of that rice-paper wall. So little is needed for the miracle to be accomplished, for your love of enigmas to push you into piercing the wall that is so thin and so subtle!

Then, you would no longer ask questions and you would say to yourselves, 'So that was what it was!' and you would laugh – and your laugh would astonish the Old World and the atomic bomb would seem childish alongside this childish laughter.

Nietzsche said this: Thoughts that come with doves' footsteps guide the world. An explosive, however atrocious it is, is only a little thing in comparison to our concealed bombs which explode in the heart. Take an example from the oriental races which are oppressed because they refuse to participate in the pact with the devil, in the bewilderment of figures which deceive men, since two and two do not make four; without invoking the 'two and two make five' of the poets, I invite businessmen to meditate on the 'two and two make twenty-two', the emblem of the Rothschilds.

Americans,

You brush against the real world. Your sects, your clandestine religions, your ghosts, your feverishness, your anguish, your anxiety, your crimes, and even your fear of Harlem with its beautiful dances, tell me of your desire. And you're ashamed of it. And you conceal it. And you go and sniff at it in confused shows which you keep going in secret.

I've seen you, Americans, leaving your seats at the end of Tennessee Williams' *Streetcar Named Desire,* ashamed and overwhelmed, I've observed you from the corner of my eye, imagining your wives and daughters lying in the arms of the extraordinary actor Marlon Brando. I've seen you seeking nourishment in front of the magnificent mortal sins of Picasso. I've seen you, Americans, letting your masks fall and readjusting them by machine, in the same way as records are released in your street-bars. One day, if you admit this automatism, you will order your dinner in one of those bars, you'll pay for it, someone else will eat it for you and you'll be nourished without having to chew the meat. This will be the end of your world – the end of ours – the end of the world that centuries have torn out of nothingness.

Americans,

Your role is to save the Old World, so hard, so tender, the world which loves you and which you love. Your role is to save the dignity of man. Your role is to combat and not to permit. Your role is to help with all your vast strength the few heroes who bleed the white blood of the soul and the red blood that others are freezing in your veins. Your role is to conquer the living death which is walking down the steps of the world with the evil coldness of that toy made from a spring which you play with, making it go down the stairs in your houses.

To do this you will have to shake yourselves, wake up, come to consciousness. You will have to consider art no longer as a distraction but as a priesthood. You must convince yourselves that the artist finds first and searches afterwards. If you reach this stage, if you shake off *the yoke of being too free,* you will then be beyond boredom and you will laugh at its sorry face. You will say to yourselves : So it was that sorry face that frightened me, weighed me down and filled me with emptiness. And you will name it, and because you name it, it will no longer have any hold over you.

And you will pierce the wall that separated you from the enigmas and, as you inhabit the enigmas, they will become familiar to you and you will no longer fear them, no longer court them, and you will possess them as you wish, without any need to interrogate the sphinx.

Americans,

It's my feelings of affection which address these lines to you. It's my gratitude for your welcome which begs you to take care and not read them half-heartedly, not confuse them with a newspaper article, the work of an aesthete. Not to read them while your radio is broadcasting a programme of music with the title 'Music to Read By'.

The plane's going through the aurora borealis. The air hostess is telling us about it. But I'm not looking away from the lines I'm writing, for the aurora borealis I'm hoping for is more important than the aurora borealis in the sky.

Americans,

Listen to the few men of Europe whose words have the power of deeds. Don't reproach me for my insolence. In particular I direct this insolence against my own person and I seek no excuse for the mistakes I've made and won't make again.

The only thing I'm proud of is that I'm no longer absent-minded. I devour what I look at and remember the details of it. Sin against the mind is lack of precision in words. It's the sin propagated by the press of today which believes in the efficacy of lying, just as stupid people believe that intelligence demands unkindness, that kindness is synonymous with stupidity, whereas the surprising kindness of intelligence always triumphs over the conventional intelligence of unkindness.

This is the only point on which I allow myself to give you advice. The only point on which my experience is wide and long. The only point where malice could not possibly reach me, since it is mistaken about me and torments a counterfeit effigy of me which cannot do me any harm whatever.

Pay attention, Americans. I mean, be attentive in a less scholastic fashion. Pay attention to the profound shape of beings more than to the enterprises which reveal the fragments of them to you. Our actions are only valid through the continuity, the stages which provoke them. It is natural that the few very rare manifestations of ours which reach you lead you to take us for weathercocks. This is the fault of badly organized exchanges, clumsy translations, the blank steppes which in your eyes must extend between one of our works and another, after they have reached you without any link between them and like the wreckage of a ship.

The fact that you attach some price to these pieces of wreckage is enough to explain to you our appreciation and our astonishment when you succeed in recognizing the shape of a maritime accessory.

It's not your attention I'm asking for, then, but your help, so that the going and coming between our people should become less insoluble, and rather than giving your attention I ask you to attract that of your leaders to the importance of organizing a free road where culture is not shattered against the obstacle of Customs and exchange control.

France is interested only in your books, to the extent of reading with passionate attention the writers of whom you think little, and I know people in New York unaware of recent American fashions which are already current among us. Do the same for us in return. Don't let the obstacle grow thicker and don't be content with a whiff of France through a rapid visit like mine. Book sales in your country are low. Very well. And what about our country? Yet your books and your poets circulate in France, translated everywhere.

It is a fact that our true literature is a form of chamber music, a secret music suitable for passing to each other under the table. It is true that your enterprises of the same order find it extremely difficult to materialize and the U.S. can more easily find billions to organize a great catastrophe than the little sum which would make a true birth possible. It is true that beauty in all its forms remains accursed and slips in surreptitiously, while things which last don't come into the world with the ease of things that don't. But you are the people who consecrate the dangerous enterprises of Europe. Your power is without limits. My last request therefore is to ask you to pay attention to novelty which has not proved itself, and, since you hang on the walls of your museums the wonderful stupidities we perpetrated when we were twenty, I ask you to allow our recent wonderful stupidities to slip into the U.S. on the feet of doves, which Nietzsche opposes to the din of troops and guns.

Americans,

I saw the first films. I heard the first gramophones. With Roland Garros I did the first air stunts. Since then, apart from the atom, progress has replaced invention. Everything's changing. A world is going to end. A world is beginning. You can decide whether it will be darkness or light. There is not a moment to lose.

What is the nightmare of your city, its waking dream, I ask you? The atomic bomb. It exists and you don't want it to exist. It's no more talked about among you than the rope is mentioned in the hanged man's house. And since you need excuses to justify its existence, you unconsciously descend this contemporary slope towards dead thought. This is the reason for the success in New York of the ballet, where gesticulation attempts to replace words. For if thought were dead, explosives would only destroy nothingness and would no longer kill anything.

I don't admire a race as a race. A race is neither bad nor good. I only like a race if it is oppressed. For, even if it is vast, an oppressed race becomes a minority. Now, for me, a minority will always win over a majority, since a majority oppresses a minority because of some superiority over it and because of remorse that this minority makes it feel.

A race which oppresses another is detestable. If the oppressed race begins to oppress in its turn, it will become detestable to me. Don't you know that we are perpetually on the wrong side of the barricade, we minority-supporters from old Europe, and that this wrong side wins in the end, something which upsets you, you who are in love with achievement and success and want to live in the present?

You will be saved neither by arms nor money. You will be saved by the minority of those who think. Through your secret minds, through your low incomes, through your madness which is epitomized by Edgar Allan Poe, in short through your poets, whatever ink they use, and your film industry is not the least important of your inks, an ink made of light which false moralities dilute with water and prevent from spreading.

Everywhere in America there is a vibrant minority which finds itself the prisoner of artificial liberty.

Only a stroke of luck is needed for your complexes, your Protestant reserve and your fears to evaporate, for your mind to blossom and multiply, to explode wildly with the giant eroticism of your Southern countryside.

Don't forget, the rhythm of the world is like your breathing, its lungs alternately dilate and contract. We are victims of a period when lungs are empty. The world is breathing out, expiring. It no longer thinks, it un-thinks. Its breath destroys its crops. Wait for it to fill its lungs again.

*

I have often written that the spirit of creation is nothing more than the spirit of contradiction in its highest form. In fact, a great work opposes the preceding work and contradicts it – which does not prevent this preceding work from living, breathing, taking root and flowering when it is due to. And so on. We should remember continually that Hebrew proverb : 'Equilibrium produces inertia. Lack of equilibrium produces exchanges.'

It is the secret of the most famous examples of architecture. Those of Versailles, Venice, Amsterdam. The plumb-line has killed the human life of façades which offered the unequal and delightful spectacle of a face. Each one was expressive and was divinely lop-sided.

There is great danger in wanting order and not putting into operation a type of disorder in which the mind can somehow discover what to do instead of drying up in lifeless straight lines.

In the country I came across an old copy of the Goncourt *Journal*. I opened it and found this note : 'A friend arrives from New York and gives us a piece of news which we dare not believe and which would be the end of everything. *The washbasins are fixed to the walls.*' At the time such a remark causes laughter. Later we think about it and we begin to fear that some of our misfortunes are due to this.

\*

... In the past people brought us water, light, food, we had no need to move. We were free not to leave our armchair and our book. Servants were countless and gracious. Everyone found what he needed. But servants have disappeared. Machinery has supplanted them. The faucet has killed the water-carrier. And there lies the drama. If faucets work well in America, they work very badly in France.

Our weakness therefore is our envy and imitation of disciplined, ordered nations. Our strength is in the fact that we admit our lack of discipline and our disorder and draw strength from it.

\*

The Earth must be much younger than people usually think and those who like to destroy or construct still have lots of time to invent strophes and catastrophes.

The Earth seems old to us. It must be sixteen years old in comparison to the length of a man's life. It is the age of fighting and playing games in school playgrounds. At the time of Ancient Egypt the Earth was no doubt at the age of making sandcastles by the seaside. At the time of the Greek philosophers it was at the age when we question our parents. Our good fortune will be in not living on Earth when it has reached the age of reason. It's the dreariest age.

I know very well that it's tedious to live during dangerous periods. I'm not naïve enough to believe that the age of wars is over, that the world can count on living hand in hand. And it's nobody's fault. Responsibility in this order of things is still a way of reassuring oneself and nourishing one's pride. When men fight they follow the example of animals, plants and microbes. But I regret the tendency to fear that one war will follow another. This fear is fatal to the enterprises which honour a globe dishonoured by war. It serves as an excuse for laziness and many people say to themselves: What's the use of working and creating since destruction is coming?

I admire your optimism. My pessimism is only a form of optimism. I would like things to happen differently from the way they do and I find myself weeping over ruins. Then I think that the ruins have great and surprising beauty and stimulate men in some unexpected direction within art. Cities in solid gold must sleep beneath the sands. The early ages are perhaps the last vestiges of highly developed civilizations. Let us accustom ourselves to becoming modest before this incomprehensible mechanism, and since we cannot use the angels' ladder, let us resign ourselves to our own ladder, we owe it to ourselves to climb to the very top.

It is very odd, moreover, to talk of decadence on an Earth which is the result of decadence. In fact light comes only from decay. As soon as a star reaches the end of the nebulae stage (when it ages in some way), it decays and catches fire. When the fire dies down low, the star scars over. It becomes decadent and life forms. It seethes with vermin : us.

\*

I speak to you as one of the last free men, free with all that this entails of solitude and lack of electors. I cannot aspire to the support of any group, any school, any church, any party. My platform is in this ether which the plane's propellers are ravaging, a platform surrounded with cruel stars and sleeping people who all have a milieu and an opinion. I have neither opinion nor milieu. I address myself always to those who try desperately to be free and who, like me, must expect slaps from everywhere, to the point of asking themselves, when they receive compliments, if they have not been guilty of some error.

Americans,

I'm going to try to sleep and dream. I like to live my dreams and forget them when I wake. For I inhabit a world where there is still no supervision. It *will* exist if your slope is lengthened. Your dreams will be supervised – and it won't be the supervision of psychiatrists, it will be that of the police. Your dreams will be examined and punished. Acts of dream will be punished.

Goodnight.

Of all the mental escape-routes discovered by man opium has the longest and most respectable history. Its use is probably as old as civilization itself and much attention has been given in recent years to its effect on the creative imagination. In the 1920s opium smoking was fashionable in certain European circles. As far back as 1913 Louis Laloy, the French musicologist, had written his influential *Livre de la Fumée* which Cocteau naturally read. He probably began to smoke under Laloy's influence in 1924, when he was going through a period of depression following the death of Raymond Radiguet. Four years later he was still smoking, had persuaded his new lover, Jean Desbordes, to smoke also, but then decided he would stop, under medical supervision. Prolonged smoking had made him weak and ill. He wrote *Opium* during the winter of 1928-9 in a Paris clinic, where his treatment was paid for by Gabrielle ('Coco') Chanel, and dedicated the book to Jean Desbordes. It was published in 1930.

Cocteau's *Opium* is of course about Cocteau, and only incidentally does it describe the delights of the addicted and the miseries of the cured. About opium itself Cocteau does not discover a great deal that is new, either from a scientific or a personal angle. Many of his remarks naturally appear paradoxical and unexpected, even if Thomas De Quincey, writing a hundred years earlier, had in several cases reached the same conclusions. Cocteau's methods form an interesting contrast to those of his predecessor, who wrote several pages proving that the effects of alcohol were quite different from those of opium. Cocteau came to the same conclusion, but he needed only two sentences.

The value of Cocteau's remarks about opium lies obviously in the way he makes them, in that sad and splendid aphoristic turn of phrase that marks everything he writes. In one sense Cocteau lost the battle with opium; he could not give himself to it entirely, the cost was too great. The plea in this book that medicine should learn to make opium harmless rather than deal passively with its after-effects is that of an intelligent person. It is not original, and here again De Quincey in his rambling way had made the same suggestion in his book. But Cocteau's description of the actual cure, the stages in being 'weaned', as he says, from the milk of Paradise, has an undeniable value. This aspect of the journal contributes something that cannot be found in any medical treatise or in any of those flat, dull books whose authors try to communicate their experiences with drugs.

*Opium* is not easy reading, and it was not easy writing. If Cocteau had merely been making descriptive notes of how he felt from day to day it would still have required a considerable effort to write them; but along with physical change he was attempting to describe what can only be called spiritual adaptation. Elusive, subtle, changing from hour to hour, his thoughts and feelings needed clarifying, and this could only be done by writing them down. Many writers would have left only disembodied jottings which might have been a useful record but nothing more. Cocteau's journal is often staccato, obscure and without any apparent continuity. And yet, because it is written by Cocteau, it has the deeply hidden yet satisfying unity of a strange poetry. After two or three readings its themes, expressed in different keys and played at varying speeds, emerge in the simplicity of their original conception, while the orchestral *bravura* dies away.

There are other reasons why this *Journal of a Cure*, collection of notes though it is, occupies a place of its own in Cocteau's world. He regards *La Difficulté d'Etre* as the key to his house, yet *Opium* could be a useful guide-book. It stands on its own, at least as far as any of the autobiographical *poésie critique* does so, but amongst its own leaves lie tendrils which have grown across from other plants. It illustrates the vital interdependence of Cocteau's work and the degree to which one's enjoyment of his writing is increased and illuminated by knowing it thoroughly. In *Opium* he looks forward and backward, and we see just how closely he identifies himself with his work. There is the fascinating description of how *Les Enfants Terribles* came into being, how Jacques Chardonne urged him to write a full-length work, how the end of the book came into his head first, how a poem and a tune stimulated him. The novel was published just before these notes were written, and Cocteau says, 'My next work will be a film.' *Le Sang d'un Poète*, first shown in 1932, contains a mysterious but poetic version of the snowballing episode which is such an integral part of *Les Enfants Terribles* Then, in 1950, Cocteau created the striking film based on the novel itself. Going back once more, but forward in time from *Opium*, in

*Portraits-Souvenir* he describes the Cité Monthiers, Dargelos and the snowball fight once again. Thus scenes and incidents which occupy a central place in Cocteau's mythology appear in a novel, two films and at least two sections of the *Poésie Critique*, including *Opium*.

Cocteau's detractors have often remarked that the interdependence of his work is nothing more than an absence of self-discipline, a paucity of ideas and a tedious, interminable attempt to justify himself. This criticism is meaningless, for Cocteau's discipline is exercised in another realm. Justify himself he does, remaining strangely patient before a dense and unsympathetic public. Something of his supposed and his genuine attitude can be understood from the pages about *La Voix Humaine*, which was successfully produced at the Comédie Française while *Opium* was being written. In fairness to Cocteau it must be admitted that he works just as hard to explain his successes as his failures, although from his point of view this arbitrary division into black and white does not exist.

Since *Opium* is a microcosm of Cocteau, nearly all his favourite themes recur there, like a whole row of King Charles' heads. They range from the role of the poet as a seer, and the necessity for remaining in the deep creative sleep of poetry, to the fact that 'Victor Hugo was a madman who believed himself to be Victor Hugo', or the problems of realism in the theatre. The Cocteau enthusiast will be delighted to hear so many favourite stories again and to recognize that unmistakable voice saying quite seriously, 'I detest originality. I avoid it as much as possible.'

*Opium* could perhaps be recommended as an introduction to Cocteau's work in the sense that it appears to be about something, about opium. One can enjoy it without wishing to learn anything about that time-honoured nepenthe. If one already knows something about it then Cocteau adds his usual paradoxical illumination, his poet's interpretation. If one knows nothing about opium one will learn only a little. If one knows nothing about Cocteau, then one will want to know and read a great deal more.

*Opium* is not a long book, but its shorthand style makes for slow, concentrated reading. It has been much quoted, the moral and philosophical aphorisms are perpetually stimulating. Cocteau once wrote that attempts to shorten a work only lengthen it, and as usual his paradoxical statement is correct, for cuts tend to mean the addition of explanations. Here then is all that the book has to say about opium itself, and indirectly about Cocteau.

I became addicted to opium a second time in the following
circumstances.

To begin with, I could not have been thoroughly cured the first
time. Many courageous drug addicts do not know the pitfalls of
being cured, they are content merely to give up and emerge ravaged
by a useless ordeal, their cells weakened and further prevented from
regaining their vitality through alcohol and sport.

Incredible phenomena are attached to the cure; medicine is
powerless against them, beyond making the padded cell look like
an hotel room and demanding of the doctor or nurse patience,
attendance and sensitivity. I shall explain later that these
phenomena should be not those of an organism in a state of decomposition but on the contrary the uncommunicated symptoms of a
baby at the breast and of vegetables in spring.

A tree must suffer from the rising of its sap and not feel the
falling of its leaves.

*Le Sacre du Printemps* orchestrates a cure with a scrupulous
precision of which Stravinsky is not even aware.

I therefore became an opium addict again because the doctors
who cure – one should really say, quite simply, who purge – do not
seek to cure the troubles which first cause the addiction; I had
found again my unbalanced state of mind; and I preferred an
artificial equilibrium to no equilibrium at all. This moral disguise
is more misleading than a disordered appearance : it is human,
almost feminine, to have recourse to it.

I became addicted with caution and under medical supervision.
There *are* doctors capable of pity. I never exceeded ten pipes. I
smoked them at the rate of three in the morning (at nine o'clock),
four in the afternoon (at five o'clock), three in the evening (at
eleven o'clock). I believed that, in this way, I was reducing the
chances of addiction. With opium I suckled new cells, which were
restored to the world after five months of abstinence, and I suckled
them with countless unknown alkaloids, whereas a morphine addict,
whose habits frighten me, fills his veins with a single known poison
and surrenders himself far less to the unknown.

*

I am writing these lines after twelve days and twelve nights
without sleep. I leave to the drawings the task of expressing the

tortures inflicted by medical impotence on those who drive out a
remedy which is in process of becoming a despot.

*

Opium leads the organism towards death in euphoric mood. The
tortures arise from the process of returning to life against one's
will. A whole springtime excites the veins to madness, bringing
with it ice and fiery lava.

I recommend the patient who has been deprived for eight days
to bury his head in his arm, to glue his ear to that arm, and wait.
Catastrophe, riots, factories blowing up, armies in flight, flood – the
ear can detect a whole apocalypse in the starry night of the human
body.

*

Do not expect me to be a traitor. Of course opium remains
unique and the euphoria it induces superior to that of health. I owe
it my perfect hours. It is a pity that instead of perfecting curative
techniques, medicine does not try to render opium harmless.

But here we come back to the problem of progress. Is suffering
a regulation or a lyrical interlude?

It seems to me that on an earth so old, so wrinkled, so painted,
where so many compromises and laughable conventions are rife,
opium (if its harmful effects could be eliminated) would soften
people's manners and would cause more good than the fever of
activity causes harm.

My nurse says to me, 'You're the first patient I've seen writing
on the eighth day.'

I fully realize that I am planting a spoon in the soft tapioca of
my young cells, that I am delaying matters, but I am burning
myself up and will always do so. In two weeks, despite these notes,
I shall no longer believe in what I am experiencing now. One must
leave behind a trace of this journey which memory forgets. One
must, when this is impossible, write or draw without responding to
the romantic solicitations of pain, without enjoying suffering like
music, tying a pen to one's foot if need be, helping the doctors who
can learn nothing from laziness.

During an attack of neuritis one night, I asked B : 'You, who do
not practise and are up to your eyes in work at the Salpêtrière and
are preparing your thesis, why do you attend me at my home day
and night? I know doctors. You like me very much but you like
medicine more.' He replied that he had at last found a patient who

talked, that he learnt more from me, because I was capable of describing my symptoms, than at the Salpêtrière where the question 'Where does it hurt?' invariably brought the same reply : 'Don't know, doctor.'

\*

The reawakening of one's senses (the first clear symptom of recovery) is accompanied by sneezes, yawns, sniffling and tears. Another sign : the poultry in the hen-house opposite exasperated me and so did those pigeons which trot up and down the tin roof, their hands behind their backs. On the seventh day the crow of the cock pleased me. I am writing these notes between six and seven in the morning. With opium nothing exists before eleven o'clock.

\*

Clinics receive few opium addicts. It is rare for an opium addict to stop smoking. The nurses only know the counterfeit smokers, the elegant smokers, those who combine opium, alcohol, drugs, the setting (opium and alcohol are mortal enemies), or those who pass from the pipe to the syringe and from morphine to heroin. Of all drugs 'the drug' is the most subtle. The lungs absorb its smoke instantaneously. The effect of a pipe is immediate. I am speaking of the real smokers. The amateurs feel nothing, they wait for dreams and risk being seasick; because the effectiveness of opium is the result of a pact. If we fall under its spell, we shall never be able to give it up.

To moralize to an opium addict is like saying to Tristan : 'Kill Iseult. You will feel much better afterwards.'

\*

Opium cannot bear impatient addicts, bunglers. It moves away, leaving them morphine, heroin, suicide and death.

\*

If you hear someone say 'X has killed himself smoking opium', you should know that it is impossible, and that this death conceals something else.

\*

Certain organisms are born to become a prey to drugs. They demand a corrective, without which they can have no contact with the outside world. They float. They vegetate in the half-light. The world remains unreal, until some substance has given it body.

It does happen that these unfortunates can live without ever finding the slightest remedy. It does happen, too, that the remedy they find kills them.

It is a matter of luck when opium steadies them and provides these souls of cork with a diver's suit. For the harm done by opium will be less than that caused by other substances and less than the infirmity which they try to heal.

*

When I speak of young cells I am not speaking of nerve cells which are created once and for all and never change.

*

With a man, the awakening process of weaning manifests itself physiologically, but with a woman the symptoms are mainly psychological. With a man the drug does not put his heart to sleep, but his sexuality. With a woman it arouses her sexuality and puts her heart to sleep. On the eighteenth day of weaning a woman becomes tender and whimpers. That is why, in clinics for drug addicts, the female patients all appear to be in love with the doctor.

*

Tobacco is almost harmless. After combustion the nicotine disappears. It is customary to confuse nicotine, which is a white powder, with the kind of yellow paste produced by the pyrotechnical change in the combustible materials. It would take four or five big cigars a day to produce a heart-attack. Most of the notorious ravages of tobacco are spasmodic phenomena without real danger. They are exaggerated, as Michelet wondrously exaggerates the role of coffee.

*

Young Asia no longer smokes because 'grandfather smoked'. Young Europe smokes because 'grandfather did not smoke'. Since, alas, young Asia imitates young Europe, it is through us that opium will return to its starting-point.

*

A letter from H, who gave up opium on his own with unheard-of courage. I knew the effort was useless, I knew the confusion between giving up oneself and giving up the drug, and I expected pessimistic news after the first optimistic letters.
1. Too much exercise; 2. Recourse to alcohol (the letters just before the last); 3. (the last letter) The breakdown. 'I feel ill – how am I to describe it to you? – in my "great divide".' Do you recognize the great sympathetic nervous system, the terrible mountain chain of nerves, the armature of the soul?
If the organism rejects the drug, this is its last refuge. Drive opium off the ship, and it hides in the engine-room.

*

A car can massage organs which no masseur can reach. It is the only remedy for the disorders of the great sympathetic nervous system. The craving for opium can be endured in a car.
Clinics for addicts should have attached to them, in the first place, a medical masseur and electrical massage equipment. With hydrotherapy it is not the water from the shower which calms, but the spray. Baths can be upsetting, they drove me mad.

*

I remain convinced, despite my failures, that opium can be good and that it is entirely up to us to make it well disposed. We must know how to handle it. Nothing is worse than clumsiness on our part. A strict régime (laxatives, exercise, perspiration, rest-periods, care of the liver, keeping hours which do not encroach on one's night sleep) would permit the use of a remedy jeopardized by half-wits.
Let no one say to me : 'Habit forces the smoker to increase the dose.' One of the riddles of opium is that the smoker never has to increase his dose.

*

The drama of opium, as I see it, is none other than the drama of comfort and the lack of comfort. Comfort kills. Lack of comfort creates. I am speaking of the lack of both material and spiritual comfort.

To take opium without yielding to the absolute comfort which it offers is to escape, within the domain of the spirit, from the stupid worries of life which have nothing to do with the lack of comfort in the domain of the senses.

*

If a hermit lives in a state of ecstasy, his lack of comfort becomes the height of comfort. He must relinquish it.

*

There is in man a sort of fixative, that is to say, a sort of absurd feeling stronger than reason which allows him to think that the children who play are a race of dwarfs, instead of being a bunch of 'get out of there and leave room for me'.

Living is a horizontal fall.

Without this fixative any life perfectly and continually conscious of its speed would become intolerable. It enables the condemned man to sleep.

I lack this fixative. It is, I suppose, a diseased gland. Medicine takes this infirmity for an excess of conscience, for an intellectual advantage.

Everything convinces me of the functioning, in others, of this absurd fixative, as indispensable as habit, which conceals from us each day the horror of having to get up, shave, dress and eat. Even if it were only the photograph album, one of the most comical ways of turning a helter-skelter into a succession of solemn monuments.

Opium gave me this fixative. Without opium, plans, marriages and journeys appear to me just as foolish as if someone falling out of a window were to hope to make friends with the occupants of the room before which he passes.

*

The mortal boredom of the smoker who is cured! Everything one does in life, even love, occurs in an express train racing towards death. To smoke opium is to get out of the train while it is still moving. It is to concern oneself with something other than life or death.

*

If a smoker, damaged by the drug, questions himself sincerely, he will always find some fault for which he is paying and it turns opium against him.

*

The patience of a poppy. He who has smoked will smoke. Opium knows how to wait.

*

Opium chastens one's ambitions.

*

One of the wonders of opium is to transform instantaneously an unknown room into a room so familiar, so full of memories, that one thinks one has always occupied it. When addicts go away they suffer no hurt because of the certainty that the delicate mechanism will function in one minute, anywhere.

*

After five pipes an idea would become distorted, diffused slowly in the water of the body with all the noble whims of Chinese ink, foreshortened like a black diver.

*

A dressing-gown in holes, stained and burnt by cigarettes, gives the addict away.

An extraordinary photograph in a sensational magazine : the beheading of a Chinese rebel. The execution and the sword are still blurred like an electric fan as it stops. A spray of blood shoots out of the trunk, quite straight. The head, smiling, has fallen on to the rebel's knees, like the smoker's cigarette, without his noticing it.

He will notice it tomorrow by the bloodstain, like the addict by the burn.

*

One always speaks of the slavery of opium. The regularity it imposes on the passing hours is not only a discipline, it is also a liberation. Liberation from visits and from people sitting round in circles. I would add that opium is the opposite of the Pravaz syringe. It reassures. It reassures by reason of its luxury, its rites, the anti-medical elegance of its lamps, furnaces, pipes and the age-old perfection of this exquisite poisoning.

\*

Even without any spirit of proselytizing, it is impossible for a person who does not smoke to live with a person who does. Each would inhabit a different world. One of the few protections against a relapse will then be a sense of responsibility.

\*

For two months I have been discharging bile. The yellow race: bile implanted in the blood.

Opium is a decision to be taken. Our only error is wanting to smoke and to share the privileges of those who do not smoke. It is rare for an addict to forsake opium. Opium forsakes him, ruining everything. It is a substance which escapes analysis – living, capricious, capable of turning suddenly against the smoker. It is the barometer of a diseased sensibility. At times when the weather is humid, the pipe drips. If an addict goes to the seaside, the drug swells and refuses to burn. The approach of snow, a storm or the mistral, destroys its efficacy. Some noisy surroundings can take away all its virtues.

In short, there is no mistress more exacting than this drug which takes jealousy to the point of emasculating the addict.

\*

In preparing raw opium the alkaloids are combined quite haphazardly. It is impossible to foresee the consequences. By adding the dross one increases the chances of success, but risks destroying a masterpiece. It is the beat of a gong which breaks the melody. I do not recommend a drop of port or *fine champagne*. I recommend a litre of old red wine in the water where the raw pill is soaking, afterwards avoid bringing it to the boil, strain seven times and keep at it for eight days.

\*

If he takes care of himself, an addict who inhales twelve pipes a day all his life will not only be fortified against influenza, colds and sore throats, but will also be far less in danger than a man who drinks a glass of brandy or who smokes four cigars. I know people who have smoked one, three, seven, up to twelve pipes a day for forty years.

*

Some people will say to you : 'The discriminating throw away the dross.' Others : 'The discriminating make their boys smoke while they smoke only the dross.' If one questions a boy about the drug's dangers, 'Good drug make fat,' he replies. 'Dross make sick.'
The vice of opium-smoking is to smoke the dross.

*

Just as one must not confuse a cure and its typhoid-like convalescence with a suppression by means of various substitutes (physical exercise, walking, winter sports, cocaine or alcohol), so one must not confuse addiction with habit. Some people only smoke on Sundays. On Sundays they cannot do without the drug; that is habit. Addiction ruins the liver, affects the nervous cells, causes constipation, makes the temples like parchment and contracts the iris of the eye. Habit is a rhythm, a singular hunger which can upset the addict but causes him no harm.
The symptoms of the craving are of so strange a kind that they cannot be described. Only the nurses in clinics succeed in forming some impression. (The symptoms do not differ from serious ones.) Imagine that the earth is turning a little less fast, that the moon is coming a little closer.

*

A wheel is a wheel. Opium is opium. Every other luxury is mere ingenuity; as if man, not knowing the wheel, had made the first carriage, after the style of a horse, with mechanical legs.

*

Let us profit from insomnia to attempt the impossible : to describe the craving.
Byron said : 'Love cannot withstand seasickness.' Like love, like seasickness, the craving penetrates everywhere. Resistance is useless. At first a malaise, then things become worse. Imagine a silence equivalent to the crying of thousands of children whose mothers do

not return to give them the breast. The lover's anxiety transposed into nervous awareness. An absence which dominates, a negative despotism.

The phenomena become clearer. Flashes like moiré before the eyes, champagne in the veins, frozen siphons, cramps, sweating at the root of the hair, dryness in the mouth, sniffling, tears. Do not persist. Your courage is to no purpose. If you delay too long, you will no longer be able to take your equipment and roll your pipe. Smoke. Your body was waiting only for a sign. One pipe is enough.

*

It is easy to say: 'Opium arrests life, anaesthetizes. Well-being comes from a kind of death.'

Without opium I am cold, I catch cold, I do not feel hungry. I am impatient to impose what I invent. When I smoke, I am warm, I do not know what colds are, I am hungry, my impatience disappears. Doctors, reflect on this riddle!

*

Opium is the 'femme fatale', the pagodas, the lanterns! I do not have the strength to undeceive you. Since science does not know how to distinguish between the curative and the destructive properties of opium, I must yield to it. Never have I regretted more profoundly not having been a poet and a doctor, like Apollo.

*

We all carry within us something folded up like those Japanese flowers made of wood which unfold in water.

Opium plays the same role as the water. None of us carries the same kind of flower. It is possible that a person who does not smoke may never know the kind of flower that opium might have unfolded within him. One must not take opium too seriously.

About 1909 there were artists who smoked without talking about it and who no longer smoke. Many young couples smoke without anyone suspecting it; colonials smoke to combat fever and stop smoking when circumstances force them to stop. They then experience the discomforts of a heavy dose of influenza. Opium spares all these addicts because they did not and do not take it seriously.

Opium becomes serious to the extent to which it affects the nerve centres which control the soul. Otherwise, it is an antidote, a pleasure, an ultimate siesta.

The danger is smoking as a defence against some moral dis-equilibrium. Then it is difficult to approach the drug in the way it must be approached, as wild beasts should be approached – without fear.

*

Opium perpetuates itself across the centuries like the royal cubit. Helen of Troy knew recipes as long lost as the mysteries of the Great Pyramid. Gradually they are all brought together again: Ronsard tries the poppy in all its forms and tells us about it in an alarming poem. He knew a Helen : he no longer knew how to prepare the poppy.

*

I am not one of the cured who is proud of his effort. I am ashamed to have been expelled from that world, compared with which the world of health resembles those nauseating films in which ministers unveil statues.

*

It is hard to feel oneself dismissed by opium after several failures: it is hard to know that this magic carpet exists and that one will no longer fly on it; it was pleasant to buy it, as in the Baghdad of the caliphs, from the Chinese in a sordid street hung with washing; pleasant to return home quickly to try it out in one's hotel, in the room between the columns where George Sand and Chopin lived, to unroll it, stretch out on it, open the window on to the port, and take off. Undoubtedly too pleasant.

*

The addict becomes as one with the objects which surround him. His cigarette, a finger, falls from his hand.

*

The addict is surrounded with slopes. Impossible to keep the spirit on the heights. It is eleven o'clock in the evening. One smokes for five minutes; one looks at one's watch : it is five o'clock in the morning.

\*

Countless times the addict must return to his point of departure as the ball in the rifle-range returns to the trough. The slightest untimely noise blows the egg off the fountain.

\*

Grey matter and brown matter make the best harmony.
The addict's optimism is not a drunkard's optimism. It emulates the optimism of health.

\*

Picasso used to say to me : *The smell of opium is the least stupid smell in the world*. The only smell one can compare with it is that of a circus or a seaport.
Raw opium. If you do not shut it up in a metal chest but content yourself with a box, the black serpent will soon have crept out. Be warned ! It hugs the walls, goes down the stairs and the floors, turns, crosses the hall and the courtyard, passes through the archway and will soon coil itself round the policeman's neck.

\*

The slow speed of opium. Under the influence of opium one becomes the meeting-place for the phenomena which art sends to us from outside.
The addict can become a masterpiece. A masterpiece which is above discussion. A perfect masterpiece, because it is fugitive, without form and without judges.

\*

... Now the need for self-expression, for contact with the outside world, disappears with the hedonist.
He does not seek to create masterpieces, he seeks to become one himself, the most unknown, the most egotistical.
To say of an addict who is in a continual state of euphoria that he is degrading himself is like saying of marble that it is spoilt by Michelangelo, of canvas that it is stained by Raphael, of paper that it is soiled by Shakespeare, of silence that it is broken by Bach.
Nothing less impure than this masterpiece, an opium addict.

Nothing more natural than society demanding a share, condemning him like an invisible beauty without the shadow of prostitution.

*

The painter who likes to paint trees, becoming a tree. Children carry within them a natural drug. The death of Thomas the Impostor is a case of the child playing at horses turning into a horse.

All children possess the magic power of being able to change themselves into what they wish. Poets, in whom childhood is prolonged, suffer a great deal when they lose this power. This is undoubtedly one of the reasons which drives the poet to use opium.

*

If an addict who has been completely cured starts smoking again he no longer experiences the discomfort of his first addiction. There exists, therefore, outside alkaloids and habit, a sense for opium, an intangible habit which lives on, despite the recasting of the organism. This sense must not be taken for the regret felt by an opium addict who has become normal again, although this regret does constitute part of the appeal. The dead drug leaves a ghost behind. At certain hours it haunts the house.

*

An addict who has been cured keeps defences against the poison within himself. If he becomes addicted again his defences come into action and force him to take stronger doses than those of his first addiction.

*

Opium is a season. The smoker no longer suffers from changes in the weather. He never catches cold. He suffers only from the changes in drugs, doses and hours, in everything in fact which influences the barometer of opium.

Opium has its colds, shivers and fevers which do not coincide with cold and heat.

*

Doctors would have us believe that opium dulls us and takes away our sense of values. But if opium takes away the old scale of values from under our feet, it sets up another for us, superior and more delicate.

*

(1930) One cannot say that opium, by removing all sexual obsessions, weakens the smoker, because not only does it not cause impotence, but what is more it replaces those somewhat base obsessions by others which are somewhat lofty, very strange and unknown to a sexually normal organism.

For instance a type of mind will be sensed, sought out, and linked across the centuries and the arts, against all appearances, and will haunt the untended sexuality across the most dissimilar sexes and social backgrounds (Dargelos, Agathe, the stars and the boxers in Paul's bedroom).

*

All animals are charmed by opium. Addicts in the colonies know the danger of this bait for wild beasts and reptiles.

Flies gather round the tray and dream, lizards with their little mittens swoon on the ceiling above the lamp and wait for the night, mice come close and nibble the dross. I do not speak of the dogs and monkeys that become addicted like their masters.

At Marseilles, among the Annamites, where one smokes with implements calculated to confuse the police (a gas-pipe, a sample bottle of Benedictine with a hole in it, and a hat-pin), the cockroaches and the spiders form a circle in ecstasy.

*

*... But the young Annamites do not smoke. In Indo-China the people don't smoke any longer. It's only in books that they smoke aboard ship.*

When I hear one of these phrases I close my eyes, I see again the boys' berths on board the *X*, one of the largest steamers on the Marseilles-Saïgon line. The *X* was waiting to get under way. The purser, one of my opium-smoking friends, had suggested the escapade to me. At eleven o'clock at night we crossed the deserted docks and climbed up the ladder on to the deck. We had to follow our guide at full speed and avoid the watch. We climbed over cables, worked round columns and Greek temples, crossed public squares, labyrinths of machines, shadow and moonlight, we mixed up the companion-ways and the corridors so much and so well that our poor guide began to lose his head, until, softly, that powerful strange smell put us on the right path.

Imagine enormous berths, four or five dormitories, where sixty 'boys' lay smoking on two tiers of planks. In each dormitory a long table filled up the empty space. Standing on these tables, and cut in two by a flat, unmoving cloud half-way up the room, the late-comers were undressing, tying up the cords where they liked to hang up their washing, and gently rubbing their shoulders.

The scene was lit by the dim lights of the lamps, and on top of them burnt the spluttering drug. The bodies were wedged against each other and without causing the slightest surprise, or the slightest ungraciousness, we took our places where there was really no place left, with our legs doubled up and our heads resting on stools. The noise we made did not even disturb one of the boys who was sleeping with his head against mine. A nightmare convulsed him; he had sunk to the bottom of the sleep that stifled him, entering into him through his mouth, his large nostrils and the ears which stuck out from his head. His swollen face was closed like an angry fist, he sweated, turned over and tore at his silken rags. He looked as though a stroke of the lancet would deliver him and bring forth the nightmare. His grimaces formed an extraordinary contrast with the calm of the others, a vegetable calm, a calm which reminded me of something familiar. What was it? On those planks lay the twisted bodies in which the skeletons, visible through the pale skin, were no more than the delicate armatures of a dream.... In fact, it was the olive trees of Provence which those young sleepers evoked in me, the twisted olive trees on the flat red earth, their silver clouds hanging in the air.

In that place I could almost believe that it was all this profound lightness which alone kept this most monumental ship floating on the water.

\*

I wanted to take notes during my stay in the clinic and above all to contradict myself in order to follow the stages of the treatment. It was a question of talking about opium without embarrassment, without literature and without any medical knowledge.

The specialists seem to be unaware of the world which separates the opium addict from the other victims of poisons, 'the drug', and drugs.

I am not trying to defend the drug; I am trying to see clearly in the dark, to make blunders and to come face to face with the problems which are always approached from the side.

I imagine that young doctors are beginning to shake off the yoke, to revolt against the ridiculous prejudices and follow new developments.

A strange thing. Our physical safety accepts doctors who correspond to the artists whom our moral safety rejects. Imagine being cared for by someone like Ziem, Henner or Jean Aicard.

Will the young doctors discover either an active type of cure (the present method remains passive), or a régime which would enable us to withstand the blessings of the poppy?

The medical faculty detests intuition or risks; it wants practitioners, forgetting that they only arise thanks to discoveries which in the first place come up against scepticism, one of the worst forms of comfort.

There will be objections – art and science follow different paths. This is not true.

*

The half-sleep of opium makes us pass down corridors and cross halls and push open doors and lose ourselves in a world where people startled out of their sleep are horribly afraid of us.

*

Opium may make us slightly visible to the invisible, may make spectres of us to frighten spectres in their own haunts.

Opium is really effective once in every twenty cases.

*

Never confuse the opium smoker with the opium eater. Quite different phenomena.

*

After smoking, the body thinks. It is not a question of the *confused thinking* of Descartes.

The body thinks, the body dreams, the body becomes soft and flaky, the body flies. The smoker embalmed alive.

*

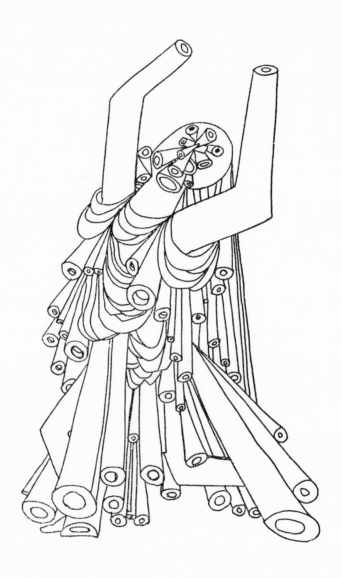

The smoker has a bird's eye view of himself.

\*

It is not I who become addicted, it is my body :
'... as certain chemical substances, essentially unstable when in their pure state, seize hold greedily of an element capable of giving them stability'. (Julien Benda)

My nature needs serenity. An evil force drives me towards scandale, like a somnambulist on the roof. The serenity of the drug used to protect me against this force which compels me to sit on the stool of repentance at a time when the mere reading of a newspaper would destroy me.

\*

Everything is a question of speed. (Immobile speed. Speed in itself. OPIUM : speed in silk.) Beyond plants, whose speed is different from our own, revealing only a relative immobility, and the speed of metals, which show us an even greater relative immobility, lie other realms, whose speed is too slow or too fast for us even to see them or be seen by them. (LE CAP, the angel, the fan.) It is not impossible that the cinema will one day be able to film the invisible and make it visible, adapting it to our rhythm as it adapts the gesticulation of flowers to our rhythm of life.

Opium, which changes our speeds, procures for us a very clear awareness of worlds which are superimposed on each other, which interpenetrate each other, but do not even suspect each other's existence.

\*

I do not condemn the music of words and all that it brings with it by way of dissonance, harshness and new sweetness. But a modelling of the soul attracts me much more. To oppose a living geometry to the decorative charm of the sentences. To have style and not *a* style. A style which does not allow itself to be imitated in any way. One would not know how to grasp it. A style which would only be born by cutting something from me, from a hardening of thought during its brutal passage from the interior to the exterior. With a frightened halt like the bull as it comes out of the *toril*. To expose our phantoms to the spray of a petrifying fountain, not to learn how to improve on ingenious objects, but to petrify, in passing, anything shapeless which comes out of us. To make concepts acquire volume.

Opium enables one to give form to the unformed; it prevents, alas, the communication of this privilege to anyone else. Even if it means losing sleep. I shall watch out for the unique moment in the process of cure when this faculty will still function a little and, inadvertently, will coincide with the return of the power of communication.

\*

Once a poet wakes up he is stupid, I mean intelligent. 'Where am I?' he asks, like ladies who have fainted. Notes written by a poet who is awake are not worth much. I offer them only for what they are worth, at my own risk. One more experience.

\*

The lung is a sack of globules. Each globule is divided into alveoli which lead direct to the bronchi. One globule imitates the entire lung of a frog. The smooth internal surface is tapestried with a network of blood capillaries. In this way, if the lung were spread out and ironed over, it would cover 200 square yards. You have read aright.

Smoke, therefore, impregnates at one stroke 150 square yards of pulmonary surface.

The blood mass of the lung, which is only 7/1000ths of a millimetre thick, amounts to two pints.

Given the speed of pulmonary circulation, one can imagine the quantity of blood which passes through the respiratory apparatus.

Hence the instantaneous effects of opium on the smoker.

The smoker rises slowly like a balloon, turns again slowly and falls back on some dead moon whose weak pull prevents him from leaving.

Even if he gets up, talks, acts, is sociable, and appears to live, his gestures, gait, skin, looks and words do not reflect any the less a life subjected to other laws of paleness and gravity.

The return journey will take place at his own risk. The smoker first pays his ransom. Opium releases him, but the return is unattractive.

However, having returned to his planet, a nostalgia remains.

\*

Death separates completely our heavy waters from our light waters. Opium separates them a little.

\*

Opium is the only vegetable substance which communicates the vegetable state to us. Through it, we get an idea of that other speed of plants.

\*

One can say : the sun is big, this bit of dust is small, because they depend on our scale of values. It is foolish to say : God is big, an atom is small. It is very strange that hardly anyone lives with any feeling for the centuries which pass between each breath we take, of the worlds created and destroyed by our body, that the idea of our body's darkness conceals the fires which inhabit it, and that a difference in measurement renders incomprehensible the fact that these worlds may be civilized or dead; in brief, that the infinitely small may be a discovery instead of being an instinct.

It is the same for the infinitely big (big, but small by comparison with us), since we do not feel that our sky, our light, our spaces, constitute but a dark spot for the being whose body contains us and whose life (short for him) takes up centuries for us.

In spite of faith, God would sicken us. The wisdom of Moses was to confine men to their tiny houses.

\*

It is difficult to live without opium after having known it because it is difficult, after knowing opium, to take earth seriously. And unless one is a saint, it is difficult to live without taking earth seriously.

\*

After the cure. The worst moment, the worst danger. Health with this void and an immense sadness. The doctors honestly hand you over to suicide.

\*

Opium, which smooths out a little the tight folds which allow us to think we live a long time, by minutes, by episodes, first takes away our memory.

The return of memory and the feeling for time (even in my case where they barely exist in a normal state).

*

The spirit of the smoker moves without moving, like watered silk.

*

Opium lightens the mind. It never makes one witty. It spreads the mind out. It does not gather it up into a point.

*

## SIX WEEKS AFTER WEANING

For a week I have looked well again and the strength has come back to my legs (Jouhandeau has pointed out one thing that is true: my hands still look ill). Now, I find that for a week I have not been able to write any more about opium, I do not need to any more. The opium problem is receding. I would have to invent something.

I was therefore eliminating through ink, and even after the official elimination there was an unofficial elimination with a flow which became solid through my desire to write and draw. I allowed these drawings or notes only the value of frankness, and they seemed to me to be a derivative, a discipline for the nerves, but they became the faithful graph of the last stage. Sweat and bile precede some phantom substance which would have dissolved, leaving no other trace behind except a deep depression, if a fountain-pen had not given it direction, relief and shape.

Waiting for a period of calm to write these notes was trying to relive a state which is inconceivable as soon as the organism is no longer in it. Since I have never granted the slightest importance to the setting and since I was using opium as a remedy, I was not unhappy at seeing my state disappear. Whatever one renounces is a dead letter for those who imagine that the setting plays a part. . . . I hope that this reportage finds a place among doctors' pamphlets and the literature of opium; may it serve as a guide to the novices who do not recognize, beneath the slowness of opium, one of the most dangerous faces of speed.

*

Now that I am cured, I feel empty, poor, heartbroken and ill. I float. The day after tomorrow I leave the clinic. Where should I go? Three weeks ago I felt a sort of pleasure. I was asking M questions about altitude and about little hotels in the snow. I was going to come out.

But it was a book that was going to come out. A book is coming out, is going to come out, as the publishers say. It is not. I could die ... the book does not care. The same game always begins again and every time one allows oneself to be taken in.

It was difficult to foresee a book written in seventeen days. I had the illusion that it was a question of myself.

The work which exploits me needed opium; it needed me to leave opium; once more, I will be taken in. And I was wondering, shall I take opium or not? It is useless to put on a carefree air, dear poet. I will take it if my work wants me to.

\*

And if opium wants me to.

2 Septembre
1950

Dear
Mary
Dans 4
jours je
plonge à pic dans
l'eau sombre
et mystérieuse
( et froide )

de mon film
Pense à moi et
priez pour moi
Jean

# Letters to Mary Hoeck

Mary Hoeck translated many of Cocteau's poems, including *Crucifixion* and *Un Ami Dort*. Her translations were approved by Cocteau and much admired by Edith Sitwell. She also translated Cocteau's last full-length play, *Bacchus*, introduced to English-speaking audiences through its broadcast by the BBC in the mid-'fifties.

Mary Hoeck, a Scotswoman of his own age, was in close touch with Cocteau for the last fifteen years of his life and naturally always consulted him about any translation problems. They exchanged many letters and discussed a wide variety of subjects, and while Cocteau was making the film *Orphée* he wrote to his English translator nearly every day about the progress of his work and about his own feelings. Cocteau was a prolific letter writer and wrote, in his own hand, to a great many people, but he rarely sustained a correspondence as he did with Mary Hoeck. This group of letters allows us to see how his mind worked and how he lived at the Villa Santo Sospir, as well as in and near Paris, in 1949 and during the early 1950s.

Milly, Seine et Oise
15th July, 1949

My dearest friend,

Here I am alone in my house and my garden – that is to say, I live in them with you. I have received the two consignments of writing. I go across the little bridge into my wood and I'm in your Botanical Garden. Do you know that no one, none of those around me, knows anything about our correspondence, I mean they don't know that it even exists. Not that I hide it from them deliberately, but I find that fairyland disappears if one mentions it and that words lose their strength when we let others see them. So here I am alone and your letter has reached me telling me of your translation of *L'Acteur* and of *Un Ami Dort*. What are you asking me? How do you think I can tell you what to do? My poems don't belong to

439

me. They belong to you, and it is for you to decide which poem is important and which one runs easily through your veins. Yesterday I worked on *Orphée* and I shall do so tomorrow. Today I am resting, but my heart is at work.

*Orphée* will be very simple. I have given up the idea of working according to new-fashioned dogmas. I let myself follow my own line, up a rising slope rather than digging into the depths. The theme will be the absorption of the poet in his own being, rather than in causes and parties. This creates great disorder on earth, and at the end, Death, who loves Orphée, sacrifices herself by throwing him back into the grime in which men like to live.

I would like to go to Nice to see you there, but apart from the fact that I shall be shooting a film, I no longer have the kind of springs needed for the Côte d'Azur. I get worn out there. What I need is Brittany or your Edinburgh climate, something sharp which whips one up. So much of my life is lived out in space, that I am afraid of places which make me lose my foothold. At the end of July and the beginning of August I shall be in Biarritz, where I shall be presiding at the Festival of damned films (films which are non-commercial).

All my love,

Jean

22nd July, 1949

My dearest friend,

When I came back to the country I found dead leaves and your living leaves which fell from our beautiful tree.

Each time this means diving into the enigma of another language, and I have to translate back again into my own words through you. These are intuitional exercises which give one strength. I am heart-broken that my work takes me to Biarritz instead of Cannes. But I don't like the Cannes Festival, which is a mixture of politics and snobbery. Try to see Picasso at Vallauris or Antibes. I'll make corrections and send the manuscript back to you. I'm busy all the time on the preliminary work for my film *Orphée* or 'La Nuit des Temps'.

It's no doubt you, my poor friend, who will have once again to do the sub-titling for it in English.

My love to you,

Jean

PS. I'm stunned. In my treasure-house there's no 'Ange Heurtebise' nor any 'Incendie'. I have corrected the rest.
'Dormeurs jouant à l'Hombre', the game of Hombre, is spelt with an 'H'.

Milly, Seine et Oise
August 1949

Dearest friend,

On reaching the country, there was your kind letter and the poem. I'm aghast at the Festival notice. However much I turn over in my mind *Le Jeune Homme et la Mort*, I can't imagine what can be found shocking in this *lied* in the Baudelaire-Heine style. The ballet (mimed tragedy) has not shocked anyone anywhere and I tell the whole story in *La Difficulté d'Etre*.

Our house here is short of rainwater, so we ought to do a bit of exchange in catastrophes. Here there's a drought and I'm afraid that when it comes to September and the outdoor scenes of my film there will be lashing rain. This film makes me ill. Can I manage to make it really intense and yet give it a life which is half real and half unreal. Pray for me. I look to you to help me a great deal and have faith in your influence to give me the necessary strength to overcome all obstacles.

Loving thoughts,

Jean

PS. I'm going back to Paris on Thursday to 36 Rue de Mont-pensier.

Milly
1st October, 1949

My dearest friend,

I have your letter from Nice and am re-reading it once more in my garden, which has mistaken the season and where flowers are blooming again in the sun. At the moment (except on Sundays) I'm shooting my film at night amongst the ruins of the St Cyr barracks at Versailles. That's where I've placed the no-man's-land between life and death. I'm sorry the film has not been shot in colour. Bombs have made a really artistic job of it, as art consists of spoiling materials. The whole place is pinkish beige, as if hanging out of the sky. Next week I'll be inside the studio. I think of you all the time and send you my love.

Jean

Milly
14th October, 1949

My dearest friend,

I found your letter here on my return to Milly from the film which is working me to death, but which brings me all the time nearer to you, since in it I am telling you a beautiful story.

Don't ever go near a psychiatrist. You would be telling him what to do and looking after him. Besides, anyone who thinks intuitively is incomprehensible to those who think with their brains and all your difficulties proceed from this perpetual misunderstanding. 'Things happen in their own way.' We should meddle with them as little as possible and live with one foot on the ground and one in space. That's what I call limping.

I'm glad you like Picasso. I didn't know you were in Paris. I always think of you as being in Scotland. No, I have not been conscious of the presence of your Merlin, which shows that there is no real struggle and that his influence is not strong enough to do any harm.

Your letter shows that you trust me and that you know I am speaking to you as you write to me. Your secrets fill my heart. I lock them away in it with mine. The phosphorescence this produces inspires me in *Orphée*.

I've done a little more than half the film. I've finished off the most difficult things, the beginning and the end. Now I'm tackling the middle bit.

Today the bees and wasps and flies and dragon-flies have all been cheated. The sun is shining as it does in May. And I have cheated myself, and if by some miracle you walked into my garden I would say to you : it is springtime, come for a walk.

Your

Jean

Milly
October 1949

Very dear friend,

It's raining and I'm writing to you before going back to work, which I do thinking of you and of your loving letter of last week. You seemed to have been shocked by my sentence 'art consists ... of spoiling materials'. That's because you make too much of it. I only meant that marble or canvas, on which anyone is working hard, thinks : 'They're spoiling me, they're messing me up, they're breaking me up.' It's true that ruins gain by deterioration, by fire, by something which dies.

They're talking of my plays for the next Edinburgh Festival. I have accepted the suggestion, thinking that in this way we can be together in the setting of our dreams. We should then be side by side while the actors are rehearsing and the décors taking shape. What do you think of this as an idea? Don't be surprised that my letters are so short and so scarce. I can only write on Sundays. During the week I give my hands and the ink of my veins to this 'Orphée' which must be a success.

Dear Mary, let me embrace you and wish you a good week till our next Sunday together.

Jean

Milly

All Saints' Day 1949

My dear Mary,

As always a warm letter from you was awaiting my return to my refuge. I had to stop work on the film for four days. I was ill with bronchitis which shook me up and undermined my health. I got up for Colette's *Chéri*, in which Jean Marais plays the lead, and so I had to get on the stage at the end and say nice things about her on behalf of everyone else. The emotion of appearing like this had the effect of creative shock-treatment (just time to appear to speak and to get recognition for this wonderful woman who is practically bedridden). After that my bronchitis came back worse than ever. I started work again the day before yesterday and now the country and your letter comfort me.

*Orphée* is progressing. I have noticed a strange thing. Each time that I miscalculate anything, without even noticing it, a technical accident (of the camera or of lighting) makes it necessary for the shots to be retaken. It seems that the film is making itself, producing itself and acknowledging me from afar, just as the soul uses the body. I do my work humbly in a sort of dream-state in which actors and mechanics co-operate with me.

And above all this, nearly all the time, you are watching over me and your advice guides me without waking me up. So it is your work as much as mine.

I have no doubt that it will be misunderstood, and that it will be considered fantastic, but not for one minute does this thought get in my way. It must live, whatever happens. This mutual penetration of two worlds, one with the other, exacts a constant rigorous watchfulness. The rest no longer matters.

I have warned you about the great danger of being too transparent, which is a kind of vanity and which prevents the mysteries from passing through us and making contact with our limitations.

Wisdom consists in not being too wise (not noticing the presence of wisdom). Everything that is put into words evaporates and leaves us with our hands empty.

But you know better than I the nature of good manners face to face with the Unknown. I'm going to have lunch and then for a walk with you in this fair weather which lingers with us after the summer is spent.

My love to you,

Jean

Milly, Seine et Oise
November 1949

My dear Mary,

It's a hard job getting rid of this beastly bronchitis. Our studio
is very cold and very dusty. But I'm working hard to get what I
want to do finished and worthy of you who follow what I do,
thanks to unseen threads and wave-lengths.

I'm getting near the end, an end that isn't an end because it is
at the end of a film that questions arise concerning the thousand
and one problems of noises off and music.

I shall be meeting the director of the Edinburgh Festival this
week. He wants two plays of mine, *Les Parents Terribles* and *La
Machine Infernale*. This will entail a tremendous amount of work,
reshaping and getting things going, but it's the only way I can see
of meeting you in the atmosphere which suits you. *Orphée, Les
Enfants Terribles, Le Bourgeois Gentilhomme, Phèdre* at the Opéra,
it's a lot of work for one man who has only two legs, two hands and
a load of weariness.

With love from

Jean


Milly, Seine et Oise
13th November, 1949

My dear Mary,

Can even a criticism from me (if I dare make one) be a way of
expressing my tenderness towards you? I find the article less free
than the beautiful writing of your letters, as you let yourself go
between the Botanical Garden in Edinburgh and the orchard in
Milly. I should have liked you to write a letter to Goffin in Brussels
as if you were writing it to me, one that would show people how the
thing we are doing is not a question of writing but comes from the
heart and from the soul in its deepest sense. This work will be the
first in which anyone has made a serious study of me. Your presence
in it is essential. And perhaps you could include the translation of
a poem, the one you like best. With this as a focusing point, you
could explain how you translate me, which would make those who
think they translate us understand what a translation ought to be
like. You don't give me any news of yourself, so it must be good. My

bronchitis is going. I have finished Orphée's room in which so much takes place, so much that I know so well. It is going to be taken to pieces tomorrow. It will only exist now like a ghost in images. Tomorrow I start the garage scene in which Orphée tries to make contact with the unseen.

I work thinking of you and your Ariadne's thread. From the bottom of my heart.

Jean

19th November, 1949

My dearest Mary,

I'm back in the country, free of bronchitis, in spite of the dreadful dust of the studio, so don't worry about me. I finished the film yesterday. I still have one thing to do – four days' work – with cars and transparencies (scenes shot from cars) and then I'll have to write, that is to say link together the pictures, sounds and words.

I'm rather unhappy and slightly worried as I always am when I disband a company which has been in love with what it was doing. Over and above this, there is an autumn haze and the anguish of having drawn a huge monster out of oneself.

Your article (the end of it) is very beautiful, but once again nothing equals your letters, in which your writing flows as quickly as your mind. I would have liked one of these real letters for the Belgians, to explain to them the feeling between a poet and his translator. But no doubt that's too much part of us.

Dear Mary, I have no recent news from the Festival. The Directors should have come to see me last week.

I kiss your hands,

Jean

This is a short letter because of the disease called sleep, not a serious sickness, but I've had it since yesterday. I dream of dreaming and sleeping for ever.

Milly, Seine et Oise
November 1949

My dearest friend,

I finished work on the film *Orphée* the day before yesterday, You would have laughed to see me trundling around 300 kilos of mercury into which I wanted the gloved hands (of Death) to sink. Tomorrow I'll begin to work up the 'style', that is to say to link the pictures together. Your letter-study is very beautiful and I'm very proud of it. You should add a few lines on the link between the real translator and the real poet, which seems to join them together with gossamer threads stronger than a marine cable. Send the study to Goffin who has also done a very fine study of my work.

What you say about Edinburgh could be applied in other ways to the cities of Europe. Sometimes frivolity, light-mindedness or unawareness take the place of puritanism, but it's the same sin against the spirit. My dearest wish would be to be sure that our relationship brought you that freedom which is absolutely necessary for some human beings. If I have been guilty of taking refuge in work, it has been in order to avoid contamination by outside contacts. The very day that the shooting of *Orphée* was finished I began to have a look at *Les Enfants Terribles* which I had entrusted to Melville. But the atmosphere is not the same as the other. Journalists are milling round it and photographers insulting the youth of the actors. Melville is shooting scenes this week in his own flat, which is like the strange confusion of certain dreams.

You speak of translating *La Machine*, but I think it's been done already. It was given by a company of young actors in London and on television – same for *Les Chevaliers, Orphée, La Machine à Ecrire, Les Parents Terribles,* etc. I said the other day to my agent that only your translation of *Les Chevaliers* was near to my heart. But he spoke of contracts and signatures. As regards the poems, they belong to you, and I intend to send you an official letter, giving you the exclusive rights to them. Tomorrow, in all the hurly-burly of the film, I shall think of the silence around you and absorb its peace.

Love from

Jean

Milly, Seine et Oise
December 1949

My dearest Mary,

Don't be worried by my letter-silence, which is not a real silence, and, even more important, don't worry about my health, of which I have nothing to complain at present. But I'm working during the day (*Orphée*) and in the evening (*Les Enfants Terribles*), which does not leave me a moment of peace. Last Sunday I was working in the studio and every five minutes I said to myself, I must send a wire to Edinburgh. But meantime I was looking at the 'Enfants' living in their untidy room and felt you sitting beside me, beneath the cameras, and I was happy seeing those youngsters, born at the time I wrote the book, giving it a new life, and so, as I was babbling to you all day long I could not imagine that you would think I was silent. Your letter, which I found this morning, moved me to the bottom of my heart. It proved to me once again that poetry is not a question of writing or of the mind, but a bubble rising from the spirit, springing up from the depths and able to play the role of the poet. Don't be afraid to tell me all that goes on in your heart. If we were not free to express our essence to each other, my God, who would be?

My scanty letters tell you little of what I really think and feel and, once again, they are only supplementary to the countless conversations which take place between us during the week. Tomorrow we leave the Pigalle Theatre in which they set up the décor for the bedroom. We are going into the corridor at the end of the film and I'll take you there with us. I am sure you must often feel our presence and hear the sound of our voices.

Believe in my love,

Jean

Milly, Seine et Oise
December 1949

My dear Mary,

What a lot of things I'd like to hang on your Christmas tree, things invisible, sweet and sparkling. I hate the kind of life which deprives us of the adorable feast-days of childhood. On Christmas Day I shall be in the country with my cats and dogs. In the past I could hardly imagine a Christmas without snow. Is it snowing in Edinburgh? With us there is less and less snow and the first chapter of *Les Enfants Terribles* has a mythlike quality. We shall have difficulty in making the abstract concrete in the film.

Your last manuscript for Belgium moved me deeply. Have you sent it to them? They only speak of the other one. Do send it to them.

I am really excited by your new work on *Léone*. Once the poems have got to the right stage, I'll get out a perfect edition. It will be our secret triumph. Dear Mary, I'm lighting for you all the candles of my heart, my mind and my soul.

Your

Jean

Christmas 1949

Dearest Mary,

The poet, his dog and his five cats send you their most tender greetings.

His star is with you and protects you in the Edinburgh gloom. Dream dreams that lead you into this house in Seine et Oise.

The Enfants Terribles join me in kissing you under the lighted tree.

Jean

Milly, Seine et Oise
1st January, 1950

I hope that 1950 will be like you, that is to say that it will bring nothing but those treasures of the soul and heart which the mind knots together. I am almost dead with weariness, but I won't grumble, because others are weary from lack of work, whereas I am weary from too much work into which I try to mould my being. I found your dear letter this morning, touched by sunlight on the table. The sunlight of *Léone*, which is the moon, added its ghostly sweetness. This is my New Year's Day. The dog, the four cats and the two little water-tortoises which I brought back this evening and whose faces are tatooed in green and red. I should like distances, barriers and dates to have no being and to be able to visit those I love like the angels of the Renaissance who know so well how to greet others and how to seethe up out of the ground.

My dearest Mary, my love to you,

Jean

8th January, 1950

My dearest Mary,

This time work has 'got me' as we say. I'm wandering about in a dream and wondering whether I shall reach the end of the tunnel. Yes, there is a Siamese in the company of cats. She's cleverness itself and clings to one, as she can't bear loneliness. There are : the Siamese, the blue Persian, the stray cat and the white cat which appears and disappears at will. All this lovely cat-world is watched over by Martin, son of Malouk (Jean Marais's celebrated dog), a fine snow-coloured creature.

What you say about *Léone* excites me very much. My fatigue disgusts me. I ought to be flying over to you.

Love from

Jean

Milly
Sunday, 15th January, 1950

My dearest Mary,

Your warm letters give rhythm to the syncopated life I lead, as we are shooting *Les Enfants Terribles* at times in one corner of Paris and at times in another and the company goes about like a troupe of gypsies. Tuesday I am recording the music of *Orphée*. You will be sitting beside me in the hall.

I am curious to see 'Léone' in her Edinburgh dress, walking through the wonderful Botanical Garden with her step which is like that of Time. Did I tell you that Ezra Pound wrote to me from America on New Year's Day : 'I have just read *Léone*, you've saved France.'

I know Spender, whose portrait I painted in Paris. You might submit your translations to him if you want help, which between ourselves I don't think likely, but he might take pleasure in seeing them. The cats and dogs are marvellously well and the tortoises are scrambling about in tepid water. My one-time secretary has decamped with all his furniture, which leaves a bedroom and a large between-room empty. I shall refurnish them having you in mind, so that you would be able to stay here for a few days of peace.

I couldn't make out very well the title of the play you were listening to on the radio. Unfortunately I know very little about the contemporary English stage. Yesterday I wired Vivien Leigh asking her to play *Streetcar* in Paris, while our company went over to London. We are already making plans to celebrate the hundredth performance. Jean Marais, who is like a son to me, continues to fill the theatre with Colette's *Chéri*. So, everything is as it should be, as all that I ask from life is happiness and good luck to those I love. You can imagine from that what wishes I shower down on Inverleith Terrace.

Jean


Sunday, January, 1950

My dear Mary,

What a lovely surprise, here amongst my cats, to find *Léone*, who has borrowed Sunday-time from them to float across the Channel, and your photograph (naturally it's the latest one I like best) which I have slipped into my pocket-book. Nothing in it would prevent things from flowing, there's nothing flabby or inert about it, everything is firm, without being sharp, everything cuts without harming, everything has been confirmed but not coarsened by age. Everything seems to be of gold and silver.

I'll tell you later about coming to Milly, because I may be leaving France for a time when the films are finished, to stretch my mind and legs. *Les Enfants Terribles* is nearly finished. There's only the Cité Monthiers to do, and a furniture dealer is trying to stop us from doing that – besides, we need the snow, which is now falling in Nice.

Tomorrow at 2 p.m. I am recording the music for *Orphée* – after that all my strands of exhaustion will have to be bound together to make a firm bundle of strength.

The type of work required for *Les Enfants Terribles* obliges me to be my own stage manager, so that with the turn of a hand (a hand-spring?) with anything I can find to right or to left, I can make fresh scenes; in this way the décors are like my worries which I set right with anything that comes to hand, and so they are more living than real décors which cost so much. The cats and dogs have been kissed and petted as you told me to do. This morning there is lovely icy sunshine and flowers scent the rooms. I shall get into a chair at the given time and follow the meanderings of *Léone*. On Friday I'm giving a talk in Brussels. How I should like a breathing space, but I'm afraid it would be fatal for faces like ours.

I greet you and embrace you,

Jean

Sunday, 29th January, 1950

My dear Mary,

You naturally know and foresee everything; you knew I was ill before I knew it myself. Too much 'all round the clock' work. On Friday I had to give a talk in Brussels to three thousand people. I thought I should never get through. I was speaking lower than, and to the left and to the right of my lips and mind. It was frightful. Then there were banquets and lunches at the Embassy. One had to pretend to be alive. I vomited up some bile and at nine o'clock tomorrow morning I shall tackle all the practical things which eat up people who are not themselves practical.

Just these few lines, as I should hate to let Sunday pass without sending you a sign of love. If some day this should happen, don't jump to any unpleasant conclusions. Nothing will ever prevent me from telling you my troubles and whispering them into your ear.

Love from

Jean

4th February, 1950

My dearest friend,

I've finished the mixing of sound and music for *Orphée*. No doubt I shall finish shooting pictures of *Les Enfants Terribles* next week. After that I shall relax, and fatigue will set in, as it only comes to the top when one rests.

1. I'm not speaking to you about *Léone* because I'm keeping it, fingering it, impregnating it, but alas, my English is not equal to doing more than absorbing its magic ink.

2. You translate with your inner being. Therefore it is only your being which must be expressed.

3. I think they want to consolidate your letter-study in our language.

I'm sure of the nature of your inner springs. They do not grate and they are perfectly flexible. Mine nearly let me down in Brussels. One has to accept these things. No one can go on for ever.

All my love,

Jean

Milly
February 1950

My kind Mary,

I hope to be able to cure you some day of your nightmares about me. If my letters are not constant, my heart is. At times I write short letters but talk a lot to the absent one. I even talk to my dead.

Radiguet and Christian Bérard give me instructions all the time, because I ask their advice and they answer me, since I know their reactions and follow them so that they in turn can drive me on.

It's very odd for me to be playing the role of healer, as if a friend is five minutes late for an appointment I always think he's under a bus. So you can laugh at my wisdom and say I have a mania for preaching instead of practising.

Yesterday I listened to the Bach-Vivaldi Concerto in A flat for four pianos. Buy it in Edinburgh. I'm thinking of linking it with the film-takes of *Les Enfants Terribles* and so give them that step that Destiny has, climbing swiftly up the stairs or coming down slowly. This music gives me wonderful peace, it's worth more than anything from the chemist's.

I did not send you *Maalesh*, as I was busy every moment of the day and the few copies that Gallimard sent me were on a table in my country place. This shows once more that books only reach those who want to read them and that the habit of giving away copies is rather silly. A book should float out on waves. I'm going back to Paris tomorrow to attend the funeral mass for Bérard.

Then I return to work, offering myself to this praying mantis which loves and devours us.

My dear kind Mary, I have your lovely photo in my pocket and it takes care of me. If I could protect you against the nasty tricks your mind plays on you, I should be very happy.

Love from

Jean

Milly

20th February, 1950

My dearest Mary,

Now it's my turn to scold you, as your letter seems to show a kind of anguish and disorder which are not worthy of your beautiful face, as integrated as a Bach fugue. My sufferings are not important. They come from feeling tired after a period of mental and physical strain, in which intuition directed everything. I had a bad ear, which made it hard to record my script, as I could only hear my voice from the inside. My cats and dogs had the same trouble, no doubt out of sympathy. They nursed us together, they said. This morning it's all gone, and I'm listening to Mozart records and to the wonderful Bach-Vivaldi Concerto in A flat which I'm going to put on to the sound-track of *Les Enfants Terribles*. Yesterday morning I saw the second version of *Orphée*. I think that this film will prove worthy of us and of our friendship. I'm longing for you to see it. Here, your snow turns into strange April sunshine and a delightful temperature which is all wrong for the time of year and for nature. The trees are in bud. I'd like to idle the days away. But unfortunately I have to write a very difficult article. I'll write it as a continuation of this letter and no doubt that will make it easier.

Be strong, that's how you'll keep me in shape.

Love from

Jean

Sunday, 26th February, 1950

My dearest Mary,

This has been a day of complete idleness, neglecting all my chores, neglecting all my letters, playing with the dictaphone newly received from New York, recording music, voices, laughter and the purring of my cats. I did not reproach you for complaining but for what motivated your complaints. You must live up to your face which is not that of a complaining person but of one who lives courageously surrounded by the enigma of life. I forgot to tell you that this morning I was studying English, re-reading *Renaud et Armide* through you, syllable by syllable. Beware of one thing. The lines of this play *seem* to flow, but they don't. I have worked it out so that the dough quickly hardens and makes a series of road-blocks. You'll have to find the corresponding line to 'Le cheval du malheur vers les bords que je crains'. I don't think that 'grey sea' evokes the strong dark picture conjured up by these words. I know that you can bring any miracle into being, that's why I should like you to go over it again, a bit at a time, and harden the lines. I'm taping the music of the Bach concerto on Saturday morning. I shall listen to it with you by my side. Are you sure that this record is not to be found in London? That would surprise me. If not, buy what can only be found in London, Purcell's trumpet music. And please get another record of it for me. Someone brought it from London for *Les Chevaliers*. It was used as a fanfare to usher in Blancharmure. These fanfares are sublime, celestial.

I have so much to do that my head's going round. Every night I make up my mind to sleep well and be at peace. I do manage it, although the films run all night long, and I count and recount and stick things together, until sleep overtakes me and shows me another film.

Dear Mary, I leave you for this seed of sleep and send you my love.

Jean


5th March, 1950

My dearest Mary,

I've come back to Milly with the two young *Enfants Terribles* actors, and they *are* Enfants Terribles, filling the house with the din of the records they have recently bought. The Mrs D you mention must be one of those scandalmongering concierges who sully France with their false tales. Jean Marais is a sort of arch-angel made of solid gold, who has such a beautiful soul that shafts don't get through his armour. As regards Josette Day, she's a perfectly adorable, well-brought-up young woman, incapable of anything underhand, indiscreet or wrong. She adores me and I her. She could have been annoyed with me for not giving her the part of Eurydice but, on the contrary, yesterday she sent me an affec-tionate telegram, completely true to type, from Cannes, where she had seen my film. I'm sorry for your lady, but I'm angry with her too for having given you a moment's anxiety and tarnished your mirror. *Orphée* will probably not be released till September. There is a whirlwind round *Les Enfants Terribles*. I recorded the Bach-Vivaldi concerto this morning. I was alone in the Salle Gaveau, like Louis of Bavaria, and shared with you the health-giving rhythms. We have to throw the film to the mob on the 17th and everyone is trying to do their best, in their own way, to make the impossible possible. So there you are. Last Tuesday, as it was going round the Rue St Didier at full speed, a car caught me up like a scarf, and I was thrown to the ground like Cégeste in *Orphée* – that's what happens when art gets mixed up with one's life. Everything is going well in the best possible way. I kiss you with all my heart and won't scold you any more, as your suffering is only another form of peace, worthy of you.

Jean

Milly
12th March, 1950

Dear Mary,

The second instalment is very beautiful, I'm divided between reading it and the letter which came with it. Tomorrow at nine o'clock I shall be present at the mixing – mixing Bach and the words spoken by the youngsters in *Les Enfants Terribles*. Once again in this work you will be present unseen, but seen by me with your fine serious face. This evening I'm showing *Orphée* to a handful of friends and you will again be there too and I know your responses. I have nothing to learn now about the way your inner being works, except that there are still some remnants of old anxieties; but if you look after me I'll look after you, and send you messages that don't use the post.

Your Botanical Garden will soon be very beautiful. The sap is rising and is ready for its work. It has the deep thoughtful look of someone preparing a speech. After the work has come to an end I hope for a few days alone with the cats and dogs. I am working 'like a machine', as Madame de La Fayette said. Thanks for getting the 'Trumpets', which I am impatiently expecting, for nothing is more sublime.

Love from

Jean

Thursday, 16th March, 1950

My dearest friend,

Thank goodness I can now spend four days in Milly, something which didn't often work out while the films were on. I've seen the *Enfants* going up into the 'heaven of legend' accompanied by the magnificent Vivaldi music and I'm resting. Monday went off very well, but friends brought their friends and the little hall was much too full. Your place was of course left empty, but you were every-where. Amongst the audience many felt that something was taking place which was more than cinematography. You know what happens next – those who think they are seeing 'the best film of the year' and all the usual silly things that people say. The best I could hope for. I know now all that you will say about the film, that's the proof of how we understand one another and of those strong gossamer threads which reach from Edinburgh to Paris.

We have the same flowers as you and the rose-bushes are beginning to take on life once again. The birds encourage them. It's a wonderful feeling being here after the montage and the din of the moritone (the machine which shows the film in miniature both on the right and wrong sides). My God, why do you wish me to scold you? Naturally the peace I speak of is not 'peace', our vocabulary, yours and mine, rarely has anything to do with the way others use words. Peace in the midst of storm, to me, that's the real peace. What people call peace is nothing but self-indulgence, in which they stretch out their toes peacefully without ever having walked the tightrope on them.

I can't judge the part of *Armide* which you don't like. I find it difficult to distinguish between what is tight and what slack in English, but you must be careful because tragedy easily becomes flabby if one is not perpetually watchful of the thread which I try to stretch from one end of the work to the other. Don't burden yourself with the 'Trumpets'. Get them to send the record from London when you are there. They are well embedded in my ears, and I only want them for the joy of getting them into the ears of others who don't know them. Your letter arrived by a miracle at the same time as I did, just a minute or so after I arrived amongst my cats.

I would very much like to put you in touch with the firm which is handling *Orphée*, so that you can do the sub-titling. No one but you could really find the indispensable words. And besides, this would let you see the London copy at once. I am writing by this very same post to Emile Doulon so that he can get in touch with you. The trick of this business consists of translating each section within a given number of letters. The German woman translator did it very well, so you will do it marvellously, as the script has been part of you since you were born.

Till Sunday,

Love,

Jean

Milly

27th March, 1950

My dear Mary,

Here the garden is making a wild effort to work its way free of the wood and make its sap creative through different channels, its leaves and flowers. It's at work everywhere, under the earth and in the branches. I can guess how your Botanical Garden is shouting for joy and doesn't care a hoot about the Edinburgh reserve of which you speak. I have been doing nothing for four days, except yesterday when I changed the ending of *Les Enfants Terribles* by phone. The book had been followed too closely, and Paul died twice over because the camera had gone back while taking the Chinese room which constituted a sort of ending. I had left the picture as it was but had taken out the script. At that time it was wrong for the author to intervene, except through the actions of the main characters. The poster for *Orphée* will be very fine. The faces of the stars are placed in Rodin's great marble hand. At the base, which in this dimension looks like a steep rock, Cégeste is stretched out full length, thrown there by the motor cyclists. It is a photographic montage which has real poetry. Thursday I'm going to

Zurich to show the film. I'm not very hopeful about a German-Swiss audience, but a few words from me may make people avoid inattention more than they usually do in the case of films.

Thank you for going to London for the sub-titling. Its method consists of counting letters, enough to make you bash your head in, a puzzle which will irritate you, but without which you might turn into a catastrophe. They've tried what you suggest : comment to take the place of dialogue, but it draws the attention of the audience from what is taking place, instead of immersing them in it. You'll see what I mean for yourself when you've been in touch with the experts. What is essential is for you to see the film before others and for you to feel it has a message intended for you.

The cats are in Paris at the cat-show. They're coming back tomorrow. The tortoises seemed dead, but a Brazilian came along and said they were not, that it's only their hibernating season. Sometimes they lie floating on their backs for six months at a time.

I'm telling you all these little things about Milly, because the big important ones about Paris bore me to death and I always try to turn blind eyes and deaf ears to them. I'm putting the manuscript of our *Renaud* together and I'll make your corrections to it later. Poetry has enough majesty in itself to stop us from worrying about what may happen to it. The main thing is that the river should flow and roll on. Dear Mary, I embrace you,

Jean

Milly<br>2nd April, 1950

My dearest Mary,

We've returned from Zurich, where I gave them *Orphée* in an odd but quite warm atmosphere (enthusiasm or torpor?). *Les Enfants Terribles* is getting the same treatment in Paris, insulted by philistine critics. All this is very trying, but the trees flourish, the cats grow fat and the world goes on turning accompanied by flying saucers.

I eagerly split your envelopes open, thinking you had seen the film and not being able to wait to know whether it had touched you.

Tomorrow I go back to Paris and have to get busy, on *Phèdre* at the Opéra. I wish for nothing better than to be free of all these things which we throw to the public and which critics criticize. I

hope to run away to the South at the end of April.
I haven't yet received the 'Trumpets'.

My love to you,

Jean

Milly
9th April, 1950

My dearest Mary,

You must have felt that I was there beside you during the film and that this film was not a film in the ordinary sense, but blood which flowed, the white blood of the soul, this likeness of the soul, and that the actors had become letters, syllables, words, full stops and commas. It does not matter whether it is understood or not. For instance, look at *Les Enfants Terribles*, which the press tries to kill but which the audience loves and hates so thoroughly that they quarrel about it in the auditorium and all the way out into the street. Nothing disgusts me more than these picture-houses full of people eating ices and coming in and going out, as if it were a public lavatory. But even those who have seen *Orphée* without understanding it, are impressed and go on thinking about it. In front of my window the white cherry tree is like a wedding bouquet. There's sunshine in the wind and my bronchitis goes on. I'm coughing and I should like to be in the South.

The best thing for you to do would be, as soon as you reach France, to give me a ring at Richelieu 55.72, or else Milly, Seine et Oise 28. We'll arrange our meeting straight off. Everything depends on the Opéra. If the Opéra leaves me free I'll go to the country. If the Opéra requires my presence I shall be in Paris. I'll know in a day or two. I have just written to Lifar that I refuse to be kept in the dark. Will you have a car or shall I have to arrange for one? It's quite easy. Wire me.

We'll have so much to say to one another that we shall be unable to speak and my eyes will be full of tears,

Your

Jean

*Mary Hoeck writes of her subsequent visit to Paris and Milly*

Jean met me at the airport accompanied by Francine (Madame Weisweiller) and Doudou (Edouard Dermit, 'Cégeste' or 'Doudou' in the letters, who became Jean's adopted son and who is his sole legatee).

I had not seen Jean in the flesh before but I recognized him at a distance, because his walk (*la démarche d'un poète*) had the same rhythm as his poetry. Although he is not 'consistent' in the ordinary sense, he is 'all of a piece'. The skin of his face has the same delicacy as the outline of his drawings, his hands have the exquisite wonder of his verse.

During the visit I was shown round the tiny Paris flat including the famous 'red room'. I met Madeleine, the housekeeper who looks after Jean and adores him. We all sat on his bed discussing plans in his bed-workroom with the low half-moon window looking on to the Palais-Royal. As Francine said, it was unhealthily devoid of air – she was planning to take him to Saint-Jean-Cap-Ferrat, which became his third home for many years.

At Milly it was like walking through the Garden of Eden before the serpent foisted the 'knowledge of good and evil' on man. Jean showed me every inch of the house, 'La Maison du Bailli', even the attic with all the trunks which had gone on his theatrical tour of the Middle East. He wanted me to have an exact picture of it for my disincarnate night wanderings. He brought me bundles of cat (that's the only way I can describe how he picked them up and deposited them delicately in my lap). One cat was missing, but was found later busily allowing its kittens to be born while we all looked on in wonder at life emerging. Then Jean took me across the bridge over the moat and we walked in the little wood. We had lunch in the 'school-room' with the grown-up children (Francine and Doudou). Later he asked me to join him in recording the poem published in French and English by Empreintes of Brussels. He read it in French and then he steadied me with his arm round my shoulders while I read my translation. When it was played back I was (like everyone who hears his or her own voice recorded for the first time) horrified at my speech. But Jean said he loved it, that we should not entirely lose accents, that he could not lose his Parisian one, etc., and that at any rate my French was perfect – in fact everything to put me at my ease. This is one of his unrecognized keynotes, the perfect politeness and consideration he gives to others. I saw its effect later in Nice, on the bemused wonder-struck staff in a shop selling artists' materials where 'everything stopped for Jean' and where they assured me that he was always the same, always the ideal customer. He never condescends, he is always on everyone's level, like the angels he speaks of 'who billow down from the sky', like the Greek gods who 'walked on earth with men'. He took his cue more directly than most other Christians from the Carpenter's Son.

But people who prefer destructive gossip like to seem knowledgeable about the red room – it requires less insight, which they probably killed out of themselves in their youth or even their childhood. Jean's miracle lay in keeping the sophisticated heart of a child.

# Beauty Secrets

This text, which so far as I know can be found only in the *Coupures de Presse* included in Volume X of Cocteau's so-called 'Complete Works', expresses succinctly his attitude to life, and life for him meant poetry. Here he describes with intensity and simplicity what poetry is, how it is written, how a poet should live and work.

*Beauty Secrets* (Secrets de Beauté) contains many echoes of the early aphoristic *poésie critique*, notably *Le Coq et l'Arlequin*, *Le Secret Professionnel* and *Le Mystère Laïc*. It is, however, more straightforward in style and there is no acrobatic word-play. The writing is less aggressive than in the earlier essays, the author is now more contemplative than critical, and his glance tends to move backwards rather than forwards. The themes included in this piece are not new to the Cocteau student and it is their continued repetition which proves how important they were to him. Rarely, however, did he express himself so clearly and so memorably.

The last few lines make a fitting end to what Cocteau decided should be his 'Complete Works'. *Beauty Secrets* is Cocteau's world in microcosm.

All too often a kind of rhythmic prose, arranged in the shape of a poem, is called poetry. These spurious poems always fascinate the public. A poem consists of such a delicate balance and loss of balance, it has a gait so stiff and light that inattentive and disjointed minds cannot distinguish one aspect from another.

\*

A poem is not written in the language used by the poet. Poetry is a language of its own and cannot be translated into any other, even into that in which it seems to have been written.

\*

The great solitude of a poem is to be the height of autocracy and the height of anarchy. The great solitude of the poet is to be completely invisible and visible to an extreme degree (to be laughed at).

*

Even if it seems pleasant, a poet's life is ghastly, it takes place among tortures and he cannot avoid a single one of them.

*

Poetry cannot act like a physical enchantment, which is made up of a quantity of details indistinguishable in one glance, unless it is impossible to ask some other person, who is distracted by his own preoccupations, to introduce himself into a labyrinth of a style, appreciate the slighest turnings within it and lose himself there.

*

Poetry stops when ideas come. All ideas kill it. Poetry is an idea in itself, it could not express one without becoming poetic, that is to say without destroying itself.

*

It is the poetic aspect of a poet which strikes his contemporaries. Poetry hides beneath this mask. It is natural for subtle minds to despise a great poet during their own period, when they only see the dead matter which will disappear one day and free the poetry.

*

Baudelaire: *Les Femmes Damnées, Les Fleurs Etranges, La Charogne*, etc. . . . Hugo (one always comes back to Gide's remark, 'Hugo, alas!'), the decorative masses in which the most astonishing of encounters can occur.

*

I have just seen, in Picasso's studio, the sketch for a large canvas which represents a charnel-house. This sketch is given depth as it were by the countless lines which the painter has erased. These lines are the proof of a search which is not for a better line but for the only line there can be. As a result the entire surface of Picasso's pictures does not show a single syntactical error which is his own and shows us handwriting in which a graphologist would read his mind like an open book. The whole sketch has an intense life and the slightest section of a line lives with the same intensity as the whole. Everything is false and everything is true. A hand, a shoulder, a mouth, a head, a neck, an elbow, a breast, a knee or a big toe are expressed in such a way that they acquire the power of a coat of arms. They recount the nobility of the painter and the lofty deeds which ennoble him.

\*

It is against the grain for me to call out to Picasso : 'Stop ! You couldn't go any further.'

He will go further. He will finish. He will paint. But perhaps in finishing and painting he will reach that secret defence of which I speak and which conceals poetry beneath masks whereby the public can satisfy its thirst for prose and decorative ornament.

\*

The poet's disorder becomes an order which is rejected by conventional disorder. The poet will always answer the accusations against him badly. If he answered well according to the Church, he would betray God.

\*

The poet is clumsy. He is only skilful within his clumsiness. This remarkable clumsiness causes him to be accused of being skilful in everything.

\*

Poetry always causes a scandal. It is a stroke of luck that nobody notices it. It only becomes visible, alas, a long time afterwards, when events imitate it and disturb the world.

\*

Writers are always responsible, but not for what they are accused of. They are responsible for the régime which accuses them and which, without knowing it, is influenced by them.

\*

The tragedy is that politics always lags far behind the revolutions of poetry and as a result the poets who take part in it find themselves side-tracked into a period which is dead in relation to the period when they are living, and they run the risk of being dragged away to death.

A poet is always occupied by the enemy and resists. This

clandestine resistance is the basis of his work. The resistance of 1944 was only a visible image of this perpetual enterprise.

\*

Heroism (the heroic act) is prolonged only by myth. To say what one is going to do means that one no longer does it. To say what one has done means that one has no longer done it.

\*

It can happen that the intuition which replaces intelligence in the poet assumes the form of intelligence and causes him to be regarded as intelligent. This spurious intelligence will discredit him in the eyes of people who do not allow the poet to possess it and will protect him against an immediate success, which is a source of death.

\*

Poetry is not holy just because it speaks of holy things. Poetry is not beautiful because it speaks of beautiful things, and if we are questioned on why it is beautiful and holy, we must answer as Joan of Arc answered when she was questioned too far : 'Go on.'

\*

In order to read poetry one must be inspired.

\*

The word poetry is abused, it is used for everything which seems poetic. Now poetry would be incapable of being poetic. Anything poetic takes advantage of the light given off by poetry.

\*

A poet's violence could not be lengthy. Joan of Arc was brief.

\*

The poet is the servant of forces which he serves without understanding. He must keep his house clean. His progress can only be moral.

\*

There is no visible success for the poet. The clandestine cannot become official without ceasing to be clandestine. Those who believe they are bringing a secret out into the open are mistaken. They are driven out from the shadow in which poets live. A new form of clandestinity takes shape behind them.

\*

Every poet is posthumous. This is why it is very difficult for him to live. His work hates him, it eats him, it wants to get rid of him and live alone as it pleases. If he comes to the fore, his voices leave him.

\*

The case brought against poets is inevitable. If they avoid it, it is because they abjure it. They cannot be reproached for weakness and doubt. The example of Christ and Joan of Arc would be enough to absolve them. But they must undergo the rejection of men until the end.

\*

It is only by dying through injustice that one can aim to be reborn.

\*

I have only written one poem in my life in which luck never left me until the end : it is *L'Ange Heurtebise*.

\*

If luck abandons us we must win it back, struggle and begin again. It is the passages when luck leaves us which please others and allow poems to take root in people's memories. One day these passages displease and luck appears.

\*

Baudelaire's contemporaries saw only the airs he affected and only admired these airs. Beyond these airs his gaze journeyed slowly towards us like the light from the stars.

\*

The left cannot turn to its right. If it seems to do so, then it has become right, it is no longer left. It is finished.

\*

Lack of constraint, lyricism and words lead young poets to their downfall. I recommend to them an old-fashioned régime, a very simple form of hygiene : they should write upside-down, join the letters together, look at the sheet of paper in the mirror as they write, make a geometrical design, place the words at the points where the lines meet and fill the spaces afterwards, turn a famous textbook upside-down by inverting the meaning, etc. ... in this way they become athletes and develop the muscles of the mind.

\*

Strong goodness is stronger than wickedness which is regarded as strong. We must overcome this conformism. We must be good.

\*

Poetry is so much subjected to individual laws that a serious man, capable of feeling himself a poet, can give the illusion of being one through knowing these laws and studying the mechanisms which produce what is unusual or beautiful.

\*

Beauty limps. Poetry limps. The poet limps when he emerges from wrestling with the angel. The poet draws his charm from this limping.

\*

If poetry did not limp it would run and it cannot run because it counts its steps and interrupts them with halts.

\*

A poem is the reverse of all that a man usually regards as the best way of expressing what he thinks. One must therefore be very humble in order to read a poem and not fight against it as though it were an enemy.

\*

There is nothing more humble than a poet. He is only a vehicle. What gives him an air of pride is that he defends the strength that dwells within him, as Joan of Arc defended the cause of God.

\*

Paul Claudel says in a fine article that man has a right not only to justice but to injustice. Through a small degree of luck the poet is rewarded for a long effort.

\*

The masses can only like a poet through some misunderstanding.

\*

Poetry is the only market value which has not been devalued. It is the only nourishment really needed by man.

\*

Radiguet found that all publishers have made a fortune thanks to a poet.

\*

Poetry of the cinema. I am often asked what I think about it. I think nothing about it. I do not know what it is. I have seen films made without the slightest preoccupation with poetry, and poetry emanates from them; other poetic films where poetry doesn't happen.

The poetry of films arises from the unusual relationships between objects and images. A mere photograph can obtain these relationships. I possess photographs taken in the depot where the Germans melted down and destroyed our statues. The most mediocre statues assume greatness in them.

Poetry proceeds like lightning. Lightning undresses a shepherd and takes his clothes several miles away. It prints the photograph of a young girl on the shoulder of a ploughman. It pulls down a wall and neglects a tulle curtain. In short, it creates the unusual. The poet does not premeditate his acts any more than lightning does.

Poetry borrows astonishing contrasts by chance, it transplants things, it accidentally sets up a new order.

\*

The surrealists would have been my public. Since I have quarrelled with them, I no longer have a public. But my role consisted of loving them and following them in spite of their attacks. Our dramas were love dramas. Seeing anything sordid in them is a serious mistake. At the present time my best friends are surrealists. The politics of literature no longer affect us. Only our memories of the fight remain. We mention them as little as possible, as happens with true fighters. The reasons for our quarrel would remain a dead letter for anyone trying to understand them, since an enemy cannot be chosen outside the family. They formed a group, I was free. I could and had to defend myself only through my work.

Today I am constantly described as a surrealist in articles. *Le Sang d'un Poète* is described as a surrealist film. None of this matters any longer.

I have never been able to obey any order which did not come from within myself.

The essential thing is not to lose oneself in embraces. Remain sharp at all costs. Remain pointed. Do not become rounded.

\*

Poetry is a precision instrument. A shot at long range.

\*

People say to me : 'You don't change.' I reply : 'I'm too absent-minded.'

\*

A poet should be preoccupied only with poetry.

\*

Poets receive love-letters only.

\*

A man who does not possess a drop of *light blood* will never be a poet.

\*

Before he was shot B... wrote poems. A man who wants to outlive himself thinks only of writing poems.

\*

The 'event poems' of which Apollinaire used to talk to me. Every poem should be an event. It can happen that between two events one carries out exploitation work. It is these intermediary poems which people always notice.

\*

The absence of rules in poetry forces the poet to find methods for himself which give his work the prestige of a ritual from some sacred cult.

\*

Style is not a dance, it is a gait.

\*

One should not recognize a poet by his style but by his gaze.

\*

If by accident you show some sign of intelligence to the public in a poem or a play, they notice it and the rest escapes them immediately.

*

I have heard Charlie Chaplin complain apropos *The Gold Rush*
that people only mentioned the dance with the bread rolls.

After *Orphée* everyone congratulated me over an image which
I had been weak enough to leave in.

*

The vulgarity of images. People like to see something for the
second time, seeing for the first time tires them. This explains
the success of 'as' in poetry.

*

It is a privilege to be born a poet. Many writers of the race of
Encyclopédistes attack poets from bitterness at not being poets
themselves. They try to overcome the obstacles and that produces
hybrid books. An entire generation of youth is deceived by this
and falls into the trap.

*

Not being born a poet made Barrès ill.

I have sometimes been moved by this invalid who wants to get
up from his chair.

*

A poet is at first not read. Then he is read inaccurately. Then
he becomes a classic and habit prevents people from reading him.
All in all, he keeps for ever his few early lovers.

*

The sunshine of fame crushes outlines and shapes. Works flatten
themselves against them.

*

In poetry what matters is neither what is said, nor the way in
which it is said, nor the meaning, nor the music. Something else
matters and it cannot be analysed.

*

A poet should have the politeness and the memory of kings.

*

A poet should not refuse honours. He should act in such a way
that people do not think of offering them to him. If they are

offered to him it is because he has made some mistake. He should therefore accept what is offered to him like a punishment. If he refuses the honours which are offered him, he is taken in and takes in others, for his work accepts them to some extent and it should be his work which refuses them; he will then search out in what way his work accepts them (he certainly knows this already) and will steel himself against this weakness.

He is probably suffering through having undertaken work without having received the order from inside, and because this work has rendered visible to the eyes of the Prince what should for the moment remain invisible.

This is what Erik Satie was trying to express when he said : 'The important thing is not refusing the Légion d'Honneur, it is deserving it.'

\*

Honours are only admissible for the poet if they are addressed to his person and to the air of responsibility that the works earn him, whether he wants it or not.

'One must not be known for what one does,' Max Jacob used to say and he exemplified this remark. 'Give Max Jacob a decoration then,' X or Y would say to some minister who would decorate him without reading him.

\*

The popes and Louis XIV regarded Michelangelo, Racine and Molière as workmen in their pay. They were interested in the visible side of these people, not the invisible. They would have been greatly surprised and even angry if they had guessed that their fame would eclipse their own and that their work would be more powerful than their reigns.

\*

Young people make no mistakes about this. They like us for what allows us to escape from the Prince. They fraternize with the youth that clings to works which are not entirely produced by us.

\*

A poem results from marriage between the conscious and the unconscious, between the will and the non-will, between inaccuracy and vagueness.

\*

All fine handwriting is automatic.

*

A poet must be a saint, a hero, but without anyone knowing it. He must have no fear of death. He must be on close terms with it.

*

A poet hates himself. He respects within himself only the vehicle.

*

The poet's laziness : waiting for voices. A dangerous attitude. This is because he doesn't do what he should to make voices speak to him.

*

Discover a physical and moral hygiene. Be always in a state of grace. The poet's religious exercises.
Sleeping means going back into the stable. Do not sleep too much.

*

*Le Sang d'un Poète* has been the object of endless interpretations. Recently again a whole generation of youth has seen in it the Passion of Christ. What can I do about it? These young people translate this film as we try to translate nature. This poem in pictures has been made in a state of half-sleep. I was only trying to capture the themes which move me, to introduce myself as little as possible into this unwinding of unreal documents. There is not one symbol to be found in it. This is what allows one to symbolize. I am a cabinet-maker. I make a table, you are free to make it turn and speak.
*Le Sang d'un Poète* is a film 'which cannot be contrived'.
The poet is an enigma. He does not set enigmas. He recounts a world which he inhabits, a virgin world which tourists cannot reach and cannot litter with pieces of sticky paper.
There are poets among the public. My film is addressed to them. They guess that our world exists and collect information. This Tibet is within us and around us. It is our birth, our sleep, our youth, our loves, our blood. It is the world where we are, without the loss of shape imposed on it by the shameful fear of discomfort.

*

It is the break with this comfort of cowards that makes any spectator see flashes of poetry in a war where current events impose monstrous spelling mistakes, and snatch him by force from the school bench where he had assumed he would live and die.

\*

A poem is a series of accidents suitable for demoralizing comfort.


## SOLITUDE

Discomfort is proper to the poet. His universe is almost inhabitable. People sense this. They come into it as little as possible, as quickly as possible and only through curiosity.

\*

I once used for the poet a detective's advertisement : 'Sees everyone, hears everyone, nobody suspects it.'

\*

A poet is never free enough. Everything that he hoards turns against him. It is a stroke of luck if people rob him, devour him, abandon him, empty his house and drive him out of it.

\*

The poet is reassured by things that frighten others. Acts of violence reassure him and give him gentleness.

\*

Formlessness is unbearable to the poet.
The poet has a truth of his own which people take for a lie.

\*

The poet is a lie which tells the truth.

\*

In the long run revolutionary minds turn to poetry, even though they should despise it most.

\*

Revolution has always an air of poetry because poetry is revolution.

\*

Through whom did the Resistance of 1944 express itself? Through poets.

## MADNESS – GENIUS

When I wrote, 'Victor Hugo was a madman who believed he was Victor Hugo', this was not a witticism. Hugo's greatness is that he was mad and nobody in the world suspected it. The general style of his work did not allow him to write the things which astonish us without an organic disorder proved by endless details of his inner life. (Seen at Jean Hugo's house in Fourques : notebooks, drawings and innumerable monograms where the V and the VH are combined with the frightening concentration of a maniac.)

Goethe is often ridiculous with the sense of the ridiculous. Goethe is the reverse of Victor Hugo.

\*

It is neither Rimbaud's 'rampart with wallflowers' nor Baudelaire's 'jugs of wine behind the groves' which cause their fame. Their fame comes from the exoticism contained in *Bateau Ivre* and from erotic exoticism, beneath which Baudelaire is still concealed.

It is through the ornaments which one day fall from his work that the poet takes hold of human beings and journeys towards those who discover him.

\*

Nothing to discover in Musset. What he was, he remains. He deceives no one. He reassures. This is why he has so many statues in Paris.

\*

The poet runs no risk of copying. It is through the extent of his failure to do so that he expresses himself. Before Radiguet wrote *Le Bal du Comte d'Orgel* he said to me : 'I'm going to copy *La Princesse de Clèves.*' Apollinaire admitted to me that he was trying to write like Anatole France. Racine copied Euripides. Molière Molina.

In writing the poems in *Opéra* (*Musée Secret*) I thought I was copying the Civil Code, with *Thomas l'Imposteur, La Chartreuse de Parme.*

\*

Apollinaire chanted his poems while writing them and they enchant us. These old-fashioned secrets are more worthwhile than Aristotle.

*

For a poem, a play or a film one must imitate the oyster and form an excrescence. The pearl takes shape on its own, round about it.

A poem always unties itself too quickly. You must tie it and retie it firmly.

*

As from a certain moment you can no longer make any sign without significance.


## LES FORAINS

With a few rags, four poles and four old canvases Bérard creates a sumptuous spectacle. In the theatre and the cinema everything is too expensive and too rich.

Picasso's *Mercure* (*Le Bain des Grâces*), a sumptuous spectacle. There is only an oilcloth curtain, an imitation marble well-head, a sloping surface pierced with holes and, emerging from these holes, unshaven scene-shifters combing out old wigs and wearing pink tights with huge stuffed breasts. That is theatre.

*

Certain languages are poetic and unsuited to poetry. The French language is a language for poetry, because it is precise and does not sing. It is the piano without pedals mentioned by Gide. It is only through a combination of hardness, points and dryness that one achieves this rhythm which no longer has any connection with the terms one employs, none with the things that one expresses.

*

Poets should fear adjectives like the plague.

*

This decisive way of saying in French things that strike no French intelligence, except a certain intelligence of the heart.

*

Seriousness that asserts itself. Never believe in it. Never confuse it with gravity.

\*

Poetic behaviour is the element whereby the poem keeps its colour, its freshness and life. A poem breathes in it like a marine plant.

\*

A poem is a thinking jewel.

\*

A remark made by Pierre Reverdy : 'There is no love. There are proofs of love.' I add : 'There is no poetry, there are only proofs of poetry.'

\*

Almost all children have the genius of a poet, which is soon spoilt. Confusion in relationships forms within them spurious contacts which provoke a flash of poetry.

\*

Childhood. The protection and preservation of childhood are the poet's biggest concern. Youth is nothing. It is the age when everyone is a poet and no one is a poet. Rimbaud was never young. He was a child and a man. At twenty Rimbaud died old. His death was that of a child.

\*

Silence is the basis of a poem. A poem is the way in which silence is contradicted, offended, deceived, tormented, struck, wounded and vanquished.
Sometimes silence is absent-minded. Too late ! The poem is there.

\*

Poem blood of silence.

\*

Poem cry of silence.

\*

Poem cry that is written.

\*

Canvas hates being painted. Colours hate serving the painter,

paper hates the poem and ink hates us. From these struggles there
remain a place for warfare, a famous date, evidence of heroes.

*

A masterpiece is a battle won against death.

*

It's not by writing the word table that you will express 'table'.
It's not by writing the word tree that you will express 'tree', it's not
by writing the word love that you will express love.

*

Pushkin is a good example of the inimitable rhythm of poets. In
translation nothing of him remains. Now his magic (in the precise
meaning of the term) holds sway over Russians, whatever they are
like. It cannot be a question of verbal music, for in that case
Pushkin would go out of fashion. It cannot be a question of meaning, since in translation this meaning is mediocre. It can only be a
question of an internal rhythm which Pushkin owed perhaps to
a drop of black blood.

*

Eluard's pure water reflects the nature of his soul and lovingly
distorts it. Those who imitate it can only reflect a reflection.

*

More and more I find immense difficulty in making contact with
the realism of life. Especially in the morning, when I leave a life
of dream which has no connection with mine. That is why I like
working on a film where the overwhelming responsibilities force me
to be present. That is no doubt why a film as simple as *L'Eternel
Retour* gives so much dreaming to the countless unknown people
who are consumed with solitude in the provinces and write letters.

This unrealism makes it difficult and almost impossible to write
the memoirs that people continually ask me for, the memoirs of a
fairly extraordinary life, but less extraordinary than that of my
sleep which I am obliged to forget immediately. This life of sleep
would disturb the effort of each moment which consists of clinging
to life, something that gives me an active and sociable air.

People who live with their feet on the ground and want to have
an air of dream are no use to poetry. Poetry walks with one foot in
life and one foot in death. This is why I say it limps and it is
through this limp that I recognize it.

\*

The trial of Joan of Arc was the trial of a Resistance leader by collaborators. I am surprised that nobody emphasizes more strongly what a great writer Joan of Arc is. Each word she utters is in place. One could not utter any others. She says exactly what she means. Poetry is within her and expresses itself in addition.

\*

The poet's intelligence is only intuition. Bergson was the first to have within himself 'the intuition' of the outside, that is to say of his universe which is not ours.

\*

I realize the incalculable number of pages one must have written before a word can strike, before one can remember some detail. The truth is that people judge our house by a window-hasp. In realizing this I feel a kind of dizziness that makes me lazy.

\*

I could not survive without saying that Georges Limbour's poem entitled *Motifs*, in *Soleils Bas*, is one of the finest in the French language. Equal in perfection to Apollinaire's *Colchiques*.

\*

Max Jacob tries to overturn silence. Sometimes he even says simply anything to make silence remain quiet. In the same way I used to see the Comtesse de Noailles wave her hand at table, while she drank, in order that people would not interrupt her.

\*

Why do these notes come to me, since I don't like writing. It is no doubt because I am writing them while on the road, during a breakdown, in the street in Orléans, in a third-class carriage which shakes me about. I find this work that I love on book-jackets, the backs of envelopes, tablecloths, that wonderful lack of comfort in which the mind is stimulated.

\*

A room paralyses me, a table kills me. How many works have composed themselves in my head when it was impossible to take notes for them? If I tried to write afterwards they would evaporate like a dream, there would remain only a vague outline of them, only the empty façades of the Place d'Orléans.

*

Letter from J. F. L. P., written from Antibes. He tells me that he had made a pilgrimage to Villefranche. When he arrived he was very happy to find Villefranche intact, the Hôtel Wellcome in its place. He rushed along to it. He went in. Alas! Only the façades of the Hôtel Wellcome remain, the interior no longer exists.


## ACTOR-POETS

This is the rarest thing.

The actor-poet does not prove himself by the timbre of his voice, or by his face, or by his gestures, but by a certain conduct of the soul which brings unusual qualities into action and embarrasses the majority of spectators.

Jean Marais's sportsmanlike physique protects him somewhat against the hate people feel for poets and deceives many of them. Alain Cluny is less well equipped for the creation of this misunderstanding. Charlie Chaplin was protected by laughter. When he causes less laughter he causes fright. His first films are as terrible as Kafka.

*

Debussy's *Pelléas* is a poetic masterpiece. Maeterlinck's text is a masterpiece of poetry. The poetry that is distilled from the opera is due much more to the dramatist than to the musician. But people don't realize it. They believe that the poet is inferior to the music and even, without the music, slightly ridiculous and old-fashioned.

It is in fact precisely the part of Maeterlinck which still displeases people that saves him, and the over-rapid and over-unanimous movement of the élites towards Debussy's music proves to us that it is poetic prose upon the prose poetry of Maeterlinck.

*

Picasso says : 'Music is prose.'

*

It is said in a fairy-tale by Madame d'Aulnoy : 'The Prince had his portrait painted in order to send it to the Princess and the painter was so clever that the portrait could utter a few words.' One can imagine the Princess's emotion.

I have been able to read a few of the hundreds of letters that film stars receive. They consist entirely of spelling mistakes (one always finds the same one : *dédicasse*). These uncultivated letters fail to correspond to a certain passionate understanding of what the women letter-writers have seen.

This world without spelling is not concerned with knowing who made the film. The only things that count are the actors and the heroes they incarnate. This uncultivated world receives sensations all the stronger because they come through portraits which talk and allow people to dream of the originals.

\*

The poet's task is to conceive, in order to live in it, a universe where time, space and volumes are not organized as in the human universe. The result is a kind of invisibility.


## MEMORY OF CHILDHOOD

Flour betrayed us. We were hidden in the windmill, we emerged from it black from head to foot.


## MEMORY OF YOUTH

We shut ourselves up in the coal-mine and rolled about in it. Coal betrayed us. We were white from head to foot.


## END OF THE JOURNEY

Here is the cold dawn, its bells, cock-crows, coughing and beard growing. Now is the moment to cling to life and believe in it. There's something to laugh about! Now is the moment to live *a little*.

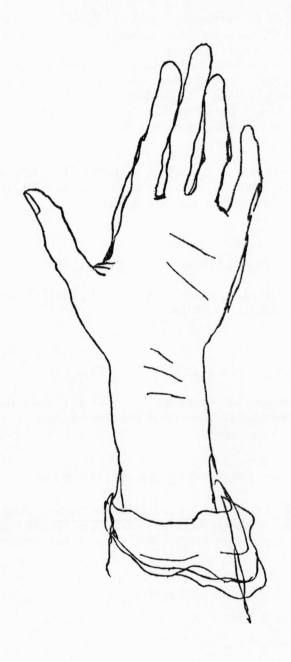

# CHRONOLOGY

1889    On 5th July, birth of Jean Cocteau at Maisons-Laffitte, Seine et Oise, near Paris. His sister, Marthe, was twelve at the time; his brother, Paul, eight. His father had practised as a lawyer but had private means and did not continue with his profession.

1898    Cocteau's father commits suicide.

1900-4    Cocteau attends school, first at Le Petit Condorcet, then at the Lycée Condorcet. He was removed from the school at the request of the headmaster. He attended the Cours Fénélon for a time, then studied with private tutors.

1906    Cocteau begins to go regularly to the music-hall and falls in love with a young performer, Jeanne Reynette. During this and the following year he failed the *baccalauréat* examination three times.

1908    Cocteau's first contacts with the literary world. His poems are read in public for the first time and he becomes a social success.

1909    Publication of his first book of poems, *La Lampe d'Aladin*, which he later rejected.
Becomes engaged to the actress Madeleine Carlier, but his family objected to the association.
First meeting with Diaghilev, the Russian impresario who first brought the Russian Ballet to Paris.
Publication of the luxury revue *Schéhérazade*, edited by Cocteau and Maurice Rostand.

1910    Publication of a second book of poems, *Le Prince Frivole*, also rejected later.
Cocteau and his mother come to live at 10 Rue d'Anjou in Paris.
First meeting with Stravinsky.

1912    Première of the ballet *Le Dieu Bleu,* for which Cocteau, in collaboration with 'Coco' Madrazo, had written the scenario.
Publication of the third (and likewise rejected) book of poems, *La Danse de Sophocle*.

1913-14    Cocteau writes *Le Potomak*, finishing it while staying with Stravinsky.

1914     War service with an ambulance unit. First flights with the well-known aviator Roland Garros.

With Paul Iribe Cocteau launches another luxury revue, *Le Mot*.

1915     He meets Apollinaire, Picasso and Erik Satie.

Further war experiences at the front.

1917     Première of the ballet *Parade*, devised by Cocteau, music by Satie, décor by Picasso and choreography by Massine.

1918     Cocteau arranges the first performance by the group of composers known as *Les Six*. He writes *Le Coq et l'Arlequin* which is published by the firm founded by himself and the writer Blaise Cendrars.

1919     Publication of *Le Potomak* and *Le Cap de Bonne-Espérance* (poems).

First meeting with Raymond Radiguet, who was then fifteen.

1920     *Le Boeuf sur le Toit* is performed in Paris and London.

1921     Cocteau spends much time with Radiguet. They write a short play together and it is performed in Paris.

Cocteau's *comédie-ballet Les Mariés de la Tour Eiffel* is performed in Paris, with music by *Les Six*.

1922     A bar called Le Boeuf sur le Toit, named after Cocteau's ballet, is opened in Paris.

Publication of *Le Secret Professionnel*.

1923     Cocteau gives a talk at the Collège de France which he calls *D'un Ordre Considéré comme une Anarchie*.

Publication of *Le Grand Ecart* and *Thomas l'Imposteur*.

Death of Radiguet.

1924     Cocteau begins to take opium regularly.

He acts the part of Mercutio in his adaptation of *Romeo and Juliet*.

Publishes several collections of poems. Meets Jacques Maritain, the Catholic writer, and Maurice Sachs, later famous for his book *Le Sabbat* and for his association with Violette Leduc. Cocteau also meets Jean and Jeanne Bourgoint, the brother and sister who may have been the inspiration for *Les Enfants Terribles*.

1925     Cocteau undergoes a first cure for opium poisoning. At Villefranche he meets the artist Christian Bérard.

1926     Publishes his *Lettre à Jacques Maritain*, in which he attempts to reconcile his own personal 'religion' with

Catholicism. Maritain published a reply in which he rejected Cocteau's thesis.

Cocteau's play *Orphée* performed in Paris.

He meets Jean Desbordes, a young writer, and hopes the latter will replace the friendship of Radiguet.

Publication of *Le Rappel à l'Ordre*.

1927  First performance of Stravinsky's oratorio *Oedipus Rex*, for which Cocteau had written the words; they were afterwards translated into Latin.

In a second performance of *Orphée* Cocteau plays the part of Heurtebise.

Publication of *Opéra* and other collections of poems.

1928  A second cure for opium poisoning at Saint-Cloud.

Publications include *Le Livre Blanc*, *Le Mystère Laïc* (about the painter de Chirico).

1929  Publication of *Les Enfants Terribles*.

Private performance of *La Voix Humaine* at the Comédie Française.

1930  Cocteau works on his first film scenario, *Le Sang d'un Poète*.

Publication of *Opium* (dedicated to Jean Desbordes) and *La Voix Humaine*.

1931  Cocteau goes to live in the Rue Vignon in Paris.

1932  The film *Le Sang d'un Poète* is shown at a film gala.

Love-affair with Natalie Paley.

Publication of *Essai de Critique Indirecte*.

1933  Cocteau meets Marcel Khill. Jean Desbordes leaves him.

Publication of *Le Fantôme de Marseille*.

1934  Performance and publication of *La Machine Infernale*.

1935  Serial publication in *Le Figaro* of *Portraits-Souvenir*, followed by book publication.

1936  Journey with Marcel Khill, Cocteau's account of which was later published by *Paris-Soir* under the title *Mon Premier Voyage*. The trip followed the trail set by Jules Verne in *Around the World in Eighty Days* and was the result of a wager with the newspaper.

1937  Cocteau brings back Al Brown, former world boxing champion, to the ring.

Meeting with Jean Marais, the actor, who scores a triumph in Cocteau's play *Les Chevaliers de la Table Ronde*, produced and published this year.

1938    Al Brown again becomes world boxing champion.
        Performance and publication of the play *Les Parents
        Terribles*.

1940    Première of the play *Les Monstres Sacrés* in Paris, along
        with the curtain-raiser *Le Bel Indifférent*, specially written
        for Edith Piaf.
        Cocteau moves to 36 Rue de Montpensier, in the Palais-
        Royal, and becomes a neighbour of the writer Colette.
        Publication of *La Fin du Potomak* and *Les Monstres
        Sacrés*.

1941    Première of the play *La Machine à Ecrire* in Paris,
        followed by attacks on Cocteau by journalists writing for
        the collaborationist press. A new production of *Les
        Parents Terribles* was greeted in the same way.

1942    Cocteau defends Jean Genet in court. He also publishes
        an article praising the German sculptor Breker.
        Acts a role in the film *Le Baron Fantôme*, directed by
        Serge de Poligny.

1943    Cocteau's play *Antigone*, with music by Honegger, pro-
        duced at the Opéra.
        Death of Cocteau's mother.
        The verse play *Renaud et Armide* produced at the
        Comédie-Française.

1944    The film *L'Eternel Retour* made and shown.
        Cocteau is deeply upset by the death after torture of Jean
        Desbordes, who had been working for the Polish Under-
        ground movement.

1945    Cocteau makes the film *La Belle et la Bête* and writes a
        journal while doing so.

1946    Cocteau creates the ballet *Le Jeune Homme et la Mort*
        for Jean Babilée, produced in Paris and subsequently in
        London.
        Film of *La Belle et la Bête* receives the Louis-Delluc prize.
        The play *L'Aigle à Deux Têtes* produced in Brussels,
        Lyons and Paris.
        Publication of *La Belle et la Bête: Journal d'un Film*, the
        play *L'Aigle à Deux Têtes* and the poem *La Crucifixion*.
        The Swiss publishers Marguerat begin publication of the
        so-called *Oeuvres Complètes*.

1947    Roberto Rossellini makes a film of *La Voix Humaine*.
        Cocteau meets Edouard Dermit, later to be his adopted
        son.

Film made of *L'Aigle à Deux Têtes*.
*La Difficulté d'Etre* is published.

1948    The films of *L'Aigle à Deux Têtes* and *Les Parents Terribles* shown in Paris.
Publication of various poems, also of *Reines de la France* with illustrations by Christian Bérard.

1949    Cocteau flies to New York for the première of his film *L'Aigle à Deux Têtes*. He writes most of the *Lettre aux Américains* on the flight back to France.
He tours the Middle East with a company of French star actors and actresses, presenting three of his own plays and three other famous French dramas.
He is made a Chevalier de la Légion d'Honneur.

1950    The film *Orphée* is shown in Cannes and wins the International Critics' prize in Venice.
The film of *Les Enfants Terribles* is shown in Paris.
Cocteau's ballet *Phèdre* is performed at the Opéra.

1951    Cocteau's play *Bacchus* is presented in Paris and attacked by François Mauriac.

1952    Cocteau presents Stravinsky's *Oedipus Rex* with *tableaux vivants* and masks, and his narration is received with hostility by the public.
*Bacchus* and *Journal d'un Inconnu* are published.

1953    First production of Cocteau's ballet *La Dame à la Licorne* in Munich.
Cocteau makes his first visit to Spain.

1955    Cocteau takes the place of Colette at the Académie Royale de Belgique.
He is elected to the Académie Française.

1956    He is awarded an honorary doctorate at the University of Oxford.
Decorates the chapel at Villefranche-sur-Mer.

1957    Made an honorary member of the National Institute of Arts and Letters in New York.
Publication of *La Corrida du Ier Mai*.

1959    The ballet *La Dame à la Licorne* is presented at the Paris Opéra.
Acts a part in his own film *Le Testament d'Orphée*.

1960    Presentation of *Le Testament d'Orphée*.

1961    He is made Commandeur de la Légion d'Honneur.

1962    Première of *L'Impromptu du Palais-Royal*, presented by
        the Comédie-Française in Tokyo. The play is published
        the same year. Other publications include *Le Cordon
        Ombilical* (souvenirs).

1963    A television programme about Cocteau recorded at his
        country house at Milly-la-Forêt.
        He dies at Milly on 11th October.
        His book *La Comtesse de Noailles oui et non* published
        posthumously.

For help in my work on this anthology, I am particularly indebted to the following books :

Jacques Brosse, *Cocteau*. Paris : Gallimard, 1970.

André Fraigneau, *Cocteau par lui-même*. Paris : Gallimard and Editions du Seuil, 1957.

Elizabeth Sprigge and Jean-Jacques Khim, *Cocteau: The Man and the Mirror*. London : Gollancz, 1968.

Francis Steegmuller, *Cocteau: A Biography*. Boston : Atlantic Monthly-Little, Brown, 1970; London : Macmillan, 1970.

M. C.